T0304113

The Origins of National Financial Systems

Since the nineteenth century, there has been an accepted distinction between financial systems in which commercial and investment banking are carried out by separate types of firms and those in which "universal banks" carry out both kinds of operation. The purpose of this comprehensive collection is to establish how and why financial systems have developed – this is important since establishing how financial differentiation occurred in the nineteenth century may well afford insight into whether or not the contemporary process of liberalization of financial systems will produce changes in banking structure.

In the 1950s Alexander Gerschenkron argued that universal banks evolved in late-industrializing nations in order to take advantage of structural incentives for economic growth. This book poses a systematic challenge to the Gerschenkron thesis. With contributions from leading scholars such as Ranald Michie and Jaime Reis, this well-written book provides solid and intriguing arguments throughout.

The Origins of National Financial Systems will be of interest to students and academics in several fields, including economic and financial history as well as international finance in general.

Douglas J. Forsyth is Associate Professor of History at Bowling Green State University, Ohio, USA.

Daniel Verdier is Associate Professor at the European University Institute, Florence, Italy.

Routledge Explorations in Economic History

The Origins of National Financial Systems

Alexander Gerschenkron reconsidered

Edited by
Douglas J. Forsyth and
Daniel Verdier

Routledge
Taylor & Francis Group

LONDON AND NEW YORK

First published 2003
by Routledge
2 Park Square, Milton Park, Abingdon, Oxon OX14 4RN

Simultaneously published in the USA and Canada
by Routledge
711 Third Avenue, New York, NY 10017

Routledge is an imprint of the Taylor & Francis Group, an informa business

Selection and editorial matter © 2003 Douglas J. Forsyth and Daniel Verdier;
individual chapters © the contributors

Typeset in Times by
HWA Text and Data Management Ltd, Tunbridge Wells

British Library Cataloguing in Publication Data
A catalogue record for this book is available from the British Library

Library of Congress Cataloging in Publication Data
The origins of national financial systems: Alexander Gerschenkron
reconsidered / [edited by] Douglas J. Forsyth and Daniel Verdier.
        p. cm. – (Routledge explorations in economic history ; 23)
    Includes bibliographical references and index.
        1. Banks and banking – History.   2. Investment banking –
History.   3. Universal banks – History.   4. Gerschenkron,
Alexander.   I. Forsyth, Douglas J.   II. Verdier Daniel, 1954–
III. Series.

    HG1601.O75 2002
    332.1–dc21   2002026932

ISBN 0-415-30168-8

In memory of Audrey Paige Verdier, 1958–2001

Contents

Figures

Tables

Contributors

Deeg, Richard. Associate Professor, Political Science, Temple University, Philadelphia.

Forsyth, Douglas J. Associate Professor, History, Bowling Green State University, Ohio.

Jonker, Joost. Lecturer and Research Fellow in Social and Economic History, Utrecht University.

Knutsen, Sverre. Associate Professor, Center for Business History, Norwegian School of Management, Oslo.

Lescure, Michel. Professor of History, Université de Paris X-Nanterre.

Lindgren, Håkan. Professor, Institute for Research in Economic History, Stockholm School of Economics.

Michie, Ranald. Professor of History, University of Durham.

Polsi, Alessandro. Professor of History, Scuola Normale Superiore, Pisa.

Reis, Jaime. Senior Research Director, Instituto de Ciências Sociais, University of Lisbon.

Rowney, Don K. Professor of History, Bowling Green State University, Ohio.

Sjögren, Hans. Professor, Department of Management and Economics, Linköping University, Sweden.

Verdier, Daniel. Associate Professor, Political Science, European University Institute.

Acknowledgements

We would like to acknowledge financial assistance from the European Association for Banking History, e.V., Frankfurt a. M.; the Bank of Italy; and the Crediop in Rome. At the EABH our thanks go to Prof. Dr. Manfred Pohl. Prof. Franco Cotula was instrumental in securing financial support for our project from the Bank of Italy. Dr. Antonio Pedone supported our application to the Crediop. Other individuals who have worked to secure support for our project include former Prime Minister Giuliano Amato, Prof. Marcello De Cecco, Prof. Gerry Feldman, Prof. Jaime Reis, Prof. Hermann van der Wee, and Prof. Gabriel Tortella. We would like to thank Prof. Yves Mény, Ms. Monique Cavallari, and the staff at Robert Schuman Center at the European University Institute for hosting a conference 2–4 March 2000, where first drafts of the papers in this volume were presented and discussed. We thank also the commentors and participants in that conference: Prof. Marcello De Cecco, Dr. Alfredo Gigliobianco (Bank of Italy), Dr. Nobert Walter (Deutsche Bank), and Prof. Dieter Ziegler. Forsyth's research was also supported by the Policy History program at Bowling Green State University, by a German Marshall Fellowship, and by an appointment as Visiting Professor at the Centro de Estudios Avanzados en Ciências Sociales, Instituto Juan March de Estudios e Investigaciones, Madrid, during 1997. We would like to thank Rob Langham and Terry Clague at Routledge Press for their assistance in shepherding our manuscript through the production process. Thanks are also due to four anonymous reviewers at Routledge; revisions undertaken to meet their criticisms have improved the final product offered here. Jim Buss at Bowling Green helped standardize the bibliography and notes. Needless to add, the editors and authors are solely responsible for any errors or omissions.

Introduction

Douglas J. Forsyth

The problem

The purpose of this volume is to reopen an old and venerable debate in political economy on completely new terms. At issue are the origins of the distinct features of national financial systems. Since the nineteenth century, it has been common-place to distinguish between financial systems in which commercial and investment banking are carried out by separate types of firms and those in which "universal banks" carry out both kinds of operation. Britain is often considered the paradig-matic case of a country in which commercial and investment banking evolved separately, and Germany as the paradigmatic homeland of universal banking. Many of the other countries examined by the contributors to this volume fall somewhere between, with France and the Netherlands falling closer to the British end of the spectrum, Italy and Portugal closer to the German end, and Norway, Sweden and Late Imperial Russia somewhere between. Once in place, these financial systems have proved remarkably robust. Most industrial nations still have today financial systems conforming to the broad type they developed by the end of the nineteenth century.

Establishing how and why national financial systems have developed along different lines could be important for two reasons. First, if there are differences in the relative efficiency of universal vs. functionally segmented banking systems, it should matter a great deal how these systems came into being in the first place. Let the reader be advised, we do not attempt to resolve the efficiency issue here, but other scholars have debated, and continue to debate, this question with great intensity. Second, establishing how financial system differentiation occurred in the nineteenth century may afford insight into whether or not the contemporary process of liberalization and international standardization in the regulatory framework for the financial system will produce changes in banking structure.

Two rival explanations

Beginning in 1952, Alexander Gerschenkron argued in a series of influential essays that universal banks evolved in late-industrializing nations in order to take advantage of a set of structural *incentives*, and in order to compensate for a set of structural *impediments* to economic growth. The incentives included the possibility for rapid growth through imitating technologies and organizational forms that already existed in more advanced countries. One of the impediments to economic growth was capital scarcity. In poor countries universal banks channeled scarce resources into industrial investment. Further, in a cultural environment in which information was unreliable and entrepreneurship weak, they provided client firms with valuable information and strategic advice.[1]

For over forty years, Gerschenkron's arguments have stood at the center of historical research on the development of financial institutions. Among the principle theoretical questions at issue have been: Did relative backwardness call into existence universal banks as compensatory institutions? How important was the contribution of financial institutions to the process of late development? And related to this: Did the universal banking model produce greater or more efficient investment, and thus more rapid growth than financial systems that separated commercial and investment banking (R.H. Tilly, 1966; R.H. Tilly, 1986; Cameron *et al.* (eds), 1967; Cameron (ed.), 1972; Neuberger and Stokes, 1974; Sylla and Toniolo (eds), 1991b; Lamoreaux, 1994; Calomiris, 1995)?

Criticisms of and exceptions to Gerschenkron's thesis have emerged in this vast literature, but until recently, one looked in vain for an encompassing alternative explanation for the origins of difference between national financial systems. However, in a series of papers and a recently published book, Daniel Verdier has been developing just such a systematic challenge to the Gerschenkron thesis (Verdier, 2002a; Verdier, 2002b; Verdier, 1998; Verdier, 1996). For Verdier, relative economic backwardness is irrelevant in determining differences in the development of national financial systems. Instead, he argues that bankers' choices were shaped decisively by two variables. The first is how governments regulated and structured national deposit markets. Where governments promoted the growth of non-profit financial institutions (e.g., savings banks and cooperative banks) and hence prevented private, for-profit, joint-stock banks from capturing a predominant share of the national deposit base, the latter were forced to rely more heavily on share capital and shareholders' reserves as their liabilities base. They needed to worry less about a depositors' run, and tended to combine investment with commercial banking activities. Where commercial banks were successful in capturing a substantial share of the total deposit market, and deposits constituted most of their liabilities, they abandoned the long end of the market, concentrating on short-term commercial lending.

The second variable invoked by Verdier to explain bankers' choices is exercise of the lender-of-last-resort function by central banks at a relatively early date. Despite higher ratios of share capital plus shareholders' reserves to deposits, universal banks remained vulnerable to a run on deposits in the event of a financial panic. They could only flourish, therefore, in countries where bankers could be reasonably certain that the central bank would step in to provide liquidity if the system came under stress.

For Verdier, all banking systems were segmented, but along different lines. Where deposit-taking banks specialized in short-term commercial lending, segmentation was between commercial and investment banking; where universal banking prevailed, segmentation was between private, for-profit institutions on the one hand, and various types of non-profit savings and cooperative institutions enjoying special tax privileges on the other.

Following Stein Rokkan, Verdier suggests that political support for non-profit institutions was more likely to emerge in polities where the agricultural periphery was strong enough to impede the centralization of economic institutions and activity (Rokkan and Urwin, 1983). Thus, commercial/deposit banking developed in Britain and France, nations where political power was centralized relatively quickly. Universal banks developed alongside a strong non-profit sector in what Verdier refers to as "semi-centralized" polities: Austria, Germany, Italy, and Switzerland fit his model most closely. Meanwhile, fully decentralized polities, according to Verdier, tended not to meet the second necessary precondition for universal banking, namely a central bank with an expansive view of its responsibilities as lender-of-last-resort. This accounts for the absence of universal banking in the United States and in Australia.

The analytical framework for this project

The present volume is the product of a collaborative research project that was originally constructed in order to test the alternative Gerschenkron and Verdier theses against qualitative evidence, in the form of essays by experts on the financial history of key countries in the samples of both. We tried to recruit as contributors the sort of scholars who know relevant archival collections inside out. We wanted to get these empirically minded individuals to think critically about rival synthetic explanations for financial differentiation and review their applicability to the national cases they know so well. As our project developed, we realized as editors that in order to explain why banking developed along different lines in different countries, we would need to examine also how securities markets developed in tandem with banking. Consequently, in addition to the case studies devoted to individual countries, we recruited two authorities on securities markets, Ranald Michie and Joost Jonker, to write additional comparative essays for us. Our exchanges with the contributors have, in turn, sharpened and broadened our understanding of the range of variables that have shaped national financial systems.

Our object all along has been to organize an open debate. Participants were required to agree neither with Gerschenkron nor with Verdier; a wide range of opinion and argument consequently is offered here. We have, however, devised a common analytical framework within which we believe one can think more clearly about rival explanations for the development of national financial systems.

In our view, an alternative to Gerschenkron's thesis must be articulated along two vectors. The first vector is best understood by putting oneself in the place of a late nineteenth-century banker, and considering the set of constraints and incentives that might have induced him (and nearly all bankers in this era were male) either to confine himself to short-term lending or to combine commercial with investment banking. A good way to understand the banker's strategic decisions would be to arrange the constraints and incentives he faced according to whether they affected the *assets* or the *liabilities* side of his balance sheet.

From this perspective, we recognize immediately that Gerschenkron's explanation is based on factors that affect the *assets* or *demand side* of the banker's ledger. In a relatively backward country, the banker has an incentive to lend long, because firms suffer from capital scarcity, and their potential for rapid growth is high. In a more developed country, firms can find investment capital through retained profits or on the securities markets and thus they are less in need of the banker's assistance. Further, a more developed country, according to Gerschenkron, will produce a high volume of short-term commercial transactions that bankers can finance. In a relatively backward country, little information is available about economic opportunities and firms need strategic advice that bankers can provide. There is little trust among economic actors, and a close relationship with a respected banker can overcome information asymmetry problems. Bankers monitor the performance of entrepreneurs and vouchsafe the reliability and solvability of their clients. In a more developed economy, meanwhile, information is more plentiful and minimum standards of honesty are higher; entrepreneurs and investors, therefore, can dispense with monitoring by bankers. Bankers, in turn, can extend short-term loans to clients with whom they do not have continuous and intimate relationships, with reasonable prospects of repayment and profit.

Our analytical model induces us to ask whether there are other incentives and constraints affecting the demand side of the balance sheet that might influence bankers' choices, in addition to those advanced by Gerschenkron. For example, what opportunities for short-term investment were available to bankers other than the steady stream of commercial bills, thought by Gerschenkron to be characteristic of more developed economies? What sources of investment capital were available to entrepreneurs in late developing economies apart from those managed by the banks?

And finally, how did the behavior of the central bank affect the investment choices of commercial bankers? In countries where the central bank developed an expansive interpretation of its lender-of-last-resort responsibilities at a comparatively early date, commercial bankers may have had more latitude to engage in long-term lending, knowing that they ran less risk of being caught short in a depositors' run. In countries where bankers could not rely on the central bank to act as lender-of-last-resort, or where it was clear the central bank would deny assistance to commercial banks with frozen long-term asset portfolios, it was presumably imperative to specialize in short-term commercial lending.

Alternative explanations for the origins of universal banking would look at incentives and constraints that affect the *liabilities* side of the banker's ledger; in other words, they would offer a *supply-side* account of differences in bankers' choices. The key issue here is whether commercial bankers rely primarily on deposits to finance their lending activity or whether they rely to a significant degree on share capital and shareholders' reserves. Bankers that rely heavily on deposits must structure their asset portfolios so as to remain solvent in the event of a depositors' run; bankers who rely more extensively on share capital and shareholders' reserves can afford to hold a larger share of long-term or less easily liquidated assets. The core questions for a supply-side explanation of how national banking systems develop, therefore, become: How are bank *deposits* held within a particular national economy? Are they held primarily by for-profit commercial banks or do other classes of institution, including non-profit savings and cooperative banks, government-run postal savings bank networks, or the central bank, primarily hold them? Do for-profit commercial banks derive their resources overwhelmingly from deposits or do share capital and shareholders' reserves constitute a substantial share of their liabilities? To what extent are national savings diverted into institutional forms other than bank deposits? For example, are household savings channeled directly into purchases of either public or private securities? Do they remain stuffed in the mattresses of savers, because of distrust in banks or because of political hostility to those who run the banking networks? What are the consequences for banking in a national economy so poor that a market for savings deposits barely exists?

The second vector along which an alternative to Gerschenkron's thesis can be articulated is the distinction between *state-centered* and *market-centered* explanations for bankers' choices. The fundamental dichotomy can be articulated in these terms: Did universal banking develop because the set of incentives and constraints facing market actors in relatively backward countries were different from those faced by bankers in early industrializing nations or did it develop primarily because of the manner in which government regulation shaped financial institutions?

Casting Gerschenkron in the role of champion of market factors over the state in the shaping of financial institutions may strike the reader at first glance as counter-intuitive. After all, Gerschenkron had a great sensitivity for the role of the state in economic development in relatively backward countries. The defining feature of his native Russia, he believed, was the combination of military competition with the West, which served as the impulse for modernization, and relative economic backwardness. For Gerschenkron, Russian economic development differed from that in Western Europe above all because it was managed by a coercive state that was preoccupied with building a modern military establishment (see the essay by Rowney in this volume for an extended discussion of these issues).

However, if the reader looks closely at Gerschenkron's account of the origins of universal banking in Continental Europe, it becomes clear that markets take precedence over regulation. German capitalism may have been more organized than British capitalism owing to relative backwardness, but it was organized by private market actors, notably bankers, and not by the state. German bankers organized their business to take advantage of the incentives for rapid growth offered by the possibility of imitating technological processes already developed elsewhere, and the exploitation of natural resources, and to overcome the constraints created by insufficient capital, and cultural backwardness.

Our analytical model induces us to ask whether there were market incentives and/or constraints other than those invoked by Gerschenkron that might explain bankers' choices. For example, did the existence of broad and deep securities markets shape the investment opportunities available to bankers? What about highly developed informal credit markets? How did domestic interbank markets or the availability of international capital influence the choices of commercial bankers?

The counterfactual to Gerschenkron's thesis, meanwhile, would posit that it was not differences in market incentives that were decisive in structuring national financial systems, but rather differences in state policy, including regulation of the financial sector.[2] The core questions for a state-centered explanation for how financial systems developed would include: Did non-profit institutions, including savings and cooperative banks benefit from tax privileges, subsidies or other regulations? What were the consequences for for-profit commercial banks? Did regulation impose a particular kind of segmentation on the national banking system? Were mergers between institutions of different classes prohibited? Was unit banking (banks without branches) sustained by regulation or public policy? Did regulation impede financial flows within interbank markets? Did state-owned financial institutions, including postal savings banks, enjoy any particular privileges? How did government fiscal policy affect the banking system? For example, how did the state structure relations with its creditors? What were the consequences for the banking system? How did central banks, which were either state-owned or enjoyed special privileges, interpret their responsibilities within the financial system, including their roles as lender-of-last-resort?

Before turning to the individual contributions to this volume and the arguments they propose, it is necessary to offer a generalizable definition of universal banking. As noted, universal banking is most commonly associated with Germany. German universal banks developed a set of peculiar features that can be found in its entirety only in a few neighboring countries. They engaged in industrial promotion, making loans to start-up firms that were recovered later through the flotation of securities by the banks. German universal banks held equity stakes in the firms they promoted. They occupied seats on corporate boards. This practice was facilitated by German corporate law, which required joint-stock companies to establish managing (*Verwaltungs-*) and supervisory (*Aufsichtsräte*) boards. The bankers' presence tended to be concentrated on the latter. Where possible, German bankers created a *Hausbank* or exclusive relationship with client firms. In other words they looked after most of the firms' day-to-day commercial banking requirements while also playing the leading role in long-term financial operations. The constant stream of information about firms' profitability and prospects derived from this complex and intimate relationship was supposed to allow the universal bank to provide finance at lower cost than would have been possible if the relationship were more sporadic or arms-length.[3]

For the purposes of this study, a narrow definition of universal banking based on the classical German model as sketched out above would be inappropriate. Among the other countries discussed by our contributors, only Italy had banks with managing and supervisory boards, and even in Italy the double board system was neither generalized nor mandated by law. Some of the countries in our sample, one thinks of Portugal, hardly had functioning securities markets, and we would have had to exclude them if we limited our definition of universal banking to institutions that floated securities.[4]

Consequently, we are proposing a broad definition of universal banking here. For our purposes, banks that accept deposits, and engage in both short- and long-term lending are universal banks. While this definition allows us to make broad cross-national comparisons, we recognize that it has its own shortcomings. Long-term lending can be disguised as short-term transactions in a banker's balance sheet. Credits that were initially extended as short-term advances can become frozen if economic conditions change. Bankers that try to stay out of the long end of the market might be reluctant to drive their clients to the wall in the event of a crisis. As Ranald Michie observes in his contribution, the recent literature on British provincial banks has discovered that they were more involved in the long end of the market than the stark differences between ideal types of British and German banking used by the theorists would allow. German banks, in turn, were anxious to secure collateral for long-term loans that could be sold in a crisis. But, as Håkan Lindgren and Hans Sjögren point out in their contribution to this volume, even if the actual differences in practice were not as stark as the ideal types might suggest, not just scholars today, but also contemporary observers in the late nineteenth century, believed that there were profound differences in the practices of British and German bankers, and that these differences concerned primarily their respective attitudes toward long-term lending.

It is also necessary to add a few words about periodization. As noted, major differences between national financial systems were clearly in place by the end of the nineteenth century so 1900, or better 1914, might serve as a convenient end point for our study. A few of our contributors follow specific threads of development into the 1920s, but we have chosen not to deal with the major changes introduced in the financial sector by legislation in the wake of the Great Depression. We have asked our contributors to take the perspective of the commercial banker, as he made strategic choices about how to employ his resources, and about how his choices were shaped by environmental constraints and incentives. The key period for us therefore, begins in the years following legislation that made it relatively easy to form joint-stock banks. Across most of Europe, that occurred in the middle of the nineteenth century. This volume deals primarily with the period running from the middle of the nineteenth century through the outbreak of World War I, therefore, although some contributors have found it necessary to trace the decisive variables shaping the behavior of commercial bankers farther back in time.

The essays

The specific arguments made by the contributors to this volume offer highly varied and often nuanced responses to the questions posed in the analytical framework above. They propose both demand- and supply-side, and both market- and regulation-centered explanations for outcomes in different countries. Many contributors propose multi-variable explanations that lie on both sides of our two dichotomies.

8   *Douglas J. Forsyth*

Balance Sheet of a Commercial Bank

Assets	Liabilities

Demand-side accounts: → **Supply-side accounts:**

Long / *Long*

1. 'Gerschenkronian' incentives for rapid economic growth afforded by relative backwardness (Lindgren-Sjögren for Sweden; Rowney for Russia).

2. 'Gerschenkronian' constraints: information asymmetry (Deeg for Germany, Lescure for France, Polsi for Italy. All three find this applies especially to local banks).

3. Active lender-of-last-resort favors long-term lending by banks (Lescure for local universal banks in France; Rowney for Russia; Verdier).

8. Local non-profit banks protected and promoted by legislation capture most of deposit market (Deeg and Michie for Germany; Knutsen for Norway; Polsi for Italy; Verdier).

9. *Banques des dépôts* drive local universal banks out of the deposit market (Lescure for France).

10. Postal savings banks capture deposits (Lescure, elsewhere, for France).

11. Central bank captures deposits (Martín-Aceña, elsewhere, for Spain).

12. Public debt captures savings that would otherwise be deposited in banks (Polsi for Italy; Reis for Portugal).

13. Economic poverty and cultural distrust limit bank deposits (Reis for Portugal).

14. Restrictions on securities markets reinforce banks' role in long-term lending (Jonker for Germany).

Short / *Short*

4. Absence of lender-of-last-resort deters long-term lending (Knutsen for Norway; Verdier).

5. Call market offers banks opportunities for short-term lending (Michie for Britain).

6. Foreign investors provide investment capital (Knutsen for Norway; Rowney for Russia).

7. Highly developed formal or informal securities markets provide investment capital (Michie for Britain; Jonker for Britain, France and the Netherlands; Knutsen for Norway).

15. The interbank market drains resources from savings to commercial banks (Lindgren-Sjögren for Sweden).

16. **Policymakers** and bankers imitate German banking practice, because of that nation's impressive record of economic growth. (Lindgren-Sjögren for Sweden; Rowney for Russia).

Figure 0.1 A schematic account of arguments linking environmental incentives and constraints to strategic decisionmaking by commercial bankers.

The range of explanation articulated within the volume is set out schematically in Figure 0.1. The spatial organization of the panel assigns variables affecting the assets side of the banker's balance sheet to the left side of the table, and variables affecting the liabilities side to the right side. Variables inducing bankers to extend their lending activities into the long end of the market appear at the top of the table, and variables encouraging them to confine themselves to the short end of the market appear at the bottom. Fonts illustrate the distinction between market-

and state-centered explanations for bankers' strategic choices: the standard font indicates market-centered explanations and boldface indicates state-centered explanations.

Gerschenkron's classic demand-side, market-based explanations for the origins of universal banking appear under rubrics 1 and 2 in the upper left-hand corner of the figure. The two components of Verdier's thesis appear under rubrics 3, 4, and 8 (rubrics 3 and 4 are opposites of one another). Verdier's argument that the distribution of deposits between the for- and non-profit sectors within national banking systems will affect for-profit bankers' choices is a liabilities or supply-side variable; the absence of a lender-of-last-resort is an assets or demand-side, albeit non-Gerschenkronian variable. Both of the principal variables identified by Verdier involve state regulation, as opposed to market incentives or constraints.

Our model captures 15 of the 16 variables invoked by our contributors; the 16th lies outside the analytical model proposed here and thus appears alone at the bottom of the chart. To add some additional depth to our analytical framework, Figure 0.1 references two articles published elsewhere (under rubrics 10 and 11). Let us now review each contributor's essay in turn, and explore how it relates to our common analytical framework.

The comparative essays by Ranald Michie and Joost Jonker develop arguments distinct from, but complementary to, those of Verdier. Verdier argues that one cannot understand the strategic choices of *commercial bankers*, without considering how they are shaped by the choices of actors in the *non-profit banking sector*, and by the *central bank*. The essays by Michie and Jonker argue that banking structures are determined also by the manner in which *securities markets* are regulated and structured. Like Verdier, Michie and Jonker argue that financial systems have been shaped decisively by government regulation and intervention.

Ranald Michie offers a comparative essay on Britain and Germany. National legislation is a key variable for him in explaining different outcomes in the two countries. In Britain government did little to regulate the securities markets, fostering their growth. Until 1825, in contrast, the Bank of England exercised a legal monopoly on joint-stock banking in England and Wales, and its choices substantially shaped the British banking system. The Bank of England failed to develop an extensive national branch network, and it prevented other institutions from doing so. It turned its attention primarily to the London market, fostering the growth of specialized institutions there. Provincial banks took the lead in developing branched networks once the Bank of England's monopoly was revoked. By then investment banking business was firmly in the hands of London-based institutions, and the branched joint stock banks eschewed this line of activity in favor of short-term commercial lending.

In Germany, Michie points out, a broad market even for government securities did not develop until the second half of the nineteenth century, because of political fragmentation, and because of the tardy assumption of responsibility by state parliaments for the public debt. Even after German unification in 1871 securities markets remained more heavily regulated in Germany than in Britain, restricting their growth. Meanwhile, Michie argues that a nationwide network of branched commercial banks failed to develop in Germany for two reasons. First, late political unification hindered the development of branched networks. Second, dovetailing with Verdier, Michie argues that government encouragement of the non-profit sector kept a substantial part of the deposit base out of the hands of the commercial banks.

Michie also makes an interesting argument about how the existence of a broad, deep securities market in Britain affected the choices bankers faced in structuring their asset portfolios. In Britain banks could place funds medium-term and even short-term on the call market. In Germany, where securities markets were weaker, there was less short-term paper, and this reinforced the tendency of banks to engage more heavily in long-term lending. It is worth calling attention to this, since few banking historians have much understanding of securities market sophistication, and its implications for bankers' choices.

Joost Jonker examines the development of securities markets and banks in four countries: the Netherlands, Britain, France and Germany. He uses a functionalist argument developed by Robert Merton and Zvi Bodie to explain what financial systems do as his theoretical point of departure (Merton and Bodie, 1995). Following them, he argues that a fully developed financial system must perform six core functions, to wit: 1) provide ways of clearing and settling payments, facilitating trade; 2) provide a mechanism for pooling resources and for subdividing shares in various enterprises; 3) provide ways of transferring economic resources through time, across borders, and among economic sectors; 4) provide ways of managing risks; 5) provide price information, in order to coordinate decision-making in various sectors of the economy; and 6) provide ways of dealing with incentive problems created by information asymmetries.

Jonker's own argument, however, is anything but functionalist. He seeks to show how the exercise of these six functions came to be institutionalized in very different ways in four countries. In order for financial systems to develop vigorously, the state needed to intervene in the economy to provide three prerequisites. First, it needed to bring about a successful financial revolution, i.e. a switch from enforced loans or the contracting of government debt out to private business in the form of personal obligations, to a system of publicly accountable debt management with transferable securities. Second, the state needed to provide an open, flexible and generally accepted system of commercial law, including safeguards for private property. Third, it needed to create a firm currency largely free from official interference. Otherwise, financial innovation was best secured, in Jonker's view, when the state stood aside, letting financial markets develop through a spiral of innovation fostered by competition.

Jonker feels that in the absence of extensive regulation, banks tended to develop functional specialization and securities markets tended to stand at the core of national financial systems. The Netherlands takes chronological precedence in his account because it was the cradle of the modern financial revolution. It firmly established a system of public finance tied to representative government by the end of the sixteenth century. The creation of a market for government securities paved the way for publicly quoted joint stock companies issuing transferable shares and bonds. Broad, deep securities markets, Jonker argues, involved forging a close link between the money market and the securities market. In the Netherlands, a seamless range of facilities from short-term lending to long-term investment was created. He informs us that a technique known as *prolongatie*, or the lombarding of securities for a month, tacitly rolled over until one of the parties cancelled the transaction, became so common in the Netherlands that deposit banking never really developed there until World War I. The Netherlands represents the only country in our study where the development of deposit banking was retarded by the sophistication of securities markets!

The English financial revolution of the seventeenth century, in Jonker's view, bore many similarities with the earlier Dutch financial revolution. It is of crucial importance for our volume, however, that banks acted as intermediaries between savers and the securities markets in Britain. Banks and bankers functioned as hinges between the system's functions, and between England's regions in a way that Dutch bankers never really could, he notes. Deposits became more central to the English system. London developed a call-money market that was bill-based, rather than securities-based, like Amsterdam. The Bank of England influenced the development of the banking system crucially. In contrast to the Dutch Wisselbank, it acted as a "flywheel," not merely as a "facilitator," according to Jonker.

France was of course late in bringing its financial revolution to conclusion. However, by the Restoration in 1815, parliamentary responsibility for the public debt was established, and a market for government and private securities developed apace. Jonker notes that the official securities market in France was highly regulated, but in his view this was not of great importance, since the unofficial *coulisse* market was allowed to operate more or less unhindered. Jonker treats France's experiment with universal banking after the founding of the Crédit Mobilier in 1852 as an aberration. The expansive claims made for the Crédit Mobilier's contribution to French economic development by Gerschenkron and by Rondo Cameron have been discredited by the research of subsequent generations of historians, he points out.[5] By the early 1870s the Parisian *haute banque* was clearly specialized in company finance and stock exchange floatations, leaving deposit banking to other specialized institutions.

In Jonker's account Germany is the outlier. It failed to develop broad deep securities markets for two reasons. The first is late state development. It was not just that Germany unified late; even more importantly it established parliamentary responsibility for the public debt late, and this retarded the development of securities markets. Moreover, even after parliament's responsibility for finance was enshrined in the constitution, first of Prussia, and later of the Reich, German officials continued to harbor a deep suspicion, and even outright hostility toward the Berlin stock exchange as likely to undermine public confidence in the state.

The attitude of the public authorities toward futures markets, and trading in options and other financial derivatives is of decisive importance to Jonker. Futures trading provided a vital hinge between the money and capital markets; where it was limited the securities markets tended to lose their vitality and their functions were assumed by other institutions or by foreign exchanges. In the Netherlands the authorities never regulated futures transactions substantially. In Britain futures transactions could not be enforced through the courts as normal commercial transactions. Rather than suppressing futures trading, this provided an impetus for stockbrokers to form the Stock Subscription Room, a private club with controlled membership in 1801. According to Jonker, the legitimacy of futures trading in France was firmly established by the 1820s. In Germany in contrast, lawmakers intervened repeatedly to restrict futures trading, in certain periods outlawing it altogether. It was still a sideshow in Berlin by 1890, he suggests, and not an integral part of operations, as in Amsterdam, London or Paris. In 1897 the *Börsengesetz* or Exchange Act imposed far-reaching restrictions on futures trading. The balance between the stock exchange and the commercial banks in Germany now shifted decisively in favor of the latter. The big German banks moved futures operations entirely to London, Paris or Brussels. The big banks dominated German stock exchanges and internalized many transactions that occurred over markets elsewhere. "What could have been the system's lungs," Jonker writes, "became the appendix, not quite useless but without a clearly defined function for the body economic." "German banks," Jonker concludes, "became universal not ... because of market imperfections, as argued by Gerschenkron and others, but because of deliberate restrictions on competitive markets introduced by a government wary of free markets for political reasons."

It is interesting to note that farming interests, united in the powerful *Bund der Landwirte* (BDL) spearheaded the campaign against the stock exchange in the 1870s and 1880s. This provides us with yet another link to the argument of Verdier, since agricultural interests in Germany sustained both the non-profit banking sector while also hindering the development of the stock market.

Now we turn to the single-country case studies. Among the essays in this volume, those written by Richard Deeg on Germany and by Alessandro Polsi on Italy dovetail most closely with Verdier's arguments. Both insist on the primacy of politics in producing and sustaining universal banking in the two countries in question. Both argue that the domination of the national deposit market by non-profit banks prevented commercial banks in Germany and Italy from specializing in short-term commercial banking on the model of their counterparts in Britain.

Deeg's contribution illustrates how fully legislation and regulation reinforced and perpetuated social and regional segmentation in German banking. The big private universal banks developed a close association with heavy industry. Insofar as they drew deposits from households, it was primarily from the wealthy. The financial needs of small and medium-sized enterprises, the German *Mittelstand*, meanwhile, were met by regional for-profit universal banks, cooperative banks, and especially after the turn of the century increasingly by the savings banks. Thus the segmentation in the German financial system corresponded closely to and perpetuated the segmentation in German manufacturing that has come to light in the recent literature.[6] The cooperative and savings banks, moreover, played a key role in sustaining Marshallian industrial districts consisting of a myriad of small and medium-sized firms.

Deeg and Polsi leave us with no doubt that banking segmentation was maintained by legislation protecting the non-profit sector. Not only did savings and cooperative banks enjoy tax privileges, the laws applying to them also made mergers between banks of different types next to impossible, impeding the rapid spread of branch banking. In Germany an extensive interbank market developed in the late nineteenth century, but it was segmented between the three types of institution. The cooperative and savings bank movements both developed their own central institutions (*Girozentrale*); only for-profit commercial banks lent excess funds to the *Groß-banken* in Berlin. In Italy, Polsi informs us, the interbank market remained highly fragmented. In Germany each type of institution ran its own payments network; in Italy, the central bank ran one payments network, in which many private, local banks participated, while the big commercial banks in Milan ran another, virtually independent network.

The major differences between Germany and Italy that emerge from these two essays concern the functionality and stability of the two systems. Deeg depicts a financial system that produced favorable results with respect to economic growth and stability. Polsi depicts a fragmented system that yielded sub-optimal results with respect to efficiency and stability. This divergence illustrates an important limitation to the arguments advanced in this volume: while we seek to explain how and why different financial systems developed historically, we have little new to add to the old debates about the relative efficiency and stability of different systems – on this more below.

Both Gerschenkron and Verdier have invoked French evidence in support of their contrasting explanations for the development of banking systems. Gerschenkron used the involvement of the Crédit Mobilier in the financing of French railway construction in the 1850s and 1860s as an illustration of the contribution of universal banking to industrialization in a relatively backward country. Verdier, meanwhile, draws support for his argument from the fact that the great Paris-based deposit-taking banks (*banques de dépôt*) turned away from universal banking in the 1870s and 1880s, confining themselves to short-term lending. France, Verdier points out, did not have a strong non-profit banking sector and the *banques de dépôt* successfully captured a preponderant share of the national market for deposits.

Michel Lescure's essay on France does not offer unequivocal support for either Gerschenkron or Verdier. Lescure points out that while functional segmentation between *banques de dépôt* and *banques d'affaires* emerged in the French capital in the 1870s and 1880s, smaller private banks in the provinces continued to practice universal banking well into the twentieth century. They were sustained by the Banque de France, which offered liberal rediscounting facilities and support as lender-of-last-resort. Although conceived by Napoleon as an agent of centralization, the Banque de France wound up supporting provincial unit banking in the late nineteenth century because of rivalry with the big *banques de dépôt*. The latter refused to hold reserves or rediscount paper with the issue bank; they also encroached upon the Banque de France's lending operations by offering lower rates and better terms to its non-banking customers. The Banque de France thus saw both its profitability and its ability to determine market interest rates threatened; the alliance with the provincial banks helped it parry both of these threats.

Despite the centralized nature of the French political system, Lescure points out that the French economy remained highly fragmented along regional lines in the late nineteenth century. In many cases small to medium-sized firms clustered in specialized industrial districts. Local banks were better placed than the Parisian institutions to overcome information asymmetry problems and offer long-term finance at competitive rates to neighboring firms, he argues. Indeed, Lescure suggests that the disappearance of these institutions in the 1920s and 1930s, after the Banque de France adopted a less generous rediscounting policy in its dealings with them, may have dealt a fatal blow to small and medium-sized manufacturing firms in many parts of France.

The success of the *banques de dépôt* in capturing the lion's share of the deposit market, meanwhile, may have strengthened the inclination of local banks to engage in universal banking. They tended to have high ratios of capital and shareholders' reserves to deposits, and thus had to worry less about maturities mismatches than institutions in which deposits constituted a greater share of liabilities.

One encounters similar institutions in other contributions to this volume. Polsi describes how the Banca d'Italia built a similar alliance with local and provincial for-profit banks in Italy. Like Lescure, he feels that the information asymmetry argument applies better to local banks and to small and medium-sized firms than it does to the largest firms and banks. In Germany, as Deeg's essay makes clear, local and provincial universal banks were an important source of finance for small and medium-sized firms. However, from the late nineteenth century through the 1920s, the *Großbanken* based in Berlin absorbed them. The amalgamation movement in Germany was largely amicable and it built upon correspondence relationships that had developed earlier on. In some cases, Deeg points out, cooperative and savings banks made inroads into the industrial clientele of provincial institutions as the latter lost their independence. In contrast to France and Italy, the Reichsbank maintained a more cooperative relationship with the largest for-profit institutions, and it made no attempt to play off local banks against the *Großbanken*.

To summarize, Lescure's essay proposes segmentation in France between large *banques de dépôt* and local and provincial universal banks. This banking structure conforms neither to the functional segmentation characteristic of Britain nor to the segmentation between for- and non-profit sectors characteristic of Germany. Lescure's explanation for the development of the French banking system combines demand-side arguments (information asymmetries sustain universal banking on the local level) and supply-side arguments (the *banques de dépôt* crowd local for-profit banks out of the deposit market). The crucial role of the central bank in sustaining local institutions in France illustrates the importance of state intervention in shaping the banking system; the happy marriage of Marshallian industrial districts with provincial universal banking, in contrast, points to the importance of market variables.

Sverre Knutsen's essay on Norway offers little support for a Gerschenkronian interpretation of banking development, but also a less than perfect fit with Verdier's thesis. As was noted above, commercial bankers in Norway constructed asset portfolios that put them somewhere between the British and German ideal types. Long-term lending, he informs us, was largely in the form of rollover credits.

Norway appears to have been a perfect environment for Gerschenkron-style universal banking. It was a very backward country in 1850, and it enjoyed one of the world's highest growth rates during the late nineteenth century. Banks were not, however, the most important sources of investment capital during Norway's "big spurt". Retained earnings were of greater significance. Growth in Norway's merchant shipping industry, one of the largest in the world, was financed also through informal partnerships until the turn of the century and increasingly on the organized capital market in Christiania (Oslo) after that. Heavy industry, notably electro-chemicals and metallurgy, meanwhile, was financed on foreign capital markets and through foreign direct investment. Thus the Norwegian case illustrates that demand for capital in a relatively backward economy does not necessarily call into being universal banks.

At first glance, the Verdier thesis also would appear to predict the rise of universal banking in Norway. Savings banks had sprung up across the country prior to the 1870s, when the first big wave of commercial bank foundings occurred. The non-profit savings sector held on to a significant share of total deposits in Norway: 64 percent in 1870, and 49 percent in 1913. This was a larger share in both years than in the other Scandinavian countries, Knutsen points out. Moreover, the Norwegian banking system was highly fragmented territorially; unit banking was the rule, and local agricultural interests were instrumental in defeating the efforts of the larger institutions based in the capital from establishing extensive branch networks. Why, under these circumstances, were commercial banks reluctant to expand aggressively into the long end of the market? Knutsen notes that the Bank of Norway did not take an expansive view of its role as lender of last resort until the turn of the century. Thus the second of Verdier's two preconditions for the emergence of universal banking was not met here.

The Swedish case, as described by Håkan Lindgren and Hans Sjögren, offers some support for both the Gerschenkron and the Verdier theses. The early development of a non-profit savings bank sector would appear to put it in the set of countries for which Verdier predicts the emergence of universal banking. However, Sweden's savings banks had anomalous features. First, they enjoyed no privileges vis-à-vis for-profit institutions, apart from not having to earn a profit for their shareholders or owners. Until 1892, the savings banks enjoyed almost complete discretion in their investment policy as well; some acted like commercial banks.

Another anomaly of the Swedish banking system concerns the interbank market. No regional or national federation of savings banks emerged, much less regional or national *Girozentrale*, or clearing institutions, as in Germany. The savings banks acted in some respects almost as subsidiaries of for-profit commercial banks. They deposited their funds in current or time accounts with the commercial banks; they acted as correspondents for commercial banks and utilized their notes (note-issuing was restricted to the Riksbank only in 1903) in their local business activities.

In no other country in our sample in which savings banks established themselves widely in the nineteenth century, in advance of commercial banks, did they enjoy such weak legal and regulatory protection as in Sweden. Moreover, legislation in 1892 severely limited not only the types of lending operation in which they could engage, but also set maximum limits for individual savings accounts. Not surprisingly under these circumstances, the savings banks held only about a third of total deposits in Sweden by 1913, with for-profit commercial banks holding most of the remaining two-thirds.

Verdier's model would predict that Swedish commercial banks would specialize in short-term lending, given their success in capturing the lion's share of the deposit market. For much of the nineteenth century, Lindgren and Sjögren note, that was the case. However, after the turn of the century Swedish commercial banks increasingly began to imitate German universal banks in their lending strategy. A new banking law in 1912 facilitated the trend toward universalism; it relaxed earlier restrictions on purchasing and holding industrial shares by commercial banks.

The authors offer two explanations for the turn toward universal banking in Sweden at the end of the nineteenth century. One is a straightforward Gerschenkronian account of how the growth of heavy industry created a demand for long-term finance. Indeed, among the contributors to this volume Lindgren and Sjögren most explicitly embrace Gerschenkron's classic thesis. They qualify this argument somewhat by pointing out that Germany's industrial success spurred imitation of the German financial model in Sweden. In other words, the power of example, especially the tendency to imitate successful nations, must be included as an important explanatory variable shaping banking structures.

This cannot be situated comfortably in the analytical structure we are proposing in this volume. As we have seen, by the late nineteenth century, British and German banking practices were widely understood as competing models. As Germany's economic growth outstripped that of Britain at the end of the nineteenth century, bankers and policymakers in other countries were tempted to imitate the German model. This phenomenon can be found not just in Sweden, but also in other countries, including Italy, Russia, and even the Netherlands.[7] As Germany's economic fortunes waned again during the Weimar Republic, and in particular in the wake of the German and Austrian banking crises in 1931, policymakers and bankers in other countries once again discovered the virtues of the British model.[8] As Ranald Michie points out in his essay, advanced industrial countries have gone through another cycle of imitation of *"Modeldeutschland"* in the 1970s and early 1980s only to embrace the British or the American financial model, as it is now widely understood, in the 1990s.[9]

The essays by Don K. Rowney and Jaime Reis deal with the most backward countries in our sample: Late Imperial Russia and Portugal respectively. Russia, of course, assumed a prominent position in Gerschenkron's thought as an example of a country that was so backward in the late nineteenth century that universal banks were inadequate to serve as compensatory institutions. Instead, direct intervention by the state was required to set in motion the process of industrialization. However, even in Russia Gerschenkron was inclined to assign a developmental role to the mixed banks a generation after the initial "big spurt" of industrialization in the mid-1880s. By 1907, Gerschenkron argued, Russian development had reached a level that made it possible for the state to withdraw from the direct financing of industry, and German-style mixed banking appeared in St. Petersburg.

Rowney points out that despite political centralization, Russia had a banking system that was highly segmented along regional lines on the eve of World War I. In St. Petersburg universal banking predominated, and the larger institutions maintained intense relations with heavy industry. In Moscow, in contrast, banks tended to concentrate on short-term commercial lending. Moscow, in turn, was a center of light manufacturing. This might suggest a Gerschenkronian demand-side explanation, with light industry calling into being commercial, and heavy industry calling into being universal banking, and Rowney offers this as a hypothesis. However, he also notes that universal banks were founded in St. Petersburg after the Russo-Japanese War with very direct state encouragement. Indeed, ex-bureaucrats and ministers were prominently represented on the boards of these banks alongside the managers and owners of firms that were heavily dependent on state contracts for their survival. The *Gosbank* (State Bank) favored the development of these banks by offering generous rediscounts and taking an expansive view of its responsibilities of lender-of-last-resort. It is possible, Rowney suggests, to argue that universal banking came into being in Russia because the state willed it into existence. Even the Moscow banks, Rowney makes clear, owed their existence initially to generous support by the state. Thus it is possible to argue that both for-profit sectors in Russia's regionally segmented commercial banking system were shaped primarily by state regulation, and not by the demand of industry for finance. According to this scenario, English-style banking was established in Moscow in the 1880s because state bureaucrats looked to Britain as a model at the time; universal banking developed in St. Petersburg after 1907 because Germany was now the model for Russian officialdom. Regional segmentation would reflect the chronological layering of government initiatives.

In Russia the non-profit sector held only about a third of total bank deposits on the eve of World War I. Most of this was in the hands of the State Savings *kassy*, "whose hundreds of teller windows led directly back to the State Bank." Although modest as a percentage of total deposits, the *kassy* held 70 percent of savings in savings accounts in the Russian Empire. The Russian market for deposits, in other words, was highly segmented along class lines, like those in Germany and Italy. Depositors were exempted from some capital gains taxes and registration fees; the state guaranteed deposits. Together with cooperative credit and loan-savings associations, peasant small savings and loan communal associations and *zemstvo* savings banks, the *kassy* acculturated artisans, petty merchants, peasants and the more highly paid workers to putting their savings in banks.

Portugal was even more backward and less economically dynamic than Russia on the eve of World War I. In his essay on his native country, Jaime Reis concludes that Portugal tends to defy Verdier's predictions, while Gerschenkron's are inapplicable. Portugal was a centralized polity, with a weak non-profit banking sector. According to Verdier, we should expect the development of extensive commercial banking networks, and deposit banking. Instead, unit banking along universal lines prevailed. Why? There seem to be two principal reasons. The most important was poverty. There was not a very large deposit market for banks to capture in Portugal prior to World War I. The country was poor and savings rates were low. Moreover, there was little trust in financial institutions, especially outside of the two major cities. This lack of trust was fully justified by the performance of the few banks that existed in provincial centers, according to Reis's analysis. Even the Bank of Portugal had a hard time staffing its provincial offices with honest personnel. To the extent that individuals and households did save in rural Portugal, Reis speculates, they must have put their savings in their mattresses. The second reason for the underdevelopment of a deposit market was the high Portuguese national debt. In 1910 it amounted to three times the aggregate of bank deposits. 85 percent of interest payments were made to residents of Lisbon and Oporto, so the public debt crowded out banks on the liabilities side in the cities, but not in the countryside. Portuguese banks had high capital plus reserves to assets ratios, and comparatively modest deposits. This constituted a necessary if insufficient precondition for universal banking. Reis also notes that another necessary, but insufficient precondition posited by Verdier was present in Portugal: a central bank that exercised lender-of-last-resort responsibilities.

On the supply side, Reis suggests that opportunities for short-term lending for the few banks that existed were relatively scarce; either one practiced universal banking or one had no banking business at all in a backward country like Portugal.

All of this might suggest an affirmation of Gerschenkron's classic theses. With the exception of the possible crowding out effect of a large public debt on bank deposits in narrow urban markets, the structure of the Portuguese economy seems to have been the determining factor in the structure of banking, not government intervention or regulation. Similarly, demand-side variables seem to be paramount, not supply-side variables. However, as Reis points out, Gerschenkron was not really interested in backward nations like Portugal with stagnant economies. He believed that universal banks could be agents for rapid development under certain conditions, but he never suggested that they would exercise this role everywhere.

Within our study, Portugal looks like something of an anomaly. The crowding-out effect of a large public debt on the development of a deposit market is observable in at least one other country in our sample as well, i.e. in Italy, as the essay by Polsi indicates. Even so, Portugal stands out because of the late development of a market for bank deposits. The Verdier thesis hinges crucially upon how bank deposits are held within a national economy. It appears to be irrelevant in countries so poor and so backward that they have not developed a substantial market for bank deposits in the first place.

As noted above, to add some additional depth to the larger argument, Figure 0.1 contains references to two articles published elsewhere. Rubric 10 refers to an article by Michel Lescure in which he argues that the postal savings network in

France crowded provincial for-profit banks out of the deposit market, prolonging their involvement in the long end of the market.[10] Rubric 11 refers to work by Pablo Martín-Aceña, arguing that the domination of Spain's deposit market by the central bank induced commercial banks in that country to practice universal banking (Martín-Aceña, 1995).

The results

This volume does not offer a systematic destruction of Gerschenkron, nor was it intended to do so. The general conclusion of our work, however, is that constraints and incentives on the *liabilities* side of bankers' balance sheets and *government regulation* have been more important in shaping financial systems than *assets-side* and *market constraints* and *incentives*, although evidence for the influence of both emerges in the various country studies. Thus we do, collectively, "stand Gerschenkron on his head," although some of us do so with greater determination than others.[11]

One more core idea has emerged from this project. It is that national financial systems need to be understood in their entirety, and this requires at a minimum examining securities markets, central banks, for-profit banking, including local institutions, the non-profit banking sector, and the interrelationships among all of these sectors. For too long, historians of banking have ignored the non-noble sectors of banking, including savings banks. Historians have tended to focus too exclusively on the largest for-profit institutions, and as a result they often have failed to appreciate how the strategic choices of the latter have been influenced by the activity of other institutions. As Richard Deeg notes in his essay on Germany, all three sectors of banking in that country, i.e. the for-profit universal banks, the savings banks, and the cooperatives, tend to have their *Haushistoriker*, and the English-language literature in particular is overwhelmingly about the big private banks.

Similarly, our study underscores the necessity of studying banks and securities markets as a totality. As Ranald Michie observes in his essay, historians, especially those who, following Gerschenkron, have assigned a crucial developmental role to universal banks, frequently have investigated the banking system alone, and then assessed it in terms of its contribution to economic development. The results of this *modus operandi*, he points out, inevitably tend to favor universal banks, for they can be seen to be providing the most comprehensive service to their business customers. Michie also points out that although securities markets at times functioned as an alternative to banks, the relationship was also in part complementary. Thus the distinction commonly made, particularly in the political science literature, between "market-based" financial systems, such as that in Britain, and "bank-based" systems, such as that in Germany, fails to capture crucial relationships between the two.[12] Securities floatations were an important part of the business of universal banks, he points out. Bank loans could scarcely have fully substituted for securities in any case, he continues, if one considers that in 1913 $158bn in securities existed, between three and four times the total amount of bank deposits worldwide at the time.

Another important result of this volume is the illustration of how important interbank markets are in structuring national financial systems. In Germany funds did not flow from the savings bank to the commercial bank sector via interbank markets; in Sweden they did, and this may have influenced the decisions commercial bankers made in structuring their asset portfolios.

Still another result of this volume is to call attention to the importance of information asymmetries in sustaining the practice of universal banking on the local level in France, Germany and Italy. Gerschenkron associated a poor information environment with relative backwardness. In our volume, in contrast, Deeg, Lescure, and Polsi associate information asymmetries, and the successful practice of universal banking, with local and regional institutions, and with Marshallian industrial districts, embracing clusters of small and medium-sized firms with similar product specializations.[13]

In order to derive the maximum heuristic benefits from this study, it is important to set out clearly the issues about which our study *does not* afford important new insights. Chief among them is the old question concerning the *relative efficiency* of German-style universal banking versus British-style specialized banking. An explanation for the *origins* of different national financial systems does not resolve the issue of relative efficiency unequivocally. As was noted above, scholarly and popular opinion has tended to shift in favor of German-style banking in periods in which German economic growth has outpaced that in Britain and the United States. In periods in which Germany's growth has lagged, including the last decade, opinion tends to become more favorable to US and British institutions once again. Some contributors to this volume, most notably Ranald Michie and Joost Jonker, express open skepticism about the thesis that German institutions are or were more efficient. Others, notably Richard Deeg, feel that German institutions produced elegant solutions within the context of the German political economy, without seeking to generalize the usefulness of German practice to other countries. In the view of the editors, the fact that national financial systems have maintained such different institutional form for so long, without one set of countries having gained clear advantage over the other, suggests that any efficiency advantage must be subtle, capable of being offset by relative efficiency differentials in other areas of the political economy, including labor market institutions and education.[14]

Future research agenda

We hope that the analytical framework and arguments proposed in this volume will stimulate further research. If the arguments made here by Verdier, Deeg, and Polsi are right, and the manner in which the non-profit banking sector is structured is of crucial importance for the development of the for-profit, commercial banking sector, then it is high time for scholars to study systematically and comparatively the development of non-profit banking. The evidence that Lindgren and Sjögren offer here concerning the anomalies of the Swedish non-profit sector illustrate how important this endeavor could be. Similarly, we hope that our findings will encourage financial historians in the future to devote greater attention to the development of interbank markets, a virtually non-existent field of inquiry up to now. Further, our volume calls attention to the need to investigate the relationship between Marshallian industrial districts and local or regional universal banks.

This volume has offered primarily qualitative evidence to test the rival theories of Gerschenkron and Verdier. We hope, however, that the debate initiated here will entice econometrists to devise new quantitative tests that could shed light on our arguments.

Finally, yet another important task that we hope other scholars will take up is to explore how additional countries fit into or do not fit into the model we are proposing. A case study of the United States would be particularly useful. Among European countries not considered in this volume, we would welcome work on several where universal banking developed, including the Habsburg Empire, Switzerland, Belgium, and Spain. Studies of Denmark and Finland would enhance our understanding of Scandinavia. We would welcome also work on late-late developing countries, including those in Latin America and East Asia.

Contemporary implications

Our study may afford some insight into the *direction* in which financial systems will develop in the near future, in an environment characterized by liberalization and international convergence in the regulation of financial institutions. As a thought experiment, let us put ourselves in the position of a contemporary commercial banker, as she thinks through how new opportunities and constraints on both the assets and the liabilities side of her balance sheet, and how changes both in markets and in the regulatory environment, will affect her strategy.

If the burden of opinion and argument in this volume is correct, and regulation has been a more decisive force shaping financial systems than market incentives, then the current process of regulatory change should promote *convergence* among national financial systems. Our hypothetical banker would want to focus on two sorts of changes in particular. First, if she operated in a country in which savings banks or other non-profit institutions have enjoyed substantial privileges, she would need to monitor changes in that protective legislation carefully. Even a scholar like Richard Deeg, who takes a favorable view of German financial institutions, feels that removal of the regulatory privileges of savings and cooperative banks in that country would produce massive change in the entire system. Whether or not this will actually occur is another question. Our study of the historical evidence also indicates that differences in national financial systems have proved remarkably robust over the past century and a half.

Second, our study would confirm another trend that our hypothetical commercial banker would be quite aware of already – the trend toward securitization. The removal of international financial controls and the liberalization of national financial markets since the 1980s has produced explosive growth in securities markets. The findings of this volume suggest that the logic of this process mirrors developments in the nineteenth century, and suggest that in the absence of generalized re-regulation of securities markets this process will continue.

Notes

1 Gerschenkron's essays are collected in Gerschenkron, 1962. Gerschenkron's primary aim, it should be pointed out, was to explain the pattern he saw in European industrialization at the country level. Only one part of his work related to banking and finance, but that part has become foundational for scholars seeking to explain the development of national financial systems.

2 Needless to add, it has long been appreciated by scholars that regulation and other forms of state economic intervention have played an important role in shaping financial systems. Sylla and Toniolo (eds), 1991b is structured squarely around this proposition. What is missing from the previous literature, including this volume, however, is the development of a convincing counterfactual to Gerschenkron's thesis predicated on the primacy of regulation over market incentives in shaping divergent paths in the development of national financial systems. Indeed, many of the contributions to the Sylla–Toniolo volume take the validity of Gerschenkron's thesis for granted, and incorporate it into their own explorations of how regulation has affected finance.

3 Classic studies of universal banking in Germany include, in addition to the sources cited above, Riesser, 1911; and Whale, 1968 [1930]. Within the more recent literature see Wellhöner, 1989; Gall *et al.*, 1995; and Fohlin, 1997a.

4 On Italy see, in addition to the essay by Polsi in this volume, Confalonieri, 1977–80; Confalonieri, 1982; Hertner, 1984; and Forsyth, 1991; on Portugal see Jaime Reis's essay in this volume.

5 In addition to the work by Cameron and Gerschenkron cited above see also Cameron, 1961.

6 See for example Herrigel, 1996.

7 On Italy see Confalonieri, 1977–80; Hertner, 1984; and Forsyth, 1991; on Russia, in addition to the contribution by Rowney in this volume, see Bovykin and Anan'ich, 1991; and Yudanov, 1997; on the Netherlands see Vanthemsche, 1991.

8 See for example the essays in James, Lindgren and Teichova (eds), 1991.

9 Critiques of British banking, using *Modeldeutschland* explicitly as a comparison include Ingham, 1984; and Kennedy, 1987. For a recent comparative study more favorable to Anglo-American practice see Story and Walter, 1997.

10 Lescure, 1995a. See also Lescure and Plessis (eds), 1999.

11 Verdier's expression, 1996.

12 See for example Zysman, 1983.

13 Their observations on this score tend to dovetail with those made by Naomi Lamoreaux in her work on New England. See Lamoreaux, 1994.

14 For a recent review of the literature on financial systems and efficiency see Levine, 1997.

1 Explaining cross-national variations in universal banking in nineteenth-century Europe, North America, and Australasia

Daniel Verdier

A universal banking system is defined as a system in which banks engage in both lending and the underwriting of securities. In contrast, a specialized banking system keeps the two activities under separate roofs. Universal banking is commonly believed to have existed before 1913 in Belgium, Germany, Austria, Italy, whereas specialized banking was mostly encountered in France and the Anglo-Saxon countries. The purpose of this chpater is to explain this variation.

In 1952, Alexander Gerschenkron offered what is still the most ambitious explanation for cross-national variations in banking systems in Europe. The more capital was needed in the shortest amount of time, the less could equity markets cope with the task of allocating long-term financial capital; instead, banks and state had to step in, causing cross-national variations in banking structures.

In this essay, I shift the emphasis away from the asset side of the banks' balance sheets – loans and the demand thereof – to the liability side – deposits. I draw from Adam Smith's famous argument that the division of labor is only limited by the extent of the market.[1] I argue that universal banking was a rational response to the segmentation of the deposit market. Wherever the deposit market was allowed to develop unshackled, banks tended to specialize. Market segmentation was a necessary but not sufficient cause for universal banking. A second condition had to be met in the form of the existence of a lender of last resort. Universal banking was less liquid than specialized banking. Its survival required a stabilizing agent in the form of a modern central bank. These two conditions (segmentation and central banking) in turn were two consequences of one single cause – the degree of centralization of the state. Segmentation was found along with decentralized state institutions, whereas central banking first appeared in centralized states. As a result, universal banking was most likely to emerge in states that were neither so centralized that local banks were displaced by center banks, nor so decentralized that there was no central bank.

I first lay out the background for the argument: the state of the deposit market in the first half of the century and how it changed in the second half. I then show the existence of a cross-sectional relation between state decentralization and market segmentation. I then argue, and show systematically, that market segmentation and central banking were two necessary and sufficient conditions for the emergence of universal banking. I survey the unexplained residual in the last section.

The deposit market during the first half of the nineteenth century

The market for individual deposits was separate from the payments system. The payments systems operated on the basis of the bill (acceptance and domestic bill of exchange) market and current bank accounts – in addition to bank notes. Professions involved in the exchange of goods and services had their current account credited whenever they discounted a bill and had it debited whenever they settled a debt due on a prior purchase.[2] In contrast, the market for individual savings was controlled by savings banks. Savings accounts were opened by individuals, not businesses, and were always creditor – they could not be used to grant credit. Savings were kept out of the payments system until the middle of the century, earlier in Belgium and England (even earlier in Scotland).[3]

Initially, savings banks were non-profit organizations, created in the early 1800s by philanthropic individuals and local municipalities to instill the saving habit among the urban poor; savings banks invested their customers' savings in mortgages and safe, government paper. The anticipation or consummation of crises raised the question of government guarantee and regulation. The answer reflected state structures. In Britain, France, and Belgium, the solution to the savings banks crisis came from the center. In Britain, the 1817 Statute provided for the mandatory deposit of all savings banks' deposits in an account with the Bank of England (Horne, 1947; Moss, 1997). French and Belgian savings banks spontaneously invested all their deposits in *rentes sur l'État*. Anticipating the depreciation of this asset, however, the *Caisse d'épargne de Paris* petitioned and obtained the right in 1829 to re-deposit all its resources in a current account earning a fixed rate of interest with the Royal Treasury.[4] The Belgian solution was more radical: the failed savings banks were allowed to be taken over by joint-stock banks.[5]

Similar setbacks in decentralized countries drew the opposite response. The banks were rescued by, and became the *chasses gardées* of, fiscally-strained local governments. They invested their profits in local government projects, and their resources (individuals' deposits) in mortgages (local land). In some areas, they also held communal bonds among their assets. This was current practice in Italy and Prussia in the early part of the century.[6] In Geneva, the cantonal Caisse d'Épargne held more city bonds than Confederal bonds until 1873 (Hiler, 1993: 188). In Austria, the savings banks were allowed to make short-term loans to towns (Albrecht, 1989: 77). In the United States, in the states of Massachusetts and Maryland, savings banks were prohibited from investing in bonds of other States (Vittas, 1997: 150). In Denmark, until the end of absolutist rule in 1848, the savings banks were forced to place their deposits at interest in the treasury; the following Liberal governments discontinued the practice, and savings resources were mainly invested in mortgages (Hansen, 1982: 590).

State custody was not favorable to the long-term expansion of the savings banks. State officials in Britain and France harbored mixed feelings; they benefited from managing the savings banks' ample resources but had little control over operating costs. Support existed at the ideological level – succor the poor, combat poverty. But that principle in the end worked against the savings banks, for it denied them the possibility to become the banks of the petite bourgeoisie – which is where the money was. The British and French governments contained the development of savings banks, reducing the interest rates that these banks could pay to their depositors and capping the amount of each account.

Municipalities in decentralized countries proved better custodians of the long-term interest of the savings banks than the state in centralized countries. Having at heart the welfare of the local economy, local governments supported the savings bank administrators' requests for an extension of their activities. Although in many cases the local imperative clashed with the central regulator's ideological wishes, the decentralized nature of the regime insured that local wishes would in the end prevail.[7]

In sum, even though savings banks started off as local endeavor to succor the poor, by 1850 the local logic had dethroned the class logic in decentralized countries. Only in centralized countries did the philanthropic motive retain pride of place, albeit as a convenient justification for the central treasury's lack of ambition for savings banks.

The rise of deposit-branch banking

The neat separation between the current account and savings markets was progressively questioned by a ubiquitous change in the payments system – the check and wire transfer dethroned the bill as principal instrument of the money market. The change rested on three related innovations – the joint-stock bank, the branch-bank network, and the individual deposit. Joint-stock banking, along with limited responsibility of shareholders, made it possible for banks to develop countrywide networks of branches, tap individual deposits five times at least over the size of the initial capital, and finance assets with individual deposits. Deposit banking took market share away from banknotes and coins, as checks and wire transfers reduced the amount of cash kept on hand for payments purposes. It also cut into the bill market, as banks no longer needed to rely on rediscounting to maintain adequate liquidity.

What made deposit banking irresistible, however, is not so much that it was more efficient than past modes of payments, but that it brought within the payments system three segments of the economy – the periphery, industry, and the petite bourgeoisie – until then excluded from it. The eighteenth-century bill market was centrally located in Amsterdam, London, Paris, New York, and so forth. This concentration reflected economies of scale but was also a source of discrimination against business located on the periphery, for which credit information was more difficult to obtain. The success met by the country branches of the Banque de France when it was forced by the government in the early half of the nineteenth century to extend its branch network to the countryside attests to the limits of the bill market mechanism at including the periphery within the money market.[8] Although the British and Dutch money markets may be considered as having been able to overcome this problem, in most other countries, however, the countryside was left out of the money market.[9]

Deposit banking also brought industry into the payments system. Manufacturing had a slower inventory turnover than trade and thus required a type of financing that was not strictly dependent on the shipping of goods to purchasers. The solution was provided by the overdraft, an advance that the bank financed through deposits and that it could renew at its own discretion, without having to obtain the sanction of a third party, as such was the case with rediscounted bills of exchange.

Last, deposit banking brought the savings of the petite bourgeoisie into the payments system. As the benefits of industrialization began to penetrate deeper into the middle strata, the demand for deposits accounts, both short and long, grew (J. Wysocki, 1997: 22). Risk-averse and uninformed, these new strata at first took their newly-earned savings to the savings banks, which typically re-invested them in long-term placements such as mortgages and public debt, until private bankers understood that they could finance investment by tapping the vast store of popular savings. Bankers also saw in deposit-taking a way of improving profitability, as depositors typically earned less than bank shareholders.

The change was quick and ubiquitous. With the exception of North America, in which joint-stock banking was liberalized from the outset in the United States, 1821 in Canada, and the isolated case in Europe of three Scottish banks, joint-stock banking is a mid-nineteenth century occurrence. Joint-stock banks first flourished in Britain after the passage of legislation permitting it beyond a 65-mile radius of London from 1826 until 1833, and anywhere thereafter. Limited responsibility was granted in 1855. A parallel evolution occurred on the continent, charters being granted by governments sparsely before 1852 (the Belgian Société Générale and Banque de Belgique in 1822 and 1835 respectively, the Swedish Enskilda banks from 1824 on, Spanish banks in the 1840s), liberally after 1852, the founding date of the French Crédit Mobilier, which spawned dozens of imitations throughout the continent, and was completely freed sometime after 1860 (1863 in France and Italy, 1864 in Sweden, 1869 in Spain, 1870 in Germany, 1881 in Switzerland, and so on). In countries without note-issuing monopoly, the thus-chartered joint-stock banks were given the right to issue notes as well as collect deposits.

The rising importance of deposits created a liquidity problem for the banks. Deposits were short-term resources, since even an early-withdrawal penalty scheme would hardly stop a poorly informed, panic-prone depositor confronted with the danger of a bank run from cashing his savings rather than facing the risk of losing it all. The problem was compounded by the popularity of overdrafts. Overdrafts were better remunerated than bills, but they were easily renewed and could not be readily recycled through rediscounting at the central bank. Therefore, relying on more volatile resources (deposits) to finance less liquid assets (overdrafts), banks were caught in a liquidity squeeze, of which they became aware in the wake of a string of banking crises, during which deposits were withdrawn in exchange for coin and central bank notes. Hence, after each crisis in England and Wales, the most severe being the crash of the City of Glasgow Bank in 1878, the banks tended to maintain a higher proportion of very liquid assets. The crash of 1882 in France served to disqualify loans to industry in the eyes of Henri Germain, the director of the Crédit Lyonnais (Collins, 1991: 41; Bouvier, 1968: 221). Meanwhile, banks scrambled for "good paper," that is, standard, short, and readily disposable assets, thereby reviving the competition between the central bank and the deposit banks.[10]

The higher demand for good paper, along with the drive to provide improved payments services to customers, elicited new profit-making strategies – amalgamation, centralization, and internationalization. Amalgamation allowed banks to take advantage of the internal scale economies released by the move toward standardization. Centralization allowed banks to capture external scale economies in the form of central clearing and greater breadth of the market (Kindleberger, 1978: 72–5). Centralization also allowed banks to enter lucrative and rather safe lines of activity, such as the underwriting of government and railroad loans. Internationalization gave banks access to foreign government paper, short-term government debt especially.[11] The upshot was the founding of the gigantic joint-stock banks of today, also known as deposit banks.

The main source of market segmentation: local and non-profit banking

The unleashing of private banking fortunes into deposit banking threatened to deal severe redistributional costs to local banks. Access to the center allowed the large banks to offer their clientele of investors instruments that were more diverse and that generated higher returns than local banks could. Their branch networks and membership in a clearing association also allowed them to offer efficient payment services to their clientele in all banking places in the country. If left to the interplay of market forces, the joint-stock banks threatened to sweep the field, branching out across the periphery, drawing depositors from savings banks and mutual credit societies, taking over local commercial banks, and forcing the rest out.

The local banks' clients, the small and medium-size firms, which were not large enough to raise external capital on the equity markets, would be hurt by the disappearance of local banks and the center banks' disengagement from long-term lending to industry. The monopolizing of deposit-taking by a handful of risk-averse, center-located banks, each at the head of a countrywide network of branch offices, threatened to drain local districts from individual savings and channel it instead into national and foreign government-backed paper. Local governments would find it harder to finance infrastructure projects by local investors while the industrial vitality of regions with a concentration of small and medium-size firms would be depressed.

The potential losers were not necessarily condemned, but their fate depended on their local governments' power, that is, both the extent to which local governments could interfere with capital flows on their own, free from state supervision, and the power that local governments had, acting together, to block the central state from assuming greater regulatory power at the detriment of local regulators.

As a result, joint-stock banks did not capture their country supply of deposits with uniform ease and to the same extent. They managed to do so only in centralized countries, in which local governments possessed little or no power. In decentralized countries, in contrast, non-profit and local banking sectors managed to check the joint-stock banks' inroad into deposits by various means: subsidies to non-profit banking, geographic limits on branching, and the continuation of free banking until 1905 in Switzerland, a country where note-issuing banks were formally linked to local governments.

Data on market shares support the claim that political protection of local and non-profit banking in decentralized states fragmented the fast-growing market for individual deposits. Figure 1.1 plots the deposit market share of non-profit banks (adding to it the market share of State-chartered banks in the United States) against a proxy for state centralization. State centralization is proxied by a fiscal ratio: revenues going to the central government as a proportion of all government revenues, central and local, circa 1880. The two variables show a negative relation. Australia is a real outlier, for its capital market, which London structured after the British model, predated its state structure, which ended being rather decentralized.

A secondary source of market segmentation: state banking

The commercial banks were also in competition with the state. Treasuries viewed the collection of savings as a supplementary means of financing the debt. They chartered postal savings, a formidable competitor to the already existing savings banks. The British and French governments had no difficulty overruling the opposition of the savings banks, in 1861 in Britain, and in 1883 in France. The

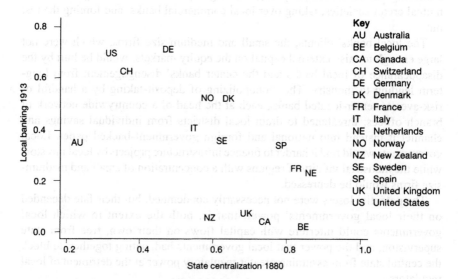

Figure 1.1 Local banking and state centralization.

Belgian government too, upon the failure or near-failure in 1848 of the handful of joint-stock banks that had taken over the old savings banks, consolidated all savings banks into one state-owned body, the *Caisse Générale d'Épargne et de Retraite*, founded in 1865. No such centralizing posture could be as easily assumed in less centralized countries. Governments refrained from competing for local capital through postal savings in Denmark and Norway, or did so with little success in Germany, Austria, Sweden, and Spain. Postal savings were non-existent in Switzerland and insignificant in the United States. The only decentralized state to fully exploit postal savings was Italy. Note too that all Australasian governments, except South Australia, established post office savings *before* they joined the Australian Commonwealth.

State banks belong to what the French call the "*circuit du trésor*," a network that is separate from other banking networks, and thus constituting a further source of segmentation of the capital market.[12] Although limited in 1913, the relative size of state banking was not randomly distributed. A necessary, though not sufficient, condition for state banking was state centralization – the relation between the two variables is heteroscedastic.[13]

The first requisite for universal banking: market segmentation

Segmentation of the deposit market, irrespective of its origins, was the first requisite for universal banking. Following the revolution in mode of payments, the joint-stock banks moved along a secular trajectory from investment banking toward modern deposit banking. When allowed to capture the market of individuals' deposits unhindered, joint-stock banks became deposit banks, leaving the business of investment banking to institutions especially created for that purpose – trustee banks, investment banks, and the stock market. They abandoned the field of investment banking altogether in order to match the maturity of their assets with that of their newly-gained short liabilities. The outcome was specialized banking.

However, if frozen in mid-course, because local commercial or non-profit banks were entitled to corner the market for smaller depositors, the center banks were left to cater to a wider clientele of large, industrial depositors, with whom they found both their most profitable lending opportunities and, as loans make deposits, their most abundant sources of deposits (Riesser, 1911). Unable to fully capture the field of deposit banking, joint-stock banks were forced to rely on their own resources to a greater extent than pure deposit banks. Their liabilities showed a greater share of "own resources" relative to individual deposits (this ratio is used to measure universal banking below). The greater cost of "own resources" – shares earned more than deposits – was an additional reason to stick to investment banking, a more profitable, because riskier, line of business. Consequently, unlike joint-stock banks in centralized capital markets, joint-stock banks in segmented markets could not completely vacate the field of investment banking.

In decentralized states, the development of universal banking was accompanied by the development of relationship banking among local savings banks. By keeping joint-stock banks out of entire regions, social strata, or sectors of activity, and thus turning peripheral banks into de facto local monopolies, market segmentation created a gap that savings banks filled. Savings banks in decentralized systems began to lend to business firms; such lending was short at first, and long thereafter (Hansen, 1982: 583, 589; Feldman, 1991: 69; Deeg, 1999; Michel, 1976; Nygren, 1983: 33, 43–4; Nordvik, 1993: 69; Egge, 1983: 281). The growing competition of the non-profit sector was generally condemned by the universal joint-stock banks, which regularly denounced the unfair advantage enjoyed by non-profit banks, but was consistently upheld by legislators and state regulators who were partial to the non-profit banks and their clientele of farms and small business. In addition to developing a commercial capability, savings banks in decentralized states founded their own clearing organizations, regional at first, national later on. These clearing organizations progressively assumed the functions of savings banks' banks, through which locales with an excess of savings would lend to locales with a shortage (Brück *et al.*, 1995: 52, 101, 231, 282; Michel, 1976: 37; Deeg, 1999). This way, peripheries developed a vertically-integrated credit network separate from, and parallel to, the commercial bank network (crowned by the central bank), with both networks equally present in the center and the periphery, although in reverse proportions.

Because market segmentation was the cause for universalism, banks in universal banking systems (and also in the United States) were, in fact, "specialized" in terms of whom they lent to. Money center banks lent to large national firms and local banks lent to small local firms.[14] The banks were also "specialized" in terms of whom they borrowed from. The upper bourgeoisie banked with center branch banks, whereas peasants and artisans banked with local banks, savings banks, or mutual credit societies. In sum, capital mobility was territorially and socially bound; Siemens, for example, could not raise capital from the lower classes to finance its heavy immobilizations. In contrast, joint-stock banks in Britain and France would lend short to any firm, irrespective of size, and draw resources from all depositors without regard for social strata and area of residence. As Adam Smith would have it, product specialization was inversely related to customer specialization. Universal banking went hand in hand with customer specialization.

The second requisite for universal banking: liquidity guarantee

Fragmentation of the deposit market was a necessary, but not sufficient, condition for the stabilization of universal banking. For this to happen, a second condition had to be met as well: the existence of a liquidity guarantor.

Mixing long- with short-term assets, universal banks had difficulties matching the maturity profile of their assets with that of their liabilities. The source of the problem was not so much that assets were systematically longer than liabilities; all banks took advantage of the information and collective action costs faced by their creditors to engage into maturity transformation. Rather, the issue was one of cyclicality. Cyclical business downturns typically froze assets (the bank couldn't recall advances or sell securities but at an unacceptable loss) while melting liabilities (actual terms of deposit grew shorter), thereby worsening the mismatch in maturity profiles between the two sides of the balance sheet. The extent of the problem depended, of course, on the intensity of the crisis, but also (and this is why universality presented higher risk than specialization) on the range of maturity between the most and least liquid assets. Mixing 1-day-long with 1-year-long assets made the bank more vulnerable to an illiquidity crisis than mixing 1-day-long with 3-month-long or 6-month-long with 1-year-long.

Balance sheets were uninformative. They would not reveal the actual solvency of a bank, all the more so that they were regularly window-dressed to hide profits from shareholders. Outsiders could only tell post facto, after crises weeded out insolvent banks. The impenetrability of balance sheets removed an important means that bankers needed to elicit depositors' trust – the capacity to commit to certain liquidity targets. Absent such a commitment, depositors would invariably suspect that mixed banks were placing the interests of the industries in which bank directors had vested interests above those of the banks' depositors.

Universal banking was therefore unstable. The unpredictability of crises, combined with the cyclicality of most assets and liabilities made universal banks either unprofitable during booms (they were in a sense financing a greater proportion of easily liquidable assets with highly stable liabilities) or insolvent during slumps (they were financing less liquid assets with more volatile liabilities). This uncertainty plus the high monitoring costs faced by depositors made universal banking an unlikely occurrence. Without a lender of last resort committed to tiding universal banks over periods of economic slowdown, the universal banks could not elicit depositors' confidence.

The decisive step toward the institution of a liquidity guarantor to joint-stock banks in times of financial crises was the creation of a central bank.[15] Historically, a central bank is a private note-issuing monopoly – a rent the ruler would concede in exchange for emergency cash and the underwriting of treasury paper (North and Weingast, 1989; Brewer, 1989; Hoffman and Norberg, 1994; Broz, 1998). Central banking helped promote universal banking in two ways. Its first and more basic contribution was to monopolize note-issuing, taking it away from commercial banks. Banks that finance a sizable part of their business by issuing notes must hold many liquid assets (bills of exchange bearing more than one signature) in order to be able to redeem their notes in cash when they are presented for payment. Systems of free banking (four only were left by the turn of the century: Canada, Australia, New Zealand, and Switzerland), in which commercial banks were banks of issue, could not afford the illiquidity of universal banking. The few attempts to mix the two, in Belgium before 1850 and in Switzerland before 1905, were unsuccessful, ending in a crash in the Belgian case and fueling recurring crises and depressing the exchange in the Swiss case.[16]

Second, central banks helped stabilize universal banking by assuming the role of lender of last resort in the event of a depositor run. Though less volatile than notes, deposits were not predictable enough to serve as a basis for underwriting or for building durable relationships with firms. Unfortunately, the extension of a liquidity guarantee to commercial banks is not an event that one can easily observe and precisely time. As Ziegler (1990a) in his study of the Bank of England reminded us, a note-issuing monopoly is not necessarily a liquidity guarantor. It may become one at the government's request, usually in the wake of a serious banking panic, for the central bank, after all, owes its rent to the government. Complicating the matter is that central banks are deterred from extending any automatic guarantee, lest they invite moral hazard.

It is still possible to identify a relation between state centralization, the early creation of the central bank, and the early extension of the liquidity guarantee. First, the timing of central-bank creation was related to the timing and depth of state formation. Note-issuing monopolies were granted earlier in centralized countries (Britain 1684, France 1800) than in decentralized countries (Switzerland 1905, Australia 1911, United States 1913, and Canada 1934).[17] It usually took a strong political center (or, as in Denmark and Norway, a military and financial debacle) to impose an English-type central bank on its unwilling periphery. Indeed, the centralization of note issuing diminished short-term capital available for commerce and industry located at the periphery. Having to make its notes as good as gold, a central bank typically invested in commercial paper of high quality – issued by a reputable merchant or industrialist and endorsed by a reputable banker, mostly based in the center. Governments in Britain and France would press in vain their central bank to open branches in the countryside; the bank would either refuse to create regional branches or, when it did, it would discriminate against them.[18] Another negative distributional consequence of central banking for the periphery stemmed from what is called nowadays the "too big to fail" doctrine, according to which the beneficiaries of the liquidity guarantee tend to be the largest banks, mostly based in the center. Last, with its deeper involvement in foreign business, the financial center had a lower preference for monetary slack than the agrarian periphery (United States, National Monetary Commission, 1911: 506).

As a result, wherever agrarian peripheries had the power to do so, they blocked the creation of a private central bank. It took fifteen years (1891–1905) of trial and a couple of referenda to the Swiss *Großbanken* to overcome the opposition of local interests in alliance with the left who supported nationalization (Zimmerman, 1987). While it took three attempts for central banking to take root in the United States, and the final outcome fell short of a central bank, as money-center banks conceded a plurality of reserve banks to the local states (Broz, 1997). In Sweden, where the periphery was strong, though not decisively so, the agrarians pressed for a government-run central bank and successfully managed to gain control over it against the opposition of the money-center banks, whose own objective was a privately-owned central bank, independent from the state (Nygren, 1983: 34). In Germany, where state building was too advanced for the periphery to oppose the creation of a privately-owned central bank, the agrarians kept pushing for ever-tighter Reich regulations on the Bank.

Second, the timing of the liquidity guarantee was also related to state centralization. For instance, although Scandinavian countries had early national banks (Sweden in 1688, Norway and Denmark in 1816 and 1818 respectively), the pull of the agrarian periphery was such that it was not until the end of the century (slightly earlier in Denmark) that each state could force its bank to take on the function of liquidity guarantor (Johansen, 1985: 165; Hansen, 1991: 25; Nygren, 1983: 34; Egge, 1983: 273–5; Goodhart, 1988). In the case of Spain, a country torn by political and territorial rivalries, the liquidity guarantor came long after (1924) the national bank was created (1874).

To test how systematic the relation between the timing of the liquidity guarantee and state centralization was, I built a variable, using Broz's timing of the advent of last-resort lending for ten early central banks (UK 1860, Netherlands and Portugal 1870, Austria-Hungary 1878, France, Germany, Denmark 1880, Finland, Sweden, Norway 1890). I only postponed the Norwegian datum by a decade (setting it to 1900), to reflect the fact that relations between the central bank and the commercial banks escalated into an open conflict in the 1890s, with some banks creating their own central bank – hardly a propitious climate for last-resort lending (Egge, 1983: 278). I supplemented Broz's list with a second one, including central banks that were created to extend a liquidity guarantee to unstable banking systems. In the latter case, the advent of last-resort lending corresponded with the creation of the note-issuing monopoly, making its timing interpretation-free (Belgium 1850, Italy 1893, Switzerland 1905, Australia 1911, the United States 1913, New Zealand 1930, and Canada 1934). The date used for Spain is 1924.[19]

I then reversed the timing-of-the-liquidity-guarantee variable, so that higher values correspond with earlier (and stronger) liquidity guarantee. The formula for the inversion is given by the formula

1934 – year of initiation of last-resort lending,

with 1934 the year of creation of the Canadian central bank, the last in the sample.

The bivariate scattergram between the thus-inverted variable and the state centralization variable reveals a rather strong linear correlation, spoiled by three outliers (Figure 1.2). In Canada and New Zealand (and Australia as well), the lateness of the central bank did not reflect domestic state institutions, but the international status of these countries as British dominions – the de facto central bank was the Bank of England. The Spanish observation is more difficult to account for and will be the object of a special discussion in the last section.

I have argued in this section that universal banking needed a liquidity guarantor to remove note-issuing from commercial banking and stabilize deposits. I have argued and shown that the existence of a liquidity guarantor, in turn, reflected the existence of a strong financial center, able to impose its preference against the opposition of the agrarian periphery; the more centralized state structures, the easier for the center to overcome the opposition of the periphery.

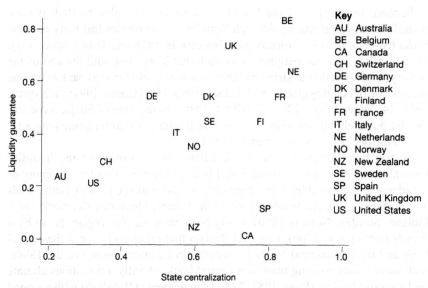

Figure 1.2 Timing of liquidity guarantee and state centralization.

Universal banking as an inverted-U function of state centralization

We can now bring the two necessary conditions for universal banking together. Segmentation of the capital market and the existence of a central bank extending a liquidity guarantee together yielded universal banking. But if one of these conditions was not met, specialized banking obtained. The segmentation condition was not met in fully centralized polities in which the agrarian periphery was very weak; the liquidity-guarantee condition was not met in very decentralized polities in which the agrarian periphery was very strong. Only in the intermediate category of semi-centralized states, in which center and periphery were balanced, were the two conditions jointly met and universal banking thus made possible. Universal banking was an inverted-U function of the degree of state formation.

The inverted-U function can be represented in the form of a graph, with the horizontal axis representing the relative power of the center and the vertical axis measuring the likelihood of universal banking (Figure 1.3). The segmentation effect is captured by a negative linear function; a more powerful center generates a lesser need for universal banking. In contrast, the liquidity-guarantee effect is captured by a positive linear function; a more powerful center favors the provision of the liquidity guarantee (without which universal banking is unsustainable). The product of the two linear functions generates an inverted-U function.

Evidence

The present argument yields two observable propositions about cross-national variations in universal banking. The first (the *joint-product hypothesis*) bears on the immediate origins: universal banking was the joint product of market

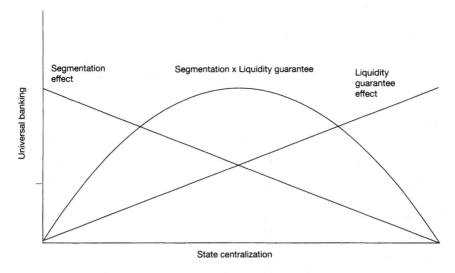

Figure 1.3 Universal banking as an inverted-U function of state centralization.

fragmentation and liquidity guarantee. The second hypothesis (the *inverted-U curve hypothesis*) bears on the indirect, distant origins: universal banking is an inverted-U function of state centralization.

I generated a comparative measure of universal banking, using aggregate balance sheets of large commercial banks. The equity-to-deposit ratio is the ratio of a bank's least liquid resources (capital plus reserves) to the most liquid ones (individual deposits, savings, and notes, when any). Behind the measure is the idea that commercial banks that are specialized in short-term lending usually have little need for long-term equity, but do finance most of their activity with cheaper short-term deposits, savings (and notes for banks possessing note-issuing rights), without risk of illiquidity. In contrast, commercial banks with long-term positions in industry must employ dear long-term resources.[20] The ratio is bounded upward, for too high a value would indicate a specialization in investment banking.

The data for the year 1913, shown in Table 1.1, track the overall sense of historians: at one extreme, the specialized Anglo-Saxon banks (UK, Canada, and the USA), at the other the universal type (Germany, Italy, Austria-Hungary). Spain is definitely an outlier; it has a 5 to 1 equity-to-deposit ratio, reflecting an investment banking specialization. I dropped the Spanish observation from the present analysis and will come back to it in the next section. The only real surprise is the Netherlands, a country with no documented consistent long-term banking up until World War I, and yet for which the ratio is inexplicably high.[21] I will also come back to this case in the next section.

I first plot the joint-product hypothesis (Figure 1.4). The hypothesized independent variable is the product of market segmentation and liquidity guarantee, both in 1913. The first term (segmentation) is the aggregated market shares of non-profit, state, and, where fitting, local banking (see percentage values in Table 1.1). The

Table 1.1   Dataset.

	Deposit market shares of the four banking sectors, 1913 in %				Central government revenues, circa 1880 in %	Year of initiation of liquidity guarantee	Equity-deposit ratio, 1913
	Profit, center[a]	Non-profit, private[b]	Non-profit, state[c]	Profit, local[d]			
Australia	65	34	1	0	25	1911	0.35
Austria-Hungary	37[e]	58[e]	5[e]	0[e]	–	1878	2.00[e]
Belgium	59	1	40	0	85	1850	0.72
Canada	92	3	5	0	75	1934	0.19
Denmark	49	51	0	0	64	1880	0.32
France	66	8	26	0	83	1880	0.43
Germany	28	71	1	0	49	1880	0.73
Italy	27	40	33	0	55	1893	0.88
Netherlands	54	22	23	0	87	1870	1.58
New Zealand	58	4	38	0	60	1930	–
Norway	49	51	0	0	60	1900	0.25
Spain	67	33	0	0	79	1924	5.00
Sweden	63	35	2	0	64	1890	0.45
Switzerland	39	61	0	0	37	1905	0.56
UK	80	6	14	0	70	1860	0.10
USA	33[g]	25[g]	0[g]	42[g]	33[f]	1913	0.25

Notes:
a   Commercial banks regulated by the central government.
b   Savings banks, mutual credit societies, mortgage banks.
c   Postal savings; savings banks in France and Belgium.
d   Commercial banks regulated by local governments (State banks in the United States).
e   Austria and the Czech Lands.
f   1902.
g   1914.

Sources: Central government revenues is central government revenues as percentage of general government revenues circa 1880. For Western Europe, excluding Spain, Flora *et al.*, 1983–87: 273. Data for Austria-Hungary could not be used, because of the exclusion of the non-Austrian part of the Empire. For Spain, Bernis, 1919: 338, 347. For the United States, United States, Department of Commerce, 1976: 1119. For Canada, Canada, Department of Agriculture, 1890: 104, 117. Data for Australia are for 1907, Mitchell, 1983: 802; Australia, Commonwealth Bureau of Census and Statistics, 1908: 668. Data for New Zealand are for 1913, Bloomfield, 1984: 333, 352.
    Year of initiation of the liquidity guarantee is the timing of liquidity guarantee, coded as 1934– (year of initiation of last-resort lending). The source for the latter is Broz, 1998: 240–1; Goodhart, 1988; and Conant, 1927.
    Equity-deposit ratio 1913 measures the ratio of own resources (capital, reserves) against individual deposits and savings. The numerator includes capital, reserves, and notes whenever appropriate. The denominator includes individual deposits and savings accounts. Unless otherwise noted, it excludes creditor current accounts, which exist for transaction purposes and are usually unremunerated. Interbank deposits (which usually constitute a relatively insignificant proportion of total liabilities) are excluded whenever possible. Data are for 1913 unless otherwise mentioned. For the United Kingdom, 43 joint-stock banks of England and Wales, Sheppard, 1971: 118. The numerator is "Paid-up Capital and Reserves." The denominator is "Deposits and Other Accounts"; it was not possible to separate current accounts from deposits. As a result, the ratio overstates the liquidity of UK banks. For the United States, 7467 National Banks, United States, Department of Commerce, 1976, Series X 634–55: 1025. The numerator is "Capital accounts"; the denominator is "Deposits" excluding "US Government." It was not possible to separate current accounts from deposits. As a result, the ratio overstates the liquidity of US banks, a bias that is further reinforced by the large number of banks included in the sample. For Canada, all Chartered Banks, Urquhart and Buckley (eds), 1965,

Table 1.1 Dataset (continued)

Series H 226–45: 240–2. The numerator is "Capital and rest fund." The denominator includes "Notes in circulation," "Personal savings deposits," Public notice deposits," and "Public demand deposits." For Australia, 21 Australian Trading Banks, Butlin, Hall, and White, 1971: 114, 120, and 131. The numerator is "shareholders' equity." The denominator includes "bills in circulation" and "deposits bearing interests." For France, 4 *banques de dépôts* (Crédit Lyonnais, Société Générale, Comptoir d'Escompte, Crédit Industriel et Commercial), archival document communicated to us in 1995 by Mr. Nougaret, Directeur des Archives Historiques du Crédit Lyonnais, Paris. The numerator is "*Dépôts*," exclusive of "*Comptes courants*." The denominator is "*Capital versé et réserves*." For Belgium, 3 among the 5 banks with the largest own resources in 1913 (Société Générale, Crédit Général Liégeois, Banque de Bruxelles); the other two largest banks were not included, the deviant Caisse Générale de Reports et de Dépôts because it was a pure deposit bank, and the Banque d'Outremer because I have no data, Chlepner, 1930: 96–9. The numerator includes "*Capital*" and "*Réserves*." The denominator includes "*Obligations*," "*Dépôts à terme*;" current accounts are excluded. For Switzerland, 8 *grandes banques* (Société de banque suisse, Crédit suisse, Banque populaire suisse, Union des banques suisses, Banque commerciale de Bâle, Banque fédérale (SA), Comptoir d'escompte de Genève, Société anonyme Leu & Co.), Switzerland, Département Fédéral de l'Economie Publique, 1927: 326–7. The numerator includes "*capital versé et réserves*." The denominator includes "*Obligations*," "*Dépôts d'épargne*," and "*Autres dépôts*"; creditor current accounts are excluded. For Germany, 9 *Berliner Großbanken*, Deutsche Bundesbank, 1976, Table 1.01, pp. 56–9. The numerator includes "*Kapital*" and "*Reserven*." The denominator includes "*Depositen*," exclusive of creditor current accounts. For Denmark, the 5 largest commercial banks, Denmark, *Statistiske Undersøgelser*, 1969: 23, 30, 32, 39, 58. The numerator includes "*Aktiekapital*" and "*Reservefond*," The denominator includes "*Folio, indlån, kontokurant og sparekasseindskud*;" it includes current accounts, overstating the liquidity of Danish banks. For Sweden, all enskilda banks, Sweden, Sverige Statistika Centralbyran, 1914, Tab. 97, 115. The numerator includes "*Fonder*." The denominator includes "*Innestäende på sparkasseräkning*" and "*Innestäende på depositions- och kapitalräkning*." For Norway, 119 commercial banks (in 1914), Norway, Norge Statistisk Centralbyra, 1975, Tab. 252, 492–3. The numerator includes "*Aksjekapital*" and "*Fond*." The denominator includes "*Innskott på tid*" (deposits subject to notice); it does not include "*Innskott på anfordring*" (demand deposits), most likely to current accounts. For the Netherlands, 5 largest (*algemene*) banks (Amsterdamsche Bank, Incassobank, Nederlandsche Handelmaatschappij, Rotterdamsche Bank, and Twentsche Bank), Nederlandsche Bank n.v., 1987, Tab. 3c, 43. The numerator includes "*kapital en reserves*." The denominator includes "*deposito's*" and "*spaargelden*" (current accounts excluded). For Austria-Hungary, 4 largest Viennese Great Banks involved with the financing and founding of industrial firms (Österreichische Creditanstalt, Allgemeine Bodenkreditanstalt, Niederösterreichische Escompte-Gesellschaft, and Wiener Bankverein), Nötel, 1984: 154. The numerator includes share capital and reserves. The denominator includes deposits (current accounts excluded). I used Rudolph's 10:57 ratio to break down individual deposits from current accounts, Rudolph, 1976: 84. That breakdown was established for the six largest Viennese great banks in 1912. For Italy, 5 major commercial banks (Banca Commerciale Italiana, Credito Italiano, Banco di Roma, Societa Bancaria Italiana, Credito Provinciale); for the Credito Italiano, Confalonieri, 1982, vol. 1: 610; for the Banca Commerciale, Confalonieri, 1977–80, vol. 3: 538; Banco di Roma, archival document; Credito Provinciale, archival document; for the Societa Bancaria, archival document. The numerator includes "*Capitale sociale*" and "*Fondi di riserva*." The denominator includes "*Depositi in Conto Corrente ed a Risparmio*"; it was not possible to exclude current accounts from deposits. As a result, the ratio overstates the liquidity of Italian banks. For Spain, 3 Catalan (Banco de Barcelona, Sociedad Catalana General de Crédito, Banco de Cataluña), 3 Basque (Banco de Bilbao, Banco del Comercio, Banco de Vizcaya), and 1 Madrid (Banco de Castilla), Tortella, 1974: 234, 274, 286, 326, 394, 408, 418. The numerator includes "*Capital desembolsado*" and "*Reserva*." The denominator includes "*Depósitos*" and "*Cuentas de ahorro*;" creditor current accounts are excluded.

For *deposit market shares*, for Australia, Butlin, Hall and White, 1971: 114, 503, 525. For Austria-Hungary, Mitchell, 1992: 774, 781. For Belgium, League of Nations, Fr. (ed.), 1931: 116; and Mitchell, 1992: 781, 784. For Canada, Canada, Dominion Bureau of Statistics, various years. For Denmark, League of Nations, Fr. (ed.), 1931: 125. For France, Mitchell 1992: 774, 782. For Germany, Deutsche Bundesbank, 1976: 57, 63, 65. For Italy, Mitchell, 1992: 774, 782, and League of Nations, 1931: 187. For the Netherlands, Nederlandsche Bank, 1987: 34, 48, 52. For New Zealand, League of Nations, 1931: 447. For Norway, League of Nations, 1931: 199; and Mitchell, 1992: 782. For Spain, Martín-Aceña, 1995: 522; and Mitchell, 1992: 782. For Sweden, League of Nations, 1931: 275; and Mitchell, 1992: 783. For Switzerland, League of Nations, 1931: 288. For the UK, Sheppard, 1971. For the United States, United States, Federal Reserve, Board of Governors, 1942.

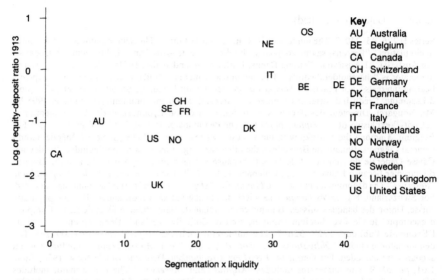

Figure 1.4 The joint-product hypothesis.

logic is that profit banks are competing for deposits with all types of sheltered banks, local and central. The second term (liquidity guarantee) is proxied by the timing of liquidity guarantee variable (used above in Figure 1.2). The plot (Figure 1.4) provides visual evidence of the strength of the findings (Spain is excluded). Note the presence of Austria, a case that we had to exclude from earlier figures for lack of data, as a country with high segmentation, early liquidity guarantee, and high universal banking.

The second hypothesis, that universalism is an inverted-U function of state centralization, is plotted in Figure 1.5. The inverted-U is observable, except in the cases of the Netherlands, Belgium, and marginally France. I explore these cases in the next section. Note also that the Australian case fits the curve for the wrong reason. It scores low on universalism, not because its decentralized political structure caused the financial market to be segmented, but because its financial market was very centralized and it had a late central bank. There are finally smaller anomalies that lessen the fit of the expected relation with the measured reality; the level of universal banking is higher than expected in Switzerland, lower in Norway. Being one more step remote, the inverted-U curve hypothesis suffers more exceptions than the joint-product hypothesis. The next section systematically goes over the unexplained residual.

Omitted variables

Several cases fit the argument in part only. The dominions, Belgium, France, Switzerland, Norway, the Netherlands are outliers with respect to the inverted-U curve hypothesis, but not with respect to the joint-product hypothesis. The Spanish case does not fit the argument at all. I go over these cases, with an eye for omitted

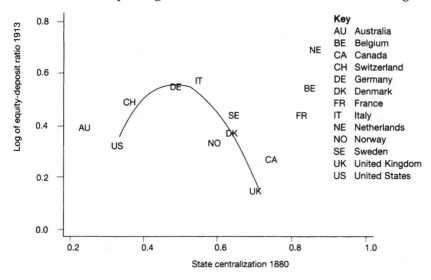

Figure 1.5 The inverted-U curve hypothesis.

variables. Four especially stand out: the international environment, liberalism, political instability, and markets.

The present theory leaves out the international dimension, even though it played a role in several ways. In the dominions, first, the financial structure was not the product of the state structure, as in the other countries, but both state and financial structures reflected British interference. All dominions had the same odd financial market structure – centralized, yet without a central bank – reflecting London's persisting centrality to dominions' finance. A condition of application of the present theory, the endogenous development of the financial market, was not fulfilled in those cases.

Swiss banks, second, were able to sidestep the liquidity constraint of universal banking in spite of the very late chartering of the central bank. They did so because they were more dependent on foreign firms and banks for their resources than on individual depositors, with the former being less subject to sunspot panics than the latter.

In Norway, third, foreign banks controlled underwriting, making Norwegian banks less universal than the theory would have expected in light of the fragmentation of the deposit market. Norwegian industrialization was dominated by the primary sector, a sector that was export oriented, highly concentrated, and in need of too much capital, too soon to be financed on the national market.

The theory fails to take into account a second important variable – liberalism. State centralization had two contradictory effects: it worked against one source of market segmentation – local banking – but promoted another – state banking. In the event that the two effects were equally strong, they would have canceled out and no correlation between state structure and universal banking would be discernible. This did not obtain because the period under scrutiny was dominated by liberalism.[22]

The Belgian case was exceptional in that respect. State banking preempted the development of deposit banking. Early nineteenth-century Belgian banks were universal banks *avant la lettre,* in that both the Société Générale and the Banque de Belgique combined investment banking with note issuing and deposit taking. They were crowded out of note issuing when the central bank was created in 1850 and from deposit banking when the state savings bank (CGER) was founded in 1865 (Chlepner, 1926: 101, 228; van der Wee, 1982: 612). The Belgian state controlled about 40 percent of the deposit market in 1913, the highest figure in our sample (Table 1.1).

A third omitted variable, one that helps make sense of the Spanish case, is political instability. A century of political instability, topped in 1897 by the disastrous war with the United States, made for a sizable public debt, which the central bank financed by expanding its share of the market for cash. It obtained an issue monopoly in 1874 and crowded out commercial banks from the deposit market – it controlled 58 percent of all bank deposits in 1900. Deposits and notes together gave the Bank control over 82 percent of all short-term bank liabilities in the country (Martín-Aceña, 1995: 522–3). Its share of bank deposits was still comparatively high in 1913. Moreover, unlike the French and English central banks, which shunned outlying areas, the Bank of Spain opened branches nationwide. It is not until after World War I that the Bank assumed the functions of liquidity guarantor and those commercial banks branched out of their regions of origin (Martín-Aceña, 1995: 504–5).

A last omitted variable is the security market. Although specialized banking and security markets were mutually reinforcing, Dutch historians have argued that the existence of a well-developed security market in the Netherlands crowded out deposit banking – commercial banks could not tap individual deposits to finance part of their activities, but remained overcapitalized (Eisfeld, 1916; Jonker, 1995: 190; Kymmel, 1996: 122). Clearly, there are many other variables that mattered and that are better captured by country studies. My purpose was to identify a cross-sectional pattern, not to account for singular cases.

Conclusion

This essay presented evidence for two generalizable propositions. The first proposition is that universal banking was the product of two conditions – market segmentation and the presence of a liquidity guarantor. This is a strong finding, the only exception to this pattern among the fourteen countries present in the sample being Spain. Spanish banking was specialized, not because its state was centralized (indeed it was), but because of political instability. The second proposition is that universal banking was (through the mediation of the two aforementioned requisites) related to state centralization. Universal banking required an intermediate dose of state formation, insufficient to overcome the agrarian peripheries' claims to maintain local control over local capital, yet enough to impose a central bank on these peripheries. This condition was met in Germany, Italy, and Sweden. In contrast, specialized banking obtained in both very centralized (the UK, France) and very decentralized countries (the USA). More ambitious than the first, this second proposition is also less robust. There were clear exceptions to this general trend reflecting omitted variables, such as the international environment (the dominions, Switzerland, Norway), state intervention (Belgium), political instability (Spain), and, perhaps, security markets (the Netherlands). State centralization was not the only factor shaping banking structures, nor was state centralization the decisive factor in all cases. My sole ambition is to have identified a cause as general as Gerschenkron's timing of industrialization.

Gerschenkron gave an asset-side account of universal banking, in which universal banking reflects firms' capital needs. Information economists also give an asset-side account, in which universal banking reflects information asymmetry between lender and borrower. The present account instead stresses the liability-side, in which competition for deposits constrains forms of lending. Of course, a full account should emphasize both sides of the balance sheet.

Acknowledgments

I am pleased to acknowledge the invaluable research assistance of Elizabeth Paulet and Thimo De Nijs. I thank Lawrence Broz, Philip Cottrell, Douglas Forsyth, Peter Hertner, Michael Mastanduno, Larry Neal, Jaime Reis, Ronald Rogowski, and Herman van der Wee for their valuable comments. I also thank Maurice Lévy-Leboyer, Mr. Nougaret from the Crédit Lyonnais, Dr. Gabriele Jachmich from the Institut für Bankhistorische Forschung E. V., Dr. Francesca Pino from the Banca Commerciale Italiana, and Dr. Sbacchi from the Credito Italiano for their help with archives. An earlier version was delivered at the 1995 meeting of the American Political Science Association, Chicago, and published as a European University Institute Working Paper. The research on which this paper is based was financed by the Research Council of the European University Institute.

Notes

1   The actual quote is: "As it is the power of exchanging that gives the occasion to the division of labor, so the extent of this division must always be limited by the extent of that power, or, in other words, by the extent of the market." A. Smith, 1976 [1776]: 21.
2   Although being the most common in trading countries, the acceptance and domestic bill of exchange were not the only money market instruments available. In the Netherlands during the nineteenth century, the dominant instrument was the *prolongatie*, a month advance against a security (public debt or the stock of a chartered-company); see Jonker, 1996. In postbellum United States, it was the promissory note, a bill without bank endorsement; see James, 1978.
3   The only significant exception to this separation between savings and payments concerns princes and principates, monarchs and governments, and wealthy private persons, whose wealth was already deposited with, and managed by, the *haute banque*.
4   On French savings banks, see Passion, 1991: 102 and Vogler, 1991.
5   On Belgian savings banks, see Chlepner, 1926: 96.
6   On Italy, see Polsi, 1993: 234, 249; on Prussia, Thomes, 1995: 151.
7   For an instance of continual tension between center and periphery on the regulation of savings banks, see Albrecht, 1990.

42 *Daniel Verdier*

8 See Plessis, 1985a: 158 and Nishimura, 1995. The Bank of England's branch network failed to meet the same success because it occurred too late, long after the local joint-stock banks had spread the use of check-banking in the countryside as an alternative to bill discounting; see Sayers, 1976: 2; see also Ziegler, 1990a.

9 On the British money market, in its relation to Lancashire especially, see Ashton, 1945 and Neal, 1994: 168. On the Dutch market, see Jonker, 1996: 105, 183.

10 On Britain, see De Cecco, 1974: 101 and Ziegler, 1990a: 135; on France, Bouvier, 1973: 160; Lévy-Leboyer and Lescure, 1991: 167, and Lescure, 1995a: 318; on Belgium, Kauch, 1950: 235, 260.

11 On internationalization, see Verdier, 1998.

12 Central banks are not part of the state banking network, but of the profit banking network, irrespective of whether they are privately or state-owned.

13 I have studied elsewhere the relation between state centralization and state banking; see Verdier, 2000.

14 This geographic specialization is emphasized by the literature on industrial dualism. For two recent contributions, see Deeg, 1999 and Herrigel, 1996.

15 Central banking is not the only form to overcome the liquidity and commitment problems faced by universal banking systems; a state regulator, armed with inspection rights, along with Treasury support, is an equally valid alternative. Although more common today, the regulatory option was only found in Sweden during the nineteenth century. Self-regulation by a corporatist association of bankers, along with ad hoc Treasury support, was also found in Canada.

16 See Chlepner, 1926: 317 and Guex, 1993: 20–38. Like Chlepner, 1943: 35 with respect to Belgium, R.H. Tilly, 1986: 122 argues that the creation of the Prussian State Bank in 1846 helped promote investment banking in Prussia.

17 For a similar argument, see Broz, 1998: 242.

18 See Ziegler, 1990a: 131–4; Plessis, 1985a: 158, 279; Bouvier, 1988: 80. Toward the end of the century, however, the severe competition for good paper with joint stock banks led central banks in many countries to rediscount larger quantities of country paper.

19 Based on Martín-Aceña, 1995: 504.

20 Surely, the existence of a central bank proffering a liquidity guarantee to the commercial banks relaxes the extent to which universal banks have to cover long-term loans with equity. But it does not eliminate it altogether, for this guarantee is never complete for two reasons: (1) the supply of liquidity to the banking system is constrained by the central bank's obligation to stabilize the currency; (2) wary of moral hazard, the central bank exercises discretion in extending its guarantee to each individual bank, and thus can induce commercial banks to maintain what are considered in national banking milieus as safe levels of equity.

21 Although most historical accounts point to the emergence of universal banking right in 1910–1911, that alone cannot account for the 1913 datum. Vanthemsche, 1991: 107 and Jonker, 1991 date the Dutch move toward universal banking to 1910; van Gor and Koelewijn, 1995: 158 to World War I.

22 Things would change with the two wars; see Verdier, 2000.

2 Banks and securities markets 1870–1914

Ranald Michie

There can be little doubt that a strong and direct correlation exists between a country's per capita income and the financial system it possesses. Wealthy economies generate savings, which are either short term, as in the seasonal or cyclical surpluses of individuals and businesses or long term, as in the need to provide for capital replacement or retirement. Conversely, wealthy economies also generate demands for funds to finance a variety of activities, whether consumer spending on automobiles, homes and holidays; business expansion involving new mines, factories, shops and offices, or the state's obligation to provide defence, infrastructure and social services. The function of the financial services sector in advanced economies was to match supply and demand of savings and to do so in a way that lenders and borrowers were appropriately rewarded and charged in order to allocate scarce resources as efficiently as possible (Crane *et al.*, 1995: preface, viii). However, if per capita income were the only criterion dictating the development of financial systems in individual countries then it would be expected that a high degree of similarity would exist among advanced economies. Clearly this is not the case. Instead, considerable divergence exists which both needs to be explained and its implications for national economic performance assessed (Merton and Bodie, 1995: 3–4). Even in terms of the relative size of the financial services sector in apparently similar economies, large differences existed. Whereas in the year 2000 the provision of financial services generated 7 percent of national income in Britain, the figure was only 5.5 percent in the United States and 3.5 percent in France (*Financial Times*, 2 August 2000). A direct correlation between financial services and per capita income would have suggested both rough comparability and a different ordering.

Furthermore, closer scrutiny of financial systems in countries at similar stages of economic development reveals major differences in their nature and composition. Though all such economies possessed both banks and securities markets, the importance and role of each varied enormously. In 1998, for example, stock market capitalization, as a percentage of GDP, ranged from a high of 143 percent in the UK and 122 percent in the USA through to 64 percent in Australia, 62 percent in Canada, 52 percent in Japan, 51 percent in Germany and 38 percent in Italy. This position was also reflected in the popularity of the equity (shares/common stock) culture in these countries. Whereas 54 percent of the adult population in Australia owned shares, either directly or through a managed fund, and a similarly high proportion was to be found in Canada (52 percent), USA (48 percent) and Britain (40 percent), the proportion for Germany was only 25 percent (*Financial Times*, 18 October 1999; 9 February 2000).

This is not a new phenomenon for such differences between the financial systems of advanced economies already existed at the beginning of the twentieth century. On the eve of World War I there was a group of economies where banks played a dominant role, led by countries such as Germany and Italy, and another group led by Britain and the United States, in which securities markets had come to occupy a central position within their financial systems. Using the data compiled by Goldsmith, it is clear that in advanced economies around 1913 financial assets comprised around 40 percent of national assets, ranging from a low of 30.8 percent in Italy to a high of 57.5 percent in Denmark, but with most being in the 35–45 percent range. However, when the nature of these financial assets is examined in further detail much greater differences between countries emerge. In judging the relative significance of financial institutions in individual economies the range is from one where banks controlled 73.2 percent of financial assets in Denmark down to 33.5 percent in South Africa, with Germany registering a share of 67.6 percent compared with Britain's 43.2 percent and the United States' 39.6 percent. On that judgement banks appeared to play a more important role in the economies of Continental Europe and Japan than they did in Britain and the United States. Conversely, when the proportion of securities in financial assets is measured the reverse position emerges. This is especially so when the focus is upon corporate stocks and bonds rather than public debt. In countries such as Italy, Germany and Switzerland corporate securities comprised around 10 percent of financial assets while in Britain they totalled 27.6 percent and 38.1 percent in the United States (Table 2.1).

The conclusion from this evidence is that there were long-standing and fundamental differences between the financial systems in place in different countries which were not explained either in terms of relative per capita income, as between the rich and the poor, or in terms of more recent historical experience such as the impact of revolutions and wars upon the financing of economic activity in the twentieth century. In turn this places the focus of research on the century before 1914, and especially the period after 1850 for that was when modern financial systems took shape in the leading economies of the world, such as Britain, France, Germany and the United States. The nineteenth century witnessed a great flowering of both banks and stock exchanges as financial intermediation became an increasingly important part of advanced economies. Fundamental forces were at work generating a need to collect and mobilize the savings being generated by populations in receipt of higher incomes, and to provide the credit and capital required by governments and businesses around the world. At the same time the growing separation between those who generated savings and those who required them, which was taking place in terms of space, function and time, created profitable openings for those who could match supply and demand. One important result of this was a proliferation of banks, both by number and activity, though the particular

Table 2.1 Comparative financial systems, 1912–14.

Country	1 Financial assets	2 Financial institutions	3 Transferable securities	
			Total	Corporate
Belgium	39.4 %	44.4%	36.5%	22.1%
Denmark	57.5%	73.2%	21.3%	15.6%
France	39.3%	47.1%	37.4%	21.6%
Germany	39.5 %	67.6%	20.0%	10.3%
Italy	30.8%	51.6%	36.5%	4.6%
Norway	41.3%	72.6%	19.8%	11.7%
Switzerland	48.4%	69.8%	21.9%	14.4%
UK	47.4%	43.2%	35.6%	27.6%
India	13.3%	21.1%	10.8%	4.0%
Japan	38.0%	53.4%	21.6%	12.7%
South Africa	34.0%	33.5%	31.4%	27.8%
USA	42.9%	39.6%	42.2%	38.1%

Notes:
1 Financial assets as a proportion of national assets.
2 Assets/liabilities of financial institutions as a proportion of financial assets.
3 Government debt/foreign assets (net or gross) corporate stocks and bonds as a proportion of financial assets.

Source: Goldsmith, 1985: Appendix A.

form that this took varied enormously across the world. In some countries the pattern was a large number of individual banks while in others it was a small number of banks possessing a large number of branches. What banks provided also differed, for some confined themselves to the provision of short-term credit whereas others supplied long-term capital. However, irrespective of the particular form it took, banks had come to play a central role in all developed economies by World War I. A similar development took place in securities markets for they also grew enormously in number and activity during the nineteenth century. Prior to 1800 the use of transferable securities was little employed, outside government, as a means of raising finance, and few in society invested in stocks and bonds apart from occasional and short-lived speculative outbursts. Reflecting this, trading activity in securities in the eighteenth century was largely conducted in open markets, such as the mercantile exchanges, and involved little in the way of organization and regulation. In contrast, by the early twentieth century virtually every major city had its organized stock exchange housed in an imposing building and supported by trained staff, and that was where the numerous stocks and bonds issued by governments and major business corporations from around the world were traded. However, like banks these stock exchanges also exhibited substantial differences, as with who was permitted to join, what securities were traded, what investors were catered for and how business was conducted.[1]

Lying behind these differences was the fact that the development of national systems was conditioned by the historical experience and contemporary practices of the individual countries within which they operated, as well as the specific supply and demand requirements they had to meet. The financial system that developed in a small market economy open to international challenges and opportunities, and where the state played a limited role, was likely to be fundamentally different from that in a large closed economy where the state was of major influence. No financial system was thus immune from the unique set of circumstances that determined its particular characteristics, irrespective of the importance of the general economic forces creating a need for the functions it embodied. This can be seen from a brief review of Britain's banking system, for the successful establishment of the Bank of England in 1694 influenced the way the banking system subsequently developed. The Bank of England concentrated its activities in London, where it acted for the government, but enjoyed a monopoly of joint-stock banking in England and Wales until 1825. It did not create a nation-wide banking network, and as it prevented any other bank from doing so, it was necessary for London and provincial private banks to establish their own national networks, so facilitating payments and the employment of idle funds. Consequently, there developed in Britain a devolved banking structure divided between the Bank of England, private banks throughout England and Wales, and a group of Scottish joint-stock banks not bound by the Bank of England's monopoly. As many of the provincial private banks collapsed in the monetary instability that followed the end of the Napoleonic wars in 1815, whereas the major Scottish joint-stock banks did not, the Bank of England's monopoly over joint-stock banking in England and Wales outside of London was eventually ended in 1825. This and subsequent legal relaxations, led to the establishment of numerous English joint-stock banks, before new restrictions on bank formation were introduced in 1844. The result was competition between these new joint-stock banks and the established private banks for business, with the Bank of England focused more and more on its functions as the government's bank and as banker to the London money market. In order to compete successfully against the private banks the joint-stock banks cultivated deposits, whereas the private banks had traditionally operated on a large private capital provided by a small number of partners. No matter the wealth of the individual partners in a private bank they found it increasingly difficult to compete against the lending power of the joint-stock banks based on these deposits. As the joint-stock banks learned how to structure their assets and liabilities so as to survive financial crises, involving sudden withdrawal and defaults, so they could better compete against the private banks. Hence there appeared the traditional British joint-stock banks with numerous branches collecting deposits and making loans, supported by a head office managing the whole operation, and employing a large reserve of funds in the London short-term money market. In turn, there developed in London, because of the size of its money and capital markets, a group of specialist financial intermediaries that employed these short-term funds, relying on the fact that any reduction in supply by one bank would be marked by an increase from another, so maintaining the overall level (Anderson and Cottrell, 1974: 9–11, 151–7, 243–9).

The financial system that evolved in Britain was a response to the varied economic and political forces at work rather than a simple product of supply and demand in a developed economy. In particular, the privileges extended to the Bank of England and the facilities for employing funds in the City of London, were instrumental in creating a functionally specialized financial system. In 1913 the *Banking Almanac* listed 239 banks as having offices (head offices or branches) in London and these included banks with numerous branches either in Britain or abroad as well as banks with only one office but specializing in particular financial activities such as investment banking or money broking. Furthermore, there was a host of other financial intermediaries operating in London, including thousands of brokers and dealers in such areas as securities, commodities, insurance, bullion and foreign exchange. There was a self-reinforcing process present in the British financial system during the nineteenth century for the more specialized its components became the more successful it was at meeting the needs of both lenders and borrowers, so expanding the volume of business to be done, and so encouraging new entrants and further specialization. The *Banking Almanac* for 1913 also listed 1,356 banks from around the world that were either directly represented in London with their own branch or were present indirectly through an arrangement with a bank which did have an office there. By then the City of London had emerged as the foremost financial centre of a world economy that was increasingly integrated in terms of financial and commercial flows. The City of London was at the very centre of a dense network of global connections and payments systems, so making the British financial system unlike any other in the world at that time.[2]

Consequently, in no case was the financial system of one country identical to that of another, and nor should one expect it to be so, given the importance of economic development, historical experience and government legislation in determining the role and nature of both banks and securities markets.[3] Though Britain and the United States, for example, are usually regarded as having comparable financial systems, because of the importance of securities markets, there were fundamental differences between the banking networks of each country. In 1913 Britain had 104 banks and these controlled a total of 8,156 branches through which deposits were collected and loans made. This was a nation-wide banking system largely directed from head offices in the City of London. In contrast, in 1913 there were 24,514 banks in the United States and they possessed only 548 branches. Though those US banks located in New York were the largest and most important they had no direct control over the direction and management of the banking system. As Canada had a banking system closely resembling that of Britain, with 24 banks and 2,962 branches, it is evident that the way banking developed in the United States owed much to the influence of political and social factors, rather than geography and economics.[4]

An even greater contrast can be drawn between Britain and Germany (Table 2.2). In Britain commercial banks dominated the banking system, and they largely operated on short-term deposits provided by savers, which greatly restricted their ability to make long-term loans and forced them to maintain highly liquid positions. In Germany commercial banks were only one part of the banking system, for savings banks dominated the collection of deposits from savers. As a result the commercial banks operated much more on the capital provided by their

Table 2.2 Banking in Britain and Germany: a comparison, 1913.

A) Deposits

	Total	Commercial	Savings
Britain	$6,728.9 m	$5,483.6 m (81.5%)	$1,245.3 m (18.5%)
Germany	$7,212.6 m	$2,525.2 m (35.0%)	$4,687.4 m (65.0%)

B) Assets

	Cash and money at call	Loans, advances, discounts	Investments
Britain	24.5%	60.7%	12.6%
Germany	4.4%	81.9%	11.9%

C) Liabilities

	Capital and reserves	Deposits
Britain	8.5%	91.0%
Germany	23.6%	74.7%

D) Gearing

	Capital/Deposits	Cash/Loans and investments
Britain	10.7%	3.0%
Germany	3.2%	21.3%

E) Liquidity

	Deposits/Cash	Loans and investments/capital
Britain	3.7%	8.6%
Germany	17.0%	4.0%

Source: Tables 2.3–2.6.

shareholders, plus their own reserves, which allowed them to make long-term loans as they had less need to cover sudden withdrawals. Germany had only been united in 1871 followed by currency unification in 1873, or some 166 years after Britain, so the conditions supporting the emergence of nation-wide branch banking hardly existed. In addition, the attitude of the German government, expressed through legislation, protected the position of the local savings banks and stunted competition from the large Berlin-based banks. Therefore, there emerged in Germany a particular type of bank that became known as a Universal bank. This bank had few branches but attempted to provide the whole range of financial services that its customers, especially businesses would require. It provided not only the short-term credit that a business needed to finance its daily operations but it also extended long-term loans to finance such items as factory extensions. Furthermore, the bank could also arrange the conversion of a business into a joint-stock company and handle the issue of the resulting securities to investors through its contracts with its other customers. In Britain these functions would be split between commercial banks, investment banks and stockbrokers.[5] In the same way as Britain's historic experience and economic circumstances had created a particular financial system, so the same had happened in Germany.

However, the focus of research has not been on the way each country's financial system responded to the demands made upon it, with judgements made accordingly. Instead, it is banking systems alone that have tended to be investigated and then assessed in terms of the contribution they made to the finance of economic development. Inevitably the results of that research have tended to favour the Universal banks for they can be seen to be providing the most comprehensive service to their business customers. The very concept of a Universal bank involved the provision of not only the short-term credit that a business needed to carry out its daily business but also the long-term capital required to finance further expansion. Furthermore, Universal banks also included an investment banking and brokerage function so that they could issue securities on behalf of their business clients, when additional long-term finance had to be raised, while their network of customers provided the investor base to which such securities could be sold. In contrast, a more disaggregated financial system, involving separate banks providing credit and capital, and the existence of independent brokerage houses, appeared to offer a greatly inferior service, as comparisons involved only one part of the system being provided.[6]

To a large extent there has been a predisposition to accept research findings that favored Universal banks because it was easy to understand the role that they played – namely the mobilization and allocation of finance under the guidance of knowledge and trusted bankers. In contrast, the logic behind a disaggregated financial system was less easy to understand, involving as it did an unwillingness by credit bankers to provide long-term finance to their own business customers. Instead such businesses were required to pay fees to investment bankers in order to persuade investors, who had little knowledge of them, to buy the securities issued on their behalf. In turn that exposed them to the market sentiment guided not by a familiarity with the business but short-term considerations.[7] This pre-disposition to find in favor of the Universal banks was also encouraged after the World War II by the association of such banks with some of the most successful economies during the golden age of expansion between 1950 and 1970, namely Germany and Japan. In contrast, disaggregated financial systems were identified with lagging economies, notably Britain and the United States.

Thus, for much of the post-war years a consensus has existed in which the Universal bank, especially on the German model, was regarded as the ultimate form of financial institution, valued especially for the contribution it made to supporting long-term economic growth. In contrast, specialized financial systems were seen to be deeply flawed, encouraging a short-term attitude towards investment because no single component had a long-term commitment. However, such a judgement now requires serious revision. On the one hand much greater research has been conducted into the relationship between German Universal banks and their customers, especially after 1945, and the conclusions that have emerged tend to refute the idea of them playing a long-term, supportive role. Similarities rather than differences between German and British banking practices have tended to emerge, undermining the view that the different economic performance of the two economies can be attributed to the nature and behaviour of their banking systems. That has also been extended to other countries where Universal banks were considered to have played a central role. In Italy recent evidence suggests that the Universal banks there had their strongest connections with the building and agricultural sectors rather than manufacturing industry.[8] On the other hand the convergence of the economic growth rates in the leading advanced economies, and even the relatively poor performance of Germany and Japan compared with Britain and the United States since 1980, have undermined many of the assumptions concerning the superiority of the Universal banking model for financial provision. What became increasingly clear in the late twentieth century was that both banks and securities markets were essential components of the financial system of any advanced market economy. Though competition between banks and securities markets existed they also complemented each other in the financial services that they provided in order to meet the diverse and complicated needs of a sophisticated economy. Securitization of bank assets for instance became increasingly common in the 1980s and 1990s, as banks sought to balance assets and liabilities in a more volatile and competitive world. It should never be assumed that any particular financial system suits all countries at all times, for each is the product of the conditions that created it and allowed it to flourish. This is not to say, however, that the financial system that a country possessed at any one time was the best that could be achieved, for the very fact that it had been, and continued to be, moulded by forces other than the supply of savings and the demand for finance meant that it was a sub-optimum solution to the economy's needs.

Nevertheless, for much of the nineteenth and twentieth centuries there did appear to be a rough division between those countries where savings and investments were largely channelled through the banking system and those where the securities market undertook much of this activity. The League of Nations, for example, noted in its survey of commercial banks, published in 1931, that: "In some countries, savings are of considerable extent directly invested in industry and trade or in public securities, while in others they are largely deposited with a bank, which then invest them in loans and discounts, or in bonds and other securities" (League of Nations, 1931: 9).

To them, as to many others, what mattered were the relative merits of a financial system where individuals chose between the competing attractions of diverse companies and a financial system where those investment decisions were left in the hands of bank officials. However, this is to miss the point that the financial systems of advanced economies possessed both banks and securities markets for both were required and neither were perfect substitutes for the other. Certainly the 50 years before World War I experienced an enormous expansion in banking across the world. By 1913 there were numerous banks conducting a purely local business all around the world. One indicator of the spread of banking provision in Asia, Africa, Australia and Latin America was the fact that London-based overseas banks, which provided part of the banking services in these areas, had grown from 15 in

15 in number with 132 branches in 1860 to 25 in number and 1,327 branches in 1913, or a ten-fold expansion (G. Jones, 1993: Tables A1.1, A1.3). For the more developed economies it is possible to compare deposit statistics in 1880 and 1913, in order to obtain a better measure of the use being made of banks. In Europe, for example, in 1880 savers had placed an estimated \$4.6 billion on deposit in banks, whereas by 1913 the amount had reached \$27.3 billion, or a six-fold increase. World-wide, it can be suggested that this increase in Europe reflected the general picture as banking provision only appeared in many countries during this period (Table 2.3). Altogether, by 1913 it is estimated that world bank deposits had reached \$43 billion but around 95 percent of this was to be found in Europe and North America. Thus, despite the expansion of banking world-wide in the late nineteenth/ early twentieth centuries, as exhibited by the position of the British overseas banks, when deposits are examined it is clear that banking remained largely confined to Europe and European areas of settlement, especially the United States and Canada but also including Australia, New Zealand, South Africa and Argentina (Table 2.4). In addition this distribution of world banking had implications for national financial systems for it implies that only a few countries could generate the level of savings necessary to support sophisticated money and capital markets, and those who served them. Taking the position in 1913 it is clear that the United States had the greatest accumulation of bank deposits with \$13 billion or 30 percent of the world total, followed by Germany (\$7.2 billion or 17 percent), Britain (\$6.8 billion or 16 percent) and France (\$3.3 billion or 8 percent). These four countries alone were responsible for 70 percent of the world's bank deposits (Table 2.3).

However, there were major differences in the nature of banking world-wide, and this was not simply between branch and unitary banks. Of major importance was the role played by savings banks in different countries. In Germany in 1913, 65 percent of bank deposits were held by savings banks compared with only 33 percent in France, 29 percent in the USA and 18 percent in Britain. As savings banks tended to adopt different lending policies from commercial banks (including Universal banks) this had major consequences for the financial systems of each country. Savings banks collected the deposits of smaller savers, maintained a large cash balance, and adopted a cautious lending policy, favoring deposits in other banks, lending on mortgage, and substantial holdings of government debt. This was certainly the case not only in Britain but also in Germany and France. Essentially savings banks were risk-averse financial institutions whose priority was to avoid losses and pay a moderate rate of interest to those who saved with them. This meant that they directed their funds towards the government and contented themselves with a relatively low rate of return and thus made little direct contribution to economic growth (Thomes, 1995: 151–2; Tortella, 1999: 171).

In contrast commercial banks were more business orientated, both in terms of the deposits they received and the loans they made. Commercial banks could expect a much greater turnover in deposits as businesses, including other banks like the savings banks, found themselves with temporarily surplus funds or had to draw down their liquid positions. The reverse was also true in their loans and advances as businesses looked to their banks to provide them with credit not only to cover

Table 2.3   World bank deposits, 1880–1913 ($ M) (current prices at 1913 exchange rates).

Region	Country	Commercial banks		Savings banks	
		1880	1913	1880	1913
Europe	Austria	–	853.3	152.0	1,465.3
	Belgium	102.3	449.0	29.8	394.8
	Bulgaria	–	32.7	–	9.8
	Denmark	20.9	241.0	68.1	230.0
	Finland	6.4	119.0	–	1.7
	France	–	2,192.3	246.2	1,121.0
	Germany	126.0	2,525.2	622.6	4,687.4
	Greece	–	39.8	–	112.3
	Hungary	–	967.1	53.1	864.5
	Italy	–	326.9	141.0	904.4
	Netherlands	–	116.8	14.8	125.6
	Norway	21.7	158.7	37.2	162.7
	Russia	39.8	488.3	1.5	324.0
	Spain	33.7	73.3	11.0	96.2
	Sweden	72.1	453.6	39.1	268.4
	Switzerland	–	353.3	–	340.6
	UK	2,410.7	5,483.6	339.4	1,245.3
	Total	**2,833.6**	**14,873.9**	**1,755.8**	**12,354.0**
North America	Canada	42.0	381.0	15.0	97.0
	USA	2,222.0	9,249.0	819.0	3,749.0
	Total	**2,264.0**	**9,630.0**	**834.0**	**3,846.0**
Australasia	Australia	73.3	284.9	38.2	379.9
	New Zealand	41.4	125.2	5.4	92.5
	Total	**114.7**	**410.1**	**33.6**	**472.4**
South/Central America	Argentina	–	271.3	–	–
	Bolivia	–	2.3	–	–
	Brazil	–	154.2	–	70.8
	Chile	–	45.8	–	19.2
	Ecuador	–	0.7	–	–
	Guyana	–	–	–	1.2
	Mexico	–	17.3	–	–
	Peru	–	1.6	–	–
	Uruguay	–	2.3	–	–
	Venezuela	–	1.9	–	–
	West Indies	–	–	–	5.7
	Total	–	**497.4**	–	**96.9**
Asia of which	**Total**	–	**526.5**	–	**182.9**
	India	–	292.5	–	75.3
	Japan	–	227.5	–	96.0
Africa of which	**Total**	–	**114.5**	–	**37.5**
	South Africa	–	112.0	–	28.2

Source: Mitchell, 1998. (Original data is in national currencies. It was converted to US dollars using official 1913 exchange rates.)

Table 2.4   Distribution of world bank deposits, 1913.

A) By type of bank

Country	Total	Commercial banks		Savings banks	
World	$43,042.1 M (100%)	$26,052.4 M	(60.5%)	$16,989.7 M	(39.5%)
Europe	27,227.9	14,873.9	(54.6%)	12,354.0	(45.4%)
N. America	13,476.0	9,630.0	(71.5%)	3,846.0	(28.5%)
S/C America	594.3	497.4	(83.7%)	472.4	(16.3%)
Australia	882.5	410.1	(46.5%)	472.4	(53.5%)
Asia	709.4	526.5	(74.2%)	182.9	(25.8%)
Africa	152.0	114.5	(75.3%)	37.5	(24.7%)

B) By region

	Total	Commercial banks	Savings banks
Europe	63.3%	57.1%	72.7%
N. America	31.3%	37.0%	22.6%
S/C America	1.4%	1.9%	0.6%
Australia	2.1%	1.6%	2.8%
Asia	1.7%	2.0%	1.1%
Africa	0.4%	0.4%	0.2%

Source: Table 2.3.

the period between expenditure and receipts but also seasonal and cyclical fluctuations. Thus, commercial banks had to balance constantly the funds flowing in and out so that they were always able to meet, on the one hand, withdrawals by depositors and increased borrowings from regular customers and, on the other hand, employ remuneratively the funds placed with them. Failure in the former could jeopardize their survival, while failure in the latter could undermine their profitability and thus the return enjoyed by their owners or shareholders. Consequently the location of the deposits within a financial system had profound implications for the way that system developed and operated. Thus, if only commercial bank deposits are compared, which totalled $26 billion in 1913, it is clear that the United States with $9.3 billion or 36 percent of the total and Britain with $5.5 billion (21 percent) are in different leagues from either Germany ($2.5 billion or 10 percent) or France ($2.2 billion or 8 percent) (Table 2.3).

Furthermore, the way the commercial banks operated in the various countries also had implications for the rest of the financial system, for major differences between them do emerge. Banks in Continental Europe tended to retain a very small proportion of their funds as cash or near cash (money at call). Instead they lent out a high proportion by way of loans, advances or discounts to either personal or business customers. In contrast, banks in Britain, the United States and European settled areas overseas, tended to keep a high proportion of their funds in cash or money at call, so reducing the proportion available for lending to customers. As a result Continental European banks were regarded as being much more supportive to business because of their willingness to lend out a higher proportion of their funds, than banks in Britain (Born, 1983a: 70, 88). Even in the United States only 13.5 percent of funds were retained as cash or its near equivalent in 1913 compared with 24.5 percent in Britain (Table 2.5).

However, considering that bankers had to always balance the amount and type of loans against the amount and type of the funds they had available, any judgement based solely on the distribution of such loans is inadequate. The money that the banks had available for lending came from two sources, namely the capital provided by those who owned the bank, plus the reserves accumulated from profits, and the deposits of savers attracted by the convenience and return offered. When a bank operated on its own capital it had a source of funds that could not be withdrawn, only its ownership transferred from one holder to another. As a result that capital could be lent out on a long-term basis because there were no circumstances in which it would have to be repaid. In contrast when a bank operated on deposits it was constantly aware that these could be withdrawn, often without notice, by savers. It had to be in a position to repay, for any refusal would lead to all savers trying to reclaim their deposits. As a result such funds

Table 2.5 Commercial banks: assets and liabilities, 1913/14.

Country	1 Assets			2 Liabilities	
	Cash and money at call	Loans, advances, discounts	Investments	Capital and reserves	Deposits
Austria	2.4%	86.5%	9.9%	22.7%	75.2%
Denmark	2.9%	75.0%	20.5%	22.9%	75.5%
Finland	2.4%	90.2%	4.4%	17.7%	80.5%
France	7.7%	86.0%	4.8%	18.0%	80.3%
Germany	4.4%	81.9%	11.9%	23.6%	74.7%
Hungary	1.7%	87.8%	8.6%	15.6%	83.0%
Italy	5.5%	83.1%	9.6%	22.0%	76.5%
Netherlands	4.0%	81.3%	13.4%	29.3%	68.5%
Norway	1.9%	90.1%	6.9%	15.5%	84.5%
Sweden	2.7%	89.9%	7.0%	24.2%	75.8%
Switzerland	1.5%	90.7%	6.7%	16.7%	83.3%
UK – E/W	24.5%	60.7%	12.6%	8.5%	91.0%
Canada	15.6%	74.9%	6.8%	14.7%	84.3%
USA	13.5%	67.0%	16.9%	16.1%	81.5%
Argentina	24.7%	71.4%	1.1%	27.7%	71.0%
South Africa	15.3%	75.4%	6.6%	13.9%	86.1%
Australia/New Zealand	28.6%	62.4%	5.9%	16.3%	83.7%

Notes:
1 Figure for premises omitted.
2 Figure for profit/loss omitted.

NB: There is a lack of consistency whether short-term loans are classified as money at call or as loans/advances/discounts.

Source: League of Nations, 1931.

could only be employed in such a way as to ensure that a significant proportion was available in cash or near cash form, so as to meet any sudden increase in withdrawals. Under these circumstances the lending policies followed by each bank had to reflect the nature of the funds upon which they operated. If a bank employed too high a proportion of the deposits placed with it in long-term loans then it became highly vulnerable to sudden withdrawals by savers. Hence the collapse of banks during a financial crisis when the failure of businesses to which banks had lent generated rumours on the stability of the bank, leading to a rush of savers attempting to recover their deposits. Banks all over the world learnt to adjust either their lending to suit their deposit base or their capital base to suit their lending in the late nineteenth century, and so avoided collapsing like so many banks had during previous financial crises. This was something that British commercial banks had become experienced at doing earlier in the nineteenth century, though the collapse of the City of Glasgow Bank in 1878 through overlending to a few large clients with unsaleable assets as collateral, indicates that the techniques of successful banking took a long time to learn. Generally, by the late nineteenth/early twentieth century, British commercial banks had become so experienced at balancing assets and liabilities that the financial system experienced no serious financial crisis between 1878 and 1914. In that period only 0.2 percent of British bank loans to industrial firms resulted in a loss to the bank, because of a failure to repay, and even then the loss was only 0.19 percent of the total amount lent (Newton, 1996: 70, 79; Collins, 1998: 21; Baker and Collins, 1999: 21, 23; Merrett, 1997: 188; S. Jones, 1994: 65, 74; Cleveland and Huertas, 1985: 28). Such care was essential in a banking system where deposits were of major importance. In 1913, 91 percent of the funds used by British commercial banks came from depositors and only 9 percent from their shareholders. In contrast, it can be seen that German commercial banks, like the Universal banks, obtained 24 percent of their funds from their shareholders and 75 percent from depositors (Table 2.5).

From this analysis emerges a clear division in the nature of banking in different countries during the years before World War I. In Continental European countries such as Germany the tendency was for banks to develop that had a low gearing in terms of the ratio of deposits to capital but were highly geared in terms of the ratio of their loans and investments to cash. It was not until 1901 that deposits exceeded capital in Deutsche Bank even though it had been formed back in 1870 (Gall *et al.*, 1995: 2). Simply put, such banks had less need for cash because such a high proportion of their funds was in the form of capital and accumulated reserves. In contrast banks in the English-speaking world, and especially Britain, were highly geared in terms of the ratio of deposits to capital but had a much lower gearing in the ratio of their loans and investments to cash (Capie and Collins, 1997: 165). Again, simply put, such banks had to maintain a high proportion of their funds in cash because of the need to repay depositors at any time. The converse picture for each type of bank emerges from a comparison of liquidity ratios for Continental European banks were relatively illiquid whereas banks in English-speaking countries maintained highly liquid positions. The reasons for such a situation are fairly obvious when it is recognized that financial crises were regular occurrences and all banks had to adopt strategies to cope with them if they wished to survive the risky environment in which they were operating. The study of individual banks in countries like Britain, France, Germany, the United States, Australia, South Africa and Japan confirms that those which survived, adjusted their gearing and liquidity in order to do so. Those that did not could not meet withdrawals by savers during a financial crisis and either collapsed or were saved by the state. For those that came near to collapse but survived a financial crisis the subsequent response was to adjust both gearing and liquidity so as to be better positioned when the next crisis occurred, which they did regularly from the mid-nineteenth century to World War I (Marichal, 1997: 344–53; Born, 1983a: 171; Checkland *et al.*, 1994: 3–5; Gall *et al.*, 1995: 28; Hansen, 1994: 62–4; Tortella, 1999: 161–2, 171; Balogh, 1947: 231; Merrett, 1997: 188; Merrett, 1995: 73; S. Jones, 1994: 65–74; Lazonick and O'Sullivan, 1997: 119, 127) (Table 2.6).

Inevitably, such marked differences between banking systems, as with Britain and Germany, had major implications for the securities market. The securities market fulfilled two major functions in the financial system. Of these the most

Table 2.6 Commercial banks: banking ratios, 1913/14.

Country	1 Gearing		2 Liquidity	
	Capital deposits	Cash/loans and investments	Deposits/ cash	Loans and investments/ capital
Austria	3.3	40.2	31.3	4.2
Denmark	3.3	32.9	26.0	4.2
Finland	4.6	39.4	33.5	5.3
France	4.5	11.8	10.4	5.0
Germany	3.2	21.3	17.0	4.0
Hungary	5.3	56.7	48.8	6.2
Italy	3.5	17.8	14.7	4.2
Netherlands	2.3	23.7	17.1	3.2
Norway	5.5	51.1	44.5	6.3
Sweden	3.1	35.9	28.1	4.0
Switzerland	5.0	64.9	55.5	5.8
UK–E/W	10.7	3.0	3.7	8.6
Canada	5.7	5.2	5.4	5.6
USA	5.1	6.2	6.0	5.2
Argentina	2.6	2.9	2.9	2.6
South Africa	6.2	5.4	5.6	5.9
Australia/New Zealand	5.1	2.4	2.9	4.2

Notes:
1   The *higher* the number, the *higher* the gearing.
2   The *higher* the number, the *lower* the liquidity.

Source: Table 2.5.

obvious was a means by which governments and businesses could raise the long-term finance they needed. Wars, in particular, always put a strain on government finances, as it was impossible to finance any prolonged conflict from current revenue. The solution found was to issue transferable securities which could not be redeemed until some distant date, if ever, but on which interest was paid and which could be transferred from one holder to another. Hence the importance of the securities market, for without the ability to buy and sell such securities quickly, easily and cheaply there would be an understandable reluctance among investors to purchase such securities when issued by the government and its agents. The existence of such a market was thus vital if government was to obtain the long-term finance that it required, for there were few in society who could, or were prepared to, provide the vast sums required to wage war without any expectation of recovering that money when required for another purpose, no matter the rate of interest paid. Thus in the eighteenth century securities markets were largely associated with the securities issued by governments for non-productive purposes rather than the finance of economic growth. In the nineteenth century railways had similar requirements to government for they needed large amounts of finance in order to construct complete systems. Only then would they become profitable – hence their use of transferable securities. Finally, the conversion of established companies into the joint-stock form, and the subsequent issue of stocks and bonds to investors, provided a simple and convenient way of transferring the ownership of the business to the next generation as they outgrew the ability of any single individual, or even a small group, to own and manage an enterprise on such a scale. Once such a conversion had taken place these joint-stock companies were now in a position to issue even more securities, so furthering their own expansion. Again, in all these cases the existence of a market in securities was of paramount importance in persuading investors to employ their funds in this way. Thus, in the nineteenth century securities markets made an important contribution to economic growth through the funds that could be provided to business, especially railways (Michie, 1992b).

Altogether, the result of the increasing use made by governments and business of issues of securities to raise long-term finance was an enormous expansion in the amount in existence. The value of securities quoted on the London Stock Exchange, for example, rose from £1.2 billion ($5.8 billion) in 1853 to £11.3 billion ($54.9 billion) in 1913, or over nine-fold at a time of steady or falling prices. That amount alone was greater than world bank deposits in 1913. Overall, an estimated $158 billion in transferable securities was in existence by 1913, or between 3 and 4 times the level of world bank deposits at that time. Judging from the securities quoted on the London Stock Exchange in 1913, and it was the world's largest and most international, 44.4 percent of these securities had been issued by governments but these were now almost matched by those created to finance the construction of the world's railway systems for these were now 37 percent of the total. The remainder was distributed among a wide variety of other enterprises such as urban utilities, industrial and commercial companies and mines (Michie, 1999: 4, 88–9). From being an almost exclusive preserve of governments at the beginning of the nineteenth century, the use of transferable securities had come to pervade economic life in all advanced economies and had proved essential in the financing of the world's railway system. Clearly, with the paid-up capital of the railways quoted on the London Stock Exchange alone totalling around $20 billion by 1913 such a financing operation would have been impossible for banks to have carried out, let alone meeting the needs of governments created by such events as the American Civil War, the Franco-Prussian War and French Indemnity, or the Russo-Japanese War. Thus, securities markets added a dimension to the capital market, which was beyond banks for they provided the means of raising long-term finance in large amounts, as with governments and railways. That is why they came into being and then flourished. Certainly banks could also provide long-term loans, as the Universal banks did, but this did not compare with the amounts raised by the issue of securities. A focus on industrial finance, which has tended to be the case, ignores where the great bulk of long-term finance was required, namely governments and railways, not industry and commerce (Michie, 1994).

However, the role of securities markets was not confined to the capital market, where they added a dimension that banks were not in a position to provide. The very fact that securities were transferable made them money market instruments, for they could be bought and sold whenever required. This facility made the most marketable securities ideal repositories for funds only temporarily available, even though they were long-term investments. Fixed interest securities, for example, would tend to rise in price as the date when interest was paid gradually approached, as they had to be held for less and less time before the return was obtained. Thus they could be bought for cash and sold forward, with the price difference providing the return, minus the dealing costs. Practice and experience made it possible to conduct such operations as these with little risk, especially when the securities chosen were the most actively traded in the most liquid markets. Thus banks reluctant to commit funds for too long a period were attracted to the securities markets as they obtained a return and maintained liquidity. There also built up a system where banks lent to market specialists who then employed the funds they obtained in holding securities. Short-term loans could be obtained from banks at low rates of interest, because they had to be repaid at short notice, while fixed interest securities paid a higher rate. Banks, for example, would lend idle funds at rates of interest no higher – or even less – than they paid deposits in order to obtain some return. Market professionals then used their experience and connections to employ the loans to carry the securities and so profit from differential in yield. If the loan was withdrawn and a replacement could not be found from another bank, the securities could be sold and the money repaid (Michie, 1987: Chapters 5 and 8).

Though banks provided such loans to brokers and others in all advanced economies, the practice was most prevalent in those countries where the banks needed to maintain a highly liquid position, as in Britain and the United States. British banks, for example, are estimated to have lent around 11 percent of their funds to members of the stock exchange in 1913 (Balogh, 1947: 57–60). In New

York the call money market on the Stock Exchange played an even more important role, while in the Netherlands the practice even went so far as to by-pass banks. There, savers lent directly to brokers through a network of contacts, who then employed the funds to carry marketable securities (van Zanden, 1997: 130; League of Nations, 1931: 342). The ability to buy and sell marketable securities at will played an essential role in maintaining the liquidity of banks in countries like Britain and the United States while at the same time allowing them to employ productively the deposits placed with them. Conversely, the funds they provided made it attractive for governments and businesses to issue securities in these centres for they were readily taken up there. Hence the development of the London Stock Exchange as the premier international securities market in the world, serving the interests not only of British investors and British borrowers but also investors and borrowers from around the world. Of the securities quoted in London in 1913, 21.3 percent had been issued by foreign governments while another 30.7 percent belonged to railways operating abroad, especially in the United States. There was a direct connection between the growth and nature of banking in countries like Britain and the United States and the importance of securities markets in these economies. It was no accident that the most active securities markets were located in the most active money market centres, namely London and New York (Michie, 1992a).

Both money and securities markets were essential components of a financial system where banks were highly geared in terms of deposits and so needed to be highly liquid. If that was not to be achieved by maintaining large cash balances, and thus immobilizing much of the savings entrusted to them, a method had to be found to lend large amounts of money remuneratively for very short periods. The transferable nature of securities and the development of markets where they could be traded provided an ideal outlet. In contrast, banking systems, which were much less highly geared, did not have the same liquidity requirement and had thus less need for the facilities provided by an active securities market. Nevertheless, that need still existed. Even the German Universal banks and the Japanese Zaibatsu banks were keen to persuade their business customers to provide securities as collateral for the funds that they borrowed, as they could be sold in a crisis. In turn, this meant that even these banks had a vested interest in building up a market for these securities, so providing the bank with a prospective exit from its long-term loan. This became an increasing priority in Continental European banking after the financial crises of the middle decades of the nineteenth century. During these crises, many of the European banks that had lent extensively to finance early railway or industrial development found themselves in a highly illiquid position when those who had borrowed could not repay. Even with substantial capital these banks could not meet withdrawals from depositors and so were bankrupted or rescued by the state. Bankers the world over were only too aware of the risks that they ran, positioned as they were between short-term deposits and long-term loans and so developed strategies to cope with the situation. As the experienced German banker, Jacob Goldschmidt, of the Darmstädter und National Bank, observed in 1931, when asked the question "Do I understand that the German banker, like the

English banker, does not like to have his money tied up permanently in industry?", his response was "No, the German banker dislikes that as much as any banker in the world" (Great Britain, Committee on Finance and Industry, 1931, Minutes of Evidence, Q 7285). Even British bankers who on the surface made few long-term loans, usually rolled over short-term loans to their business customers when required to do so because of economic circumstances. Otherwise, they would lose these customers through bankruptcy or to a competitor bank. The business of banking was to lend money and, where this took place in a competitive environment, bankers had to compromise their principles in order to survive. British banks rarely refused to roll over loans to a business customer facing difficulties and also tailored their loans to meet the needs of their customers, as long as it did not endanger the solvency of the bank. This even meant that loans were given for as long as 3 to 5 years when it was necessary and prudent to do so, as in the case of shipping and shipbuilding, where an easily marketable asset like a ship was provided as collateral.[9]

Consequently, the existence of securities markets was vital for those bankers operating largely on deposits, and of major importance even to those banks whose funds came from shareholders' capital and accumulated reserves. In 1913 German commercial banks had an estimated 11 percent of their lending in the form of loans where securities were provided as collateral, so providing them with a means of realizing assets either in a crisis or to meet the needs of another customer. A similar situation prevailed in other European countries, with the proportion being 12 percent in Switzerland and 21 percent in the Netherlands (League of Nations, 1931: 138–49, 192–9, 269). As a result the securities market did not merely supplement the financial provision available from banks, as was the case with government borrowing and infrastructure investment, but it also contributed to the operation of banks themselves.

Thus, the London securities market, as the world's largest and most liquid before 1914, attracted business from banks from around the world, directly and indirectly. London was the one place where temporarily idle balances could be always employed in a safe and remunerative way through call loans, secured on the most marketable of the stocks and bonds issued by companies and governments from around the world. Banks in countries like Australia, New Zealand, South Africa and the Latin American republics, as well as India, China and Japan all made extensive use of the London money market. As no Continental European centre could match the money market facilities available in London, even French and German banks, with Paris and Berlin readily available to them, made extensive use of London. This was further boosted in the case of Germany by legislation, which restricted the development of the call-money market on German stock exchanges. In North America, New York was similarly used by Canadian banks despite the existence of established securities markets in both Montreal and Toronto, because they did not possess the volume of turnover in marketable stocks and bonds that permitted rapid entry and exit and so a safe use for borrowed funds.[10]

Clearly securities markets before 1914 had become essential elements in the global financial system, playing a central role in both the money and capital markets.

Absent from this, however, was any significant role in the market for corporate control, which was to become such a prominent feature of stock exchange business after 1945 with mergers and take-overs. What that reflected was a switch in the functions performed by stock exchanges away from being a market largely of fixed interest securities and towards catering mainly for equities (Mayer, 1994). Most of the securities quoted and traded on stock exchanges before 1914 were fixed interest stocks and bonds issued by governments and railway companies. As such they offered no opportunity to control a company's affairs unless it was unable to pay the interest when it came due, for only then did bondholders have the right to intervene and replace the management. Consequently, the role attributed to securities markets of providing a mechanism for trading ownership, so influencing management behaviour and facilitating change, was not one that had much relevance to the pre-World War I era. Therefore, the criticism that the ease with which a company's shares could be bought or sold, which encouraged their management to adopt policies aimed at maximizing short-term profits, and so please the market, is also largely irrelevant for the pre-1914 situation, whatever its significance for the post-1945 era. As long as a company could service its long-term debt it was immune from the judgements of the market, unless its ordinary shares were widely held and particularly badly performing. Even where shares or common stock were widely held, as with railway companies, the utility nature of the business they were engaged in tended to generate a fairly stable income so that the return on these securities was relatively stable. Thus, the securities market before World War I provided little in the way of a constant monitoring mechanism for the companies that used it to raise finance, as illustrated by the large number of failures among many new concerns operating in such areas as mining and new technology. There the role of the market was to help provide the speculative capital that any high-risk enterprise required, and investors were betting on the outcome in the hope of enjoying spectacular gains. Mining shares did generate much activity on stock exchanges all over the world, as their prospects waxed and waned with each new development, but in terms of the overall value of business in the securities markets it was tiny in comparison to the regular turnover in government and railway stocks. Between 1853 and 1913 the paid-up capital of the mining companies quoted on the London Stock Exchange never rose above 0.7 percent of the total (Michie, 2000; R.H. Tilly, 1999; Burt, 1998: 728; Phimister, 2000: 23, 38).

Judging from the documented experience of the Crédit Mobilier in France and the regular difficulties that banks in all countries were exposed to through over-lending to businesses, especially large long-term loans to individual firms, it has also to be questioned whether banks, and those that managed them, were any better than the interested public in differentiating between those companies looking for finance. Successful investors, like successful banks, were those that confined their investments to businesses about which they had knowledge through experience and connections, while at the same time ensuring that their holdings were reasonably well spread. Evidence now abounds that investors did not blindly direct their savings into corporate securities but did so informed by a knowledge acquired through proximity to the enterprise, related business experience, direct connections through trade and employment, or social networks involving family, friends and associates. These networks could even be international in scope, linking investors in one country with companies in another; such was the scale of the human diaspora in the decades before 1914 and the ability to stay in touch. This even took an institutional form from the mid-nineteenth century onwards in Britain with the formation and multiplication of investment trusts and companies. By 1913 the investment, trust and finance companies quoted on the London Stock Exchange had a paid-up capital of £228.7m ($1.1bn) or 2.6 percent of the total (Paulet, 1999: 74, 125, 130, 133; Michie, 1987: 88–97; Burt, 1998: 711–28; Burt, 1997; C. Jones, 1997: 26, 31; Schmitz, 1997: 60; Boyce, 1992: 182–91). The bank-based investment networks identified in countries like Germany and Italy were not unique developments but were commonplace in advanced economies.

Conditioned by history, legislation, and different economic structures, national financial systems developed differently before 1914. At the core of these financial systems were banks and it was the way they developed that was instrumental in determining the role played by securities markets. Nevertheless whatever the pattern of banking that did develop – unitary/branch or deposit/universal – securities markets were of increasing importance before 1914. It was only they that provided a means of mobilizing the savings required to fund the vast capital requirements of the world's railway systems. In addition, securities markets provided an essential mechanism whereby banks could both employ short-term funds in long-term investments and avoid locking up their available capital in a small number of long-term loans. This facility provided by securities market was increasingly appreciated by banks all over the world, encouraging the appearance of different types of stock exchanges, whether catering for industrial securities in provincial centres or highly marketable issues in the money markets of the world. Even speculative mining shares, traded simultaneously in more than one financial centre, provided a convenient means of adjusting monetary balances between economies through reciprocating sales and purchases. The intrinsic value was irrelevant for all that mattered was that the transaction resulted in a movement of funds (Michie, 1988b; Michie, 1998a).

Thus, even in Germany the Universal banks began to resemble their British counterparts as they sought to attract deposits from the public and reduce their exposure to a small number of large loans to a few business clients. Recent research, for example, has found that the industrial securities held by banks in both countries amounted to a similar proportion of their assets. Conversely, research into the actual lending made by British banks to industrial firms has revealed that they did make extensive long-term loans. Though 59 percent of loans to industrial firms were for less than a year, and 79 percent for less than 2 years, no less than 13 percent were for over 3 years, in the 1875–1914 period (Fohlin, 1997c: 14, 18). Nevertheless, it was unlikely to lead German banks to exactly replicate British banks in the way they operated, though the differences were clearly becoming smaller, and were much less than has been portrayed in the literature. Banks, and the financial systems that they were part of, were very much the product of each country's development. As such there was no perfect model for a financial system to which all could be compared and judged accordingly. Instead each financial system was a compromise and before 1914 the one that appeared to offer the best combination for mobilizing savings and employing them productively, while limiting the consequences of financial crisis, was the one that incorporated an active securities market. Banks by themselves, even Universal banks, were no substitute for active securities markets. In their absence the state had to play a much larger role in economic life, both in supporting the system during financial crises and supplying the funds for long-term infrastructure investment. This was to be much more the case after 1914, for two World Wars and a world economic collapse did much to destroy the role that securities markets had played in the financial systems before World War I. What has been re-appearing, since the monetary difficulties experienced in the 1970s, has been a financial system in which securities markets have played an increasingly important role, while the role of the state has become much more that of a regulator rather than a substitute for banks and markets. The consequence of this is likely to be that the financial systems that evolve in different national economies, and the exact relationship that exists between banks and securities markets, will be dictated much more by basic economic forces and the increasingly integrated nature of the global economy rather than national considerations driven by the dictates of individual governments. What this means is that the successful financial institutions of the future will be those that respond to the needs of the markets they serve instead of those that try to preserve some out-of-date model driven by the power of the past or the dictates of national governments.

Notes

1 For more on these points see the following: Michie, forthcoming b; Michie, forthcoming a; Collins, 1998: 7.

2 The *Banking Almanac* for 1913. Cf. Merrett, 1995: 70–2, 75, 80–2; Di Quirico, 1999: 9, 11; Tullio and Wolters, 1996: 426, 430, 440, 442.

3 For the importance of the state in influencing the pattern of financial provision see Sylla, R.H. Tilly and Tortella (eds), 1999.

4 For the data see Capie and Webber, 1985: 576–7; United States, Department of Commerce, 1976: 1037; Urquhart and Buckley (eds), 1965: 246.

5 Cf. Deeg in this volume. For a parallel in the Austro-Hungarian Empire see the chapters by Eigner, Hájek, Natmeßnig, Pogány, Štiblar, Szász and Verdonk in Teichova, Gourvish and Pogány (eds), 1994. Cf. Collins, 1998: 16–17.

6 For a discussion of this see Michie, 1998b.

7 For a recent empirical view in support of Universal banks see Marmefelt, 1998: 1–6, 12, 17.

8 See in particular, Edwards and Fischer, 1994; Vasta and Baccini, 1997: 152–5.

9 Gueslin, 1992: 68, 73, 87; Asajima, 1990: 81 (Japan); Hashimoto, 1990: 100 (Japan); Ziegler, 1990b: 193 (Germany); Bussière, 1997: 120 (France); Ziegler, 1997: 136 (Germany); Teichova, 1997: 219 (Austria-Hungary); Lundström, 1994: 6 (Sweden); Edwards and Ogilvie, 1996: 429; Capie, 1995: 50, 53; Collins, 1998: 13–15; Capie and Collins, 1996: 27–39; Boyce, 1992: 200–1; Lazonick and O'Sullivan, 1997: 119–20, 127–9.

10 See Michie, 1999, Chapter 3. See also Born, 1983a: 172; League of Nations, 1931: 342, 353–4, 365, 404, 411, 424; Myers, 1936: 1, 52, 158; R.H. Tilly, 1999: 140–1; Michie, 1988a; Merrett, 1995: 83; S. Jones, 1994: 67, 75.

3 Competing in tandem

Securities markets and commercial banking patterns in Europe during the nineteenth century

Joost Jonker

Introduction

The concept of universal banking used to be a contentious one. Some economists, banking theorists, and financial historians, hotly defended it as far more efficient and conducive to economic growth than simple commercial banking. Others have condemned it with equal vigor, as an anathema, as being fundamentally unsound, and crisis prone because of its inherent instability. The historical issues concerned have attracted wide attention in academic circles and far beyond, but the question about the merits or otherwise of universal banking remains largely unresolved.[1] Yet present-day banking practice appears to have made up its mind in favor of universal banking. Banks aim to provide as large a range of financial services as they possibly can, and seek to serve their clients from the cradle to the grave, and with the current craze for financial planning, even beyond. The rationale behind this appears to be a familiar one: building large business units to achieve economies of scale and scope by internalizing markets. Most of the big European banks are universal banks now, or at least aim to be, as the international scramble to buy London brokers and merchant banks has demonstrated. In the US, plans are afoot to scrap both the Glass–Steagall Act and the restrictions on interstate branching, thus freeing commercial banks from the regulatory fetters preventing them moving into investment banking and across the continent. Only the English high-street banks still cling to the creed of a simple core business without the expensive trappings of universal banks, and the continuing profitability of, for instance, Lloyds TSB appears to prove them right, at least with regard to their own particular market – or perhaps one should say peculiar market.

The fact that universal banking has become more or less an orthodox norm rather than the anathematic deviation does not make its historical origins any less interesting, quite the contrary. How come some countries adopted this modern form of banking over a century ago, in the process of catching up with economies which had, and sometimes still have, a different and now old-fashioned looking type of banking? Was it really a matter of sophistication rising in response to the capital accumulation demands caused by the rise of corporate business, as the Gerschenkron thesis asserts? Somehow this asset-side approach fails to satisfy completely. After all, as both old and modern markets demonstrate, there is so much more to finance than banking alone. In his recent papers, Verdier has opened up the debate by analyzing the liabilities of universal banking, arguing that differences in state formation affected the degree of capital mobility across Europe, and this in turn determined the flow of deposits to various institutions. According to him, centralized capital markets such as England gave rise to specialized branch banking, whereas fragmented markets in semi-centralized countries such as Germany engendered universal banks, large unit banks with a restricted geographical spread and a correspondingly narrow deposit base. This made the universal banks vulnerable in cyclical downturns, a weakness compounded by the relatively late development of central banking in those countries (Verdier, this volume).

To me, the approach linking the evolution of banking to the development of political structures is a very inspiring one. And yet by concentrating on banking alone, it falls short of being revolutionary, and thus fails to provide a new paradigm to replace Gerschenkron's. Efforts to analyze banking systems in isolation from the markets surrounding them are not so much Hamlet without the Prince, than Romeo without Juliet. This may be remedied by putting banking development back into its context with the help of modern financial systems analysis. Rather than focusing in turn on individual components of a country's financial system, say commercial banks, investment banks, merchant banks, stock exchanges, or insurance companies, the new functional framework takes the system as a whole and analyzes it through the operations of six basic functions.[2] In this chapter I want to apply financial systems analysis to look at how the evolution of financial markets had prepared the stage for the emergence of different banking patterns in the Netherlands, Britain, France, and Germany by the middle of the nineteenth century.

Restoring coherence: a functional approach to financial systems

In the introduction to their recent book on the subject, the economists Robert Merton and Zvi Bodie set out the aims of functional analysis of financial systems. They regard the evolution of financial systems as innovation spiral, driven by markets and institutions both complementing each other and competing with each other, for greater economic efficiency in resource allocation. From this primary function, Merton and Bodie (1995: 4–5) derive six core functions:

1   To provide ways of clearing and settling payments, thus facilitating trade;
2   To provide a mechanism for pooling resources, and for subdividing shares in various enterprises;
3   To provide ways of transferring economic resources through time, across borders, and among economic sectors;
4   To provide ways of managing risks;
5   To provide price information, helping to coordinate decision-making in various sectors of the economy;
6   To provide ways of dealing with incentive problems created by the existence of asymmetric information.

Thus, the functional approach takes the economic functions performed by financial intermediaries for granted, and attempts to discover the best overall institutional structure for performing them. Private and government institutions, both operating and regulatory institutions, do matter, but by concentrating on functions rather than the institutions, the functional approach offers a framework to explain institutional change in response to the assumed competitive innovation.

In a recent article using the functional analysis framework for a wide-ranging survey of the links between financial development and economic growth, Ross Levine emphasizes the need to widen the research focus from studying particular financial instruments or institutions to the interrelationship between instruments, markets, institutions, and the provision of financial services.[3] Levine singles out the lowering of liquidity risk as the core function of financial systems. When savers can convert surplus cash into assets, and back again if and when desired, at their convenience and low cost, they will be prepared to hold long-term instruments. Consequently, financial systems offering low liquidity risk will attract more savings, and facilitate more long-term investment, whilst generating better information flows, which should improve resource allocation (Levine, 1997: 692, 695). Theoretically, lowering liquidity risk may be done either by banks or by stock markets. However, liquid markets tend to have the edge over banks: '... if equity markets exist, all agents will use equities, none will use banks ..., banks will only emerge to provide liquidity if there are sufficiently large impediments to trading in securities markets'.[4]

This does not mean that securities markets are inherently *superior* to banks, i.e. more efficient in allocating resources. Ever since the late James Tobin reiterated Keynes's grave doubts about the economic performance of stock markets and more specifically the mixed blessings of liquidity, the debate about the relative merits of either system has become increasingly abstract and mathematical, and I harbor no ambitions or indeed ability to enter it (Tobin, 1984; Levine and Zervos, 1998; Jacklin, 1987; Gorton and Pennacchi, 1990; Dow and Gorton, 1997). I would rather provide a historical perspective to the debate by applying the insights from financial systems analysis and more specifically Levine's arguments about the precedence of securities markets over banks to explore the evolution of European banking patterns during the nineteenth century. Put simply, specialized banking appeared in countries which were early in developing fully-fledged financial markets, thus starting the spiral of innovation through competition, which led to lower transaction costs, increasing volume, and further specialization. Such countries had to meet at least three crucial preconditions:

1   A successful financial revolution, i.e. a switch from enforced loans or contracting government debt out to private business in the form of personal obligations, to a system of publicly accountable debt management with transferable securities;
2   An open, flexible, and generally accepted system of commercial law, including safeguards concerning private property;
3   A firm currency, largely free from official interference.

Together, these three conditions created a growing trust in financial instruments and markets, despite recurrent setbacks in the form of crises and bankruptcies. Evidently the fulfillment of the conditions depended strongly on the processes of state formation in the countries concerned, bringing the analysis close to the work of Charles Tilly and the approach advocated by Verdier (C. Tilly, 1990; Verdier, this volume).

Conversely, universal banking emerged in countries where a delayed state formation retarded the development of fully-fledged and competitive national financial markets. The notion of universal banking as a response to market imperfections is of course central to the Gerschenkronian concept. However, the functional analysis framework now enables us to pinpoint some of the inherent penalties, for internalizing non-existent or nascent markets pre-empted the competition needed to start the innovation spiral. Moreover, governments riding the tiger of late state formation often compounded the problem of restricted competition by imposing yet more obstacles, some of them designed to give the state a hold on the financial system, others deliberate curbs on perceived free market excesses, as often as not introduced as remedies in the wake of crises. I will turn to the early developers first by a brief examination of the emerging financial markets of England and the Netherlands.

The dawn of a modern capital market: Amsterdam

For reasons that I cannot treat in any detail here, the Dutch Republic happened to be the pioneer of modern financial markets. The Revolt against Spain completed the financial revolution that the Habsburg regime of the Emperor Charles V had started. It firmly established a system of public finance tied to representative government, a key issue that had helped to spark the revolt against the centralizing policies of Philip II. The Seven United Provinces were financially independent from each other, with Provincial Estates drawn by co-optation from city councils and the rural gentry voting on budgets and debts. In their turn, the Provincial Estates sent delegates to the Estates-General in The Hague, really the Republic's representative sovereign body whose responsibilities included the Union's funding. This system of devolved representative government provided the basis for the broad acceptance of a funded and consolidated public debt. From short-term expediencies, loans became long-term securities. This led both to much lower interest rates, and to the emergence of a public willing to invest in government bonds, rather than having to accept imposed loans, widely used before.[5] The rapidly rising cost of the Eighty Years' War against Spain ensured a steady flow of bonds to buy. Since the social group of the Republic's political representatives largely overlapped with the group of investors in government bonds, loan terms were strictly kept. By the early eighteenth century, the bonds had become so well established that the payments office of the Estates-General could afford an informal moratorium on its debts without much harm to its credit rating (Fritschy and van der Voort, 1997: 70). The yields on loans issued by the various provinces had meanwhile converged to the point of being nearly identical, indicating that the

68   *Joost Jonker*

Republic's capital market possessed a considerable degree of integration (Fritschy and Liesker, 1996: 176–7).

This financial revolution paved the way for another innovation, publicly quoted joint-stock companies issuing transferable shares and bonds, of which the best known are the Dutch East India Company or VOC (1602) and the West India Company or WIC (1621). Amsterdam now quickly developed into the main financial centre of Western Europe, building up an amazing financial flexibility and capacity, which enabled the Dutch Republic to punch far above its weight for over a century. The secret behind this financial muscle lay in the forging of a close link between the money market, i.e. the place for exchanging bullion and claims to money in the form of short-term debt, and the securities market. As explained above, the importance of such a link lies in the lowering of the liquidity risk through the creation of a seamless range of facilities from short-term lending to long-term investment. Savings could always be employed profitably at the Amsterdam exchange, resulting in a large pool of available funds and consequently low interest rates, the wonder and envy of foreign observers (Dehing and 't Hart, 1997: 46–8; Dickson, 1967: 4–5; Jonker and Sluyterman, 2000: 94–7). Moreover, this link lowered the threshold for the buying of long-term securities, for investors knew they could always get cash.

Amsterdam merchants created such a seamless range by pioneering a technique known as *prolongatie*, the lombarding of securities for a month, tacitly rolled over until one of the parties cancelled the transaction. This became such a common investment for short-term liquidities that deposit banking never really developed in the Netherlands until the First World War (Jonker, 1996: 91–2). By attracting a steady flow of disposable funds, the *prolongatie* technique gave both the commodity trade and the financial market extra stretch for development, optimizing as it did the circulation of available capital. Fuelled by the easy supply of flexible credit, securities trading showed a precocious development. By at least 1608, futures trading in securities had become common enough for the first documented bear syndicate to appear.[6] Options were soon part of the repertory, for it was this technique that fuelled the extraordinary tulip speculations in 1636–1637.[7] Repo trading, i.e. buying securities with a loan secured on them, is documented from the 1640s onwards, but it probably existed as early as the 1620s (M.F.J. Smith, 1919: 61). By 1680 the market had spawned an amazingly full and modern-looking array of tricks and techniques, described in detail by the Amsterdam trader Joseph Penso de la Vega in his justly famous book *Confusion de confusiones*, published in 1688.[8] Securitized commodity loans arrived in 1695, unit trust funds in the 1770s.[9] At the end of the eighteenth century, Amsterdam possessed specialized intermediaries performing all six functions, though the provision of ways to deal with incentive problems may have been relatively poor, due to an obsession with secrecy (Riley, 1980: 67; Jonker, 1996: 131–7). By then, the techniques used at the exchange had probably spread throughout the country. Manufacturers in the eastern Twente region, about 200 kilometers from Amsterdam, bought securities with the spare cash from their firms, so they must have had access to lombarding facilities, too (Sneller, 1934: 33–118).

The authorities let it all happen without much interference. Futures trading, for instance, was officially sanctioned as early as 1610. Following pressure from the mighty VOC after the 1608 bear syndicate, the Estates-General issued an edict that introduced some regulations on futures trading, while fully accepting the principle (van Dillen, 1930: 19, 68–9). Subsequent bans equally attempted no more than to protect the VOC and WIC against bear raids (M.F.J. Smith, 1919: 57–61). Time and again, pamphleteers denounced futures trading as *windhandel* or bubble trade, but the authorities refrained from taking action. Perhaps they realized that they had no way to enforce their bans, least of all in the most powerful city of the country where commercial interests reigned uppermost. After all, the attempts to protect the two trading companies had to be repeated regularly. On the other hand, the official inaction may well have been motivated by notions of *laissez-faire* being best, or the best that could be achieved at any rate.

However, it would appear to me that this non-interference with market freedom was a natural consequence of the financial revolution. The overlap between political representatives and investors secured the market's free functioning, since interference would directly harm public confidence in the bonds. Moreover, the authorities were far from powerless and did show considerable imagination in devising practical and workable solutions when it came to taking positive action. During the late sixteenth and early seventeenth centuries city councils, notably the Amsterdam one, sponsored a string of institutional innovations including an official price current, the building of exchange premises, the setting up of the famous Wisselbank to provide a stable money of account, and the introduction of regulations concerning bills and maritime insurance. Had they wished to, the Amsterdam city fathers could well have voted to establish a body to monitor the financial markets, since they did so in the case of insurance, and somewhat later also for several branches of the commodity trade, and for whaling (Jonker and Sluyterman, 2000: 78–9). The Estates-General demonstrated a similar tenacious concern for improving economic conditions, overcoming substantial provincial opposition to pass legislation designed to protect the external value of the guilder (Dehing and 't Hart, 1997: 40–1; Jonker and Sluyterman, 2000: 95–6). The Republic's financial system, then, gyrated around the twin poles of the Amsterdam Wisselbank and the city's securities market. The former served to clear payments, its extensive facilities reaching out to customers all over Europe. The latter both supplied the innovative drive that helped the merchant bankers to build a range of sophisticated financial services, and helped to nurse a keen investment public.

Throughout the nineteenth century, the Dutch financial system retained its very high degree of specialization, its openness and competitiveness, and its strong market orientation. The market possessed an extraordinary capacity and flexibility. Government debt ballooned to an estimated 420 percent of net national income, market prices (NNImp), during the first half of the century, and yet all kinds of loans still found eager investors. Russia alone floated more than 300 million guilders on the Amsterdam stock exchange through the famous merchant-banking firm of Hope & Co., which possessed a famous network of underwriters fanning out from Amsterdam.[10] By the early nineteenth century, other bankers and brokers must have had regular customers and correspondents in the provinces as well (Jonker, 1999: 53–4). These networks proved sufficiently resilient to absorb very large issues, including those of the railways and distribute them to investors all over the country, so there was no need for big institutions to mobilize funds. By 1850 the stock exchange list gave price quotes for 112 securities, 92 foreign loans against 20 Dutch ones.[11] In addition to formal flotations at the stock exchange, there existed a strong informal capital market of underhand issues for smaller businesses and those companies wanting to save money by cutting out brokers. For example, in 1867 the shareholders in a Rotterdam gas company severely criticized the board for wasting 60,000 guilders on brokers' fees in placing a 1.2 million-guilder bond issue. They argued that it could have been done without brokers, as four years earlier a share issue worth 3 million guilders had been sold directly to investors (Jonker, 1996: 159). The securities trade remained fully open to new entrants, keeping competition keen. Consequently, there are no signs at all of any shortages in the funding of industry or other economic sectors (Jonker, 1996: 115–29, 147, 158–9, 274–8).

With the spread of more rapid communications, the Amsterdam repo system turned nationwide, with provincial stockbrokers and cashiers intermediating for clients all over the country. The consequent powerful draw on deposits meant that commercial joint-stock banking entered the fray fairly late, around 1860. Despite vigorous efforts to attract deposits, the joint-stock banks could not compete with the established system, remaining anemic and highly liquidity-oriented. Their business pattern closely resembled that of the merchant bankers. Revenue from commission, bills, and securities trading generated far more income than interest, and the banks' gearing remained very low compared with other European banks (Jonker, 1997: 111, 114–18). Moreover, the joint-stock banks probably could not compete with established national networks, for the banks began to establish branches only during the early twentieth century (Barendregt, 1999: 139–43).

The government continued to refrain from interfering, apart from setting up a circulation bank in 1814. Having taken the initiative, it left the Nederlandsche Bank to its own devices, however. The bank began to assume something like a national role only around 1850, when the board appointed its first agents outside Amsterdam. In 1863, the bank finally established a national network of branches and correspondents. Together with the national coverage obtained by the *prolongatie* system, this policy move effectively pre-empted the rise of provincial banking in the Netherlands. For the early twentieth century, there are some indications that a pronounced centralization of the financial system on Amsterdam may have restricted access to financial services in the outer provinces, a phenomenon that also manifested itself in Britain (Jonker, 1991: 127–8). Clear signs of capital shortages are absent, however, apart from largely unspecified complaints. Manufacturing industry appears to have had no problems at all in finding finance, through formal channels or on the private market (Jonker, 1995: 201–4).

After founding the Nederlandsche Bank, the government intervened twice in the system to thwart initiatives for joint-stock commercial banks, in 1837 and in

1856. However, this intervention mattered less than one would think. It could be, and was in 1858, circumvented by opting for a private limited company rather than a public limited company. The dismal fate of the Dutch *crédit mobilier* initiatives after 1863 demonstrates, moreover, that the 1837 and 1856 proposals would not have been viable anyway, whatever the official opinion. The nineteenth century passed without any legislation at all concerning commercial banking, the securities trade, the stock exchange, or limited liability companies, the only exception being the 1863 Bank Act which laid down the terms of a new charter for the Nederlandsche Bank, entrusting the bank with a monopoly on note issue and on managing the currency. With the victory of political liberalism from the 1850s, attitudes towards publicity underwent a marked change as well, resulting in far more openness about details of government finance and company performance.

Transforming Britain by Dutch finance

Now of course one may object that the Netherlands is exceptional anyway, as a small country without deep geographical, social, economic, or cultural divides, with a strong mercantile tradition and a large inherited wealth, so the peculiar evolution of its financial system has little bearing on patterns of banking development in the rest of Europe. I want to counter that objection by pointing out some of the close similarities between Dutch developments and the evolution of the English financial system.

Since Dickson's seminal work, it has been widely recognized that the key to the British political and economic success during the eighteenth century lay in its financial revolution during the last two decades of the seventeenth century, following the Glorious Revolution which brought a Dutchman to the English throne.[12] Until then, government borrowing had been haphazard, a mixture of personal borrowing by the King against very high interest rates, and formal confiscations of goldsmiths' money deposited with the Mint or with the Exchequer (Dickson, 1967: 39–46; Homer and Sylla, 1996). Under such circumstances, securities trading must have remained rudimentary, for the titles were suspect indeed. Until the 1650s, the East India Company's shares do not appear to have been traded much either, because the company's status as a continuing business enterprise remained unclear. With the reorganizations of the 1650s this became much clearer, however, and this clearly helped share trading. By the 1690s futures and options trading had also appeared in London (Neal, 1990: 195; Chaudhuri, 1978: 411–17). The establishment of parliamentary control over public finance finally paved the way for a consolidated and funded public debt. A few years later, the foundation of the Bank of England further underpinned the market by creating a strong institution for debt management coupled with such innovations as a central reserve of liquidity and banknotes to economize on gold transactions.

This financial revolution put the securities market at the heart of the English financial system, as it had done in the Republic before. It was the key defining event for both systems, though they went along markedly different paths from there. Both retained their strongly market-oriented character as established so early, which led to highly articulated, open, and competitive systems. This was partly a matter of direct intermediation. Securities markets such as those taking shape during the seventeenth and eighteenth centuries in Amsterdam and London offered a growing number of options concerning investment, liquidity, and risk management, to both private investors and to the money markets to which they were closely linked. Moreover, securities markets gradually became the hubs of national and international networks of services and information, which turned them into yardsticks for options nationally and internationally.

Until the late eighteenth century, the London securities market was, like Amsterdam, open and largely unregulated, with trading carried on in coffee houses and by a more respectable crowd in the Rotunda of the Bank of England. Apart from the restrictions on limited companies introduced after the 1720s boom, there appears to have been no legislation concerning the securities trade.[13] Admittedly, the London atmosphere was not quite as permissive as in Amsterdam. Futures trading in government bonds did take place, and presumably on a considerable scale, with an observer in 1761 for instance wondering how people could conduct such a large trade without owning anything of it (Michie, 1998a: 12). However, it was regarded as the equivalent of betting, and deals could not be enforced through the courts as normal commercial transactions. This resulted finally in stockbrokers forming the Stock Subscription Room, a private club with controlled membership, in 1801. There they could both enforce trade rules and insulate their market against bankruptcies from banking or the commodity trade spilling over. The Stock Subscription Room and its successor, the Stock Exchange, were not so much attempts at monopolizing the securities market, than efforts to professionalize it (Michie, 1999: 35–6).

The English system differed from the Dutch one in two other respects: the Bank of England, and the position of banks and bankers, particularly the city bankers. First, the operations of the Bank of England stretched far wider than those of the Wisselbank. The Amsterdam bank had a much more passive role. It had been designed to provide a stable currency, not for commercial banking operations. Merchants paid the bank commission for managing their accounts, which bore no interest. The statute forbade the giving of credit, deposits had to be kept in cash at all times, issuing bank notes does not appear to have been considered by the bank's governors at any time. Consequently, however much the Wisselbank contributed to Amsterdam's commercial and financial pre-eminence during the seventeenth and eighteenth centuries, it did so as an institution designed for consolidation, not for expansion, a facilitator, not a flywheel. By contrast, the Bank of England soon occupied a central position within the system as the main note-issuing institution, a keeper of reserve liquidity, in many ways the system's referee. Government support certainly helped in attaining this position, but the bank finally got there by overcoming fierce competition.

Second, banks and bankers functioned as hinges between the system's functions and between England's regions in a way that Dutch bankers never really could. This was, of course, partly a consequence of England's far greater geographical and economic diversity, which created a functional separation unknown in the

Republic, between country bankers and London bankers, between West End bankers and City bankers, between regional banking centers and London. However, it was also a consequence of deposits being more central to the English system than it was to the Dutch one. During the second half of the eighteenth century, London bankers developed a call-money market similar to the Amsterdam *prolongatie* system. Being principally bill-based rather than securities-based, this appears to have been a bankers' system more than a channel open to private savers, as the Dutch one was (Michie, 1992a: 69–70). The difference matters. In the Netherlands, provincial brokers would charge clients a commission for placing their money at call in Amsterdam for them. By contrast, English country bankers collected local deposits by paying interest on them, and they developed cheques to facilitate payments for their customers. The London market lent their business more scope, whereas the Amsterdam market appears to have cut the margins of provincial banking down to the level of a small commission. For all the comparative strength of English country banking, government action or inaction may have tilted the balance against them in some respect. Cameron chided the authorities for taking the wrong decisions or doing nothing at a number of key turning-points in English banking history, thus preventing the banks from boosting economic growth in the best possible way. The market created ways to surmount such obstacles as official policy chose to put in the way of banking development.[14]

The English system came of age during the second half of the eighteenth century, with a final training stage provided by the pioneering phase of securities arbitrage between Amsterdam and London. A number of Dutch Jewish brokers, including the father of David Ricardo and the founder of Raphael Zorn, crossed the North Sea and established themselves in London for this particular business (Michie, 1998a: 12). As the Revolutionary and Napoleonic Wars began to envelop the continent, London quickly eclipsed Amsterdam as the international financial centre. All the essential mechanisms were in place, and London could now command far greater muscle. In 1794, for instance, Austria issued a loan in London totaling 55 million guilders. A transaction of such magnitude would have been beyond the power of Amsterdam. During the 1780s, peak years for the foreign loan business, the market never took more than 20 million guilders a year. The biggest borrower, Russia, never issued more than 12 million guilders a year, and Hope & Co. took care to split such loans into four tranches to avoid saturating the market (Jonker, 1996: 154).

Consequently, by about 1800 the English system could and did provide the six functions defined by combining a vigorous and open market with specialized intermediaries branching out from London across the country. The basic layout of this system changed remarkably little during the nineteenth century, despite a vastly increasing volume and far-reaching institutional changes. The main achievement lay in the evolution of procedures and techniques to enable easy switches from short-term to long-term funds or claims and back, essentially merging the money market and the capital market into a single entity. By 1850 this process appears to have been well under way (Michie, 1992a: 98). Whether or not England came to possess such a vigorous private market as the Netherlands did, I frankly do not know, but the signs are that it did, at least until the early years of the twentieth century. As the Bank of England and the emerging joint-stock banks knitted the home market ever closer together on London, so the City's markets began to assume a world role. Sterling bills became standard in international trade finance, and the Stock Exchange turned itself from a dealer in British government debt into the main market for securities of more or less any kind from anywhere. By 1850 the number of quoted securities was reaching an astounding 500 (Michie, 1999: 95). Meanwhile the joint-stock banks slotted into position with banking services little different in quality from those provided by the eighteenth-century private bankers, facilitating payments, providing short-term credit, and channeling deposits through the network.

This position depended on liquidity. The excessive concern for liquidity on the part of English and Dutch commercial joint-stock banks has usually been associated with these countries' shared mercantile past and a supposedly innate banking conservatism. However, from the perspective of functional analysis it appears more plausible that it was a consequence of the early sophistication of their financial system. Savers, investors, and banks possessed a range of options to switch assets as and when required, and the open and competitive market put a premium on switching at the earliest sign of either trouble or better alternatives. The Republic had reached this phase by about 1700, and England did so somewhere during the second half of the eighteenth century. Both countries had then acquired financial markets with sufficient resilience to withstand strong shocks, such as the collapse of the Wisselbank in 1795, or the suspension of gold payments by the Bank of England in 1797. In both countries, the financial markets were essentially free markets, i.e. held in check by little more than interest rates, exchange rate fluctuations, peer pressure, and the law courts, with legislation usually extending to no further than an exclusive central bank charter, currency standards, safeguards concerning joint-stock banking, and limited liability companies. Financial instruments were left untouched, so the innovation spiral could progress untouched, providing a continuous drive for lower cost, more volume, increasing specialization, really the oxygen for the whole system.

Thus the Netherlands and Britain both ended up without universal banks in the nineteenth century, because the sophisticated financial system inherited from earlier times simply left no room for them. Key factors in the development of these systems were a funded and consolidated public debt under parliamentary control, an open market, and little government interference. The timing of these events appears to have been less important, as long as they had evolved before the mid-nineteenth century, and had been preceded by state formation. This is demonstrated by the case of France.

A revolution within a revolution: France

Amongst Napoleon's enduring legacies must be counted his successful execution of a financial revolution by reorganizing French public finance. Long-tried investors accepted his cutting the debt by two-thirds in return for more assured interest payments on the remainder. Government revenue rose steadily as the new regime managed better enforcement of tax collection, and it was further buoyed up by tributes exacted from countries conquered by the French during the Revolutionary and Napoleonic Wars (White, 1995: 251). During the early Restoration years, France still suffered from a poor credit rating, as evidenced by the low issuing rates of the 1817 reparation bonds (White, 1999: 14–15; Gontard, 2000: 143–7). With parliamentary control over public finance now firmly entrenched, however, the country's reputation soon recovered. By the early 1820s the bonds were nudging par, and Dutch observers used them as yardsticks for sentiment on the Amsterdam stock exchange (White, 1999: 12; Gontard, 2000: 175, 184; Jonker, 1996: 87).

Napoleon had also aimed to restructure the French financial system by turning the Banque de France, set up by private bankers in 1800, into a privileged note-issuing bank intended for national discount operations. In the aftermath of the Napoleonic reforms, French banking entered a phase of vigorous growth during the first decades of the nineteenth century (Bonin, 1993: 250–1). Nor had the securities trade escaped from the emperor's attention. The Paris *bourse* appears to have been rather dormant after the time of Law and the Mississippi Bubble. A Royal charter regulated trade and bestowed a trading monopoly on a fixed number of brokers, who numbered 60 towards the end of the *Ancien Régime* (Taylor, 1962: 953, 956; Vidal, 1910: 145). The foundation of the Caisse d'Escompte in 1776 marked the beginning of a trading boom, which was fuelled during the 1780s by a string of joint-stock company flotations and by a spiraling public debt (Taylor, 1962: 953, 956–7, 967–8). As stories about uncontrolled speculation began to spread, so grave public concern mounted about the perceived dangers of *agiotage* in general and of speculators cornering particular securities in particular, but repeated attempts to curb such operations failed, possibly because the debt-ridden government of Louis XVI could not afford to antagonize the securities trade for fear of endangering its precarious credit. This changed with the Revolution, however. When during 1793 the *assignat* experiment began to go wrong, the new authorities blamed the stock exchange as dangerous to the public interest, and closed its doors. Trading was allowed to resume in 1795, now under strict government control (Vidal, 1910: 10, 13, 16; Gontard, 2000: 77–9).

Napoleon's 1807 *Code du Commerce* confirmed these restrictions on securities trading. Stock broking continued as a formal monopoly bestowed on a fixed number of brokers appointed by the Government, 25 at the first instance. These brokers were made responsible for drafting the official list of quoted securities, for the trade in securities quoted, and for enforcing the legal conditions imposed on the trade. The regulations included a ban on the listing of foreign securities, an attempt to put a taboo on futures trading, and a clause aimed at rendering such deals impossible by making the completion of transactions conditional upon brokers handling both the payment and the securities concerned at the same time.

The restrictions on futures trading were to little avail, if only because the ban made transactions legally void, but unless either one of the contracting parties wanted to renege on a deal, or the authorities sought prosecution, this remained a dead letter. The official brokers themselves took little notice of the law, and futures and options trading appears to have developed rapidly. An 1816 pamphlet detailed a full range of speculative techniques available for investors at the exchange (Bizet de Frayne, 1818). In 1824 a group of bankers and traders presented a petition to the Ministry of Finance strongly protesting about a broker engaged in futures trading being convicted of gambling by a Paris court. The arguments presented are worth repeating here. The petition argued on the one hand, that such transactions did concern a true exchange of goods for money, not just a bet, so they should be accorded legal protection. On the other hand, the petitioners claimed that futures trading benefited both the government and general economic activity. Futures trading created the liquidity on which the government's credit rested; that same liquidity helped to mobilize otherwise idle funds, for investors knew they could always get cash on the collateral of securities, or else employ their money remuneratively by placing it at call (Vidal, 1910: 203, 207–9). Clearly by that date the Paris market had developed futures trading connected to a call-money system in much the same way as Amsterdam and London had before. The petitioners' arguments appear to have won the day, for no further action is recorded. When in 1833 a member of parliament tabled a proposition to take action on speculative securities trading, his suggestion was brushed aside (Vidal, 1910: 210). Even so, in 1842 bankers and traders thought it necessary to present another petition about futures trading to the Minister of Finance. Referring back to the 1824 arguments, they again stressed that these transactions were vital for the *bourse* (Vidal, 1910: 18–19, 46, 210–11).

One reason for official inaction was that enforcing the legal bounds of securities trading proved impossible. The monopoly conferred by the *Code du Commerce* on the *courtiers* immediately created a new group of clandestine brokers or *coulissiers*. Since the government-appointed brokers simply could not handle the volume of business, trading spread from the *parquet* or official trading floor to the *coulisses* (passages) around it, where anyone might trade in what came to be known as the *valeurs en banque*, or intra-bank trade. This trade was already an established feature while the *Code du Commerce* was being framed, with the official brokers protesting about it to the authorities and demanding prosecution of offenders in 1809. Gradually four distinct groups of traders emerged: the official brokers or *courtiers*; an association for cash traders; an association of futures traders; and an association of dealers in French public securities. The authorities tolerated this clandestine trade, recognizing that its own credit depended to a significant degree on business generated by the *coulissiers*. The protests from the official brokers went unheeded in 1809, and again in 1824, in 1835, and in 1842. When finally in 1859, 26 *coulissiers* were prosecuted for infringing the official monopoly on dealing in quoted securities, the price of French *Rentes* dipped sharply enough for the Government to seek an urgent settlement of the case (Vidal, 1910: 28, 217–20; Lehmann, 1997: 18–19). Meanwhile the ban on listing foreign securities had been lifted in 1823, and since then trade had widened considerably. By 1848 the official list counted about 100 securities, including stocks in insurance companies, canal companies, railways, and even a few industrial companies, in addition to French government securities and a range of foreign bonds. Such flotations were arranged by the Parisian *Haute Banque*, a group of very powerful private banking firms, with Baron James de Rothschild as its uncrowned king. These houses also dealt in inland and foreign bills (Cameron, 1967: 106; Bonin, 1993: 251; Plessis, 1996: 177–8).

So by the mid-nineteenth century the Paris stock exchange stood poised to achieve a position quite similar to the Amsterdam and London stock exchanges in their respective financial systems, despite France undergoing its financial revolution considerably later than the Dutch Republic or Britain, and despite the Government's attempts to impose restrictive legislation on stock jobbing in general and on futures trading in particular. At that point in time the *bourse* still remained very much a potential driver of competitive innovation, its actual force dimmed by the financial system suffering from a distinct lack of geographical integration. The Paris region was served well enough, but the links between the capital and the provinces were weak, as were the interregional connections. The Banque de France began to venture out of Paris during the late 1830s, having 29 regional branches in 1851 and almost 50 by 1860, i.e. by the latter date the bank had a representative in just over half the *départements* (Lévy-Leboyer, 1976a: 392). Its credit policies were rather restrictive, however, constrained as the bank was between keen competition at its home base, a jealous regard for its privileged position, the need to tailor operations to suit the government's fiscal transfers and debt-servicing requirements, and finally a tight reserve policy. With the Banque de France forced to suspend convertibility for two years following the 1848 upheavals, and veering towards inconvertibility again in 1856, one may forgive the board its conservatism in keeping a tight rein (Lévy-Leboyer, 1976b: 360–1; Lévy-Leboyer, 1976a: 392; Cameron, 1967: 104–5, 120–1, 123–5). Moreover, the more mundane side of banking business, effecting payments and collecting deposits, appears to have been rudimentary. Wide interest-rate differentials between Paris and the provinces suggest a distinct lack of geographical integration in the discount and call-money markets (Lévy-Leboyer, 1976b: 375).

This problem had been recognized as early as the 1820s, but schemes to remedy it foundered in the face of stiff opposition from the Banque de France. During the 1830s and 1840s, local initiatives to find a solution by setting up deposit and discount banks had considerable success, but they perished in the aftermath of the 1848 upheavals (Lévy-Leboyer, 1976b: 373–5). In 1852 the Pereire brothers, long-standing adversaries of the Banque de France, made a fresh attempt to change the financial system by launching the Crédit Mobilier. The Pereires' concept envisaged not simply a universal bank, but a universal bank and holding company rolled into one. The institution would attract funding by collecting deposits from the general public and by issuing a variety of bonds on the market. These funds were to be channeled to industry, with the explicit aim of nursing fledgling companies towards a stock exchange flotation, but the bank would continue holding a controlling interest, enabling it to steer economic development through close coordination of economic sectors. Cameron originally hailed the Crédit Mobilier as a key factor in regenerating French economic development through eliminating existing bottlenecks in the financial system, i.e. company finance and promotion (Cameron,

1961). This claim is no longer accepted. The Crédit Mobilier did indeed perform considerable operations; between 1852 and 1866 the bank placed a total of 14 billion francs worth of securities on the Paris market, or 14 percent of all new issues (Lévy-Leboyer, 1976c: 442). However, Lévy-Leboyer, Bonin, Plessis, and others, have demonstrated conclusively that the French system was far better developed prior to the foundation of the Crédit Mobilier than Cameron would allow.[15]

The Pereires' innovation did not lie in their bank's individual services, or in its size, but in the combination of operations envisaged. The banks active during the 1830s and 1840s had relied on mobilizing deposits, in one case experimenting with interest-bearing short-term bonds for this purpose. Their failure was mainly due to imprudent management in allowing a growing mismatch between short-term funding and medium- to long-term assets (Lévy-Leboyer, 1976b: 374–5). This problem also handicapped the Crédit Mobilier from the start, until it caused the bank's downfall in 1867 (Lévy-Leboyer, 1976c: 442–5). The Paris *Haute Banque* had specialized in the other type of operations targeted by the Crédit Mobilier, company finance and stock exchange flotations, for a long time. Indeed, in setting up their bank the Pereire brothers were clearly motivated by a desire to establish a power base to rival that exclusive club. However, the Crédit Mobilier could not really compete with the *Haute Banque* for size. The biggest of the private banks possessed assets estimated to have been worth five times the Crédit Mobilier's total means, and this was only partially caused by the restrictions imposed on the bank's funding ratios by the authorities (Lévy-Leboyer, 1976b: 383).

In the end, the Crédit Mobilier fell short of its founders' ambitions for a universal bank, and failed to attain the envisaged scope. The bank did not succeed in attracting deposits from the public, deriving most of its funding from tied deposits, i.e. cash flows generated by the companies it controlled. These flows were voluminous enough in themselves, so much so that the Crédit Mobilier could not exercise the option of attracting funds with bonds, because of the ratios set by the French government. The Pereires compounded this problem by focusing too closely on a few economic sectors. Instead of spreading risks by investing in a range of businesses, the bank concentrated on utilities, notably railroads, before becoming overexposed in property development during the early 1860s. Without the hostility aroused by the Pereires within the traditional banking community through their unorthodox operations, the Crédit Mobilier might have survived for longer than it did, but the blame for the bank's downfall lies squarely with the brothers themselves, disregarding the basic rule of sound banking of always taking care to match liabilities and assets (Lévy-Leboyer, 1976c: 442–5).

Might the Pereires' universal banking experiment have succeeded given a more prudent management and less official obstruction? Quite possibly. The development of the Société Générale pour Favoriser le Développement du Commerce et de l'Industrie en France demonstrates that it could be done, at least up to a point. Founded in 1864 by the *Haute Banque* to rival the Crédit Mobilier, the Société Générale successfully combined industrial finance with company promotion and general banking activities. The bank was much more careful in spreading its commitments, however, and after the financial upheavals of the 1870s and 1880s general commercial operations gained priority over investment banking. With this policy shift the Société Générale edged closer to the general evolutionary trend of French banking. The 1850s and 1860s saw a spate of new banks being set up in response to the remaining deficiencies in the French financial system, notably the lack of national integration with regards to discounting, deposit facilities, and payments. Bonin and others have termed this phase the second banking revolution, the first one having been the wave of deposit and discount banks of the 1830s and 1840s (Bonin, 1993: 252–4). The new crop of banks proved to be more enduring than the preceding one, for in addition to the Société Générale, several other banks dating from that era, such as the Crédit Industriel et Commercial (CIC, 1859), the Crédit Lyonnais (1863), and the Banque de Paris et des Pays Bas (Paribas, 1872), are still in existence today. Instead of embarking on universal banking, the new banks opted to specialize in either general commercial banking, as the CIC and the Crédit Lyonnais did, or in investment banking, the chosen field of Paribas for instance. Clearly by the third quarter of the nineteenth century the Paris *bourse* had obtained a key position within the French system similar to the Amsterdam and London stock exchanges in their respective countries, i.e. the commanding link between the money market and the securities market. By forcing French banks to keep a close watch on their liquidity, this factor prevented the emergence of universal banking with its attendant need for stable deposits, and led to a modal split between general commercial banks on one hand, and investment banks or *banques d'affaires* on the other.

So despite France having a late financial revolution, and despite the official attempts to control the securities trade and more specifically futures trading, the financial system had become sufficiently sophisticated by the third quarter of the nineteenth century to obviate the need for universal banks. With Napoleon having cleared the ground, the four decades following the Restoration sufficed for creating the necessary conditions. The decisive factor would appear to have been the government's understanding of the link between a vibrant stock exchange and a healthy public debt. Successive governments must have tolerated open breaches of the law concerning futures trading and the stock brokers' official monopoly because they knew themselves to be dependent on these clandestine practices, and proof was delivered in the 1859 prosecution debacle. The importance of official attitudes as a precondition becomes clear when we turn to the development of the German financial system.

Building a boat while sailing it: Germany

The German financial system that emerged from the Napoleonic Wars was not even rudimentary. No such thing existed, really, across the states and free cities loosely grouped together in the Deutsche Bund. This lack of financial development was not entirely a consequence of Germany's continuing political fragmentation, for in most commercial cities financial services had only limited scope as well. None of them appears to have offered anything near the range of six functions defined by Merton and Bodie. Of course mechanisms functioned to facilitate settlements between the commercial centers. Regional centers usually had an exchange for dealing in commodities and bills, but during the first decades of the nineteenth century, none of them had a money market of any importance. Price currents became more widespread only during the Napoleonic era. Securities trading occurred in only a handful of exchanges, notably Berlin, Frankfurt, Hamburg, and Leipzig (Gömmel, 1992: 14–35; Schäfer, 1993: 19). Business does not appear to have been very lively, trading being the preserve of private bankers, a few merchants, and some speculators, with army contractors, traditional specialists in government lending, looming large (Gömmel, 1992: 135–6). The scarce public banks in existence restricted themselves to operating on their own capital, and eschewed the issuing of notes.[16] There were a host of competing currencies, many of them functioning only as money of account because state governments could not afford to overhaul the circulation. Scarce means of payment dogged the development of trade (Kindleberger, 1984: 119–20). This situation was compounded into a structural liquidity problem by governments adopting a restrictive line in managing their currency, which remained a matter for state policy, not a commercial business (R.H. Tilly, 1967: 156–7). In 1824, the official discount rate in Berlin peaked at 10 percent, the private rate even 15 percent, levels unheard of in London or Amsterdam (Gömmel, 1992: 137). Subsequently, rates remained on average one percent or slightly more above those in London (Homer and Sylla, 1996: 208, 264). Private bankers played a key role by providing some solace in the form of acceptance credits, but such indications as we have suggest that as late as the 1840s, most firms were puny by international comparison (R.H. Tilly, 1967: 159, 161). Basic functions such as the pooling of resources, or effecting transfers through time and across borders, hardly existed, if at all.

Moreover, despite having embarked on the path towards a financial revolution, the main states failed to complete it. Spiraling debts during the Napoleonic era forced German princes to replace the old personal bonds with a funded official debt. Central governments assumed legal liability for these debts, engaging private bankers to place them on the market in standardized official bonds (R.H. Tilly, 1999: 135; Gömmel, 1992: 136–7). However, these debts did not become truly public. The German states continued to treat taxation, spending, and borrowing as prerogatives of the crown, drawing a veil of secrecy over transactions and refusing to grant their subjects political control over fiscal matters. During the Napoleonic era and the Restoration, Prussia, for example, conducted a thorough fiscal reform from above, but the repeated promises for parliamentary influence over public finance remained a dead letter. From 1815 to 1847 the government published only five rudimentary budgets, and the annual budgets appearing from 1848 still gave no more than a general idea of spending, creating an unfortunate pattern which Bismarck used to bully the Prussian parliament into condoning his budgetary policy from the early 1860s (R.H. Tilly, 1980a: 57–9, 61–3; R.H. Tilly, 1999: 135, 154). When facing strong criticism over the huge debts contracted after the Restoration, the government reacted in 1820 by setting a debt ceiling and promising parliamentary consultations if it wanted to borrow more or introduce new direct taxes.

It was again a paper promise, for the government had no intention to allow outside influence and preferred to adopt a policy of deep spending cuts and debt retirement. This helped to restore Prussia's credit rating, but at considerable cost. By sidestepping the legitimate demands for more political influence from its citizens, the Prussian government prevented the formation of that coalition between political representatives and investors which underpinned the emergence of free markets in the Netherlands, France, and Britain. As a consequence, officials developed a deep suspicion, and even outright hostility, towards the Berlin stock exchange as likely to undermine public confidence in the state. Moreover, by cutting its debt the government stunted the emergence of an investment public used and willing to hold securities. And it was this budding group that gave the stock exchanges in Paris, London, and Amsterdam their buoyancy and their capacity for absorbing an ever-increasing variety of securities, a notable bottleneck in Frankfurt and Berlin until well into the second half of the nineteenth century. The grand duchy of Baden and the kingdom of Bavaria went a little further in their financial revolutions, enshrining parliamentary control over taxation and the public debt in their newly adopted constitutions, but these states also stopped short of completing the course; budget policy remained a contentious issue between the respective governments and parliament (Ullmann, 1986: 434–7, 640–1).

During the first decades of the nineteenth century, the German financial system fairly rapidly acquired more modern traits. The Zollverein promoted a closer economic cooperation, including a currency reform dividing the Deutsche Bund into two zones. Some states set up note-issuing banks. Private bankers began to float a swelling number of bonds from state governments and cities, pioneering the conversion of short-term loans into long-term debt. Such investments attracted a growing public, notably so in Frankfurt, at that time the biggest stock exchange. Various forms of futures trading developed there, helped by the strong price fluctuations of key securities in circulation, such as Austrian government bonds and lottery loans, or Spanish and Greek government bonds, which had a dubious track record. By the end of the 1840s the stock exchange list counted just over 40 securities (Gömmel, 1992: 137–8; Schäfer, 1993: 20; Forstmann, 1996: 185). The Berlin exchange traded a wider variety, namely mortgage bonds issued by agricultural credit associations mainly for the benefit of Prussian landowners, government bonds from southern German states, and shares in various Prussian state enterprises, including the Preußische Seehandlung. Dutch, Austrian, and Russian government bonds followed. Prodded by what it regarded as speculative excesses endangering the interests of agriculture, trade, and industry, the Prussian government in 1832 issued warnings about the volume of futures trading. When this did not help to curb it, the government banned futures trading in Spanish bonds four years later, extending the ban to cover all foreign securities in 1840. The bans were effective in leading to the disappearance of the bonds in question, but speculators now moved into the newly introduced railway securities. At the peak of the railway boom in 1844 the Prussian government issued an edict on futures trading in railway warrants, resulting in steep price falls of railway securities. Berlin listings numbered around 60 by 1850, but subsequently the total rose sharply to more than 350 in 1870.[17]

Since traders could switch their business to other German exchanges, the ban on futures trading appears to have affected Berlin in particular (Gömmel, 1992: 138). Up to at least the 1860s, bankers appear to have dominated the securities trade there. Securities mainly moved between banks and bankers, public trading was really a secondary phenomenon, despite attracting so much official attention (R.H. Tilly, 1967: 164–5). This retail trade was officially the preserve of official sworn brokers, and in 1870 the Berlin exchange had 37 of them. With business booming during the *Gründerzeit*, the number of brokers trebled to 110 in 1873. However, that was still insufficient to cope with the sharply rising trade, which began to attract a growing crowd of unofficial brokers or *Pfuschmakler*. Such traders operated without the legal restraints imposed on the official brokers, the main ones being a security cover against bankruptcy, a ban on trading for own account, and a prohibition of forming partnerships. Tolerated by the authorities, the unofficial traders soon outnumbered the sworn brokers. By the early 1890s their number was estimated at between 500 and 800, against only 75 brokers (Löb, 1896: 246, 249).

As the unofficial brokers could trade for own account, they were able to engage in futures trading. Their increasing prominence at the Berlin stock exchange is closely related to the Prussian government's change of position on the subject. After a long lobbying campaign, officials from the bankers and brokers association succeeded in convincing the government that the bans had really failed to root out futures trading, the custom of a merchant's word being his bond having proved stronger than the law. Now it was time to remove the obstacles to futures trading so the Berlin stock exchange could begin to provide the economy with the functions and vigorous support that it needed. In 1860, the bans on futures trading introduced during the 1830s and 1840s were lifted.[18] By the late 1870s futures trading had once more become buoyant, with *Pfuschmakler* setting up partnerships and dedicated clearing institutions for the purpose. According to one estimate, the futures market generated 60 percent of all stock exchange transactions by the late 1880s (Gömmel, 1992: 164–5; Löb, 1896: 249, 262–4).

Even so the scope of this activity remained limited in one important respect. In 1885, for example, it concerned no more than 54 securities, predominantly foreign railway shares, out of 861 quoted. Five years later the number stood at 84 out of 1,184, with only a handful of German securities included (Löb, 1896: 246–7, 262–3; Meier, 1992: 163–4). Railway paper and in particular US railway securities were of course notoriously volatile, perfect vehicles for speculative trading. Yet German industrial shares and government bonds were also subject to price fluctuations, less extreme no doubt, but in a fully articulated market small price changes would have been enough to generate futures transactions. So if futures trading affected only a tiny fraction of the listings, and few or no German securities, this suggests that by 1890 it was still a side show in Berlin, not the integral part of operations as in Amsterdam, London, or Paris, where futures trading provided a vital hinge between the money and capital markets.

At that moment in time, the writing was already on the wall. The five big commercial banks in Germany did use the exchange for investing short money in bills and in repo transactions, such advances forming roughly 15 percent of assets in 1894 (Meier, 1992: 19). However, the bill market at the *Börse* was rapidly losing its significance, as banks, current accounts, and bank acceptances began to replace trade credit and bills of exchange (Meier, 1992: 19; Riesser, 1910: 216–17). More or less at the same time, the commercial banks also began to bypass the stock exchange in securities transactions, developing in-house facilities for matching buy-and-sell orders. Syndicates sold new issues directly to investors through the big banks' branches and affiliates, setting aside no more than a portion for selling on the *Börse*, primarily to get a public price (Meier, 1992: 19–20).

Renewed official action raised the cost of doing business at the stock exchange, buttressing these trends towards the banks' internalizing market functions. The 1870s and 1880s witnessed a more or less continuous public agitation against the stock exchange as no more than a gambling house, or a "Monte Carlo without music" in a famous contemporary phrase. Farming interests united in the powerful Bund der Landwirte (BDL) spearheaded this campaign.[19] It found a rich soil, prepared by the continuing official hostility against the securities trade, and fertilized by the government's need to pacify a key partner in the political compromise between interest groups on which the regime rested. The first result was the introduction of taxes on securities transactions in 1881, explicitly aiming to curb futures trading. Brokers had to pay stamp duty over their delivery bills to clients outside the stock exchange, 20 Pfennig for ordinary transactions and 1 Reichsmark for futures transactions. In addition, bankers owed a levy of 1.5 per thousand over the value of securities floated by them. Four years later the stamp tax was extended to a 0.1 per thousand levy on brokers' turnover, thus also raising the cost of deals between brokers within the stock exchange. These measures failed to quell the hostile sentiment against the securities trade. In 1890 and 1891 sharp price falls led to bankruptcies, notably amongst some private banking houses. A series of frauds was uncovered, one of them centering on futures transactions in Russian rouble securities and involving Deutsche Bank, and as a consequence the agitation for eradicating the irresponsible malpractices at the stock exchange flared up anew, with the BDL again stoking the fire.[20]

To appease this sentiment, the government raised the stock exchange taxes in 1894. The duty on turnover was doubled to 0.2 per thousand; the duty on new issues went up from 1.5 to 3 per thousand for home securities, and to 4.5 per thousand for foreign ones. Parliamentary proposals for punitive taxation on futures transactions failed to carry a majority, with the Reichstag opting instead to adopt a motion pleading for proper legislation on the securities trade.[21] The government responded by launching an official enquiry, briefing the commission explicitly to study the dangers of futures trading (Meier, 1992: 89–95; Gömmel, 1992: 170–1). The commission's report led to the passing of a new *Börsengesetz* or Exchange Act in 1896, which imposed far-reaching restrictions on futures trading (Gömmel, 1992: 176–7).

Of course the ever-inventive stock-broking fraternity found ways to evade the new measures. Still, the combined effect of taxation and legislation was momentous, for the balance between the stock exchange and the commercial banks now shifted decisively in favor of the latter. Dealing on the stock exchange became both more expensive, and more cumbersome than in-house transactions, however hard brokers and bankers tried to finds ways around the new regulations. Such constructs had to involve cash payments and thus inevitably tied down liquidity, forcing some provincial firms to forge an alliance with one of the big commercial banks, the prelude to further concentration in the sector (Schulz, 1994: 531–2; Löb, 1896: 267; Riesser, 1910: 464–9). To avoid costs and complications, banks opted for moving futures operations entirely to London, Paris, or Brussels, and as a consequence trading in some foreign securities disappeared completely from Germany to foreign exchanges. Deutsche Bank conducted its European arbitrage operations from the London subsidiary, which had a direct telephone line to the Paris branch, but only a telegraph connection to Berlin (Michie, 1999: 131, 134; Riesser, 1910: 466). Repeated protests from the financial community led to some easing of the restrictions in 1908, but meanwhile the damage had been done. The German stock exchanges, firmly chained to banking interests now keen to protect the internalized markets, remained rather listless considering the huge economy surrounding them, and would remain so until the 1980s (Gömmel, 1992: 176–8; Michie, 1992a: 74). What could have been the system's lungs became the appendix, not quite useless but without a clearly defined function for the body economic, bereft of that vital driving force which characterized the exchanges in London, Paris, or Amsterdam.

Conclusion

The functional approach to financial systems enables us to see the performance and development of a particular financial system in the past as an entity, rather than as a vaguely connected group of economic actors. European banking patterns during the nineteenth century must be understood in tandem with the financial markets of the countries concerned, and not in isolation. The sophistication of those markets depended on countries having had a successful financial revolution, establishing both widespread confidence in the public debt, and the principle of free markets. France, Britain, and the Netherlands went through a financial revolution sufficiently early for their respective markets to unfold in all freedom, with sophisticated stock exchanges serving as hubs of the system. Joint-stock commercial banking developed in competition with the various intermediaries established in these markets, inaugurating an innovative spiral, which resulted in functional specialization along the lines, defined by Merton and Bodie. This competition prevented the commercial banks from becoming universal banks, frustrating the boundless ambitions of the Crédit Mobilier in both France and the Netherlands. As a result, the banks came to concentrate on facilitating payments, providing short-term credit and, in the case of France and Britain, collecting deposits as well, leaving the other functions to specialist intermediaries.

The German case stands in vivid contrast to these examples, primarily because of late state formation. Continuing political fragmentation prevented the emergence of a countrywide financial system until the 1870s. At the same time, the failure to achieve a complete revolution in public finance resulted in a securities market handicapped by a retarded development, shallow roots amongst the public and across the country, and by a widespread hostility towards essential functions. Consequently, joint-stock banking encountered far less competition in assuming money market and securities market operations than similar banks did in France, Britain, or the Netherlands. However, the balance between the banks and the stock exchange finally became upset with the successive rounds of taxation and the 1896 *Börsengesetz*, which provided strong incentives for the banks to internalize functions. This stifled competition, and with it innovation, stalling the virtuous circle of lower transaction costs, more volume, and more options and products for both savers and investors. So the German banks became universal not for reasons of volume and economies of scale, as is the case today, nor because of market imperfections, as argued by Gerschenkron and others, but because of deliberate restrictions on competitive markets introduced by a government wary of free markets for political reasons.

Thus banking patterns in Europe during the nineteenth century need to be understood by analyzing the entire financial system, not just the banks, as is usually the case. The functional approach advocated by Merton and Bodie provides a very useful framework for doing so, since it helps us to understand how the different components worked in relation to each other, as opposed to the splendid isolation in which the emerging banks are generally portrayed.

Notes

1   A survey of the standpoints can be found in Verdier, this volume; see the inconclusive results of a detailed comparison in Edwards and Fischer, 1994.
2   Cf. Merton and Bodie, 1995. Rybczynski's more conventional set of five functions evolving in three phases over time is less persuasive, if only because of its determinism: Rybczynski, 1997.
3   Levine, 1997: 689. See also Levine and Zervos, 1998.
4   Levine, 1997: 693, referring to Jacklin, 1987, and Gorton and Pennacchi, 1990.
5   The basic work is Tracy, 1985; cf., for the sequel after the Revolt, Hart, 1993: 161.
6   Van Dillen, 1930. Van Dillen shows a preprinted standard form of a futures contract from 1629 between pages 12 and 13.
7   A recent account is in Dash, 1999.
8   Penso de la Vega, 1957 [1688]. On Penso de la Vega see Israel, 1990a; Israel, 1990b.
9   On securitized commodity loans pioneered by the firm of Deutz, see Elias, 1963 [1903–5]: 637, 1047–8; the history of Dutch unit trust funds in Berghuis, 1967: 46–8.
10 Cf. Buist, 1974: 498–501 for a list.
11 In 1810 the price current even quoted a total of 172 securities: Jonker, 1996: 162.
12 Dickson, 1967: 3–14; cf. Weir 1989 for an illuminating comparison between English and French public debt development during the eighteenth century.
13 This point needs further research and elucidation. The Dutch market suffered no comparable boom and bust during the 1720s, though there was a flurry of attempts to found large limited companies: cf. Groeneveld, 1940; de Slechte, 1982.
14 Cameron, 1967: 58–9. Rather than looking at the securities market as a solution, Cameron opts for seeing loopholes in the law and administrative incompetence as the way in which the obstacles were surmounted.
15 Cf. Lévy-Leboyer, 1976b: 371–7; Bonin, 1993: 251–2; Kindleberger, 1984: 108–15 for a survey of the standpoints.
16 Kindleberger, 1984: 118; specifically about Hamburg, Sieveking, 1934: 125–60.

86   *Joost Jonker*

17   Gömmel, 1992: 138–41; Forstmann, 1996: 185; Löb, 1896: 237–8; Meier, 1992: 47. A detailed treatment of mortgage bonds is in Borchardt, 1971.
18   Gömmel, 1992: 163; Meier, 1992: 48; Gebhard, 1928: 59–61. In 1858 the stock exchange began fixing term prices, i.e. the prices for specific futures transactions: Löb, 1896: 263.
19   Meier, 1992: 34 (quote), 53–6.
20   Meier, 1992: 53–4; as a consequence of the fraud, Deutsche Bank wrote off 1 million marks: Riesser, 1910: 359.
21   Meier, 1992: 237–40. In 1900, the tax rates were raised again: Riesser, 1910: 464–5.

4 On the development of universal banking in Germany

Richard Deeg

Introduction

In this chapter I re-examine the Gerschenkron (1962) late industrialization thesis in light of the German case. I take the position that Gerschenkron's explanation for the emergence of universal banking in Germany is insufficiently supported by the available evidence. A more compelling, or at least comprehensive, explanation for the particular historical form and development of German banking centers on political conflicts between the political center and periphery and their allied social and economic groups. More pointedly, to understand the emergence of universal banking as the dominant model for banking in Germany, one must go beyond Gerschenkron's narrow focus on the handful of Big Berlin banks and incorporate the savings and cooperative banks. Indeed, the central institutional feature of the German banking system is universal banking based upon a tripartite division in which private commercial banks compete against public savings banks and mutual cooperative banks. As will be argued below, the competitive dynamic among these three groups played a crucial role in making universal banking the dominant bank strategy in Germany. In other words, it is only by understanding the different characteristics of these three banking groups and their co-evolution that one can understand the particular development of the German banking system.

While several eminent German banking historians have written histories that incorporate all of these groups (for example, the work of Manfred Pohl, Hans Pohl, Karl Erich Born, and Richard Tilly), there has been a common tendency to analyze their development in isolation from each other and to discount the role of the savings and cooperative banking groups in the German industrialization process; very few scholars have attempted to assess how the simultaneous (and inter-dependent) development of all three types of banks shaped – and was shaped by – the early formation and distinct evolutionary trajectory of the German model of capitalism (for an exception see Deeg, 1999). But they could hardly be blamed, since the overwhelming majority of the literature on German banking and German industrialization – from Hilferding and Riesser to Gerschenkron and Kindleberger – focuses heavily on the Big Berlin banks (this is all the more so in the English-language literature). This surprising imbalance, even amongst Germans themselves, could be partly attributed to the fact that banking historians in Germany have often specialized in one of the three types of banking groups. Historians such as

Helmut Faust and Klaus Kluthe have developed much of our knowledge about the cooperative banks, while Jürgen Mura, Werner Henze, Adolf Trende, Josef Wysocki, and Günther Wysocki have taught us much of what we know about the history of the savings banks.[1]

The chapter is therefore divided into two parts: the first part critiques the Gerschenkron thesis in light of available evidence and recent historical analyses; the second part then provides an alternative argument for the emergence of universal banking centered upon a dynamic analysis of the interdependent evolution of the three major banking groups in Germany. The core thesis is that the emergence of three rival banking systems – achieved in good part through state intervention – precluded a movement away from the universal (mixed) banking practices developed in Germany between the 1850s and 1870s because the savings and cooperative banks themselves became universal banks in response to changed market conditions.

Gerschenkron under the microscope

Briefly and simply stated, Gerschenkron argued that Germany, like other late-industrializing countries, had to industrialize on a large scale in order to overcome its "backwardness." Industrialization had to be large both in terms of the average size of an investment and in terms of the number of sectors that must simultaneously begin to industrialize. The German solution to this need to mobilize large sums of capital for investment at a time when there was a general shortage was the universal bank: a bank able to both extend credits to firms and underwrite and own shares in them. The heavy credit dependence of firms on the banks and the presence of bankers on company supervisory boards enabled banks to influence the most important management decisions of the firms. Indeed, banks were said to have a consultant-type relationship to firms and even play an entrepreneurial role in industry. Gerschenkron acknowledged the eventual emancipation of the large firms from the tutelage of the banks after 1900, though by then the institution of universal banking was firmly embedded and their contribution to industrialization a secure legacy.

The thesis of bank dominance and universal bank-led industrialization has been criticized by a long list of historians (Riesser, 1911; Jeidels, 1905; Whale, 1968 [1930]; Kocka, 1978; Kocka, 1981; Feldenkirchen, 1979; Feldenkirchen, 1991; R.H. Tilly, 1966; Wellhöner, 1989; Petzina, 1990; Born, 1977; Wixforth, 1995; Fohlin, 1997a). Broadly summarizing, these historians argue that the power balance between banks and large firms varied widely, even in heavy industry where bank involvement was strongest. Moreover, many large firms made great efforts to avoid dependence on banks and generally succeeded.[2] In numerous cases large, financially strong industrial firms could dictate the terms of financial investment to the banks. When firms faced financial difficulty, this did often give banks influence but these were more the exceptions than the rule (Edwards and Ogilvie, 1996: 439–40).

For Gerschenkron (1962: 21) the period in which universal banking made its singular contribution to German industrialization was between the middle and end of the 19th century. Supporting his thesis, in some noteworthy cases banks were major equity investors in firms, especially in the 1850s and 1860s in heavy industry. And in some cases bankers played an entrepreneurial role for industrial firms. But in broader perspective these were a relatively small number of firms, as banks generally preferred not to hold industry shares long term, especially after the downturn of the mid-1870s (Feldenkirchen, 1991). In railway construction private bankers played a prominent role in some cases, but, especially outside of Prussia, state governments were the primary financiers of railway construction (Edwards and Ogilvie, 1996: 434–5; Wixforth and Ziegler, 1995: 257). Moreover, joint-stock banks, the banks that Gerschenkron clearly had in mind, did not come into widespread existence until the 1870s, well after industrial take-off. Since most of these banks were created by private bankers (several of whom did practice mixed banking already [see Ziegler, 1997]), and ultimately supplanted most private bankers, it could plausibly be argued that joint-stock banking was a reaction against changing industrial and political developments. In other words, creating joint-stock banks was more a long-term survival strategy of private bankers in which they were as much or more following industrial change as leading it. Ziegler (1997: 149) adds that the emergence of mixed banking was very much promoted by the state's early monopolization of note-issuing that, in the case of Germany, forced bankers "... to adjust their liabilities to fit the necessary asset structure, that is, they needed a larger portion of proprietors' capital and reliable current account balances in order to engage in the remaining promising business of financing industry both by short-term and long-term credits."

The general critique of Gerschenkron is further supported by the evidence that firms were more typically autonomous of bank influence because they essentially self-financed their investments. Feldenkirchen (1982: 287), for example, studied nine major Ruhr steel firms and found that, for the whole group, internally generated funds were more than sufficient to finance investment from the late 1870s to 1895; from 1895 to 1914 internally generated funds still represented more than 80 percent of investment. More generally Feldenkirchen (1991: 133) finds that in the period after 1895 joint-stock firms as a whole accumulated substantial amounts of liquid assets that further reduced whatever dependence they had on bank financing.[3] Moreover, the rapidly expanding size of many firms through mergers and high profitability among firms after the 1890s led to strong competition among banks for their business, thus further limiting bank influence.

When large firms did turn more toward external finance after 1895, they relied on short-term current account loans and securities issues. While current account loans often served as de facto long-term loans, bank loans generally did not serve as a source of long-term investment finance (Edwards and Ogilvie, 1996: 439; Hardach, 1984: 216, 234).[4] When firms did turn to the capital markets, they usually became part of broad bank networks. Indeed, the fact that the Berlin Banks internalized much of the securities market through their control over underwriting, trading, brokerage, and stock-exchange supervision may well have deterred firms from listing and thus hindered the comparative development of the German capital market. But bank networks were generally loose networks and only a small number of firms ended up with direct involvement of bankers via their supervisory board seats (and even fewer with exclusive, one-sided bank-firm affiliation [Fohlin, 1997a]). These few cases were almost always instances in which the bank held a significant long-term stake, but banks generally did not hold blocks long term.[5]

Hardach (1984: 216–18) has suggested that the influence of the banks may have actually been at its height in the second half of the 1920s, when widespread industrial rationalization opened the door for banks to take part in the reshuffling of corporate assets. But even *if* there is some truth in this, it was rather short-lived as rapid consolidation quickly created industrial giants independent of any bank influence. And while domestic concentration among commercial banks may have reduced competition, international competition was strong in this period (Wixforth and Ziegler, 1995: 259–60).

A central assertion of Gerschenkron is that the large universal banks came to such pre-eminence because they represented an efficient solution to the problem of late development. In modern theoretical parlance, universal banks were able to reduce the information asymmetry between lenders and borrowers because of their "insider" position within company supervisory boards and their current account relationships with firms. The access to important inside information, in turn, raises the willingness of banks to lend to firms (or underwrite share issues and make equity investments), thus boosting investment, growth and profitability. While this was probably true in some cases, as noted above, bank finance appears to be much less important than Gerschenkron (and others) believed. Fohlin (1997a: 223), in a study of 400 randomly selected joint-stock firms in 1905, also found no positive correlation between bank affiliation and growth rates and profitability. She also found no correlation between debt-equity levels and bank affiliation, thus casting doubt on the argument that bank affiliation permitted higher debt levels and that banks developed close relations to firms in order to monitor their loans.

Neither did large universal banks play a major role in mobilizing capital from small investors or savers, as they did not have significant numbers of branches and deposits until the early 1900s. Moreover, some critics have made credible (though not unchallenged) charges that the preference of the banks for investment in heavy industry – a fact fully acknowledged by Gerschenkron – disadvantaged other sectors, thereby preventing an optimal allocation of resources in the economy and keeping the German economy from reaching its maximum growth potential (Eistert, 1970; Neuburger and Stokes, 1974; R.H. Tilly, 1986: 136).

Finally, it has been argued – again contrary to a central Gerschenkron premise – that large joint-stock industrial companies were themselves not as crucial to German industrial development as generally viewed. Edwards and Ogilvie (1996: 435–7), using data from Hoffman, show that in 1860 and 1870 joint-stock companies – the primary customers of universal banks or private bankers practicing universal banking – accounted for less than 8 percent of total industrial capital stock. This portion grew significantly during the 1880s and peaked in 1910 at just under 20 percent. In other words, on the eve of World War I more than 80 percent of industrial capital stock was still accounted for by private companies, proprietorships and partnerships, none of which could issue stock or have supervisory boards.

At this point in time the significance of joint-stock companies was proportionately much greater in the UK than Germany.

Perhaps it could still be argued that joint-stock companies in Germany were qualitatively more important than these numbers suggest because of their role in technological innovation and organizational leadership in sectors (for example, Kindleberger, 1984: 129). While such firms were, no doubt, highly important in these respects in certain sectors, as already shown many of them did not rely all that much on bank finance. Moreover, as Herrigel (1996) has demonstrated, only in certain regions and sectors did large joint-stock firms play a dominant role. Other regions (e.g. Siegen, Baden and Württemberg) and sectors (e.g. textiles, chemicals, machine tools and engineering) followed a decentralized industrialization pattern (frequently Marshallian industrial districts) in which small and medium-sized firms were dominant. As will be argued in the next section, the financial needs of these regions and sectors were typically served by smaller savings and cooperative banks, both non-profit financial institutions and not true universal banks until the 1920s. Up until the early 1920s provincial joint-stock banks were also important financiers of medium-sized firms, but their industrial customers were rarely joint-stock firms and therefore did not present the requisite avenues for bank influence or leadership as posited by Gerschenkron. Indeed, even at its prewar peak in 1913 the market share of universal, joint-stock banks in the total assets of German financial institutions was only about one-quarter, and in the period between 1860 and 1880 – the ostensible apogee of Gerschenkron's universal banking – their share was stable at around 10 percent (Goldsmith, 1969: 514–15).

Did relative backwardness call into existence universal banks as compensatory institutions, as Gerschenkron argued? Aside from the problematic nature of a functionalist argument, the empirical evidence in support of the Gerschenkron thesis is limited. On the one hand, there is little dispute that private bankers founded joint-stock banks in good part because the growing capital needs of industry were often greater than a single banking house alone could finance, and many of these banks played the industrial investment banking role for firms as Gerschenkron theorized. On the other hand, when viewed across all sectors of the economy and across time, the kind of universal banking role that Gerschenkron thought so central to German industrialization actually appears to be much more limited in scope than is necessary to sustain his general thesis. Moreover, Gerschenkron gives us no argument (other than an implicit one of path dependence) as to why universal banking should persist beyond the turn of the century when, according to him, large firms achieved financial autonomy. In light of changed incentives, we could have expected the large universal banks to evolve away from this, as happened elsewhere.

One could, perhaps, salvage a slightly different thesis from the ashes of Gerschenkron; namely, a thesis that banks in Germany in general, i.e. all banks taken together, played a comparatively more significant role in industrialization through their general credit activities than was the case in Britain. Indeed, the arguments and material I develop in the second part of the chapter could support just such an argument. But I hasten to add that, in my view, this is no longer

Gerschenkron's thesis, because the vast majority of the banking system was constituted by banks, which did not play the banker–entrepreneur role that was the *sine qua non* of universal banking à la Gerschenkron.[6]

An alternative perspective on banks and industrialization

In this section I construct an alternative historical account of the German banking system that emphasizes the distinctive roles and contributions of the three major bank types that came to dominate German finance during the industrial era.[7] This account suggests that the structure of the banking system can best be understood by analyzing the social and political forces that gave rise to each type of bank and promoted and constrained their respective development. Consistent with Verdier's (this volume) thesis, in Germany one of the main lines of political cleavage that shaped the politics of banking was territorial in nature – between the center, i.e. urban-based political and economic interests tied to large-scale enterprises, and the periphery.[8] In Germany, the periphery was quite successful in developing non-profit banking in a deliberate effort to restrain the expansion of universal, joint-stock banks and counter economic concentration in general (Deeg, 1999). Thus, while universal banks may have been created by design (by private bankers), they remained so largely by default – the success of the rival banking groups limited the potential trans-formation of universal banks into commercial branch (deposit) banks.

To a significant degree, during the late 19th and early 20th centuries each banking sector was a constituent component of three distinct socio- and political-economic spheres of the nation. The large universal banks focused on sectors where large joint-stock firms predominated (coal, steel, electrical, and heavy machinery). The public savings banks were an appendage of the local governments and focused on financing local authorities and their public works projects, as well as providing loans to individuals and small firms (largely in the form of mortgages). The cooperative banks were firmly rooted in the small firm craft and agricultural sectors.

There is much evidence that demonstrates that such firms and the sectors and regions in which they were strongly present were not simply residual phenomena of a pre-modern industrialism. Rather, many of these sectors and regions proved that their more decentralized economic governance mechanisms could also be successful in a presumably mass-production world (Herrigel, 1996).[9] Reflecting regional variations in sectoral composition, substantial variation among Germany's regions in the relative strength of the different banking groups emerged in the 19th century and continued well into the mid-20th century; where the major commercial banks were strongest, the cooperative and public banking sectors tended to be weak, and vice versa (Siepmann, 1968). Thus, as suggested in the first part of this chapter, smaller firms and their financial institutions arguably made a much greater contribution to German industrialization than Gerschenkron and many others realized (see also Edwards and Ogilvie, 1996).

From the late 19th century to the present, the savings and cooperative banks not only survived, but were able to gradually expand their market share vis-à-vis commercial banks because of three factors: the supportive actions of the state, the development of cooperation in associations, and their tight links to local economies and firms.

The close, symbiotic relationship between smaller banks and smaller firms helped both succeed in competition with larger banks and firms during Germany's period of industrialization and later, since the large universal banks tended to underfund small and mid-sized firms (the Mittelstand) while savings and cooperative banks' long-term prosperity depended on the ability of their Mittelstand customers to compete successfully with large industry.

Over time these banks expanded their range of activities until they became, with some exceptions, universal banks like the major commercial institutions.[10] The ability of these banks to develop their associations and universalize – a process largely completed by the 1920s – enabled them to compensate substantially for their smaller size and compete with large universal banks. For example, the regional banks of the associations were able to attain the size and resources necessary to underwrite and trade securities on behalf of smaller banks. The association system also created internal capital markets for local cooperative and savings banks – largely on a regional basis – by providing clearing functions, liquidity, and other services. Yet the association system also gave these banks the capacity to integrate into national and international markets as needed.

Since the late 19th century the German state directly promoted the cooperative banks in order to support the lower classes, peasants, and small business and thereby preserve a more conservative and decentralized society. Similarly, from the mid-19th century onward, the Länder and communal governments promoted savings banks to both serve lower classes and promote regional/local development and autonomy. Moreover, these governments repeatedly fought off political efforts by commercial banks to circumscribe the universalization of savings banks. Thus the state as a whole expended considerable efforts to establish and maintain locally-oriented "rival" banking systems to counterbalance the commercial banking sector and the Big Berlin banks in particular. In sum, the picture I draw here is clearly consistent with Verdier's (this volume) arguments about market segmentation as a prerequisite for universal banking; for not only was the deposit market segmented in Germany, capital in general circulated to a significant extent within either regionally, sectorally, or socially circumscribed boundaries.

Bank sector development in the 19th century

In the first decades of the 19th century public savings banks were gradually established in Germany by communal governments for the purpose of poor-relief. In the mid-19th century the German states began to take a more active role in their respective savings bank sectors. The conjunctural pressures of industrialization, liberalism, and nascent socialism threatened to disrupt the existing social order and thus undermine political control by the state. In light of this the savings banks began to appear to the states – Prussia and Bavaria above all – as an ideal instrument to prevent the growth of a radical underclass by supporting production in agriculture and small firms and assisting the lower classes in accumulating sufficient wealth so as to avoid poverty (Trende, 1957: 82, 131; also G. Wysocki 1983, 169–70). But they also turned out to be indispensable for financing the rapid expansion of urban housing and infrastructure demanded by industrialization (see G. Wysocki 1983: 126–33; Weinberger, 1984). Thus, starting in the late 1830s states began promoting savings banks, primarily through the creation of a statutory framework for their establishment and governance (Henze, 1972: 34–46; J. Wysocki, 1985: 37–8).

Encouraged by these new legal regulations and directives from the states, between 1840 and 1860 over 800 banks were established (M. Pohl, 1986: 37–47). While in the first half of the 19th century many savings banks did not lend to individuals – as this was not considered consistent with their purpose of promoting savings (H. Pohl, 1982a: 98) – beginning in the 1840s personal credits to local merchants, craft workers, and farmers became a central part of their lending activities (Thomes, 1995: 152). The number of savings banks continued to expand steadily for the rest of the century, as did the savings deposits they held, but toward the end of the century the amount of personal credits they granted to small businesses and individuals declined significantly as a percentage of their total lending (though increasing in absolute terms) and current account and exchange discounting were virtually non-existent.[11] A combination of institutional and market factors led the savings banks to invest heavily in low-risk mortgage loans, state securities and communal loans (Henze, 1972: 35–46). Thus for the latter part of the 19th century it appears that the savings banks played a relatively circumscribed *direct* role in German industrialization, though their indirect role through infrastructure finance was tremendous (G. Wysocki, 1983).[12]

In the last two decades of the century the long-term viability of the savings banks was increasingly in question and intense reform discussions began within the sector. In the same period in which personal credits granted by savings banks were declining in relative terms, the savings banks were increasingly confronted with direct competition from cooperatives and provincial joint-stock banks (and to some extent the Berlin Banks through their deposit offices) which were expanding their share of deposit-taking and the small business market. This came at a time when the Mittelstand faced growing competitive pressures from large firms and required more external financing than the banking system was then capable of supplying (H. Pohl, 1983).

The single most important and divisive issue in the savings bank reform debate was over the adoption of the giro. Within the savings bank sector there were many who believed the savings banks should not engage in "commercial" activities, as this would take them away from their public mission of promoting savings and serving communal needs. Reformists, in rebuttal, saw the savings banks as having a public mission to help preserve the threatened Mittelstand and the giro would enable them to offer short-term commercial credits (G. Wysocki, 1983: 169–72; J. Wysocki, 1985: 34–43). A resolution of this issue, however, would not come until the early 1900s.[13] Fortunately for the Mittelstand, the growing vacuum in small-firm lending was filled to some extent by the cooperative banking sector.

Hermann Schulze-Delitzsch created the first credit cooperative in 1852 and became the father of the German commercial cooperative banking movement through his compelling publications. Seeking a third way between socialism and large-scale capitalism, he promoted the formation of associations of workers based on the principles of self-help and mutual liability among members (Conze, 1973). By 1859 there were 80 commercial cooperative banks (known as Volksbanken) with more than 18,000 members spread over Germany. Cooperatives also quickly formed regional associations and regional clearing banks to facilitate liquidity among banks.[14] In 1859 the first congress of Volksbanken took place in Weimar, out of which came a national federation.

In the 1860s, however, competing groupings of cooperative banks emerged, mostly divided over whether to accept or reject state aid. Thus the banks were no longer united by a single national association and numerous banks acted as clearing or central banks for different groups of cooperatives. Establishing organizational unity within the cooperative banking sector – including a sole national central bank and association – evolved gradually over the following decades. Nonetheless, in the second half of the 19th century cooperative banks proliferated rapidly, despite the fact that they could offer neither current account nor acceptance credits (M. Pohl, 1976: 36–8, 68–71). Since the liability of members was unlimited, members needed to know and trust each other a great deal. These factors limited the expansion of individual cooperatives, and this became an important issue of concern in the late 19th century when the cooperatives found it increasingly difficult to meet the growing needs of members.

During this period the state came to play an increasingly important role in the development of the cooperative sector. In the two decades preceding unification, the German states, especially Prussia, had ambiguous sentiments toward the cooperative movement, since the cooperatives' adherence to the self-help principle made them appear as potential accomplices in a liberal revolutionary movement.[15] In spite of this mistrust, the Prussian government acquiesced in 1867 to the demands of the cooperatives for a law that would help protect and solidify their organizational character. This was followed by an Imperial Cooperative Law in 1871 that was substantially amended in 1889. One of the key changes in the amended law was the possibility for limiting members' liability. This enabled the banks to offer short-term current account and acceptance credits to their members, just as the major universal banks offered to large firms. With these new forms of credit the cooperative banks (especially urban ones) made a qualitative jump in their functional and organizational character from simple "advance associations" toward more formally organized universal banks.[16]

Gradually realizing that cooperatives were largely founded by conservative social groups (farmers and artisans), toward the end of the 19th century the state now began to promote cooperatives in order to protect these social groups from unbridled market competition and proletarization. Thus, in addition to providing supportive legislation, in 1895 the Prussian government created the Preußische Zentralgenossenschaftskasse, or Preußenkasse, to act as a central bank for cooperatives. It was an independent organization under public law, capitalized by the Prussian government, and run by bureaucrats. The bank held deposits from the central banks of the regional cooperative associations, for which it paid higher than market interest rates, and lent funds to these banks at below market rates. In short, the Preußenkasse was an institution through which the Prussian government could support urban and rural cooperative banks, or more precisely, to provide subsidized credits to farmers and craftsmen.[17] In the agricultural crisis of the 1890s, for example, the government used the Preußenkasse to channel badly needed funds to the rural cooperative banks (Faust, 1977: 542–53; Kluthe, 1985: 87). The combined stimuli of the 1889 amendments and the founding of the Preußenkasse unleashed a new wave of cooperative foundings. From this time forward, the combination of cooperative "self-help" and complementary state "help for self-help" – as manifested in such institutions as the Preußenkasse and Craft Chambers – became the guiding principle of the relationship between the state and Mittelstand.[18]

In sum, by the end of the 19th century the German banking sector had undergone dramatic change. Private bankers, who had dominated large-scale commercial lending in mid-century, were rapidly ceding their markets to joint-stock banks, of which there were 118 in 1900, accounting collectively for 17.2 percent of financial sector assets. The commercial cooperatives grew to number 870 with more than half a million members in 1900, and the cooperative sector as a whole (numbering nearly 10,000 with agricultural credit cooperatives included) represented 4.1 percent of total financial sector assets. Finally, from some 300 around 1840, the number of savings banks grew to 2,685 by 1900, representing 23.3 percent of total financial sector assets (Deutsche Bundesbank, 1976: 66–7; Goldsmith, 1969: 514–15). Consistent with Verdier, the deposit market was dominated by the savings banks, which controlled 8,858 MioM (million Reichsmarks) in deposits in 1900, while all joint-stock banks had 3,128 MioM (of this 1,455 MioM was in the Big Berlin banks; the remainder in provincial banks), and credit cooperatives held 1,269 MioM (in 1901) in deposits (Deutsche Bundesbank, 1976: 57–65).

Because the savings banks were so closely tied to communal governments, virtually all of their deposits were collected and reinvested locally. Where there was excess liquidity, this was typically soaked up through investment in state-issued debentures (G. Wysocki, 1983: 116–17, 137–40). Thus until the integration of the savings banks into the national giro system in the early 20th century, the funds they collected remained largely outside any kind of national (inter-bank) money market. Likewise, the savings banks did not normally borrow funds on national money or capital markets (G. Wysocki, 1983: 137).[19] In many ways this market fragmentation was a direct result of the social and political fragmentation of Germany itself.[20] It also reflected the deconcentrated pattern of industrialization in much of Germany and thus the fact that demand for investment capital (including infrastructure) was also widespread and not concentrated in a few growth poles (see also Herrigel, 1996: 33–71). Even after unification Germany remained politic-ally quite decentralized in many respects. The savings bank sector, for example, remained under the sole control of communal governments and regulation by the individual states, and the latter – with the exception of Prussia – came to view savings banks as an important resource for sustaining federalism (as opposed to Bismarckian nation-building).[21] Conversely, the general success of the savings banks helped preserve fragmentation (or decentralization) by generating and reinvesting capital locally.

Consistent with Verdier's argument that the early creation of a central bank promoted universal banking, the Prussian central bank was established in 1846 – before the advent of joint-stock banks – and became the Reichsbank in 1875. The bank proved to be an effective lender of last resort, thus helping to stabilize the banking system (especially the universal banks) in crises. The Reichsbank, through its more than 200 branches in the late 19th century, also dominated the payments system. "Though not intended, the historical result of the almost autonomous development of universal banking and of the state-controlled central banking was an efficient division of labor between Reichsbank and credit banks with the provision of means of payment and short-term trade credits on the one hand and industrial credit and security loans on the other hand" (Ziegler, 1997: 141).

The savings and cooperative banks were not yet universal banks in the same sense as the commercial banks; real universalization was yet to come in the early 20th century. Nonetheless, both groups made significant gains in organizing their respective sectors into associations. In the early part of the 20th century these associations would solidify and become indispensable tools to wage the political battles necessary to maintain the legal and political protection of their distinct organizational principles and the sectors of society with which they were linked (J. Wysocki, 1987). They also became vehicles for integrating these banks more thoroughly into an emerging national banking system.

Banking up to the 1930s: consolidating a three-sector universal banking system

Adopting the giro in 1908 would prove to be a key historical turning point for the universalization of the savings banks, but it came only after a great deal of internal debate within the sector (Dieckmann, 1981: 49). As early as 1894 the Prussian government presented a draft law that would have permitted its savings banks to not only conduct cashless transfers (giro), but also underwrite securities.[22] With these privileges the savings banks would have become true banks offering the most modern form of credit and payment options. But the savings banks and communal governments sharply rejected this initiative because the law also contained very restrictive investment provisions, including required investments in Prussian or Imperial government bonds. The banks also believed these restrictions would place them at a competitive disadvantage, while communal governments perceived this as an attempt by central authorities to impinge on their rights to self-administration.[23]

The position of many savings banks and communal governments against the giro system was greatly softened by the efforts of Johann Christian Eberle, a mayor in Saxony who campaigned for the giro as an obligation of the savings banks to provide short-term credit to the Mittelstand in order to counter the concentration of industry and banking services in a few regions (Mura, 1987b: 51). The final catalyst for the adoption of the giro system, however, was a severe capital shortage in 1907 resulting from the Imperial government's adoption of the gold standard. To ease the shortage, as well as the drain on its gold reserves, the government sought to de-monetize the economy further through expanded cashless payment mechanisms. At this point the National Savings Bank Association lobbied the Imperial government for the inclusion of savings banks in the 1908 Imperial Cheque Law. It had finally become clear to most people in the savings banks sector that participation in the giro system was essential to their survival. Thus in 1908 the savings banks obtained the right to implement transfer and checking accounts and to operate current accounts and hold securities on deposit (M. Pohl, 1976: 64–8; Henze, 1972: 58–61; J. Wysocki, 1987: 25–7). [24]

The implementation of the giro system also had the important effect of cementing unity among more than 3,000 savings banks existing in the 1910s. To implement giro, the savings banks joined together in regional giro associations (Giroverbände) and established regional giro clearing banks (Girozentralen). In 1916 the Prussian regional associations united into a central giro association (Deutscher Zentralgiroverband) and established a central clearing bank (Deutsche Girozentrale) two years later in Berlin (Faust, 1977: 556). Thus with the introduction of the giro system, the savings banks' hierarchical association structure was solidified and extended. Like the cooperative banks, this system created a sector-internal capital market that benefited the banks and their clients. Yet if it was the giro system that started savings banks down the path to universal banking, it was probably the inflation of the early interwar years that made this progression truly irreversible.

As inflation accelerated after 1918 the traditional business of the savings banks, namely savings accounts and mortgage loans, rapidly declined. To survive, the savings banks needed to do more short-term and cashless business, and the recently adopted giro system quickly became indispensable. As inflation worsened, lawmakers and regulatory authorities of the Länder found themselves forced to liberalize further restrictions on the savings banks. [25] But these measures were not simply reactions dictated by an emergency situation, they also represented an explicit effort to improve the provision of credit to Mittelstand businesses. The Länder were concerned that the private banking sector was not providing sufficient capital to these firms (Born, 1983b: 52). Indeed, in regions where the Berlin Banks had taken over provincial banks – which they had been doing in great numbers in the early interwar period – they generally provided less credit to the Mittelstand than the provincial bank had (Gehr, 1959: 103–8; H. Pohl, 1982a: 23–7; Henze, 1972: 56). Thus, by the end of the inflationary period in 1923 the savings banks had become universal bank-like institutions and were rapidly expanding their lending to the Mittelstand and competing in other commercial market segments with the commercial and cooperative banks (H. Pohl, 1983: 304). [26]

In a parallel manner, the cooperative banks also solidified their association structure in this period and essentially became universal banks. In 1920 the two competing associations of the commercial cooperative banks managed to unite and form the German Cooperative Association (Deutscher Genossenschaftsverband), though they failed to establish a single central cooperative bank.[27] Hyperinflation turned out to be a mixed blessing for the cooperative banking sector. On the one hand, it wiped out much of their equity, and many cooperatives dissolved. The state, acting through the Preußenkasse, acted as lender of last resort and put a large number of the remaining cooperatives – and the firms which depended on them – back on their feet with an infusion of much needed capital.[28] On the other hand, when the government restructured the Preußenkasse in 1924 it allowed the cooperatives to invest capital in the bank, thereby giving them an equal voice in its management. This new role for the cooperatives represented a compromise solution over the "state versus no state" debate among cooperatives. It also represented a victory for the cooperative sector against certain groups in the Prussian government that advocated extending the direct control of the Preußenkasse over the cooperatives (Faust, 1977: 563–4). The regional clearing banks were now committed to working with the Preußenkasse, thereby making it the primary central bank for the cooperative banking sector as a whole.[29]

Thus by 1925, the cooperative sector had developed a strong three-tier association system: on the primary level were 1,349 commercial and 20,855 agricultural credit cooperatives; on the secondary level were forty-three regional banks (Zentralkassen); on the tertiary level was the Preußenkasse (Deutsche Bundesbank, 1976: 122).[30] By the 1920s the commercial cooperatives and the Zentralkassen made their breakthrough into the traditional markets of the joint-stock banks. They were increasingly oriented toward short-term credit markets and developed significant securities business (M. Pohl, 1986: 76–83). They also began establishing insurance companies, building savings societies and other personal financial services to cross-sell in their banks.

The state, acting primarily through the Preußenkasse, aided the rapid expansion of the banks in two important ways: first, the Preußenkasse pumped funds into the sector in times of crisis; and second, by pursuing a counter-cyclical interest rate policy, it attempted to maintain low and constant interest rates on cooperative bank deposits and loans. Thus while the Preußenkasse could not build a completely independent capital market for the cooperative sector, it shielded the sector from the worst ravages of the national market (Faust, 1977: 552).

Intensifying competition among the cooperative, savings, and joint-stock banks in the 1920s was also stimulated through the incursion of the Berlin banks into local markets. Seeking to expand their funding base, the Big Berlin Banks began establishing significant numbers of deposit-taking offices (Depositenkassen) in the 1890s. By 1913 the nine Big Berlin Banks together commanded over 541 branches, though their share of the deposit market was only 6.9 percent (Deutsche Bundesbank, 1976: 74, 78, 122).[31] In the period after 1914 the Berlin Banks began taking over provincial banks in large numbers in order to gain new industrial business, but also in reaction to the extreme liquidity in the early postwar years that had lessened the need of large firms for external credits (Hardach, 1984: 206). From 1914 to 1921 the Berlin Banks together absorbed eighty-three provincial banks, in the process becoming true national branch banks (M. Pohl, 1986: 85–8).[32] The Deutsche Bank, for example, went from just six branches in 1900 to 173 by 1926 (M. Pohl, 1986: 62–9).[33] Completing their transformation into national branch banks, in 1928 the Berlin Banks finally introduced savings accounts (M. Pohl, 1986: 86–9). The expansion of the Big Berlin banks also dramatically raised their share of the total deposit market to 29.9 percent in 1928. But this rapid rise in market share was short-lived; in the decade after the banking crisis of 1931 their market share (of deposits and total bank sector assets) declined by nearly one-half. In short, even at their very brief peak, the big, joint-stock banks controlled less than a third of the deposit market in Germany.[34] The stranglehold of the savings banks (and to lesser extent cooperatives) on the deposit market could not be broken, and the possibility of the Berlin Banks becoming primarily commercial branch banks receded.

The expansion of the Berlin Banks into the periphery, and the expansion of savings and cooperative banks into market segments previously dominated by joint-stock banks, created the first era of head-to-head competition among the three clearly-defined universal banking groups (though each group still focused heavily on its traditional clientele and activities).[35] Indeed, the more that bank competition became competition among groups the more each group universalized in order to compete with the other groups. Perhaps not surprisingly, the emergence of "group competition" within a (now truly) national banking market almost immediately precipitated a major political conflict between the public savings banks and private banks (Dieckmann, 1981: 66–78; see also Kluthe, 1985: 105). In the mid-1920s the commercial and cooperative banks launched a campaign to push the savings banks back into their comparatively limited pre-war role. Primarily they wanted the savings banks to get out of the short-term lending business: in 1913 public banks accounted for only 9.2 percent of short-term lending, but by 1928 they accounted for 32.2 percent of all short-term credit (Born, 1983b: 87–90).[36] The commercial and cooperative banks argued that this sort of business (particularly current account lending) was a taxable commercial activity and therefore did not belong in the tax-free savings bank sector (Dieckmann, 1981: 69). The savings banks countered that they were simply filling in the market gaps left between the commercial banks and the cooperative banks and that they alone could provide a needed counterweight to growing centralization and concentration in the commercial banking sector.

The position of the savings banks received political affirmation when, in early 1928, the Prussian government issued its new savings bank ordinances, and the Imperial finance ministry issued its new tax regulations. Both rulings made clear that the current account and Mittelstand lending (with some exceptions) of the savings banks would continue to be tax-free. Having lost the fight, the commercial and cooperative banks cut a deal with the savings banks in the form of a private (albeit state-sanctioned) Competition Accord in 1928. A key part of the deal was an agreement that the private banks would drop their opposition to the savings banks' new role while the savings banks would stay away from large industrial loans (Dieckmann, 1981: 71).

In sum, by the late 1920s the fundamental institutional features of the modern German banking system were solidified, as each of the three major banking groups became universal banks and achieved a nationally comprehensive presence: the savings and cooperative banks through their association system; and the big commercial banks through concentration into national branch banks. The presence of savings and cooperative banks – and their successful expansion – clearly constricted the ability of the major joint-stock banks to expand their market share, especially in deposit taking.

The 1931 banking crisis adversely affected all three of the bank groups. All but one of the Berlin banks were bailed out by the state (so too were a very large number of savings banks [see Hardach, 1984: 214–15]). The Berlin Banks used the crisis to make one last political effort to restrict the commercial banking activities of the savings banks but were, in fact, rebuffed in this effort by the Reichsbank and other officials who believed that the Mittelstand lending of the savings banks was highly desirable, and that the neglect of the Mittelstand by the Berlin Banks had been a major contributory cause of the crisis (Dieckmann, 1981: 82; Born, 1967: 156–7). In the wake of the crisis, the universal banking system itself was called into question by a wide range of officials, including the head of the Reichsbank who advocated the introduction of a segmented banking system (Hardach, 1984: 225–6; also Wixforth and Ziegler, 1995: 251). But the bankers lobbied heavily and successfully against such a radical change. Instead of separating commercial and investment banking, the Reichskreditwesengesetz (KWG) of 1934 introduced extensive prudential regulation and new national supervisory authorities and thereby affirmed and codified a three-sector universal banking system.

Conclusion

The central Gerschenkronian thesis that universal banking played a fundamental role in Germany's industrialization is not broadly supported by the evidence. While during the 19th century joint-stock banks and private bankers practicing universal banking were no doubt very important contributors to the development of certain firms (and perhaps selected sectors), on the evidence it is difficult to argue that the bankers' contribution was either catalytic or indispensable for the industrialization process in general. While Gerschenkron was correct in citing the importance of universal banking in Germany, it only came to be a central defining principle of the *entire* German banking system well after the period in which he thought it so significant.

In this chapter I constructed an alternative historiography of the development of universal banking in Germany and the relations between banks and industry. This argument highlighted the central role of political and social conflict in shaping the evolution of a banking system that gradually came to rest on the overwhelming dominance of three groups of banks: joint-stock or commercial banks, savings banks, and cooperative banks. Two lines of political cleavage were most central to this process: a territorial, center-periphery cleavage, and a socioeconomic or class cleavage. The effect of political conflict across these cleavages was to promote the formation and extension of alternate banking systems to serve the interests and needs of distinct social groups (farmers, craftsmen, Mittelstand) and political actors (communal and Land governments). Each of these banking types and their associated groups initially developed in a largely complementary and autonomous fashion. Thus universal banking in the 19th and early 20th centuries was also characterized by market segmentation, though of a different nature than that of specialized banking systems. By the late industrialization period these banks and groups were increasingly at odds as processes of centralization and concentration brought them into competition with each other, whether for control of economic or political resources. This competition had the effect of promoting the universalization of the savings and cooperative banks in order to secure their long-term viability. In competition with joint-stock banks, savings and cooperative banks had the advantage of closeness to their clients and they compensated for their lack of scale economies through the association system. Thus the competitive dynamic – carried out both through market and political channels – forged a system of universal banking based on three distinct types of banking institutions engaged in group competition.

Notes

1   A tremendous amount of the historical work on savings banks has been promoted and published by the national savings bank association through its own publishing house (Deutscher Sparkassenverlag).
2   Feldenkirchen, 1991: 127 states, "Hostility towards external capital in many firms still largely owned by individual families often went as far as a conscious renunciation of possible expansion and the potential advantages of borrowing capital."
3   Other studies suggest similarly high levels of self-finance in other joint-stock companies (R.H. Tilly, 1980b; Wellhöner, 1989).
4   Vitols, 1995 shows that long-term bank loans to industry (other than mortgages) did not become a significant proportion of all bank lending until after World War II.
5   Some estimates show that the securities portfolios as a percent of assets of German banks were comparable to those of British banks in the early 20th century (Vitols, 2001).
6   Ziegler, 1997 makes a similar argument about the general contribution of all banks combined, though he interprets this as mostly supporting the Gerschenkron thesis.
7   This section draws significantly from Chapter 2 of Deeg, 1999.
8   A second key cleavage was class; though the class cleavage aligned to a significant extent with the territorial in that savings and cooperative banks were the banks of the periphery and the working and agrarian classes (and, to a certain extent, the petty bourgeoisie).
9   See Herrigel, 1996: 468 for a comprehensive picture of decentralized industrial regions.
10   Though they definitely did not become the type of universal bank envisioned by Gerschenkron, since they did not underwrite firm shares or sit on supervisory boards to any significant degree (until their larger regional banks began to do so in the 1970s).
11   Generally personal loans were less than 5 percent of total assets in the early 1900s (Thomes, 1995: 152).
12   On the other hand, a significant portion of mortgage lending was to support commercial enterprises (Thomes, 1995: 153).
13   One very important success in this period was the creation of regional associations and then a national savings bank association in 1884 (G. Wysocki, 1983: 186).
14   The regional clearing banks (in which membership was voluntary) provided many essential functions for a large number of cooperatives. First, by providing credit when necessary, they helped cooperatives overcome their common liquidity problems arising out of the mismatch between long-term loans and short-term deposits. Second, they acted as lender of last resort.

Third, they provided a deposit-taking outlet for cooperatives with excess liquidity. Finally, they frequently acted as development banks for new cooperatives (Guinnane, 1997: 257).

15   In the 1860s Bismarck castigated cooperatives as "war chests of democracy" (Kluthe, 1985: 82–7).

16   Among its many provisions, the 1889 law also forbade lending by cooperatives to non-members and required the cooperatives to establish supervisory boards and issue formal shares to members (M. Pohl, 1986: 77).

17   As late as 1914 more than 1,100 savings banks were also using the Preußenkasse as a central bank (Faust, 1977: 556).

18   In a corresponding effort to promote the very social groups tied to cooperative banks, Craft Chambers were gradually established throughout German states starting in 1897. For an excellent analysis of the organizations of the craft sector, see Streeck, 1989.

19   The same was generally true of cooperatives. Deposits not used by individual cooperatives for loans were typically deposited with one of their regional clearing banks. The regional banks generally used these deposits for loans to other cooperatives or invested them in government obligations (Guinnane, 1997: 258).

20   Early on, the savings bank associations developed the "regional principle" which limits individual savings banks to conducting business only within their designated area (usually one commune, though a number of savings banks operate county-wide).

21   For most communes and counties, the "profits" of their savings banks were significant; much of it was used to pay for public expenditures. Savings banks were also important sources of credit for communes (G. Wysocki, 1983: 156–66).

22   The law was promoted by the Prussian Finance Minister Miquel, who also promoted the creation of the Preußenkasse in 1895. Together these measures suggest an increasing attempt by the Prussian government to use the savings and cooperative banks to effect its social and political goals (Henze, 1972: 39–40; H. Pohl, 1982a: 23–4).

23   In 1912 such a "forced investment law" was eventually passed in Prussia, as it had been in Saxony in 1907 and Bavaria in 1911 (Klüpfel, 1984: 117–18).

24   But savings banks, which were under the sole jurisdiction of the states, could not actually take up such business until authorized to do so by their respective lawmakers.

25   Moreover, several communal governments had begun to establish their own commercial banks in order to circumvent the tight savings bank regulations. This trend was not viewed favorably by Länder governments, as it would enhance the autonomy of communal governments (J. Wysocki, 1987: 40).

26   Reflecting the imperatives of inflation their renewed orientation to financing small business, the percentage of short-term personal credits (especially for working capital through current accounts) in savings banks' assets took off after 1921 (from 15 percent in 1913), reaching a peak of 59 percent in 1924 before subsiding (J. Mura, 1987a: 169–72).

27   According to Born (1983b: 92) the fusion initiative stemmed from the Craft Chambers which sought a more effective banking system for craft firms. Faust (1977: 282) suggests further that the tendencies toward nationalization in social democratic Weimar Germany drove the competing associations to put aside their differences in order to provide a unified front against a potential state takeover.

28   Funds to recapitalize the banks and for special credit programs for craft firms and farmers flowed from the Reichsbank through the Preußenkasse. The Reichsbank funds were guaranteed by the Imperial Finance ministry (Faust, 1977: 556–60). In the early 1920s many cooperatives began to change their legal status to joint-stock corporations in order to maintain the real value of members' shares in the bank. The cooperative association fought this trend rigorously, and with the help of some regulatory changes and the end of inflation, stopped it (M. Pohl, 1986: 82).

29   Though the Dresdner Bank continued to work directly with over 1,200 cooperative banks until 1939 when the Preußenkasse – in the meantime renamed the *Deutschlandkasse* – bought the Dresdner's cooperative division (Faust, 1977: 578–80).

30 By 1930 approximately one-quarter of all urban Mittelstand firms were cooperative members (Kluthe, 1985: 101).
31 Provincial joint-stock banks with branches had an additional 9.7 percent in deposits.
32 In 1913 there were 151 provincial joint-stock banks (Deutsche Bundesbank, 1976: 67).
33 All Berlin banks together had 1,221 branches in 1925 (Deutsche Bundesbank, 1976: 122).
34 Own calculations based on data from Deutsche Bundesbank (1976: 74, 78, 121). All Berlin bank deposits were sight and time deposits (they had negligible savings deposits) and included deposits from foreign banks. It is highly likely that a very significant portion of the deposits in the Berlin Banks were, in fact, from foreigners, especially banks, see Hardach (1984: 214), and did not, therefore, represent a mobilization of domestic savings.
35 Mergers of financial institutions from these different classes of banks were virtually impossible. First, each operated under a distinct legal and regulatory regime. Second, savings banks were not legally independent of communal governments and were not permitted to merge with non-savings banks. Finally, when some cooperative banks began to convert to joint-stock banks in the early 1920s the cooperative associations used legal action to halt this process. Thus, the cooperative and savings bank associations presented the last insurmountable obstacle to cross-type consolidation.
36 These numbers include public banks in addition to the savings banks and Girozentrale. This rapid expansion of the savings banks may well have contributed to the rapid demise of local for-profit banking in this period.

5 The early development of universal banking in Italy in an adverse institutional context, 1850–1914

Alessandro Polsi (translated by Donald A. Bathgate)

Universal banking in Italy in the early twentieth century

In 1909 a debate began to appear in Italian economic periodicals as to whether or not the Italian banking system was giving sufficient financial support to industry (Confalonieri, 1982). Many economists and observers reported difficulties in the industrial sector caused, first and foremost, by a lack of financing. Large-scale industry was to all appearances undercapitalized and in need of new investment, but the banking and finance markets seemed to be out of step with the times and the guarantees needed in industrial investment.

Was this the demise of universal banking? Many accused universal banking of having unleashed and exploited a short-lived stock-exchange boom between 1904 and 1906 and then, having got its fingers burnt, settling back into a much more conservative attitude towards investing in industry. From 1907 onwards there was a rise in call-ins of current accounts and credit-line limitations, together with a move to reinstate a more German-style mechanism of credits shifting them into equities or other securities, only partly successful because of a persistent atrophy of the stock market that left no scope for stock issues to be taken up. The universal banks themselves reported a state of malaise after 1907 because of the difficulties they had in calling in large credits. In 1911 the Italian central bank had to intervene in a somewhat unusual way as a *super partes* regulator to guide the financial restructuring of the iron and steel industry and take some weight off the universal banks.

With a slight adjustment to the classical Gerschenkron model of the role of universal banking in the industrialization process, it can be said that universal banking in Italy seemed to have lost the ability to carry out its mission to the full. It was certainly crucial to financing industry between the late 1800s and early 1900s, but it ran into serious trouble after a secondary market in securities and bonds failed to take off (Federico and Toniolo, 1991).

However, the universal bank is only one of the component parts of the Italian banking system, which, in the early 1900s, began to show symptoms of inconsistency and a somewhat excessive number of players. These were, in order of appearance:

- A note-issuing bank (The Banca d'Italia) that, together with two smaller note-issuing banks, guaranteed an efficient system of payments by corresponding with a large number of local banks. It had little relationship with the universal banks, which it viewed with suspicion for two reasons. Firstly, it feared the competition universal banks were putting up in the deposits market, straining the local bank network on which control of the internal money market rested, and siphoning off local economy resources in favor of unmonitored and in some cases speculative investments. Secondly, the Banca d'Italia made veiled accusations that universal banking was making stock-market speculation easier by allowing widespread recourse to loans against deposits of securities as collateral (Confalonieri, 1977–80; Forsyth, 1993; Zamagni, 1995).

- Two large, universal banks (Banca Commerciale and Credito Italiano) involved in large-scale transactions, but which found it increasingly difficult to manage company finance in sectors like the iron and steel industry. They generally encountered difficulty setting in motion the mechanism transforming credit into securities (stocks and bonds). Widespread use of lending against industrial securities as collateral was probably a means of creating an "unorthodox" secondary market in industrial securities (Confalonieri, 1977–80).

- Two other somewhat less universal banks, Banco di Roma and Società Bancaria Italiana, which were somewhere in between deposit banks and universal banks. They tried to achieve major territorial coverage, but problems in organization and quality of staff, linked to an overly rapid growth rate as well as to difficulties in creating space for their business area, which made it possible for local banks and large universal banks to crowd them out. They soon engaged in highly speculative activity and were repeatedly aided and rescued by the Banca d'Italia (in their case there was undoubtedly a moral hazard problem involved).

- A myriad of local banks, by and large cooperatives (approximately 1,000 plus another 1,500 "rural banks"), without branches, working the local credit market and acting as the local representatives of the Banca d'Italia on which they rediscounted part of their bill portfolio.

- A vast savings bank sector that from time to time acted as the local banks or even as a stabilizing element, in coordination with the Banca d'Italia, for keeping the national financial system on an even keel (as, for example, in 1907 when the Savings Bank of the Provinces of Lombardy took part in an important operation to rescue the Società Bancaria Italiana, not forgetting the crucial role of the savings banks as purchasers of government bonds). In other situations the savings banks acted as lenders of last resort on the local credit markets (see Table 5.1).

Local and savings banks were spread here and there over the national territory with a higher number in the North.

While despite these drawbacks universal banks lent a more sympathetic ear to large-scale industry and innovative technology like electricity, medium-sized

Table 5.1 Number of banks operational in Italy, 1890–1930.

	Universal banks	Ordinary banks	Cooperatives	Savings*	Private	Rural banks
1890	3	150	698	216	960	–
1900	3	153	795	240	–	–
1910	4	193	862	235	360^	1660^
1920	4	245	748	220	–	–
1930	3	304	625	113	316	2392
1936	–	246	358	102	187	1922

Notes:
* = including pawnbrokers/Monti di pietà.
^ = 1912.

Source: Cotula and Raganelli, 1996: 20–3; Polsi, 1995.

industry was penalized in that it was somewhat too large for local banks but below the size dealt with by universal banks. Credit for agriculture was unevenly distributed as was finance for local industry, although there was a discernible trend towards a greater density in those areas where industry was to grow in the 1900s (Conti and Ferri, 1997).

The stock exchange showed little transparency and had very little weight in the financial market. A mere 60 equities were traded on the Milan exchange in 1901. Indeed throughout the nineteenth century all sources agree that the market was asphyxiated, commonly trading in only four or five stocks (Banca Nazionale, Credito Mobiliare, Ferrovie Meridionali, Ferrovie Romane and, in the 1880s, a few building companies and little else), besides the state bonds that were the only securities dealt in to any great extent. Only these securities were also traded on the bourse in Paris; this made the markets a bit more liquid, while creating opportunities for arbitrage. Companies quoted on the stock exchange were very sparing with their balance sheet information and this did nothing to stimulate the stock market.

One may wonder whether, at the beginning of the 1900s, a banking "system" existed in Italy at all, in the sense of a network of institutions with some kind of interrelationship and territorial hierarchy, according to business and specialization, or rather whether there was a mere jumble of institutions juxtaposed haphazardly with little interrelationship, confused hierarchical organization and inefficient or murky management.

The origins of universal banking in Italy and its development are to be viewed in this context and in the light of these conclusions.

I would suggest that the reason for the lack of "coherence" of the Italian banking system is to be sought in a set of interwoven factors, that from time to time could be linked to institutional path dependence and to the crowding out of other banks, themselves heavily beset by problems deriving from the late political unification process (Verdier, 1996).

Lastly, we cannot ignore the problem of the links to the real economy, an economy apparently highly dependent on foreign markets (for exports and for financial resources), with many of the features of an economy dependent on "strong" countries.

The economic cycles

Let us take a quick glance at the major business cycles and how they affected banks.

The 1850s saw progress in agriculture, and a steep rise in silk production in the North of Italy, which led to the accumulation of significant financial resources. In my view, this paved the way for the first Italian banking system in the 1850s and early 1860s including the early crédits mobiliers, set up in 1863 to support the railway and navigation companies underpinned by generous State grants. The silk slump of the 1860s, the serious deficit in the trade balance and the balance of payments as well as in public finances, jeopardized the whole banking system, which in the event was saved by the government, when it declared the suspension of gold payments against the paper notes of the issue banks in 1866.

There was a brief economic boom between 1870 and 1873, favored by a significant improvement in the trade balance (devaluation of the lira and difficulties facing French trade) and by a speculation bubble in the stock exchange together with the start-up of many banks. In subsequent years the financial market fell into a long slump period, resulting in numerous setbacks and the failure of many attempts to set up nationwide deposit banks.

An economic recovery began in 1878, developing into a boom between 1882 and 1884 for a number of sectors of industry and a speculative bubble in the building trade, but with agriculture in serious difficulty. The next depression (1886–1894) was so severe that it overwhelmed both crédits mobiliers and note-issuing banks, which were replaced, in 1893, by the Banca d'Italia (although two smaller note-issuing banks continued to operate until 1926). The crédits mobiliers went bankrupt after failing to become real universal banks, but market needs and the vacuum in the credit system paved the way for the establishment of two new universal banks (Banca Commerciale and Credito Italiano), more similar to German-style universal banks (whose interest in these new banks led to a partial transfer of high-echelon staff and *modus operandi*). Significant industrial development (and agricultural recovery) started towards the end of the 1800s, speeding up between 1901 and 1906, when Italy endowed itself with a complex industrial structure. This was the universal banks' golden era, and for the first time a bourse market seemed to take shape.

Between 1907 and the onset of World War I industry and finance were beset by growing difficulties; the bourse shrank and universal bank intervention grew sluggish.

One important feature that Cafagna stressed almost 40 years ago was an alternation of short, sharp growth spurts with fairly long periods of stagnation or slump (Cafagna, 1989). This is a structural point that requires highly complex discussion but which, in my view, made it difficult for innovative banking and financial organizations to take root and create a tradition, and that forced bank managements to continually change strategies and aims.

The origins of the banking system in the nineteenth century

The crucial starting point is the late political unification, which started in 1859 and only reached completion in 1870.

By contrast with Germany, the pre-unification states of Italy had few economic links among themselves (with the possible exceptions of Lombardy and Piedmont), and had differing political leaderships striving towards diverging political and economic goals, especially after 1848.

The predominance of conservative agrarian élites in the governments of the single states caused serious delays on the part of the institutions in bringing commercial laws up to date. Up till 1860, only Piedmont and Tuscany allowed the constitution of joint-stock companies.

Banking was reduced to note issuing, where it was allowed (with significant activity only in Piedmont and Tuscany). Lombardy, the richest region, was unable to set up a note-issuing bank because of the outright refusal by the Austrians who governed the region at the time. According to one interpretation, Milan's private bankers were so powerful that they didn't need a note-issuing bank because they could rely for refinancing on Swiss banks.

Only the savings banks, which began to spring up in the 1820s, enjoyed healthy development. Set up by members of the dominating agrarian élite, they specialized in the accumulation of deposits and the concession of mortgages. Unlike France or Great Britain, they were not nationalized because in the early decades of the 1800s the sovereigns who ruled over Italy's states were politically weak, relying on consensus from the agricultural élite who would never have tolerated the nationalization of savings banks. In short, the savings banks soon became a means of financing agricultural and urban investment and, albeit marginally, a source of credit for commerce.

The savings banks gained virtual monopoly status in the deposits market and became widespread in the affluent North and Centre.

When the country gained unification and from 1865 on, many legal and administrative barriers to the setting up of joint-stock companies were lifted, the bank deposit market was already firmly in the grip of the savings banks and private commercial banks were never able to make substantial inroads against this (Table 5.2).

From the 1870s demand for deposits grew, but commercial banks were locked in a vicious circle; they had to offer higher yields involving taking higher risks which made them more prone to periodic bankruptcies resulting in a lack of public confidence.

Another structural point that played negatively on commercial banks was the enormous weight of the State's public debt and the high earnings it yielded (Table 5.3).

Up until 1880 private investment was at a disadvantage. The high yield of public bonds meant that the average paid interest rates were even higher, forcing banks to choose between high-yield investments (with high risks) or high-security ones with low yield. The only ones who managed to keep out of this pincer grip were the few large *crédits mobiliers* who could tap resources abroad, in France, at lower rates.

This was the reason why many banks were virtually obliged to settle for a local setting and gave up the idea of territorial expansion. The few banks that opted for

Table 5.2 Fiduciary deposits (savings deposits and current accounts not including correspondent accounts) held by savings and commercial banks in Italy. Percentage breakdown.

	Savings and postal saving banks	Commercial banks	Cooperatives
1870	68.0	26.0	6.0
1880	55.5	33.8	12.7
1890	61.9	22.6	16.5
1900	73.0	12.4	14.6
1913	67.5	15.2	17.3
1925	62.3	23.5	14.2
1932	75.6	16.0	8.4
1936	75.6	17.1	7.2

Note:
Excluding note-issuing banks.

Source: Polsi, 2001.

Table 5.3 Net yield of Italian *Rendita* 5%. Average discount rate of note-issuing banks.

Year	Yield	Discount rate
1861	6.98	6.10
1867	9.67	5.29
1872	5.98	5.00
1874	6.25	5.00
1880	4.88	4.50
1886	4.41	4.75
1892	4.76	5.20
1895	4.38	5.00
1896	4.86	4.65
1909	3.61	4.40
1911	3.67	4.96

Note:
Noted are the years in which the trend changes. The table therefore indicates the swing between minimum and maximum yield of Italian public debt bonds.

Source: Fratianni and Spinelli, 1996: 82 for yield. Discount rate from De Mattia (ed.), 1990: Table 81.

regional expansionism and a widening of deposit procurement systematically went bankrupt. Local settings enabled a narrowing of the information gap vis-à-vis debtors, an increase in depositor confidence and, to a certain extent the insulation of the local credit market from excessively sudden swings in interest rates on the national market.

Furthermore, local-level social relationships can be more conducive to debtor virtue (Arrighetti and Seravalli (eds), 1999).

These are the success factors behind cooperative banks, which, like their German counterparts, reached widespread territorial coverage especially after 1883, when

Parliament introduced a number of legal measures facilitating their constitution. At the outset of the twentieth century they numbered approximately 800. Local cooperative banks played an important part in the payment system in connection with note-issuing banks.

System of payments and the interbank market

In nineteenth-century Italy, the payments system was guaranteed by note-issuing banks – up to 1893 there were six of them – competing among themselves and eager to offer interbank-type services to other banks. They quickly spread into the main provincial towns, leaving the local banks to cover smaller towns. The influence on the money market of clearing houses (*stanze di compensazione*), introduced in 1881 and managed in the kingdom's larger towns by the National Bank and to a lesser extent by other note-issuing banks, was limited, with the exception of Milan (Brizi and Petricola, 1994). I have the impression that interbank settlements took place mainly within bilateral, correspondence agreements or by rediscounting through note-issuing banks.

The serious banking crisis of 1893–94, besides checking large-scale banking in Italy and causing the restructuring of note-issuing ones, had the additional effect of loosening the links in correspondent relationships among banks and shrinking the already restricted interbank market. Local banks turned to note-issuing ones to cash bills domiciled elsewhere and, to a lesser extent, to obtain credit. Local banks with an excess of deposits ran into serious problems investing them. By and large they entered into bilateral arrangements with larger banks in their own category or recycled resources through other banks in the same town offering lower rediscount rates than the Banca d'Italia. No real interbank market existed in the first ten years of the 1900s except in a highly local context or through agreement between banks of the same category. For example, the larger Savings and Popular Banks accepted bills from many smaller banks belonging to the same legal category as they did. These larger banks, in turn, were privileged customers of the Banca d'Italia. This primitive system of relationships, however, had territorial limits; in 1912 in northern Italy 55 percent of the Banca d'Italia bill portfolio was made up of bills rediscounted to other banks but other regions show a dramatically lower percentage. Everything points to a scarcity of links between the Banca d'Italia and the two biggest universal banks in the country – Credito Italiano and Banca Commerciale – which in turn had limited correspondent relationships with other national banks (Alieri and Cerrito, 1996: 334). The overall picture, therefore, is one of an economy that used money but that could in no way be defined as a monetary economy in the proper sense, except for small territorial enclaves.

Banks and industrial investment

Local banks were often linked to industrial investments, but these were necessarily localized episodes, unable to go above and beyond a certain threshold without jeopardizing the special relationship of debtor monitoring so important to local banks. Besides, local banks had no need of a secondary market for equities unless they were State equities, but even here they preferred to use investment in equities as collaterals to obtain loans rather than work on the secondary market.

Large-scale investment was especially concentrated in the 1860s and stemmed from a State decision. To underpin investment in railway building and the merchant navy, it was necessary to set up crédits mobiliers, which in Italy started to appear from 1863 onwards. A second wave of large-scale business happened in the 1880s with the beginnings of the iron and steel industry (State financed) and the speculation bubble involving building in the big cities.

Besides large-scale business, perhaps the main source of income for crédits mobiliers (of which only Società generale di Credito Mobiliare had strong links abroad) was placing state equities and national and foreign bonds on the savings market. Normal banking activity was scarce. A significant example was the working of the Società generale di Credito Mobiliare, more than 80 percent of whose profit and loss account was decided by profits on financial transactions (Pantaleoni, 1998: 194).

Rather than universal banks, up till the mid-1890s it is more appropriate to talk of *"crédits mobiliers,"* viz. companies with their own resources (capital and reserves) that bought and sold shares. In order to function they needed to float securities continuously; no easy task, this was achieved by manipulating the bourses (hence undermining confidence in financial markets and hampering the growth of this institution), exploiting the short boom periods to push share placement and using shares held to obtain credit through advances from note-issuing banks. They had few branches and procured deposits only from major clients on whose behalf they acted as cashier.

Universal banks, which started to appear after the bank crash of 1893, acted somewhat differently. They had a greater territorial coverage in developing business collecting and deposits and often perceived the granting of long-term loans as a means of gaining short-term business. They enjoyed only partial success, however, in attracting abundant deposits.

There was a brief period between 1905 and 1906 when the low cost of money, the fall in yield of public-debt bonds and a small-scale economic boom linked to the emergence of new industries like electricity seemed to pave the way for the establishment of deposit banks and a broader financial market. The number of joint-stock companies quoted rose from 60 in 1901 to 169 in 1907, and some provincial banks made timid forays in the bourse. The 1907 crisis, however, put a stop to this and from then on there was a slow fall in the number of companies quoted and the amount of equities traded (Aleotti, 1990: 101). The financial market had fallen into the stagnation I referred to at the beginning.

Italy and Germany – elements of comparison

While paying the price of underdevelopment, the Italian banking system manifested a structure very similar to its counterpart in Germany, the other European country that, like Italy, reached unification only in 1870. It is very interesting to compare the distribution of bank assets in the two countries according to the legal category they belong to. In Table 5.4, I did not consider note-issuing bank assets because they were significantly higher in Italy than in Germany for a number of reasons (three note-issuing banks active until 1926, a less sophisticated payment system and therefore a greater use of banknotes in payments). Table 5.4, therefore, shows the relative weight of the three major banking sectors: commercial banks, savings and mortgage banks, and cooperative banks. There are major similarities between Italy and Germany both in the relative weights of the various banking components and their development over time, and they would seem to point to a possible structural element in the composition of assets, which up to World War I attributed a market share of 30 percent to commercial banks (including the large-scale universal banks) and a 50 percent share to the savings and mortgage banks. The cooperative banks held a higher share in Italy, while the weight of private banks, though not measurable, was far smaller in Italy than in Germany. In Italy big banks had a proportionally greater weight; as our table shows, there were only four big banks in 1913 and three in all the other periods.

Therefore, the uncertainties scholars have raised in recent years, including Deeg in this volume, concerning the Gerschenkron hypothesis on the centrality of universal banking in the credit market, apply to Italy too. In support of the Gerschenkron hypothesis, however, it must be pointed out that, in any case, the greatest expansion of large-scale universal banking in Italy was contemporaneous with the most intense phase of industrialization (1900–13). It only remains to

Table 5.4 Asset distribution by bank category: Italy and Germany.

Italy	1880	1900	1913	1925	1929	1932	1936
Large-scale banks	–	9.3%	22.0%	23.7%	21.4%	22.7%	20.6%
Other credit banks	–	13.7%	8.2%	24.7%	23.2%	12.7%	10.6%
Cooperative banks	–	15.8%	18.2%	13.6%	11.7%	9.2%	7.5%
Savings banks	–	41.0%	29.8%	19.3%	21.4%	25.7%	23.0%
Monti di Pietà	–	2.4%	2.2%	1.6%	1.5%	1.0%	1.0%
CCDDPP	–	16.0%	19.0%	13.2%	12.4%	18.7%	22.8%
Private banks	–	n.a.	n.a.	2.5%	2.3%	1.4%	1.1%
Others	–	1.8%	0.7%	1.3%	6.1%	8.5%	13.4%

Germany	1880	1900	1913	1925	1929	1932	1938
Large-scale banks	8.6%	10.2%	11.9%	24.5%	22.5%	15.7%	12.1%
Other credit banks	4.3%	11.3%	19.3%	17.8%	11.8%	9.2%	13.3%
Cooperative banks	5.6%	5.2%	8.7%	14.5%	10.0%	10.0%	10.8%
Savings banks	26.4%	29.2%	33.3%	18.3%	30.4%	36.6%	41.8%
Mortgage banks	17.6%	24.4%	19.8%	5.9%	12.2%	14.4%	11.0%
Private banks	23.8%	10.8%	5.7%	8.0%	5.9%	3.8%	1.7%
Other	13.8%	8.8%	1.4%	11.1%	7.3%	10.3%	9.4%

Note:
CCDDPP (Cassa Depositi e Prestiti) was the state organization for postal savings.

Sources: Italy, my processing of data from Cotula *et al.*, 1996. Germany, my processing of data from Ziegler, 1997: Table 8.1, 143.

ascertain with what instruments this banking tradition, apparently so similar, was built up.

Institutional rigidity?

In my view, there was one highly influential factor hindering the expansion of universal banks in the early 1900s as well as the growth of large-scale deposit and commercial banks, thereby perpetuating the structural incoherence mentioned earlier, namely, the institutional and legal setting.

Italian legislation in the years from 1865 to 1900 (the commercial code, savings and cooperative bank laws) and legislation governing *Monti di Pietà* (pawnbroking institutions) had the effect of regulating the various types of banks under differing legal frameworks. There was one legislation for savings banks, one for cooperative banks and a separate set of norms for joint-stock companies. This made it *impossible* for a joint-stock company to absorb a savings or a cooperative bank. A successful cooperative bank could only absorb another cooperative, but in so doing it jeopardized the continuity of its management, who effectively discouraged mergers. The savings banks could not absorb anything. The 1888 Reform Law simply did not provide for savings banks merging with other banks or other savings banks. On the other hand, legislation itself favored these two categories (savings and cooperatives) in establishing local banks by giving them fiscal and legal concessions. Local élites strongly supported banks with managerial policies portrayed by journalists, advertisers and "disciples" of credit as nonspeculative – an appearance partly true – and more attentive to the needs of the local economy than a desire for quick profits (Polsi, 1993; Polsi, 1997). This led to a kind of positive feedback between the preferences of local élites and legislation produced by parliaments that were the expression of these very élites.

The question, however, is rather complex. Italian parliamentary legislation proved on the whole less organic and regulatory than, for instance, its German counterpart and the differences between the two legal formats emerged "naturally" from the surrounding society, following a pattern in which up to the 1920s banks were more attentive to society and the economy than the other way round. A few examples will suffice: the cooperatives were insulated from the rest of the system by the limitation (strongly advocated by the cooperatives themselves) set by rendering equities nominative, made obligatory in 1883. Transfer of equities could therefore only take place within a regular sales contract, and the limit to the number of equities that a single individual could own was an insurmountable obstacle to exchanges with the outside.

After the debate in the 1860s between the Ministry of the Interior and the Ministry of Agriculture as to whether they were commercial or charitable entities, savings banks were given a general law in 1888 acknowledging and encouraging their nature as banking enterprises. However, the law overlooked the simple possibility of mergers so that two savings banks could not merge. It was not until 1923 that representatives of savings banks started to call for a revision of the law to allow savings banks to merge, which Parliament passed in 1927 with the objective of doing away with smaller entities. Therefore, until the 1920s it was the fractionalized habits deeply rooted in local society more than the regulations that perpetuated a radical segmentation of the banking market, by geographical area and legal format, each corresponding to different social classes at the local level.

This hypothesis is confirmed by the fact that association in the banking sector was very weak, revealing a major difference between the Italian and German situations. Cooperative banks were unable to set up an effective representative association or internal organisms providing connections and compensation. In the early 1900s the "Associazione fra le banche popolari" (Association of Popular Banks), set up in 1878, incorporated fewer than 10 percent of the cooperative banks in Italy, and it was not until 1938 that the Government intervened to create a central cooperative bank. It is this very lack of internal cohesion that explains the serious decline of cooperative banks between the two World Wars, since they held a particularly weak position against the reorganization of the banking system carried out through legislation and administrative measures by the Fascist regime. The savings banks created their association in 1911, but it wasn't until the early 1920s that the association began to wield its strength in representing the category and setting up the Central Savings Bank.

It was the Fascist regime between the two wars that definitively set the legal categories and segmented the areas in which banking institutions were to operate, but it also imposed a series of horizontal links between banks in the same sector. The complex legislative structure set up between 1926 and 1936 was left virtually untouched until 1990. Fascism also put a stop to the universal banking tradition, both for large-scale and local banks.

Getting back to the key point of our discussion, namely the period between 1900 and 1913, universal banks that wanted to expand could only do so by absorbing private banks or the few joint-stock banks active on the local markets, or opening branch offices. However, opening a branch office where there already was a strong local bank meant competing with it without being able to enjoy the advantages given by the possibility of taking over from the bank and inheriting its clients. This, in my view, is the reason why universal banking did get started in the early 1900s, but only to a limited extent. On the other hand, this situation hindered the attempt to set up nationwide deposit banks, with the result that neither a universal banking nor a commercial banking tradition were able to take root in the country.

In short, I feel that in a long-term perspective, the delay in political unification explains why the Italian bank market, like its German counterpart, is highly segmented. This segmentation, in turn, produces instances of crowding out and the raising of barriers to the access of large nation-wide organisms; it makes the birth of the universal bank a necessity while, at the same time, undermining its possibilities for growth.

The universal bank was forced into existence in the early 1860s to respond to a need the State had determined through its policies of support for the railway and the merchant navy. It was reborn in 1894 following the German example, in a financial and credit market with no room for other types of institutions. It played an important part also because few alternatives existed for industrial financing, but it operated in a context that imposed rigid limitations. In the end, a lack of confidence in universal banks' capabilities of affording industrial financing prompted the note-issuing banks, in 1914, to promote the establishment of a public body for industrial financing ("Consorzio Sovvenzione Valori Industriali," Consortium to Subsidize Industrial Valuess), the first of a series of public bodies set up to provide industrial investment which played an important role in this field up until the 1980s.

After World War I, it was mainly the State, through its legislation, regulation and entrepreneurship that attempted to clear the bottleneck of this system and improve its efficiency.

6 The origins of universal banks in France during the nineteenth century

Michel Lescure

Two different accounts have been given of the origins of the French banking system.

According to A. Gerschenkron, French banks broadly complied with the general pattern of backward countries. Even though the Crédit Mobilier was an industrial bank, rather than a universal one, its development had to be "understood as emanating from the specific conditions of a relatively backward economy," i.e. an economy characterized by the scarcity of capital and the weakness of entrepreneurship. Designed to provide industrial firms both with long-term capital and strategic advice, banks were seen as compensatory institutions. In this perspective, it was "the demand-side variables" that determined the structure of French banking.

For D. Verdier, this argument is irrelevant; "rather, it is supply-side variables that are paramount." Taking into account that the French banking system was characterized by a functional division between investment and deposit banking, Verdier stresses the role of the centralization of the capital market. By contrast with countries like Germany, where the state encouraged the fragmentation of the capital market (by promoting the growth of non-profit institutions, i.e. saving and cooperative banks), France recorded a high degree of centralization of its capital market. These differences, which reflect differences in state formation (namely, in Rokkan's sense, the existence or not of a strong agricultural periphery) are said to have in turn determined the banking structure: "specialized branch banking developed in centralized markets, whereas unit and/or universal banking obtained everywhere else" (Verdier, 1997). While German joint-stock banks were prevented from capturing a large share of deposits and thus were forced to rely on their own and costly resources and consequently to remain in the field of investment banking, French banks were "allowed to capture the market of individuals' deposits unhindered" (Verdier, 1997), which enabled them to specialize in short-term lending.

Although they include two couples of opposition (universal banks versus specialized banks, demand-side explanation versus supply-side explanation), these analyses are not necessarily contradictory.

Because of his special interest in Saint-Simonians' projects, Gerschenkron's analyses are focused on the Second Empire period. Even though he limited his analysis to the case of the Crédit Mobilier, it must be recalled that many large or medium-size joint-stock banks that came into being during this period (such as the Société Générale or the Crédit Lyonnais) were shaped on the pattern of universal banks and that, at the time when he wrote his essays (1962), Gerschenkron could seem justified in emphasizing the role of this kind of bank. Not only has the Second Empire long been considered as a period of fast economic development (coming after "a long period of relative stagnation") but also the activity of these new banks really encompassed a wide range of operations including the financing of risky investments and the formation of new enterprises.[1]

Verdier's account is centered on the end of the nineteenth century. At that time, banking and economic features were quite different from those of the Second Empire . The large joint-stock banks, which had been launched during the previous period, have given up their universal bank pattern to be turned into deposit banks designed to serve as a source of short-term capital. It seems legitimate to assume, according to Verdier's view, that this evolution was made easier by the centralization of the capital market; no non-profit institutions supported by strong local authority were liable to check the large banks' inroad into deposits (Verdier, 1997).

Even though the two theses are not necessarily contradictory, they don't give a complete account of the evolution of the French banking system. In the following, we shall stress what seem to be the original features of the French banking system; thereafter we shall discuss the reasons and the consequences of this oddness.

The segmentation of the French banking system

As emphasized by D. Verdier, "all banking systems were segmented, but along different lines." In the countries where banks were shaped upon the pattern of specialized banks, the segmentation was between deposit and investment banking; where universal banks prevailed, the segmentation was between private, for-profit banks and state-supported non-profit institutions (savings and cooperative banks).

The problem is that these two segmentations are irrelevant for the French case. Although it is difficult to give even a rough measurement of the respective share of the different kinds of banks, the evidence is that during the second half of the nineteenth century large private for-profit banks and public non-profit institutions did not capture a predominant share of the total lending business. In France, the main segmentation was up to the end of the 1920s between national for-profit banks and local for-profit banks. The main originality of the French banking system lay in the size of the local banking sector. According to A. Plessis (1987), there were 2,000 or 3,000 unit banks in France by 1870, most of them small local banks; this is four to six times more than Cameron *et al.* (1967) estimate. In contrast with what happened in other European countries, where these banks were eliminated or taken over by large banks at the end of the nineteenth century, in France they strengthened their position until the late 1920s (Lescure, 1995a), so that the share of the national for-profit banks did not account for more than 50 percent of the total assets of banks publishing their balance sheets (Bouvier, 1973).

However, throughout the nineteenth century, the content of this segmentation evolved. Until the large national banks extended their branch networks (that is to say until the late 1870s), the two segments of the banking system were occupied by universal banks. The division of banking work between the two segments was geographical rather than technical: just like large banks, local banks supplied short-term credits as well as long-term loans; they made discounts while controlling industrial operations. From the early 1880s onwards, the creation of the branch networks by the large joint-stock banks brought about a growing competition between the two segments. In fact, this resulted in a technical division of the work. At the national level, the large banks that had been launched during the Second Empire tended to give up their role as universal banks to become specialized financial institutions. As a result of both the disappointing performance of the French economy in the 1880s and the extension of their branch networks, they curtailed their illiquid transactions and made discounts, the shortest-term self-liquidating credit, their most important operation. More significant industrial commitments were left to the "old bank" and to newly created investment banks, specially designed to provide long-term credits and to control industrial operations through shareholdings in other firms (Lévy-Leboyer and Lescure, 1991).

At the regional level, the same part was to be played by the local banks; in this segment, banks tended to specialize in longer-term credits and more risky operations. The basic nature of the country banks was the rolling-over of formerly short-term advances so that overdrafts were in fact often long-term credits. While the commercial portfolio/advances ratio rose from 0.87 in the 1880s to 1.3 in 1913 at the four largest banks, it fell from 2 and 3 at Crédit du Nord and Société Marseillaise de Crédit to 0.62 in 1910–13 (Lescure, 1985). However local and regional banks encompassed a wide variety of operations so that all of them can be regarded as universal banks.

Among the local banks, the share of short-term credits and more risky and illiquid operations varied according to two criteria. The first was size: the smaller the local bank the more likely it was to be committed to risky financing and other entrepreneurial functions. The larger the bank, the more liquid it was likely to be.

The second criterion was the specific conditions of regional industrialization (Table 6.1). In contrast with regions (like the north of the country) characterized by the early start of their industrialization, the small size and the family character of their enterprises, in which local banks could give the same extent to their commercial portfolio as to their industrial credits, in new industrial areas (such as Lorraine), the heavy nature of the industries and the newness of the firms made local banks devote greater resources to long-term credits; advances accounted for 82.1 percent in the assets of the Société Nancéienne de Crédit, the largest regional bank in Lorraine, compared with 41.6 percent at the Crédit du Nord, the largest bank in the North (Lévy-Leboyer and Lescure, 1991).

Table 6.1 Assets and resources structure of the corporate banking sector in France, 1900–09 (%).

	Four largest national banks	Other banks publishing their balance sheet	Crédit du Nord	Société Nancéienne de Crédit	Société Marseillaise de Crédit
Commercial portfolio	47.6	30.3	43.5	11.3	32.5
Advances	38.5	46.9	41.6	82.1	45.8
Securities	3.0	9.0	2.1	2.8	9.6
Capital and reserves	15.6	24.3	15.0	19.9	30.5

Source: Lévy-Leboyer and Lescure, 1991.

These differences were reflected on the liabilities side of the balance sheet. Taken as a whole, local and regional banks were more dependent than large banks on their own capital (capital and reserves). The most dependent were the smallest unit banks; for a lot of these banks, this dependence meant a crucial lack of resources during the opening decade of the twentieth century. At the level of the largest local banks, a growing tendency to organize the capture of individuals' deposits can be observed from the final years of the nineteenth century. The first banks to engage in this activity were those located in the old industrial regions (North, Lyon). Because their practices were not so different from those of large banks, country banks in these regions had little choice but to meet the competition from the large national banks by using their methods and by slowly turning into regional deposit banks. In the 1900s, they were followed in turn by a majority of the other banks; the renewal of the extension of their branch networks by national banks after 1894 induced every kind of regional bank to preserve its further development possibilities by setting up its own branch network. But the consequence was the same as for national banks 25 years earlier, i.e. an increase in cash ratios.

Thus, even though the characteristics of each level were changing all through the period, French banking segmentation, which was to last up to the late 1920s, was between large national specialized banks (the English model) and local universal banks (the German model). It must be added that each level tended to specialize in a specific group of customers, country banks providing small local firms with all financial services while large banks monopolized the clientele of large-sized industry.

The reasons for this unique segmentation

The segmentation between national specialized banks and local universal banks raises the question of the reasons for the long survival of French local and regional banks. In France, this survival cannot be explained by the support given by local or national authorities. In contrast with the German model, for instance, in France it was the large national banks (here specialized and not universal) which benefited first from state involvement, and it was the local banks (here for-profit universal banks, not non-profit specialized institutions) which operated most under the pressure of the market. That local banks survived without any public support leads us to the suggestion that they enjoyed a competitive advantage compared with other banks. To understand this advantage, two factors have to be taken into account.

The first factor is the problem of information asymmetry and the special character of French industrial structures. We agree with the idea of D. Verdier that there is a close relationship between the bank structure and its strategy. French local banks provide a good illustration of this. Because they relied on their own resources to a greater extent than pure deposit banks, country banks (and especially small local unit banks) could not vacate the field of investment banking; the higher cost of their resources implied a more profitable business than deposit banks. As shown by many examples, risky investments were also the only way to remunerate the meager deposits they could not afford to lose (Lescure and Plessis, 1999).

But if they could do so it is because, upstream, they enjoyed an advantage, on the demand side, coming from their efficiency in overcoming information asymmetries and transaction costs associated with the process of financial intermediation. While the creation of their branch networks has increased the worry of the large banks over their liquidity and forced them to confine themselves to discount operations, the organization of the local banks allowed them to provide local customers with financial services implying more significant industrial commitments. In contrast to hierarchical procedures operated by large banks, where the top management guided banking practices through rulebooks, local bankers had the intimate knowledge of business circles in their geographical area. This intimacy between bank and local industry can be illustrated by the Lorraine case: in this industrial region, bankers were present on the management board of 143 firms while manufacturers and merchants accounted for 60 percent of the boards of the four banks of Nancy (Jacquemard, 1911). The fact that many advances were made in the form of overdrafts enabled bankers to have a daily record of the situation of their customers. This ability to reduce information asymmetry is underlined by the fact that, in many places, a large proportion of current-account loans was granted without any security. Given the level of information available to bankers, the transaction costs for setting up guarantees might seem unrelated to the profits to be expected (Lescure, 1995b).

The fact that this advantage played a more important role in France than in other European countries can be explained by two further considerations. The first one is that in France most of the large national banks have no regional roots. Except for Crédit Lyonnais, these banks had been launched by narrow Parisian circles recruited from the most important financial and industrial groups of the country. In contrast to this, the French industrial fabric was geographically very decentralized, the most important industrial regions being located at the periphery of the country (north, east, and south-east). The centralization in Paris of financial intermediaries anticipated the evolution of industrial structures, while the evolution of local banks paralleled it. The existence of a Paris-centric banking system combined with a decentralized industrial fabric opened a wide variety of opportunities for local and regional banks.

The second consideraton is the prominent position occupied by small and medium-sized enterprises (SMEs) in French industrial structures. With 58 percent of its factory labor in plants employing fewer than 10 wage-earners and with more than 80 percent of the new companies being personal partnerships, France was, at the beginning of the twentieth century, among the developed European countries that recorded the highest proportion of SMEs and family firms. The weight of small and medium-size enterprises was the consequence of the first stage of industrialization, characterized by the abundance of well-trained workers, the high cost of coal and the compartmentalization of the markets, as well as of the role played by new small firms in the starting up of many new industries at the beginning of the "second industrialization." This weight made more acute the problem of information availability to bankers and the evidence is that this factor strengthened the theoretical advantage of local banks.

All things considered, a banking system based on small and local units was likely to be more adequate for economic structures than large Paris-centric banks.

The second factor in understanding the competitive advantage of the local banks is related to the role played by the French central bank.

Universal banks needed the existence of a lender of last resort to guarantee their liquidity. The existence of a liquidity guarantor enabled the universal banks "to hold more risky portfolios than would have otherwise been the case" (Ziegler, 1997). It allowed them to match the maturity profile of the two sides of their balance sheet, especially when cyclical downturns froze assets while melting liabilities (Verdier, 1997).

In France, the central bank went so far in this way that it became the usual supplier of local banks with funds. According to a recent survey (Lescure, 2000), local and regional banks accounted for 83 percent in 1880 and 1913 of the commercial portfolio brought by commercial banks to the Banque de France.

Just like regional banks, the Banque de France faced serious competition from large national deposit banks for discount. The growing amount of their deposits made these banks more and more reluctant to discount their bills at the 'bankers' bank.' By discounting the bills of the local banks, the Banque de France overcame the decline of its own commercial business, while it enabled country banks to extend their lending activity without their liquidity being threatened.

It must be added that, in many places, the branches of the Banque de France accepted to discount not only commercial bills (those reflecting an effective commercial transaction) but also "effets de mobilization," i.e. accommodation bills issued by regional banks to mobilize current-account overdrafts. When they were regularly renewed these bills supported medium-term financing. In this way, the Banque de France is said to have assumed the financing of 10 percent of the formation of fixed capital by 1913 (Nishimura, 1995).

Thus, while in other countries, like England or Germany, country banks owed their survival to the ties cemented by the turn of the century with the large center banks, in France they owed it to the links woven to the Central Bank.

Economic and financial consequences

The important part played by local banks had important consequences on both industrial and financial structures.

The connection between a banking system based on small and local units and industrial structures dominated by SMEs was not only theoretical. Of course, small local firms could apply to branches of the large national banks for very liquid transactions and occasionally they could get further facilities. But the fact that local banks enjoyed more flexibility, that they used to make medium-term loans and that they did not hesitate to practice personal credits, attracted more SMEs. The result is that in 1929, credits from the local and regional banks accounted for 53 percent of the total banking indebtedness of the smallest industrial firms compared with 35 percent of the largest ones (Lescure, 1992). Although few studies have been devoted to this question, local banks seem to have been very active in Marshallian districts.

Even though it is difficult to conclude that SMEs encountered no problem at all in raising external finance, it is legitimate to think that there was a structural link between the segmentation of the banking system into for-profit large banks and for-profit local banks, and that of industry into sectors dominated by large firms and those dominated by SMEs.

The buoyant activity of local banks also had consequences for the other segments of the financial system. The first one was the lagging of the cooperative banks. One reason, on the supply side, was the unfair competition that these non-profit banks faced from the saving banks. The cooperative banks could hardly afford the rates paid by the saving banks on deposits. Another reason, on the demand side, was the ability of the local banks to provide SMEs with credits. The fact that for-profit local institutions were so successful in capturing a predominant share in the field made the role to be played by non-profit institutions less crucial than in Verdier's account. The role of this variable is underlined by the fact that it was not until local banks started to decline that the question of a legislation promoting cooperative banks became a crucial political issue.

The second financial consequence was the difficulty encountered by large banks in extending their business. Just like other for-profit and non-profit institutions, these banks faced serious competition from the saving banks; from 1880 to 1895, the large banks' deposits grew on average by less than 3 percent a year, while those of the saving banks grew by more than 8 percent. In the ensuing period, the state put a break on the development of the saving banks. This new policy made easier the take-off of the large banks' deposits that occurred between 1895 and 1913. In this period, the total number of the three largest banks branches (Crédit Lyonnais, Société Générale, Comptoir d'Escompte) rose from less than 300 to more than 1500 and the amount of their deposits increased nearly fourfold (Lescure, 1995a). However it is a legitimate assumption that local and regional banks grew faster. The assets of the four largest banks as a percentage of total assets of banks publishing their balance sheets fell from 60 percent in 1891 to 50.6 percent in 1913 (Bouvier, 1973). Although the figures reflect the growing incorporation of many private small banks, they also reflect the ability of local and regional banks to keep their competitive advantage with respect to large banks.

Thus in France large banks were prevented from capturing a predominant share of the national banking business both by the saving banks on the side of supply and by local banks on the side of demand.

Conclusion

The original segmentation of the French banking system between local for-profit institutions and national for-profit institutions is due to special historical circumstances. In contrast with what happened in other countries, French banking structures did not emerge fthrough gradual evolution, with small local banks changing slowly into large and national organizations. In France, local small banks remained local small banks or eventually became regional banks, but they rarely reached the upper floors of the hierarchy. The latter were occupied by banks that had been launched during the Second Empire period by the most important financial and industrial groups of the country and with state involvement, which enabled them to be large corporations from the start (Lévy-Leboyer and Lescure, 1991); given the high density of local banks and the linkage between small banks and a certain type of industrial structure, the role to be played by large banks was uncertain.

This segmentation was to last up to the inter-war period. At that time, it was progressively replaced by a segmentation between private banks and public institutions, in which the latter tended to dominate the former; the share of the public sector (including saving and cooperative banks) in total bank deposits rose from 35.6 percent in 1913 to 55.7 percent in 1936–38 (Lévy-Leboyer and Lescure, 1991). The reasons for the decline of the private banks were the inflation of the 1920s and the economic crisis of the 1930s; although the financial public sector was designed to compensate for the decline of the private banks or to complement their activity, it has been argued that public institutions were liable to increase the difficulties encountered by these banks (Laufenberger, 1940).

Troubles concerned all kinds of commercial banks but local and regional banks were the most affected. The reasons for this were the shift in the strategy of the Banque de France and the lack of liquidity of the banks during periods of economic crisis. From 1897 onwards, the Banque de France was requested by the state to give a new impetus to its policy in favor of the French countryside and small firms (Plessis, 1985b; Gonjo, 2000). For the governments of the Third Republic, the Banque de France had to become more and more "the bank of all French people" as Georges Pallain, Governor of the Banque, put it in 1908 (Banque de France, archives). One consequence of this was the extension of the branch network of the Banque de France and the wish to give a growing importance to the direct discount, an operation by which the Banque de France was more likely than before to be in competition with local banks. This new attitude was also grounded on the idea, which emerged during the crisis of 1907–08, that local banks had no future and that the Banque de France, a semi-public institution, had to replace local banks to promote the economic development of the periphery. In fact, in spite of difficulties recorded in the 1900s (Plessis, 1985b), local and even more regional banks did have a future and they experienced fast growth during the 1920s. And until the late 1920s, they continued to benefit from the support of the Banque de France; direct discount experienced a real development only in places where the new branches of the Banque did not find enough banking business, i.e. places where local banks were absent or had been turned into regional deposit banks, that no longer needed refinancing at the Banque de France.

It was only from the late 1920s onwards that things began to change. Under the authority of its new Governor, E. Moreau, the Banque de France became more reluctant than before to rediscount the "accommodation bills" issued by country banks. On the country banks' side, many of them went bankrupt in the 1930s. Direct discount could now expand without any restriction; in 1936, direct discount accounted for 27 percent of the commercial portfolio of the Banque de France. The decline of the local banks meant that a new segmentation was to come into being, in which the division between public institutions (some of them for-profit) and private banks (some of them nationalized in 1945) tended to support the division of industry into sectors dominated respectively by small firms and larger ones.

Note

1   For a criticism of Gerschenkron's view about the French case, see Lévy-Leboyer and Lescure, 1991.

7 Banking systems as "ideal types" and as political economy

The Swedish case, 1820–1914

Håkan Lindgren and Hans Sjögren

Introduction

The issue to be discussed in this chapter is how the specific structure of the Swedish banking system was shaped in the period 1820–1914. We shall attempt to explain the differences among three abstract constructs – ideal types in the Weberian sense – of banking systems: the extremes of retail (deposit) banking, mixed or universal banking and pure investment (*crédit mobilier*) banking. Then we shall go on to discuss the causes of the development of more universal banking practices in the Swedish commercial banking system in the decades leading up to the World War I. The four sections include an overall description of development trends, structured to enable comparison between the Swedish reality and the Gerschenkron, Verdier or other theses explaining the origins of national banking systems. The approach is basically institutional, and analyzes the economic, political and social influences, formal and informal, on the banking system that acted as constraints and opened possibilities for economic action.

New aspects of international models of banking systems

Financial activities are traditionally characterized by the two poles of retail (deposit) banking and investment banking, with an in-between area of mixed or universal banking. The terminology used to describe these different banking activities has changed over the last 150 years or so. Late in the nineteenth century, the terms deposit banks (in German *Depositenbanken*), industrial banks (*Spekulationsbanken*, *Effektenbanken*) and "universal banks" (*Universalbanken*) were widely used to describe different types of commercial banks, each with its own approach to banking (Weber, 1902).

Recent research studying the history of banks' business relationships with their customers and their actual influence on industry has resulted in a more diversified picture of the pure banking systems in various countries, both before and after World War I. British banks, for instance, provided long-term credit to industry by allowing what were formally short-term loans to take on a long-term character; aggregate empirical data suggest in fact that British deposit banks held as large a share of their portfolios in non-government securities as did the German universal banks during the half century before World War I (Fohlin, 1997b).

The traditional notion of a German banking system exercising widespread control over industry has been modified by empirical studies on interlocking and networking between banking and industry before World War I. Moreover, business history case studies on the qualitative content of bank–industry relations have shown that the real impact of the major German banks on large corporations was in practice quite limited. Corporate executives, combining their control over the framing of the agenda and their informational advantage, had in fact great influence over strategic decision-making in large corporations.[1]

Likewise, a comparative analysis of the Swedish and the UK banking systems in the early twentieth century suggests that the UK was relatively control-oriented. At the same time, the Swedish case reveals a reluctance by central actors to participate in industry, i.e. a preference to keep industry at arm's length. The number of actors managing the reconstruction of large firms points to both private banks and equity holders being equally active in Sweden and the UK, and their playing a major role from the very start of the reconstruction process. Since these banks exercized their responsibilities in a way that does not fit the theory, the relation between incentive structure, bargaining power and capital structure would seem more complex than first appears (Sjögren, 1997).

From an empirical study of 26 countries it emerged that quantifiable political factors such as government centralization did very little to explain banking system design, but did give clear indications of market orientation. Nonetheless, the various individual country histories show that political forces played important roles, setting the rules of the game for the financial markets. However, results show that these political forces were inconsistent and had no traceable, uniform relationship with the overall nineteenth-century political system in place (Fohlin, 2000).

Even if modern research has shown that (1) British banks, especially rural banks, were more involved in industry than previously thought, and (2) the influence of German banks, their entrepreneurial role and their dominance of big industry has been greatly exaggerated, the mere idea that specific English and German "*Sonderwege*" existed in organizing bank–industry relations is reason enough to justify the use of the dichotomy approach in historical research. To contemporary observers on economic–political matters, the ideal types of the two different banking systems were not only ideal – they were in fact quite real. The rapid process of industrialization in Germany during the last quarter of the nineteenth century, and the successful participation of banks in that process, became strong arguments for the "catch-uppers" in the Swedish public debate who wanted to increase the growth and transformation of society by using "idle" bank capital as venture capital (Fritz, 1987).

Creating the pillars of a modern Swedish banking system

The Riksbank

The roots of the Swedish banking system go back to the middle of the seventeenth century. In 1657 an innovative Dutch merchant, Johan Palmstruch, was appointed general manager of Stockholms Banco. The bank was owned by the state and modeled on the successful public deposit banks of Amsterdam and Hamburg. Palmstruch, however, added two important innovations: he combined deposit business with lending and, in 1661, in response to economic necessity, introduced the first banknotes in Europe. However, when lending became excessive and ceased to be constrained by deposit levels, the notes started to depreciate, and the Palmstruch "bubble" burst with a bank run. The bank could not honor its obligations and closed in 1668.

A new public bank, owned, administered and run by the Swedish Parliament – Rikets Ständers Bank – was established in 1668, making this the world's oldest central bank still to be in operation. To call it a central bank, however, would be misleading. The Riksbank (renamed in 1866) was a publicly owned commercial bank, pursuing official State mercantile-oriented policies. The bank was administered by the three upper estates (not until 1800 did the peasantry start to participate), and the King was excluded from formal influence.

In contrast to, for example, Denmark and England, the Swedish Riksbank did not serve as a fiscal agent of the government in the nineteenth century. In 1789 a special public agency, the Swedish National Debt Office (Riksgäldskontoret), was created to market the rapidly expanding debt during the 1788–90 war with Russia. Similarly to the Riksbank, this office was controlled by Parliament. In the nineteenth century the co-existence of the Debt Office and the Bank of Sweden meant that Sweden had two organizations which, always separately and not infrequently at cross-purposes, were instrumental in designing national monetary and credit policies (Ahlström, 1989).

The different roles of the Riksbank and the Riksgäldskontoret are clearly demonstrated in their handling of financial crises throughout the century. Until the 1890 Baring crisis, the Bank of Sweden's avowed role was that of banker of last resort to the banking system, allowing rediscounting of commercial bills. However, as early as the 1857, 1866 and 1878–79 crises, the Bank of Sweden supported the banking system with liquidity to some extent, although the real last-resort lending function was performed by the Debt Office up to the middle of the 1870s, both vis-à-vis the commercial banks and, interestingly enough, some of the more important private banking firms (Nygren, 1989).

After conversion to the silver standard in 1834, the main duty of the Riksbank was to preserve the domestic currency and exchange rates; it did not otherwise function as a central bank (as we understand the term today). It was run as the commercial bank of Stockholm, distributing cheap credit to agriculture, trade and industry in a conservative and bureaucratic manner and was the most important instrument for implementing the Riksdag's economic policy.

In Sweden note-issuing was not a central bank monopoly until the early twentieth century. To alleviate the shortage of means of payment and strengthen the King's position vis-à-vis Parliament, the new *enskilda* commercial banks, established from the 1830s onwards, were privileged with note-issuing rights. This was a cheap way of financing their lending, and definitely had an important "monetarizing" effect on the Swedish economy; private banknotes became successful competitors of the Riksbank notes and, from the 1860s, there was a higher volume of private banknotes in circulation than central bank notes. However, the Riksbank gradually evolved into a modern central bank during the pre-1914 gold standard period, when it was much influenced by British practices. The note-issuing rights of the enskilda banks were gradually curtailed in the 1880s and 1890s, and finally abolished in 1903 (Olsson, 1997: 60–1).

The savings banks movement

The first modern banking organizations to develop outside the capital, Stockholm, were non-profit savings banks. They were set up in various provincial administrative centers throughout the 1820s, but their breakthrough in the countryside did not come until later, in the 1840s. The new mutual societies became the cornerstone of a decentralized, regional and mostly unit savings bank system. Though they generally remained small, their numbers increased rapidly, enabling them to serve the important function of institutional saving to the general public, thus creating a market for deposits.

The savings bank movement was rooted in philanthropy. The object was to encourage self-help among people of limited means by helping them to accumulate assets to be drawn on in old age or sickness. But the farmers, who were the founders of the savings banks, were also looking for cheaper loans for investments in, for example, new machinery. On the other hand it was hoped that increased personal savings would reduce the cost of poor-relief to local governments. In Sweden the growth of deposits seemed for a long time to be dominated by the savings of wealthier people, but savings banks definitely mobilized long-term regular savings from new groups of depositors as well, mainly women and children. However, since the maximum deposit amount was set relatively low, savings banks could not compete with commercial banks on deposits from merchants and the wealthier members of society.

From 1875, county administrations played the role of inspection authorities but control was not homogeneous and varied a great deal among regions. While some savings banks were regarded as semi-public institutions with active parti-cipation by the local governor, others enjoyed a more independent status. Since 1830 they had been allowed to raise funding nationally by applying for temporary loans from the central bank at a non-subsidized interest rate, no financial support or subsidies being available from the state. The required reserve fund therefore had to be built up from surpluses from strictly business-based activities. Savings banks could also make deposits in the central bank, but because the interest rate was no higher than for savings bank deposits, these transactions were less attractive. It was not until the 1870s, when savings banks used commercial banks instead, that such deposits became profitable.

There were no restrictions by law on the investment operations of savings banks until 1892, when savings banks were invited to concentrate their entire activity on the liability side. Stimulation of the credit market could not, by law, be a criterion for setting up a savings bank. County administrations could also deny savings banks the right to start up if there was one functioning well in the region already.

They were only allowed to give credit on the basis of certification of indebtedness, hence they were not allowed to handle discountable bills or offer check credit accounts.[2]

Nevertheless, savings-bank credits were important in the development of the agricultural sector. Financing of local town businesses was also a part of regular savings bank operations. Since there was no legislation that restricted their investment activities to government paper (or obliged them to place their deposits in interest-bearing accounts with the Public Treasury, as was the case for savings banks in Denmark and England), Swedish savings banks quickly got used to acting on local financial markets. Their investment behavior varied depending on the socio-economic structure of their home communities; in some regions, they initially played a more important role in industrial transformation than did commercial banks.[3]

The mortgage institutes

The first Swedish cooperative credit society specializing in the lending of money to rural landed estates was established in 1836 in Scania, the southernmost province of Sweden. Like the German *Landschaften*, it was a mutual mortgage institute, the members/clients being collectively liable for the society's debts. Later, mortgage institutes of this same kind were established in other regions, and after the severe crisis of 1857/58 in 1861 they formed a central organization, the General Mortgage Bank of Sweden. This bank was provided with state guarantee (and state control) in order to facilitate its long-term foreign borrowing.

In Sweden, as in Denmark, the regional mortgage institutes dominated the long-term credit markets, granting amortization loans for 40 years mainly within the building and agricultural sectors. To finance their lending, these mortgage institutes were allowed to issue bonds. Their status as mutual and private organizations lent them great importance in developing the domestic deposit market, and a domestic market for non-governmental bonds in general. In the late 1840s and early 1850s, the Swedish mortgage institutes financed their long-term lending by issuing short-term bonds callable in (up to) six months. The claim has been made that this practice, while increasing the risk exposure of the mortgage institutes, made the Swedish public familiar with new short-term deposit instruments. This, in turn, paved the way for the establishment of modern commercial banks which rely on deposits to finance their lending operations (Nygren, 1985: 36 ff).

Commercial banking

Regional commercial banks started to develop in Sweden in the 1830s, but it was not until the late 1850s that they coalesced into a system for national clearing and payments. The first so-called *enskilda* (private, note-issuing) joint-stock bank, Skånska Privatbanken (later Skånes Enskilda Bank), was incorporated by royal charter in 1830 and started operations during the following year in Ystad, in southern Sweden. As with all other private banks up to 1864, Skånes Enskilda Bank was a joint-stock bank producing profits for the owners who were jointly liable for the bank's total obligations. It financed its lending mainly by note issues, which made an external fund available at a cost of only approximately 2 percent (Nilsson, 1988).

However, there were still only eight *enskilda* joint-stock banks in 1855. The reason for setting up these new banks had been mainly political, and an effect of the power struggle between King (Government) and Parliament. In this context it is important to remember that in Sweden democracy and parliamentarianism were unknown; the King had the sole right to appoint his cabinet – in accordance with the Constitution of 1809, there was a clear division of power between the King and the Riksdag. Constitutionally, the Riksdag determined Sweden´s monetary policy through control of both the National Debt Office and the Riksbank. The Riksbank was the sole issuer of banknotes, the legal tender within the realm. By allowing the growth of a private commercial banking system from the 1830s, the King side-stepped these constitutional arrangements, and consequently a long struggle ensued. In 1850–51, the King's interventions were countered by Parliament. Town burghers were allowed to establish new banks, so-called branch-banks (*filialbanker*), without the privilege of note-issuing, but financed by the Riksbank and using the National Bank legal tender in their transactions. Within a few years, by 1863, the branch banks numbered 22, while the note-issuing *enskilda* banks had only increased to twelve (Olsson, 1997: 14–15).

With the growth of new industries, higher grain and timber exports, and an increase in business as a result of the Crimean War, the need grew for a more effective credit market. In Stockholm, Sweden's capital and the hub of Swedish commercial life, both the Riksbank and influential private money-lenders fiercely opposed the new banking establishments. Finally, in 1856 Stockholms Enskilda Bank was established – a trend setter in two important operational respects. Though the new commercial bank was an ordinary *enskilda* bank chartered with the privilege of note issues, it managed to capture a large part of the Stockholm deposit market by introducing new instruments for depositing. For the first time the operations of a Swedish commercial bank were largely based on stockholders' equity and deposits from the general public.

Moreover, the new bank introduced new ways to manage real and efficient payment transfers within the country. The regional *enskilda* banks were allowed to open free-of-charge transfer accounts in Stockholms Enskilda Bank. A network of commercial banks was built up which brought distant regions together into a national system for clearing and paying, making possible the transfer of capital from surplus to deficit regions. The commercial banks´ extensive development of branch banking, starting in the 1860s, further stimulated this integration process. It was therefore natural that financial intermediation, the transfer of payments and credits, should appear as the main function of the new banking institutions; on the threshold of the industrial revolution the Swedish economy was characterized both by an undeveloped infrastructure and a growing need for transactions.

The effects of foreign influence are clearly seen here. The prototype of the Swedish commercial banking system was the Scottish one, albeit "developed and adapted to the requirements of the country into which it has been adopted."[4] The Swedish commercial banks concentrated on bill discounting and short-term lending, attracting mainly liquid and short-term deposits. In both Scotland and Sweden they were organized as joint-stock banks with unlimited liability for all shareholders. In both countries they worked with note issues as well as with deposit acquisition as the basis for their lending. Owing to a less developed deposit market in Sweden, however, note-issuing became much more important to the Swedish *enskilda* banks than to their Scottish counterparts.

In the 1860s, commercial banking in Sweden developed quickly, encouraged by a wave of liberal economic policies. The anomalous, politically-motivated ambiguity that had been present in the commercial banking system since the 1830s momentarily disappeared. A majority in the Riksdag in 1863 ruled that no new branch banks were to be established and, from 1868, that the pre-existing ones would receive no new funding from the Riksbank, a decision stemming from a twofold dissatisfaction with the large subsidies granted by the Riksbank, and the disappointing performance of branch banks compared with *enskilda* banks. A free right of establishment was introduced for private, note-issuing banks, though they still were subject to Government examination and chartering. This meant that at the end of their chartered period all existing 22 branch banks were reorganized as note-issuing *enskilda* banks (Olsson, 1997: 33–4).

In 1863, following the British example of 1862, joint-stock banks with limited shareholder liability for the bank's obligations were allowed. The limited bank companies had to rely mainly on deposits as a basis for their operations, since the note-issuing business, being the exclusive right of unlimited *enskilda* banks, was forbidden. From the very beginning, the free right of establishment of limited bank companies was applied, and in 1864 the first non-issuing joint-stock bank, Skandinaviska Kredit AB (later Skandinaviska Banken) was established in Sweden (Söderlund, 1964: 1–29, 115–20).

Markets, market integration and the role of the state

If, as is commonly done, financial sector growth is measured in terms of credit volumes, total assets, deposits, or any other variable originating from the newly emerging and rapidly growing banking sector, then overstatement is an obvious danger. By the same token, the importance of the new banking institutions – savings, mortgage and commercial banks, as well as rural credit associations – that came into being during the transitional phase of industrialization will be exaggerated.

Measured in the conventional way, however, the ratio of the sum of the assets of all financial institutions (commercial, savings and mortgage banks and credit associations) to GNP in Sweden was only 15 percent in 1835, but had reached 120 percent by 1910. Clearly, the absolute size of the modern credit market in Sweden grew much faster than did total output. At constant 1835 prices, the advances of all credit institutions increased over the same 1835–1910 period

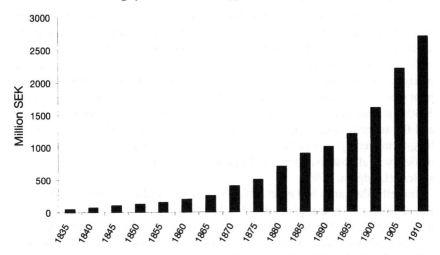

Figure 7.1 The "organized" Swedish credit markets, 1835–1910 (advances in million SEK at 1835 constant prices).

from 33 to 2,682 million SEK (see Figure 7.1), an annually compounded rate of 5.6 percent (Nygren, 1983).

The losing side: private bankers and merchant houses

There is impressive academic unanimity to the belief that viable financial markets had existed long before the emergence of modern banking institutions in the nineteenth century. Research into the workings of the eighteenth and early nineteenth centuries putting-out system has emphasized the importance of credit at all levels of the proto-industrial production and distribution system (Hildebrand, 1992: 97–108; Magnusson, 1988: 234–47). Over and above the public and semi-public national banks, the traditional Swedish financial network consisted of numerous urban dealers and brokers, as well as prosperous farmers and peasants who were part owners of rural blast furnaces. There were merchant houses and innkeepers who, besides giving loans, also accepted deposits from the public. There existed also many national, regional and local foundations and funds, established by government or private organizations such as craft or merchant guilds, that were actively seeking income-generating investment opportunities.

The general significance of the informal financial market in nineteenth-century Sweden can be seen from calculations of capital assets and outstanding loans of public and non-public funds prepared as part of the work of the 1858 Finance Committee and contained in an 1863 Parliamentary Report. On the basis of information provided by county governors, the Committee calculated that these funds had outstanding loans amounting to 37.5 million SEK in 1834 rising to 71.3 million by 1857. During these same years, the total credit provided by the modern bank-based market (including all types of private and public banks) amounted to 33 and 151 million SEK respectively.[5]

These figures give cause for reflection, especially since these public and private funds probably did not constitute a large percentage of the informal market; everything points to its total domination by private promissory notes (*reversers* in Swedish). These were executed between individuals, usually secured by mortgages or co-signers, and they could even be used as a means of payment. A pilot study of the total wealth and debt accumulation in the city of Kalmar in the 1840s, in those days southwestern Sweden's principal trade and shipping centre and the seventh most populous city of the country, shows that the volume of long-term credit provided through direct lending on the private promissory note market was almost four times as large as that channeled through the banking system (Lindgren, 1999).

Initially, the banks had great difficulty making headway against these established financial organizations which offered higher interest rates on deposits, made possible by the fewer legal maximum-interest rate constraints on this informal private market compared with those on banks before 1864. In their competition with the non-organized market, the banks received support from national, as well as from local, authorities. It was considered very much in the public interest to encourage savings among the population at large, although merchant houses and private bankers would not accept, much less pay interest on, small deposits.

County governments and rural-economy associations took the initiative in setting up most savings banks during the period between 1820 and 1850. Participation of local and regional officials in management and on the board was necessary in order to set a sufficiently high level of confidence to attract deposits. Savings banks enjoyed moral support from local and regional actors. Since legal constraints were rather bland, these networks of trust guaranteed, to a large extent, the continuance of savings banks.

The government charter, assessed and renewed every ten years, and the other regulatory measures commercial banks needed in order to carry out banking activities, could be interpreted as public recommendation and indeed as a kind of government solvency guarantee. The system of in-depth control of the banking system that evolved during the 1860s and 1870s also had as its ultimate goal the strengthening of public confidence in the new banking institutions (Lindgren, 1991; Petersson, 1998).

To a large extent, the growing demand for credit in the Swedish economy in the first half of the nineteenth century came from the expanding agricultural and construction (or infrastructure) sectors. Throughout the lengthy growth process during which industrial society evolved, traditional modes of financing commerce and transportation had seemed adequate. In Sweden, as in other countries, merchant houses were the links between primary production, exports and foreign markets. The merchant exporters were able to draw bills on their foreign customers or exploit credit facilities supplied by large banking firms in Hamburg and London, and, in turn, grant seasonal advances to domestic producers.

It is quite clear that private bankers increasingly lost market share and that in the 1890s commercial banks totally dominated the financing of the non-bank business sector in Sweden. Commercial banks replaced merchants, brokers and private banking firms, whose resources were inadequate to finance the increasing volume of transactions and stand up to the strains of recurring financial crises.

The winning side: the new banking organizations

From the very beginning commercial banks had evolved in close cooperation with the State and its government authorities. The *enskilda* banks were instruments for the monetary policy of the King in opposition to the Riksdag. They had the privilege of note-issuing rights that gave them cheap resources and the right to receive the deposits of the general public. On the other hand, their existence depended on the granting of royal charters reviewed every tenth year, and they were the focus of a lengthy political and constitutional conflict between Government and Parliament. Their close links to the State gave them a definite competitive edge over traditional money lenders and private banking firms.

Legal and ideological support by the State was essential for turning the new type of commercial bank into a success story. Underpinned by a wave of liberalism in the 1850s and the 1860s, confidence paved the way for the new banking system, implemented by radical liberals such as J.A. Gripenstedt (Minister of Finance), Mortimer Agardh and A.O. Wallenberg. The 1864 law meant not only unrestricted interest rates but also the right to set up joint-stock banks and establish branches in cities different from the head-office location. In the following year, 1865, eight new joint-stock banks were set up.

Until the 1890s both Skandinaviska Banken and Stockholms Enskilda Bank performed important central bank functions. In 1879, 21 private banks used Skandinaviska Banken as their agent of exchange. During the crisis in 1878–79 this interbank market was highly active. However, from the 1890s three factors contributed to make country-based banks less dependent on main banks in Stockholm: higher consolidation due to the long industrial boom, the establishment of branches in Stockholm, and broader rediscounting practices by the Bank of Sweden. Some smaller banks even began to use agents abroad. Although Skandinaviska Banken still played the role of agent for ten private banks in 1910, the number of transactions made was much smaller than in its heyday between 1865 and 1890 (Söderlund, 1964: 115–20, 233–7, 371–2).

Commercial banks versus savings banks: competition and cooperation

Indeed, the State exercised more control on, and gave more backup to, *enskilda* commercial banks than was the case for non-profit banks. For note-issuing *enskilda* banks, new banking laws were frequent (1824, 1846, 1864, 1874 and 1904, the last one being the first to cover both enskilda and limited commercial banks). The trend was obvious: more detailed regulation and more far-reaching control of the business behavior of the commercial banks occurred over time. The institution in 1868 of the post of Bank Expert in the Ministry of Finance, Monthly Reports replacing Quarterly Reports in 1874, and a Bank Inspectorate from 1875, are all examples of increasing State control.

By contrast, the savings bank business was in fact not regulated until 1892. Certainly, the county governors, appointed by the King, frequently set up local savings banks in the 1820s and 1830s, and there was a Normative Statute of Savings Bank Articles published by the government in 1819. Savings banks were even invited to submit the articles of the bank for confirmation by the King, and many did. The Statute was, however, very general, and scope for interpretation and establishment of local practice was very wide (Petersson, 1999: 27–38).

Parliamentary debate on savings banks was low-key and had ideological motives. While some defined them as professional actors in the capital market, others viewed them as mere philanthropical associations. In the late nineteenth century, representatives of the administration and urban upper classes called for stricter regulation. They claimed that the philanthropic savings banks had risky arrangements that jeopardized the deposits of poor people. The peasants, on the other hand, were opposed to further central regulation. A majority of the boards consisted of local farmers who declared they had clear advantages in an unregulated savings bank system. At the same time, the peasants accused the commercial banks of transferring local savings from the countryside to the growing cities (Sjölander, 2000: 100–1).

The issue of regulation mirrored the general conflict between representatives from the countryside and cities at that time. However, in the early twentieth century, categories other than urban élites argued for central regulation. The reason, this time was an observed tendency towards insider activity, i.e. granting credits to people associated more or less with the board of the bank.

The competition between savings and commercial banks in the nineteenth century has hardly been explored at all. Business histories indicate, however, that the relations between savings and commercial banks on the regional and local financial markets were characterized as much by cooperation as by competition. To an increasing degree local savings banks would deposit savers' money in a commercial bank, both giving the savings banks a decent return and reserves of money at call or short notice (Petersson, 2001: 99–101, 153–4).

In the early twentieth century, city savings banks came under Riksdag accusation of deliberately making it easier for commercial banks to operate (Sjölander, 2000: 101). One reason for this accusation was that not a few members of the local social élite were active on the boards of both savings and commercial bank branch offices. Another example of mixed interests was reflected in actual transactions. The *enskilda* banks used the local savings banks as representatives to broaden the market for their own notes, instead of opening a branch of their own (Petersson, 1999: 64, 74–7, 82–5). When commercial banks began to open their own branches from the late nineteenth century onwards, many transactions, as well as depositors, were taken over by the more aggressive commercial banks.

The result of the competition among the different banking organizations can be seen in Tables 7.1 and 7.2. At the time of the industrial upswing of the 1870s, commercial banks held 73 percent of the institutionalized deposit market. By 1880 and 1890, savings banks had increased their relative market share to over 30 percent;

Table 7.1 The Swedish deposit market, 1870, 1890 and 1910. Shares of the institutionalized market (%).

	1870	*1890*	*1910*
National Bank of Sweden	3	3	0
Commercial Banks	73 *	47	55
Savings Banks	22	37	30
Post Office Savings Bank	– **	2	2
Life Insurance Savings	2	10	12
Total million SEK	**263**	**730**	**2,630**

Notes:
* 1875.
** Founded in 1884.

Source: Sveriges Riksbank 1668–1918: Bankens tillkomst och verksamhet, Pont 5. Stockholm 1931. SCB, Historical Statistics of Sweden, Tables not published in volumes I and II, pp. 97–106.

Table 7.2 The Swedish credit market, 1840, 1875 and 1910. Shares of the institutionalized market (%).

	1840	*1875*	*1910*
National Bank of Sweden	52.5	7.0	5.0
National Debt Office	1.6	1.0	–
Commercial Banks	16.4	37.8	54.2
Savings Banks	8.2	15.9	19.1
Mortgage Institutes and Credit Societies	21.3	30.5	13.3
Insurance Companies and others	–	7.8	8.4
Total million SEK	**61**	**699**	**3,808**

Source: Nygren, 1983.

all these relative changes are to be valued in the perspective of a rapidly growing deposit market (260 percent increase just in the years between 1890 and 1910). The most interesting result is that in the period when universal banking was established in Sweden, i.e. from 1890 to 1910, commercial banks were able to increase their relative share at the expense of savings banks.

In 1840 the Riksbank was by far the largest Swedish bank in the credit market. Together with the second public-owned credit institute, the National Debt Office, it dominated the credit market with a 54 percent market share. By 1875, the public bank share had fallen to 8 percent and it dropped still further to 5 percent in 1910. The commercial banks were the real success story, starting with 16 percent in 1840 and ending in 1910 with the same market dominance as the public banks had enjoyed at the beginning. In absolute terms, the increase was over 200 percent. The savings banks grew steadily, improving their market position from less than 10 percent to almost 20 percent of the market. The credit societies, to some extent in competition with savings banks in the long-term credit market, increased their market share from slightly more than 20 percent in 1840 to more than 30 percent in 1875, but then fell back to 13 percent in 1910.

German universal banking gains ground

It is quite obvious that Swedish commercial banking developed as a response to the demand stemming from nineteenth-century growth in domestic and foreign trade. Commercial banks gradually took over the role of financing business that up to then had been played by merchants and trading houses, a process that gathered momentum during the financial crises of 1863 and 1866, when some of the most respectable money-lending and banking firms were liquidated.

A new wave of bankruptcies in the financial sector occurred during the difficult crisis of 1878–79. Savings and commercial banks – but not private bankers or banking firms – were given support by the Riksbank (through its temporary letters of credit, and rediscounting of bills) and by the Government (by granting state loans to commercial banks hit by the crisis).

Although this support was not general, nor could it be associated with any long-term guarantee, it showed the State's intention to step in to alleviate financial distress. In the case of the Riksbank, the rescue heralded a new era of more functional and progressive policies. The Riksbank began to take on a central bank identity, and for those rescued this meant survival rather than demise. However, it is likely that the actors involved perceived the State's emergency intervention as a one-off episode. In the Stockholms Enskilda Bank, lessons learned from this crisis were taken to heart and incorporated in a way that helped the organization avoid similar pitfalls for more than a hundred years.

As shown above, the early commercial banks concentrated on bill-discounting and short-term lending, financing their operations mainly by cheap banknote issues, a privilege granted by the State. A lengthy industrial transformation, however, that started in the 1830s and 1840s and took off between 1895 and 1913, gradually caused demand to shift from short- to long-term credits. This change in the make up of credit demand encouraged banks to gradually introduce new activities among their functions. Industrial bond issue underwriting for subsequent public offer became a recognized banking function. The volume of industrial and railway bonds in bank portfolios increased heavily in the boom years of the early 1870s and was a major factor in the "railway bond crisis" of 1878–79 (Boksjö and Lönnborg-Andersson, 1994).

Legal barriers to bank security holdings

Largely as a combined consequence of the expansion of banking functions and recurring financial crises, commercial and savings bank operations were increasingly subject to legislative regulation, and public supervision of bank activities grew. From the very beginning, most of the note-issuing commercial banks were, by charter, prohibited from trading or acquiring shares and real estate on their own behalf. In a new banking law aimed at enskilda (note-issuing) banks in 1874 this prohibition became very explicit. In 1886 the first banking law affecting limited liability joint-stock banks to be passed in the Riksdag contained the same prohibition. In individual savings bank charters, investing in shares was generally forbidden, and real practice seems to have corresponded to this regulation (Nygren, 1967: 203).

The primary aim of the first savings bank law of 1875 was to avoid mismanagement in accounting and to introduce public supervision by county administrations over savings banks. In 1892, however, the new savings bank law made a sharp distinction between savings and commercial banking. In order to restrict "unhealthy competition" within the banking sector, savings banks were forbidden to discount bills of exchange and offer check overdraft accounts. It was felt that savings banks should minimize their risk exposure, being primarily unit banks offering safe deposit possibilities for ordinary people. In addition, the size of individual deposit accounts was strictly limited. Thus, the 1892 savings bank regulation is a clear expression of the "democratic," depositor-security policy on savings bank operations at that time, and the non-profit tradition of the savings banks made it easy for them to fall into line with the strong Swedish people's movements of the late nineteenth and early twentieth centuries (Sommarin, 1942: 316–24).

Thus, by law and tradition, the Swedish banking system was firmly rooted in retail or deposit banking at the turn of the century. Recurring crises within the system had clearly demonstrated, it was thought, the dangers of a banking system too closely linked to the fluctuating industrial and real estate sectors. The attempt, in 1864, to establish a Scandinavian *crédit mobilier* bank with mixed Danish, Dutch and Swedish ownership failed when Skandinaviska Banken, the first non-issuing joint stock bank with limited liability, was set up. Owing to the sudden international crisis of 1863, Skandinaviska Banken became a purely Swedish enterprise, operating in the same fields as the other commercial banks. The second attempt to launch a pure investment banking concept in Sweden failed during the severe crisis in 1878–79, when the 1871-established Göteborgs Handelskompani went into bankruptcy with its London branch (The Gothenburg Commercial Co. Ltd). Besides, international investment banking was bleak elsewhere; the Crédit Mobilier bankruptcy of 1867, the failure of the German Commerz und Discontobank in 1875 and the French Union Générales in 1882 were given high profile in the Swedish media of the time; but this may also have been the result of a strong feeling of nationalism which set these events in the context of a struggle against the sway of foreign capital and foreign influence (Lindgren, 1990a: 9–14).

A precondition for the development of investment banking is the possibilities it has to occupy positions of ownership in business. Investment activity was denied to all Swedish banks from 1886. Banking laws provided for only one exception to the general prohibition; a bank was allowed to own shares if they were pledged for loans given or taken over to save what was possible of defaulted loans – but the bank had to sell the corporate securities as soon as this could be done without incurring losses for itself. Thus, after the crisis of 1878–79 and over the following decades, several major Swedish commercial banks, as principal creditors in many industrial and railway firm bankruptcies, gained experience in both financial reconstruction and long-term industrial reorganization work at both main-office and branch-office levels.

The influence of real sector demand in shaping a financial system's actual performance is clearly demonstrated in the Swedish case. Despite tradition and legislation, the commercial banks, in practice, increasingly included corporate finance and investment banking activities in their repertoire, and this they achieved through organizational innovation. Bank executives, organizing themselves in syndicates and consortia for *ad hoc* situations, borrowed money needed for long-term investment bank operations from their banks. In some commercial banks, leading figures set up investment or share-issuing companies, giving industrial bank activities a more permanent organizational form. Ultimately, the bank was the risk taker, as both the equity and the working capital of such investment companies were provided for by the associated bank. In general, bank managers and members of bank boards displayed great ingenuity in finding ways to tap into the bank's resources for the provision of venture capital to industry in breach of the spirit, and sometimes the letter, of the bank law (Lindgren, 1990a: 116).

The catching-up debate and the banking law of 1912

There was a shift in how banking functions were viewed at the turn of the century. This was due to shortages of domestic capital, lofty national ambitions to catch up with the industrially more advanced countries, and an acute awareness of the need to find answers to social problems. The prohibition against Swedish commercial banks owning shares became a subject of public controversy. Developments in Germany provided a considerable spur to this change in attitudes. After unification in 1871, the impressive growth in the German economy led many contemporary Swedes to see the successful participation of the German universal banks in the industrialization process as an ideal way of using "idle" bank funds as venture capital to promote growth and economic transformation.

A review of the entire question of share purchases by commercial banks formed part of the public debate preceding and connected to the Government's new banking bill in 1911. With its enactment in 1912, a certain freedom to purchase and own shares was granted to all joint-stock commercial banks, both the *enskilda* and those with limited liability. This freedom, however, was restricted to the larger banks, and even then it was kept within strict limits so as not to adversely affect the solidity of individual banks and the stability of the banking system (Fritz, 1987: 73–92).

The strict limitations laid down by law were, however, no serious impediment to the large-scale involvement of larger banks in providing venture capital to growing industry during the boom years of World War I. The new provisions were used by the big banks to establish subsidiary companies, in some cases with almost negligible share capital, for the purpose of acquiring shares and real estate, which were then deposited with the parent bank – frequently at high collateral values. This indirect ownership by the banks circumvented banking regulations limiting share ownership. During World War I the commercial banks, by combining loan operations with ownership responsibilities, became venture capitalists of considerable importance.

When comparing the Swedish commercial banking system of World War I with the "deposit" and "universal" ideal banking system types, it can be argued that it had features of both, as did the banking systems in many other countries. The local as well as many of the provincial banks were unmistakably deposit organizations. In the case of the larger commercial banks, however, with their diversified activities, form did not always agree with substance. Formally they were deposit banks, but in substance they clearly behaved as universal banks (Larsson and Lindgren, 1992).

The fundamental cause of the implementation of "German" universal practices into the Swedish "Scottish-influenced" banking system is to be found on the demand side, in the rapid industrial transformation of the Swedish economy during the prolonged 1895–1913 boom. Demand from the real sector for long-term rather than short-term credits increased, opening up profitable new investment opportunities to banking organizations. Shortage of domestic capital for long-term investment rapidly increased capital transfers from abroad, and the Swedish commercial banks quickly responded to these new business opportunities. By exploiting the advantage they held concerning information about various surplus capital markets in Europe (mainly Hamburg, Paris and London), and through their traditional networking relationships with various foreign banks, Swedish commercial banks gained a strong foothold as intermediaries when Swedish State and City bonds were floated on international capital markets during the decades leading up to World War I.

Influx of capital to Sweden that the big commercial banks intermediated, and that supplied them with significant additional resources while they waited for the Swedish borrower to make use of the capital, peaked during the 1905–07 boom years. The outbreak of World War I, however, dramatically changed Sweden's position on the international capital market. Thanks to growing export surpluses during the war, a substantial part of the foreign debt was paid off and Sweden emerged from the war as a capital exporting country. It is likely that the loss of the profitable intermediation business in foreign loans made Swedish bankers and bank managers more keen on developing their relationships with the banks' industrial clients by long-term agreements and interlocking directorates (Schön, 1989; Lindgren, 1990b).

Conclusions

First and foremost, the Swedish case lends support to the hypothesis that politics had a profound influence on the shaping of the modern banking system before World War I. Through the growing importance of money and credit in the economy, the formation of a national banking system stands out as one of the clearest examples of the importance of political economy in economics. Compared with neighboring countries, in the nineteenth century, Swedish bank policies were more centralized than Norway's, but less centralized than Finland's. Sweden, therefore, could fit the prototype of a semi-centralized state.

According to Verdier's hypothesis, universal banking is supposed to develop in semi-centralized states. So far, the Swedish experience supports the Verdier thesis.

But in reality the process was far more complicated.

First, local agricultural interests in politics relating to Swedish banking were much more powerful in shaping general policies after the parliamentary reform of 1865, when the four-estate Parliament was replaced by a two-chamber one. Both before and after parliamentary reform (up to 1892), non-profit banking was unregulated and did not enjoy any public support (or subsidies) at all. In Parliament, farmers' representatives were opposed to central regulation of savings banks. On the contrary, the emerging commercial banks enjoyed important privileges. These privileges were the focus of a lengthy political struggle between Parliament and Government (the King) from the 1830s to the 1890s, with a brief interlude in 1863. A conflict of interests hindered the central State from strong action on this issue.

Second, it is true that savings banks and rural credit associations had the advantage of being prime movers on the scene, developing and capturing a substantial part of the household deposit market in the 1830s and 1840s. The note-issuing rights given to the *enskilda* joint-stock commercial banks by the Government provided them with almost free resources (as the cost of their note circulation was only approximately 2 percent). Thus, note-issuing rights were an important subsidy, and can be seen as compensation for the inability to penetrate the small, undeveloped deposit market. The competition, however, did not only originate from savings banks and rural mortgage institutes; much more important for large-sum deposits was the competition with the informal, traditional market consisting of private bankers, trading houses, etc.

But the deposit market was growing. The establishment of the Stockolm Enskilda Bank in 1856 and the granting of limited liability, in 1863, to non-issuing joint-stock banks gave long-term proof that successful commercial banking based on household deposits was possible in Sweden. Relationships between savings banks and commercial banks were, on the regional and local markets, characterized as much by cooperation as by competition. When the note-issuing rights of the *enskilda* banks were gradually curtailed in the 1880s and 1890s, a new and profitable source of income, the intermediation of foreign bond loans on the international capital markets, was exploited by the commercial banks. Besides this, the commercial banks were able to increase their relative share on the deposit market at the expense of the savings banks. During this period, large commercial banks developed universal banking practices in many cases by circumventing the bank law that strictly forbade them from taking ownership stakes in firms. Also as regards active participation on the board of large firms, key features of German universal banking were more pronounced and decisive in Sweden than in Germany itself.

At the end of the nineteenth century, the entire Swedish financial system was formalized for the first time. It was also given a sectorial logic conferring specialization to various credit organizations. The institutional setting, the outcome of a protracted political debate, was designed in order to specify the relative functions of the central bank, the savings banks, the commercial banks and the mortgage institutes. New laws definitively reduced previously overlapping functions. For customers too, this clear distinction made the structure of relationships more transparent and predictable than before. From then on, the function of lender of last resort was given exclusively to the State, while commercial banks were to invest in industry.

"Relationship banking" was practiced on a large scale by Swedish commercial banks during World War I, after the granting of limited bank share-ownership in 1912. The importance of supply-side variables in determining the product mix of the big Swedish commercial banks is quite obvious in this process of take-off of universal banking. When Sweden replaced huge imports of capital with exports of capital, and the profitable intermediation of foreign loans came to an end, commercial banks became very keen on developing relationships with their industrial clients.

Having said this – bringing us to our third point – it is important to stress the demand-side variables as well. Savings banks and mortgage institutes developed in Sweden due to a growing demand from the expanding agricultural and construction sectors in the first half of the nineteenth century, whereas the development of commercial banks responded to the demand resulting from growing domestic and foreign trade during the same period. For a long time, the resources of merchants, brokers and private banking firms had been adequate to finance the increasing volume of transactions, but with the expansion of the domestic and international markets the resources of the informal banking sector clearly showed themselves to be inadequate; furthermore, the recurring financial crises highlighted the fragility of a system based on private bankers.

During the last quarter of the nineteenth century, industrial demand for long-term capital became more marked. The commercial banks responded to this not only by providing long-term credits, but also by developing banking services of various kinds for the new, expanding industrial sector: bond issues, financial and industrial reorganization of client firms in financial difficulty, interlockings, and, despite the prohibition against holding securities, organizing share issues and taking ownership stakes in syndicates and consortia, or investment companies.

Notes

1   In a sample of all German joint-stock firms in existence in 1905, Fohlin found that less than a quarter (23 percent) had joint-stock director representation on their supervisory board whereas half of them had representation by major bank directors. More revealing in a single bank domination or control context is that in most cases there were representatives from two or more banks on the same supervisory board; in only two of the 400 sampled was a major bank director the firm's only source of interlocking directorates. See C. M. Fohlin (1997b).

    For business history case studies on bank-industry relations, see Wellhöner, 1989; and Wixforth, 1988.

2   Petersson, 1999; Sjölander, 2000: 36. In 1900, a national association, Svenska Sparbanks-föreningen, was founded to look after the interests of the individual savings banks.

3   Lag angående sparbanker 1892; Petersson, 1999; Lilja, 2000.

4   R. H. Inglis Palgrave (1873), *Notes on banking in Great Britain and Ireland, Sweden, Denmark and Hamburg*, cited in Nilsson, 1981: 384.

5   *Betänkande angående Sveriges ekonomiska och finansiella utveckling under åren 1834–1860*, 9 February 1863, Stockholm, 71-8.

8 The development of a hybrid structure in Norway

Banks and economic change in the European periphery, 1870–1913

Sverre Knutsen

Introduction

This chapter is structured around two main themes. First, the development of the specific structure of the Norwegian banking system through the formative period 1870 to 1913 is discussed. When we analyze this emerging structure along two dimensions – centralized versus decentralized and universal versus specialized – the following pattern is revealed: Norwegian banking was characterized by a fragmented and decentralized unit-bank system, with local savings banks capturing a significant share of the deposit market. The commercial banks did not develop branches. In 1913, the total number of branches outside the location of the Head Office was only nine. Thus, branches hardly existed on the eve of World War I. Moreover, the chapter makes the argument that the banks only universalized to a very limited extent. Rather, the banking structure and the lending business should be characterized more as a hybrid-type, combining elements from continental style universalism with components from an Anglo-Saxon type of commercial banking.[1] The main problem I want to grapple with here is how we can explain the development of these particular characteristics of the Norwegian banking system. What were the main causes shaping the Norwegian financial structure?

The second theme discussed is the finance–economic growth nexus. Alexander Gerschenkron has developed the classic historical explanation for the emergence of universal banking, as well as the role of universal banks in European industrialization. However, Gerschenkron's interpretation does not fit the Norwegian case very well. Consequently, the chapter re-examines Gerschenkron's banking thesis in light of the Norwegian case.

Theoretical considerations

Several types of conceptual frameworks have been offered to explain why financial structures differ, especially why universal banks evolved during the nineteenth century. As already mentioned, the classical historical explanation is Alexander Gerschenkron's, explaining universal banking as an efficient response to "relative backwardness" in the industrializing process (Gerschenkron, 1962; Sylla and Toniolo (eds), 1991b). Gerschenkron also linked his explanation of the origin of universal banking with a theory of industrialization and sustained growth. According to him, late-industrializing countries faced considerably larger capital demands relative to savings than the pioneer industrializer Great Britain did. Britain had a financial system adequate to provide the entrepreneurs with capital for investment. The late industrializers lacked this precondition. To overcome this obstacle, they developed institutional substitutes like universal banks in "moderate backward countries", whereas the state substituted missing prerequisites of modern industrialization in "extremely backward countries".

Later, a more theoretical and less historical explanation has appeared: the argument based on asymmetric information. Several features associated with the operations of universal banks, it has been argued, contribute to reduce information asymmetries and improve the efficiency of financial intermediation (R.H. Tilly, 1998). Their presence in decision-making boards of non-financial firms, and hence the capacity to monitor the borrowers has been pointed out as a major instrument in the hands of universal banks in order to overcome information asymmetries in credit contracts.

Essentially, in recent literature we are offered two major explanatory approaches – information asymmetry theory on the one hand and a series of explanations referred to as "market segmentation" approaches on the other. These two approaches need not necessarily be mutually exclusive. Perhaps they are more complementary. However, the asymmetric information explanation of the origin, shaping and continuity of a country's financial structure so far appears to be unable to point to a particular explanation for why divergent solutions to the information asymmetry problems, and hence the observed variation in national banking system, evolved historically.

It seems that a theory that excludes institutional and political variables has insurmountable difficulties in explaining such variations. Richard Sylla has pointed out that "Governments, with their laws and regulations and their financial demands, shape, indeed have always shaped, financial systems" (Sylla, 1996). From this perspective, Sylla suggests a hypothesis to explain the origin of the differences between a bank-oriented German financial system and the market-oriented British and US financial systems by introducing a regulatory dimension. When a set of countries interferes with its banking, with a lot of laws and regulations, but leaves its securities markets relatively free to develop, the result would be a market-oriented system. Alternatively, we may suppose that another set of countries leaves its banking institutions relatively free to develop in accordance with market opportunities and constraints, but interferes with its securities markets, with a lot of laws and regulations. In this case, we might expect that a bank-oriented system would emerge. This was exactly what happened in US and British banking history on one hand, and in German banking hisotry, on the other, claims Sylla. Thus, systemic financial differences "were a result not only of relative advancement or backwardness, or of different stages of national development, but also of different government policy stances towards banks and securities markets early in modern economic history" (Sylla, 1996: 121). The continuity of the two different systems to the present may be explained by path dependence.

Political and legal factors seem to play a crucial role. More precisely, we should introduce institutions as central to our analysis of the origin of universal banks. Douglass North has defined institutions as the "rules of the game" structuring human interaction (North, 1990). He distinguishes between formal (legal) institutions and informal ones. Where do informal constraints come from? According to North they "come from socially transmitted information and are a part of the heritage that we call culture" (North, 1990: 37). Thus, a regulatory regime consists not only of laws and formal rules, but also culturally underpinned informal constraints. Financial structures are determined mainly by a national regulatory regime – informal constraints included – and such factors as the level of economic development. Hence, a search for the political origins of banking structures appears to be a promising approach.

To deepen the analysis, however, it would be useful to specify the political and institutional mechanisms at work in more detail. Daniel Verdier has developed a conceptual framework, drawing on and refining the center–periphery approach of the political scientist Stein Rokkan. In brief outline, Verdier's argument goes like this: Variation in the degree of state centralization was the outcome of the different paths in the process of state formation during the nineteenth century, strongly influenced by the struggle between a political core and its peripheries. Whilst the core fought for control, the periphery strove for autonomy. The control over financial resources even became an important part of this struggle (Verdier, 1996; Verdier, 1997).

According to Verdier variations in banking structures have reflected differences in state formation, with the degree of state centralization being the critical variable. The conflict between central treasuries wanting to drain capital from their peripheries and local government seeking to retain control over local capital resulted in certain typical financial structures. Verdier stresses that strong states centralized capital markets, while weaker ones dealt with multiple, fragmented capital markets. The degree of fragmentation of the capital market determined the banking structure, in the way that specialized branch banking developed in centralized markets, whereas unit and/or universal banking evolved everywhere else (Verdier, 1997). This concept of the segmentation of capital markets is closely linked with the segmentation of banking systems. In countries characterized by a centralized polity and specialized banks, the segmentation was between deposit and investment banking. In a system where universal banks prevailed, the divide was between private, for-profit banks on the one hand, and publicly supported non-profit institutions like savings banks, cooperative banks etc. on the other.

With this background information, the remainder of this chapter will explore the applicability of the Verdier thesis to the Norwegian case. Before we proceed to the empirical analysis, however, I think it is essential to discuss the notion "universal bank" a little bit further. I want to stress this point, because the content of the term "universal banking" is in a way decisive for the outcome of our discussion on the origin of universal banking as well as its relative merits.

The concept of universal banking

The economic historian Richard Tilly states that "the key element of universal banking is the institutional mixture of the commercial loan and deposit business with investment banking" (R.H. Tilly, 1998: 7). In fact, most of the literature takes the term "universal banking" as meaning a combination of commercial and investment banking. Particularly, this applies to work done by economists. Now, "investment banking" is a rather modern term, meaning an organization that specializes in the raising of capital through the issuance of new securities in the primary market and even the bringing together of buyers and sellers of existing securities in the secondary market. Currently, a very important kind of activity of investment banks is the services they offer in mergers, acquisitions and takeovers in the market for corporate control.

However, the terms "deposit bank," "industrial bank" and "universal bank" were coined already during the second half of the nineteenth century. The notion "deposit banking" covered a banking practice comprising taking deposits and providing short-term credits – also referred to as "commercial" or "retail" banking. "Industrial banking" typically denotes a type of specialized bank engaged in financing industrial investments by long-term advances, like the Crédit Mobilier de Paris. This type of bank – in Germany even called "Spekulations-banken" – was very sensitive to the business cycle because of built-in liquidity problems. The combination of industrial banking with deposit funding and advances of short-term business credit, turned out to be a more flexible solution. Consequently a system of mixed banking emerged, in particular in Germany, during the second half of the nineteenth century. This became the prototype of the so-called universal banks. But the German system of universal banking was not only characterized by the mixture of banking functions, but also distinguished by ownership relations to industry. Steinherr claims that the key feature of universal banking "is the range of activities allowed, in particular, the holding of equity shares large enough to monitor corporations as equity owners" (Steinherr, 1996: 4). This is a crucial institutional feature of universal banking from the point of view of information asymmetry, since it is argued that the equity holdings in their customers is the basic mechanism which enable universal banks to reduce information asymmetries and improve the efficiency of financial intermediation.

A survey of the literature reveals a common picture where the stylized profile of universal banking is an organizational blend of commercial banking and investment banking. Furthermore, relationship or "*Haus*" banking characterizes universal banks. Large German banks before World War II and even today, are seen as the archetype as well as the standard historical example of universal banking. Thus, an organization comprising a mixture of deposit taking with short-term and long-term lending is not sufficient to be called a universal bank, if it does not include the underwriting of corporate and government securities and other investment bank services. Admittedly, this description may be seen as a narrow definition of universal banking. Since a securities market scarcely existed in Norway and several other periphery countries during most of the nineteenth century, the narrow definition makes it very difficult to assess the existence of universalism in banking in a broader sense.

The counterpart of "universal banking" is "specialized banking". Specialized banks comprise mainly commercial, trust and investment banks, but also credit-cooperatives, specialized mortgage banks and savings banks. Furthermore, specialized banking systems are usually part of a financial system with significant securities markets, and thus are labeled market-oriented systems, whilst financial systems dominated by universal banks are characterized by a relatively weak stock market, and thus are labeled bank-oriented financial systems. The standard historical example of a specialized, market-oriented system is usually that of Britain.

Terms like universal banks and specialized banks relate to models or ideal types in the Weberian sense. As already pointed out, a narrow definition of universal banks may be of limited use for comparative and historical purposes. Thus, it would be more fruitful to operate with a broader concept of universal banking. In a historical perspective it is obvious that the most fundamental aspect of universalism in banking is the combination of deposit taking with a mix of short-term and long-term lending. Thus, a more generic working definition of universalism in banking, which I will apply in this study, is the mix of short- and long-term assets and liabilities.

The structure of the Norwegian banking system and credit market, 1870–1913

To describe the structure of the banking system and how it developed, I will first depict the prevalent institutions operating in the credit market and their shares of the loan market as well as the deposit market, and also the type of advances they provided.

The Bank of Norway was established in 1816 as the country's national bank responsible for the monetary system, but organized as a private joint-stock firm. The national bank was, however, controlled by the parliament via legislation, and even the power to appoint the board of directors. The parliament (Storting) granted the national bank a note-issuing monopoly from the outset. The Bank of Norway did not, however, act as a liquidity guarantor during most of the nineteenth century. In fact, The Bank of Norway to a large extent acted as a provider of credit to the non-financial sector. But in periods of economic crisis and distress, the national bank withdrew loans and refused to rediscount bills in order to safeguard the external value of the currency. The anchor of the currency was silver from 1842, but the country went on the gold standard in 1875, when Norway joined the Scandinavian monetary union with Sweden and Denmark. Not even during a severe banking crisis of the 1880s did the national bank act as a liquidity guarantor. It was not until a banking panic, which burst out in Christiania (the capital) in 1899, that the Bank of Norway for the first time made an effort to act as a lender-of-last-resort, although the intent to do so was stronger than the ability.

The years from 1870 to World War I was a formative period in which the structure of the Norwegian banking sector was shaped for more than half a century to come after the war. Table 8.1 demonstrates that the number of commercial banks increased especially during the period 1890–1900, when 43 new banks were established in ten years. The number of savings banks was already substantial in 1870, and this type of bank grew steadily both in assets and numbers during the subsequent decades. The substantial expansion in number of both commercial- and savings banks after 1890 and up to the outbreak of World War I mostly took part in the periphery, both in the countryside as well as in all the small towns in various districts around the long coastline of the southern and western part of Norway.

Of the four largest commercial banks in operation by 1900, three were operating in Christiania and one in Bergen. The first commercial bank in Norway – the Christiania Bank & Kreditkasse – was established in Christiania in 1848. In 1856 a commercial bank named Bergens Privatbank was established in the city of Bergen, the second largest city, whilst another commercial bank named Den norske Creditbank (DnC) opened its doors in the capital in 1857.[2] During the planning and preparation period of DnC, the ideas underpinning the Crédit Mobilier de Paris were discussed among the founders of the bank. In the statute of the bank, the aim of its operations was stated to be "the promotion and development of Norwegian trade, industry and other business enterprises" (Hertzberg and Rygg, 1907: 206). But in spite of this ambition, the bank was organized as a typical deposit bank with weight on deposit taking and granting credit, mostly by way of discounting of bills of exchange.

Table 8.1 also reveals the relative strength of commercial and savings banks in terms of assets. The commercial banks had 36 percent and savings banks 64 percent of the aggregate assets of these banks in 1870, whilst the shares were 51 percent and 49 percent in 1913. It was not until the turn of the century that the commercial banks exceeded the savings banks concerning assets. The average annual growth of total assets was 5.5 percent, which exceeded the yearly GDP growth rate. Inflation was rather low under the gold standard monetary regime; hence both commercial and savings banks increased their weight in the economy during the period under consideration.

Table 8.1 *Assets of savings and commercial banks in Norway, 1870–1913 (assets in mill. NOK).*

	Commercial banks		Savings banks	
	Assets	# of banks	Assets	# of banks
1870	51	8	91	252
1880	110	15	157	311
1890	172	33	221	350
1895	213	36	257	373
1900	427	76	344	413
1905	477	85	422	446
1910	669	102	570	487
1913	910	116	684	519

Source: Imset Matre, 1992; Norway, Central Bureau of Statistics, 1949.

150   Sverre Knutsen

Table 8.2 Relative distribution of credit in the Scandinavian countries (percent).

	Commercial banks			Savings banks			Other institutions		
	N	S	DK	N	S	DK	N	S	DK
1870	16	29	13	33	14	27	51	57	60
1880	18	33	16	36	15	26	46	52	58
1890	20	36	15	34	19	25	46	44	60
1900	30	50	18	30	18	23	40	32	60
1910	30	54	21	30	19	19	39	27	60
1913	34	–	22	30	–	18	36	–	60

Source: Nordvik, 1990.

As has been demonstrated, the Norwegian banking system on the eve of World War I was extremely decentralized, consisting of a large number of local, independent commercial and savings banks. The system was characterized by unit banking. None of the commercial banks operated nation-wide networks of branches, like for instance in Britain. Norway's oldest commercial bank, Christiania Bank, attempted to build branches outside the capital during the 1860s and 1870s, but met with fierce resistance from local élites and business communities, and had to drop the project. It should also be emphasized that the operation of the savings banks differed substantially from the way this type of bank worked, even in the neighboring countries. From the 1850s Norwegian Savings banks, although they were non-profit institutions, operated on the credit market as ordinary intermediaries, taking deposits and granting short- and to some extent medium-term loans to business. The development of savings banks to commercial bank substitutes continued in Norway after 1913, whereas in Denmark for instance, savings banks were prohibited by law (1919) from engaging in business activities.

These differences in the role of savings banks on the credit market in the Scandinavian countries are also revealed in Table 8.2. The savings banks' share of the credit market was significantly larger in Norway than in Sweden and Denmark during the whole period 1870–1913, whilst the weight of the commercial banks was considerably higher in Sweden.

When discussing the structure and development of the credit market, it is also necessary to make a few remarks on the role of government institutions. In 1850, 70 percent of known loans on the organized credit market were provided by government banks, or banks under political control, if we include the Bank of Norway. But already in 1860 the advances from private sector institutions exceeded public sector lending. This pattern continued and in 1900 the private sector's market share of the institutional credit market was 80 percent, while the shares of state banks and the Bank of Norway were reduced to 15 percent and 6 percent respectively.[3]

Let me then make a few remarks on the loan structure of the banks, as well as on their shares of the deposit market. As Table 8.3 indicates, an average of between 80 and 90 percent of the loans provided by the commercial banks were short term through the whole period in question. The long-term advances were predominantly different types of rollover credits exceeding one year to maturity. Mortgages were

Table 8.3 Commercial and savings banks in Norway: loans according to maturity (percent of total loans).

	Commercial banks			Savings banks		
	Short-term loans (%)	Long-term loans (%)	Total loans (mill. NOK)	Short-term loans (%)	Long-term loans (%)	Total loans (mill.NOK)
1870	95	5	41	n.a.	n.a.	72
1880	96	4	89	90	10	134
1890	83	17	130	67	33	173
1900	80	20	349	71	29	278
1910	89	11	524	66	34	449
1913	91	9	720	66	34	567

Source: Norway, Central Bureau of Statistics, 1949; Imset Matre, 1992.

rather rare. After 1880, the average share of long-term loans provided by the savings banks stabilized at around one third of total lending. Almost all of these loans were mortgages, and mostly loans for agricultural purposes. Until 1888, because of legislation against usury adopted in 1754 in Denmark–Norway, an interest rate ceiling was put on all loans other than acceptance credits. Hence, the rate of interest on mortgages had been pegged by the authorities and maximized at 5 percent in Norway until the restrictions were abandoned by a change in legislation in 1888. This deregulation made it more attractive for savings banks to provide loans on mortgages, and probably explains the change observed in Table 8.3.

The classification of short-term and long-term lending in Table 8.3 is based on formal criteria. All advances based on discounting of papers with less than one year to maturity have been classified as short term, whereas all other credits, chiefly mortgages, have been classified as long term. However, since the classification of credits as short term and long term is dependent on the applied taxonomy, it might be useful to explore the commercial banks' assets in more detail. We know for instance that loans, which formally are short term (less than one year to maturity), in reality can be transformed to a kind of roll-over credit and thus be altered to a form of long-term loan. Table 8.4, showing the commercial banks' balance sheet on an aggregate level, demonstrates that acceptance credits were an important part of their business. Besides discounting bills of commerce and advances against promissory notes, the banks also provided credits on so-called "bond bills."

These loans were formally short term, but very often they were transformed to medium- or long-term credits by renewal. "Bond bills" was a peculiar type of paper only in use in Denmark and Norway. This instrument was developed to circumvent the usury legislation already mentioned. If the transaction, however, was labeled "discounting" and not "loan," the lender could charge as high an interest rate as he could achieve in the credit market. Thus, it was customary that even long-term loans on personal liability were arranged formally as discounting of bond bills. If the plan was that the loan was going to be renewed on the date of maturity, it was a condition that the borrower had to pay a 10 percent installment on the loan in addition to the discount premium for the term of the bond bill. Table

Table 8.4 Composition of assets, Norwegian commercial banks (percent).

	1890	1900	1913
Norwegian and foreign bills and bond bills	47.0	32.0	21.1
Of which bond bills	–	11.0	15.7
Current drawing accounts	18.0	28.9	35.6
Mortgages	n.a.	9.5	7.5
Misc. credits (incl. mortgages)	12.0	–	–
Securities	n.a.	4.5	6.8
Norwegian and foreign banks	n.a.	8.5	9.3
Cash and Bank of Norway	n.a.	2.5	1.9
Other assets	–	3.1	2.1
Residual	23.0	–	–
Total assets (1,000 NOK)	172	427	910

Source: Norway, Central Bureau of Statistics, 1915; Imset Matre, 1992.

8.4 shows that 11 percent of the banks' assets in 1900, increasing to 15 percent in 1913, were loans on bond bills. This increase was chiefly a result of a new stamp duty on bills of exchange and promissory notes implemented in 1900. The available statistics for commercial banks is not specific enough to separate bills and bond bills before 1900. But Table 8.5, which shows data from the balance sheet of one of the major commercial banks, gives us a clue. DnC's ratio of bond bills to total assets fluctuated between 11 and 25 percent during the period 1870–1913. The 25 percent ratio in 1870 indicates the level before the removal of the interest rate ceiling in 1888. Table 8.5 reveals a rather low share for mortgages during the whole period, but the share of this type of credit was to some extent larger in other commercial banks after 1988, as indicated in Table 8.4.

Both Tables 8.4 and 8.5 reveal that credits on current drawing accounts increased as a share of total lending during the period in question. Although formally short term, even advances of this type were to an increasing extent "frozen," and in that way transformed into long-term loans of a sort (Knutsen, 1991). To sum up this analysis of the composition of assets during the period under consideration, there appears to have existed a mix of short-term and long-term lending, and thus an element of universalism in the Norwegian banking system prior to 1913. However, the banking system that emerged from the mid-nineteenth century to the eve of the World War I was not a complete system of universal banking. Large universal banks did not develop within the system. In fact the largest banks, like for example the DnC, concentrated their business on providing acceptance credit and other short-term lending. Since a modern securities market hardly existed before the turn of the century, the commercial banks were not engaged in the securities business. Hence, the narrow definition of universal banking discussed above does not match this system very well. On the other hand, our broader working definition fits better. The data revealed by our analysis suggest that the banking structure and the lending business should be characterized more as a hybrid-type, combining elements from continental-

Table 8.5 Composition of Den norske Creditbank's assets, 1870–1900 (percent).

	1870	1880	1900
Norwegian and foreign bills	37.5	55.5	36.4
Bond bills	24.7	11.2	18.3
Norwegian and foreign banks	9.5	6.9	3.6
Mortgages	3.5	–	–
Securities	12.4	5.6	6.0
Cash and Bank of Norway	5.2	5.2	5.0
Current drawing accounts	3.2	4.6	6.7
Other assets	4.0	11.0	24.0
Total assets (1,000 NOK)	10,332	24,575	46,760

Source: Hertzberg and Rygg, 1907.

style universalism with components from an Anglo-Saxon type of commercial banking. A doctoral thesis on Norwegian banking written by a German scholar in 1938 concluded its analysis of the character of Norwegian banking this way: "Man kann sagen, daß die gewöhnliche norwegische Privatbank nach einem System arbeitet, das zwischen dem englischen und dem deutschen Banksystem liegt" ("One can say that the Norwegian private bank works according to a system between the English and the German") (Stünkel, 1938).

Although registered savings banks until 1887 were given the privilege by law to charge 1 percentage point higher interest on mortgages than other banks, the discounting of bond bills was the main type of credit provided by this type of bank. In 1885, bond bills in fact made up 58 percent of their total assets. However, loans with real estate as collateral increased from 14 to almost 39 percent of total assets from 1885 to 1913, chiefly because the market now set the rate of interest. The lending policies of Norwegian savings banks clearly differed from the pattern prevailing in Britain and on the continent, where savings banks adopted a cautious lending policy favoring deposits in other banks, maintaining a large cash balance, lending extensively on mortgage, etc. The type of business that Norwegian savings banks were involved in even differed substantially from the practices of the savings banks prevailing in the other Scandinavian countries.

Banking regulation and supervision

We have seen that regulation had an important impact on the lending policies of savings banks. The first law on savings banks was enacted in 1824. The law gave savings banks, that registered various privileges. Among these were the already mentioned right to charge a higher rate of interest than other banks. Another privilege was exemption from taxation. The savings banks were also granted a monopoly to receive deposits from trust funds administering the money of minors and people declared incapable of managing their own affairs. The legislation defined savings banks as non-profit institutions. All profit had to be retained by the bank and added to its equity fund, except grants to purposes of public utility.

A new Act regulating the activities of savings banks was adopted in 1887. The main reason for this legislation was to strengthen the interests of depositors and to establish systems for internal control. The government did regard the protection of small savers and depositors as an important task. However, a government proposal to set up a separate, centralized supervisory agency for savings banks was turned down by the parliament. But in 1900, a savings bank inspectorate was finally established (Ecklund and Knutsen, 2000). The commercial banks were not regulated by separate legislation until 1924. This legislation followed a severe banking crisis. At the same time, a joint Bank Inspectorate was set up to organize supervision of the whole banking sector.[4]

Fragmentation of the deposit market

The main source of funding for both commercial and savings banks was deposits provided by savers or by firms, as in the case of commercial banks. When we turn to the liability side of the banks' balance sheets, the data in Table 8.6 illustrate further the strong position of the savings banks. Although their market share was decreasing, local non-profit banks like the savings banks took the lion's share of the individual deposit market during the whole period under consideration. Clearly, Norway had a fragmented deposit market. Thus, the savings banks were able to check the large commercial, joint-stock banks' inroad into deposits.

However, an interbank market involving foreign and domestic banks did in fact develop to a certain extent during the 1880s and 1890s, as can be seen from Tables 8.4 and 8.5. This market was a source for the commercial banks' short-term funding, but rather insignificant. It was not until during World War I that the interbank market really expanded to become an important part of the Norwegian financial system.

Cash and bills of exchange were the dominant means of payment in Norway during most of the nineteenth century. The bill of exchange functioned as a means of remittance, as current assets and as a credit instrument. However, this instrument was not very flexible as a means of payment, since it was necessary to calculate discount for every single transaction. Towards the end of the century, the use of the check expanded substantially. In 1897, legislation was passed on the use of

Table 8.6 Deposits at end of year in Norwegian credit institutions, 1870–1913.

	Savings banks	Per cent	Commercial banks	Per cent	Other institutions	Per cent	Total
1870	83	65	39	31	5	4	127
1880	140	61	79	34	10	4	229
1890	196	61	116	36	7	2	319
1900	311	54	257	45	6	1	574
1910	518	53	449	46	8	1	975
1913	620	51	592	48	13	1	1,225

Source: Nordvik, 1990.

checks.[5] The law was the result of joint preparatory work between Denmark, Norway and Sweden. Nonetheless, in order to become an efficient means of payment, it became necessary for the banks to organize a system of clearing. A clearing function was organized in England during the 1850s and during the 1880s in Germany. In Norway, Christiania Clearing House was established in 1898, including the capital's commercial banks and the Bank of Norway. The largest commercial banks in Christiania had correspondent relations with provincial banks. Thus a network for check clearing was in operation just before the turn of the century.

The political and institutional shaping of the hybrid structure

If we use the assessment of taxes distributed on central government and municipalities as a proxy to classify the type of polity, Norway can clearly be characterized as a "semi-centralized" polity, with strong local interests. In 1910 only 15 percent of taxes went to the central government, whereas 85 percent were municipal taxes.[6]

Legislation and regulatory power was centralized at the national level. But substantial space for self-governing was delegated to the municipalities in Norway, according to a reform in 1837. Moreover, the rural districts were given more representatives in the parliament, relative to the number of inhabitants, than the largest cities. The periphery in Norway was very influential and prevailed over central élites in many important matters because of its ability to form a united front along an ideological cleavage that overlapped the center–periphery cleavage.[7] This "united front" representing the interests of the periphery is still very influential in the Norwegian parliament even today. An illustrative case connected to banking is an initiative to establish a state-owned Post-office savings bank. During the 1880s, the parliament turned this proposal down several times. The majority was formed by MPs representing the periphery, and several of them were engaged in local savings banks. One of the major arguments against the plans for a postal savings bank, was that a centralized Postal Bank with headquarters in the capital would drain savings and capital from the local districts into the center. Actually, a postal savings bank wasn't established until 1948, and even then this was against fierce resistance in the parliament by representatives from the periphery (Bergh, 1975).

Taking into consideration that Norway was a semi-centralized polity with a strong savings bank sector capturing a significant share of the deposit market, the "Verdier thesis" would predict that for-profit banks should universalize. Furthermore, the banking structure should be characterized by unit banking. Our analysis has shown that a unit bank structure certainly emerged. However, the for-profit commercial banks developed hybrid-type banking practices.

The fragmentation of the deposit base and the emergence of a unit bank structure was evidently a matter of *mentalities*, underpinning informal institutions and codes of conduct, which made collective action in favor of the periphery possible on the national political level. The non-profit savings banks sector gained the privilege of political protection from both legislation and a parliament heavily influenced by a strong periphery. At the same time the absence of central, national banking legislation left local commercial banks free to develop according to an economic logic firmly rooted in a decentralized economy.

But why did for-profit banks only universalize to a limited extent? Fragmentation of the deposit base was, a necessary but not sufficient condition for the stabilization of universal banking (Verdier, 1997). Universal banks had an intrinsic propensity to develop a mismatch between the maturity profile of their mixed short-term and long-term assets with that of their liabilities. To maintain the confidence of the depositors, the existence of a liquidity guarantor was another condition that had to be met as well. Because industrial credits made up a substantial share of advances provided to the private sector by universal banks, they were particularly vulnerable to cyclical downturns. Financial fragility rose during the upturn because an increase in the share of industrial credits meant an increasing share of long-term loans. This boosted the risk of frozen assets, and thereby the danger to be forced to sell at unacceptable loss during the subsequent downturn. Combined with melting liabilities, implying that the actual terms of deposits grew shorter, the balance sheet mismatch deteriorated. Thus the existence of a central bank acting as a lender-of-last-resort was more vital to universal joint-stock banks than to specialized commercial banks. According to the analysis carried through above, the Norwegian case did not meet this condition during the formative period of the banking system 1870–1913, at least not before 1899–1900.

Banking structure, industrialization and economic growth

Although our analysis has shown that elements of mixed banking evolved in the Norwegian banking system, it did not meet Gerschenkron's picture of the classical universal bank at all – relatively large in size and characterized by equity holdings as well as presence in the decision-making bodies of client firms. Although the savings banks provided loans on mortgages, the banking system mainly provided short-term loans. In particular, it was typical that the Norwegian banks engaged in investment banking to a very limited extent. This type of activity was chiefly confined to the largest banks in Christiania and Bergen, who helped business clients to convert "frozen" short-term credits to long-term loans through arranging the issue of bearer bonds.

No doubt, in 1850 Norway belonged to the group of "extremely backward countries" as classified by Gerschenkron, although he didn't include Norway as a case. This placed Norway, Denmark and Sweden in the same group as for instance tsarist Russia. Taking for example the high rate of literacy, the far better conditions of the agricultural population and the growth and consolidation of democratic institutions in the Scandinavian countries, his typology has to be judged too rough and casual.

According to the Gerschenkronian industrial development thesis, the state should substitute the missing "prerequisites" of modern industrialization in a country like Norway, if we accept Norway being classified as an "extremely backward country" during most of the nineteenth century. As for the role of the state during the nineteenth century, state investments in industrial projects were minimal. The Norwegian state certainly exhibited some developmental traits during the nineteenth century, such as setting up so-called "discounting commissions" which provided business with short-term credit, especially during periods of economic distress. Another example is the Mortgage Bank of the Kingdom of Norway, established in 1852 and owned by the state. Initiatives and institutions like this may be seen as a compensation for backwardness and lack of prerequisites. However, the development that placed Norway among the 15–16 countries experiencing Kuznets-type "modern growth" was mainly rooted in the activities of Norwegian entrepreneurs. The most important role of the state was the shaping of a growth-inducing business environment. Being a liberal country, there was no need for direct state intervention in business to promote industrialization, and hence state involvement could stop at the building-up of the infrastructure and "facilitating the import of whatever foreign capital was needed" (Berend and Ránki, 1982).

The country started to industrialize from the mid-nineteenth century, but the breakthrough of industrialization did not occur until during the 1880s and 1890s (Hovland and Nordvik, 1997: 61–86). Rapid growth did occur in Norway during the period 1870–1914, to a great extent caused by industrialization. Moreover, this was a development common to all the Scandinavian countries. A recent comparative analysis of economic performance and convergence concludes that "Scandinavia outperformed the rest of Europe (and probably the rest of the world) in the late nineteenth century. Of that there can be no doubt" (O'Rourke and Williamson, 1999: 20). The evidence presented in this study also confirms the fact that Sweden and especially Denmark tended to outperform Norway and Finland, but not by much. Norway's compound real-GDP growth rate over the period 1870–1913 was 1.3 percent compared with Sweden's 1.5 percent and Denmark's 1.6 percent (Maddison, 1991). Scandinavian economic growth was also linked to considerable growth in real wages. The study by O'Rourke and Williamson concludes on this issue "no other country in our European sample underwent real wage growth even close to that of Sweden, Denmark or Norway."

How did this growth process relate to the banking system? At the juncture of its industrial breakthrough, Norway could hardly be classified as an "extremely backward" economy, but rather a "moderately backward" one. Consequently, Norway should have been a classical terrain for continental-type universal banks to exercise their developmental functions, hence giving impetus to industrial growth during this cycle of industrialization. But there is no such correlation in the Norwegian case, as our analysis so far has shown. In spite of the absence of large universal banks and with a modest degree of universalism in Norwegian banking practice, Norway experienced growth and modernization. Thus it seems that industrialization was financed by other means.

The scholarly discussion on the relationship between financial structure and economic development surged from the beginning of the twentieth century, starting with the works of Hilferding (Finance Capital 1910 [1981] and Schumpeter's *The*

Theory of Economic Development, published in Vienna in 1911. For Schumpeter, the banking system was regarded a key agent in economic growth by providing purchasing power to the entrepreneur and then making technological innovation possible. However, economists have offered remarkably different opinions regarding the importance of finance for economic growth. Alexander Gerschenkron, who focuses on the necessity of financial development for economic growth, has already been introduced. John Hicks pointed out that finance can play a positive "growth inducing role," and he even argued that the financial system played a critical role in initiating industrialization in England by facilitating the mobilization of capital for investment in fixed capital goods (Hicks, 1965; Hicks, 1969). Economic historians have also published several country-case studies. Rondo Cameron found in his pioneering study on banking in the early stages of industrialization that financial intermediaries played a significant role in promoting industrialization and growth. On the other hand, Joan Robinson asserts that "where enterprise leads finance follows" (Robinson, 1952a: 86). Several outstanding economists have time and again expressed the view that the finance–growth nexus is of no importance, among them Robert Lucas (1988: 6).

It has indeed been very difficult to establish a strong significant, positive link between financial structure and economic performance by using formal statistical analysis. Recent research has, however, been able to offer detailed arguments and evidence for the role of finance in promoting long-run growth. The research has also been able to establish the direction of causal links. One of these studies examines the nature of links between the intensity of financial intermediation and economic performance that operated in the United States, the United Kingdom, Canada, Norway and Sweden over the 1870–1929 period (Rousseau and Wachtel, 1998). The study finds that there is a positive relationship between increases in the intensity of financial intermediation and economic growth in all five countries. Moreover, the study demonstrates that the effect seems to go from the financial variables to real economic output, with little evidence of feedback from output to intermediation. Thus these findings support the hypothesis that finance matters.

However, our scope should not be confined to universal banks. We should rather take the whole financial system into consideration when we analyze its capacity to mobilize financial resources to productive investments. This view is even consistent with the conclusion of the seminal study by Cameron *et al.* in 1967: "One of the clearest lessons to be derived from this study of history is that no single model of a banking system is appropriate for all economies" (Cameron *et al.*, 1967: 318).

In the case I am exploring here, it is difficult to claim that the Norwegian financial system by and large was dysfunctional in terms of economic growth. Actually, it seems like the system served the economy adequately, at least during parts of the period under scrutiny.[8] The paramount question then is how long-term capital was mobilized to finance machinery and other capital equipment necessary to industrialize and modernize the economy. Between 1850 and 1900, the major part of long-term financing in Norwegian industrial firms came by way of retained earnings and equity accumulated by the entrepreneur, his family and/or partnership networks (Knutsen, 1990). An investigation of a sample of industrial firms in ship-building, mechanical engineering, electro-mechanical, and paper and pulp industries covering the period 1895 to 1913, showed that internal funds generated by retained profit were decidedly the main sources of the firms' long-term finance.[9] Detailed empirical studies exploring the mobilization of capital for investment purposes on a regional basis show that the mobilization of capital from private, non-institutionalized sources like partnership organizations in shipping, combined with a flexible system of local savings banks and commercial banks, were sufficient to secure strong regional economic growth during the period 1860–1914.[10] Essentially, the decentralized Norwegian unit-bank system was first and foremost a credit system for local trade and shipping, agriculture and small-scale industrial firms.

The securities market was not an important source for business firms to obtain long-term external capital during the period in question. In Norway, the Stock Exchange played a rather modest role in mobilizing capital for business through most of the nineteenth century. But for a period around the turn of the century, the Christiania Stock Exchange did increase its importance as a source of investment capital. Both issues of new capital and the trade in the secondary market increased steeply through the 1890s. Industrial enterprises, as well as banks, shipping companies and construction firms raised long-term finance in the capital market. Particularly for shipping companies, the Christiania Stock Exchange became an important source for financing the transformation from sail to steamships during the period from the late 1890s up to World War I. An increasing number of partnership organizations as well as individually owned firms, which was the prevalent type of ownership in Norwegian shipping, were transformed to joint-stock form during this period.

From around 1900, Norway experienced the start-up and expansion of large-scale electrochemical and metallurgical industries. These new industrial undertakings were very capital intensive. The Norwegian system of small local unit banks was not very well able to serve industry's demand for capital. But foreign capital markets, and especially foreign direct investments became a substitute for the lack of ability of Norwegian banks to provide sufficient capital for the huge investments in mining, hydro-electric power stations and power-intensive industries such as aluminum, carbide and nitrogen-based fertilizers (Table 8.7). Thus, the institutional environment shaped by the government by the way of modernization of legislation around the turn of the century, was very conducive to

Table 8.7 Holdings abroad of Norwegian share capital, 1900–13 (mill. NOK).

	1900	1905	1906	1907	1908	1909	1910	1913
Total share capital	429	507	539	596	678	695	757	954
Holdings abroad	30	37	65	105	140	155	170	210
Holdings abroad (%)	7.0	7.3	12.1	17.6	20.7	22.3	22.5	22.0

Source: Skånland, 1967.

attracting foreign direct investments to build up new large-scale industry. Furthermore, foreign banks became important providers of credit to expanding energy-intensive large industry. During the period 1895 to 1910 it is estimated that more than 20 percent of Norwegian gross capital formation was financed by borrowing abroad (Knutsen, 1991). In 1909, 39 percent of total share capital in Norwegian companies in manufacturing industry was held by foreigners (Stonehill, 1965). This shows, among other things, that the mobilization of capital to business should not be studied in a purely national context.

Summary and conclusion

The main theme of this chapter has been the emergence of the specific structure of the Norwegian banking system, which developed during the formative period 1870–1913. The study finds that the banking structure exhibited two distinctive features. First, the Norwegian banking system was characterized by a fragmented and decentralized unit-bank system. Local non-profit savings banks played a significant role within the system, and even acquired a substantial part of the market for deposits. Also the lending policies of the savings banks make it reasonable to characterize them as commercial bank substitutes. Second, although we find elements of universal banking, it was only typical of Norwegian banking practice to a limited extent. Rather, the banking structure and the lending business should be characterized more as a hybrid-type, combining elements from continental-style universal banking with components from an Anglo-Saxon type of commercial banking. The main feature of the commercial banks' lending practice is the provision of formally short-term credits. However, parts of these nominal short-term advances in reality were transformed to more long-term "roll over" credits. Our findings of elements of universal banking have to be seen in the light of our working definition of universal banking as characterized by "the mix of short- and long-term assets and liabilities." A narrower definition of universal banking, emphasizing the organizational blend of commercial loan and deposit business with investment banking does not fit the Norwegian banking system very well during the period in question. Large universal banks did not develop, and Norwegian banks only engaged in investment banking on a very limited scale.

How can we explain this development of a decentralized unit-bank structure? Our analysis has shown that Norway, being a semi-centralized polity with a strong and politically influential periphery, was very conducive to the fragmentation of the deposit market, and thus in favor of the building-up of local unit-banking. In turn this balance of power was conducive to a strong savings banks sector, as well as the development of local commercial banks. However, the development of branch banking found very limited scope for growth. But why did for-profit banks only universalize to a limited extent? According to Daniel Verdier's approach, fragmentation of the deposit market was a necessary, but insufficient, condition for the stabilization of universal banking (Verdier, 1997). In addition, a second condition had to be met: the existence of a liquidity guarantor. This chapter has shown that the Bank of Norway did not develop a central bank function until the turn of the century, when it acted as a lender-of-last-resort during the *"Kristiania-Chrash."* During the banking crisis of the late 1880s it didn't act as a liquidity guarantor at all. Our analysis points this out as the decisive factor to explain why a hybrid structure developed instead of stabilizing universal banking. I thus find that it is necessary to take institutional and political variables into consideration in order to explain the development of the distinct traits of the Norwegian banking system.

The essay also gives an assessment of Alexander Gerschenkron's late-industrialization thesis and his view on the necessity of financial development for economic growth. He emphasized that large universal banks were the crucial vehicles of channeling savings to industry in "moderately backward" countries in the second half of the nineteenth century. In some "extremely backward" countries – most conspicuously Russia – private banking was not sufficiently developed to fill this role. Hence the state had to fulfill the function of universal banks. My findings offer support for Gerschenkron's idea (partly building on Schumpeter, partly on Marx) that a rapidly growing financial system can play a key role in promoting industrialization and economic growth. On the other hand, this chapter clearly demonstrates that this financial system does not have to be a system rooted in universal banking, and particularly not a system characterized by large universal banks.

Notes

1   Actually, genuine universal banks did not emerge in the Norwegian banking sector until the 1970s–80s, when deregulation, financial innovation and technological change caused extensive despecialization.
2   DnC and Bergen Bank merged in 1989 to become the largest commercial bank in Norway and was named Den norske Bank (DnB). The second largest commercial bank, Christiania Bank, was acquired by Merita Nordbanken in 2000 to become a part of the pan-Nordic and Swedish-dominated financial group named Nordea.
3   Calculated from data in Imset Matre, 1992: Table 2a.
4   Ecklund and Knutsen, 2000, give a detailed description and analysis of Norwegian financial supervision during the twentieth century. The book was the result of a research project funded by the Norwegian Banking, Insurance and Securities Commission, the Bank of Norway and Oslo Stock Exchange.
5   Lov av 3. august 1897 nr. 8 "Om visse anvisninger (checks)."
6   Historical statistics of Norway, 1978.
7   The "united front" concept, cf. Verdier, 1996: 3.
8   Although the financial system mobilized enough financial resources to promote a growth level sufficient to bring about modern growth, systemic weaknesses can well be an important factor in explaining, for example, differences in growth patterns among the Scandinavian countries. However, I am not going to discuss such a hypothesis any further here.
9   Knutsen, 1992. The sample is not a representative one, and does not give a basis for statistically significant inference.
10 Nordvik, Nerheim, and Brandal, 1989. The region explored in this book is Rogaland County in the southwest of Norway. Rogaland is today the center of the off-shore industry in Norway.

9   Universal banking in Russia

Don K. Rowney

Introduction

Large-scale, rapid industrialization is generally agreed to have begun only in the mid-1880s in Russia, continuing, with interruptions, until World War I. The entire era of market-driven industrialization in Russia thus lasted only for one generation, and it was decisively halted by the economic collapse and changed policies that began during World War I and continued into the 1920s.[1] Following the Bolshevik seizure of power (1917), banking was the first industry to be nationalized. Thereafter, in a legal sense, the state became the only banker in the country and, during the 1920s, banking became increasingly specialized and circumscribed. As we shall see, this was not the first time that the state played a predominant role in Russian banking.

One cannot describe the whole period from the mid-1880s to the beginning of World War I as an era of uninterrupted, rapidly increasing industrial output. The 1890s, a decade of exceptional growth (with annual average industrial growth of between 8 percent and 9 percent), witnessed what Alexander Gerschenkron termed "spurts" in the output of iron ore, coal, petroleum, steel and other products – developments that were driven by linkages with intensive investment in railways (Gerschenkron, 1962; Gerschenkron, 1947). During this era also, Owen identifies one of five major growth cycles in the history of Russian corporations (Owen, 1991b; Owen, 1991a: 199). But a recession, beginning in 1899, the costly Russo-Japanese War (1904–06), and the Revolution of 1905, each dealt major setbacks to economic growth which only began to resume in 1907–08.

During this early cycle of industrialization, the State Bank (Gosbank) was the country's leading investor in industry, especially the railways. In addition the Russian state guaranteed a high proportion of private Russian and foreign investment.[2] The State Bank worked with major private banks, both domestic and foreign, throughout this period to stimulate industrial growth through long- and short-term investment and to reduce volatility in securities prices (Gindin, 1980). In the years between the end of the Russo–Japanese War and the beginning of World War I, however, investment banking is thought by some to have been taken over by several big St Petersburg commercial banks which were organized as limited liability corporations. These banks also handled substantial amounts of short-term commercial credit and provided other banking services for selected clients. As we shall see below, this view of the increasing importance of commercial banks in investment banking needs qualification – particularly as it applied to the special circumstances of financing commercial and manufacturing enterprises in Moscow and the role of foreign banks and investors. There is also a major question to be addressed that concerns the continued vigorous intervention of the state.[3]

In this last period of pre-Revolutionary industrialization, Gerschenkron thought he saw a "great *volte face*" in the state's role in industrialization (Gerschenkron, 1947; Gerschenkron, 1960). The state was withdrawing from its interventionist strategies, he thought, and Russian development was taking on a more standard European, less "Asiatic," aspect as compared with other industrial societies.

In the following pages I shall try to characterize the rise of universal banking during this period by focusing on a body of data originally published by the Imperial Ministry of Finances in combination with the findings of work already completed by scholars who (unlike me) are *bona fide* economic historians. These data focus both on the supply side of the investment equation – the deposits and savings that financed both the state's and the banks' investments – and on the demand side, where investment in industrialization, the building of infrastructure and a defense budget comparable to those of much wealthier states created huge markets for capital.

Russian banking before World War I

If we simply follow the system of classification used by the Imperial Ministry of Finances, then banking – or the activities of bank-like institutions – in Russia was divided into four major tiers and at least seven or eight formally defined subdivisions within these tiers after the turn of the twentieth century.[4] In Tables 9.1a and 9.1b we summarize this structure for the banking industry in the early twentieth century. As the reader will note, on the deposit side the four segments were identifiable as follows: the State Bank, large commercial banks, mutual credit societies, and state savings windows (*sberkassy*). On the loans side, the picture was more complicated, owing, in part, to special characteristics and influence of Russian mortgage banking and to a large variety and very large number of small institutions not technically denominated as banks by law but included by the Ministry in its data on the banking system.

Gosbank: the Imperial State Bank

The State Bank was founded under statute in 1860 but it was not assigned the role of sovereign bank of issue until 1897 in connection with the program of Ministers of Finances Vyshnegradski and Witte to join the élite international club of currencies on the gold standard.[5] The State Bank had headquarters in St Petersburg, a main office in Moscow and, at the turn of the century, some 122 provincial offices and 600 state treasury affiliates scattered across the Empire. In 1900 Gosbank reported total deposits (including current accounts) of some rs. 594 million, about 41 percent of the total reported by all major banking organizations in Russia. By 1913 this

Table 9.1a Deposits in Russia, 1900–13 (includes demand and term).

Bank tier/name	Deposits 1900 (millions of rs.)	Percent of total	Deposits 1913 (millions of rs.)	Percent of total
I. State bank	594.1	27.2%	1,228.2	19.3%
II. Commercial banks	570.5	26.1%	2,539.0	39.9%
II. Mutual credit societies	168.3	7.7%	869.0	13.6%
II. Municipal communal banks	97.2	4.5%	180.0	2.8%
IV. State savings	751.9	34.5%	1,549.8	24.4%
Total	**2,182.0**	**100.0%**	**6,366.0**	**100.0%**

Source: Anfimov and Korelin (eds), 1995: 158–71.

Table 9.1b Loans in Russia, 1900–13 (includes short- and long-term).

Bank tier/name	Loans 1900 (millions of rs.)	Percent of total	Loans 1913 (millions of rs.)	Percent of total
I. State bank	397.1	8.6%	1,064.0	9.5%
II. Commercial banks	879.0	18.9%	3,476.5	30.9%
II. Mutual credit societies	212.9	4.6%	864.9	7.7%
II. Municipal communal banks	127.5	2.7%	246.7	2.2%
III. Mortgage banks (rural)	1,756.0	37.8%	3,536.3	31.4%
III. Mortgage banks (urban)	1,196.8	25.8%	1,851.8	16.5%
III. Personal property lenders	27.0	0.6%	68.6	0.6%
IV. Peasant communal societies	46.7	1.0%	100.5	0.9%
IV. Zemstvo banks	n. d.	n. d.	37.0	0.3%
Total	**7,276.1**	**100.0%**	**16,300.4**	**100.0%**

Source: ibid.

amount had risen to rs. 1,228.2 million, but the proportion had fallen to about 26 percent. We shall return to this point.

The story of the Gosbank's role in saving Russian manufacturers in moments of crisis is an interesting component of the broad narrative of delayed industrial development, illustrating, as it does, both the state's strong commitment to development and its tolerance for favoritism and corruption. First, one must recognize that, throughout the period under discussion, such intervention was broadly illegal (*neustavnyi* in Russian bureaucratese). I.F. Gindin, a historian whose career was devoted in equal measure to narrating comprehensively and brilliantly the development of the

Russian banking industry during early industrialization, and illuminating the self-serving and frequently corrupt practices of Russian and foreign financiers, offers a detailed chronicle of both state advances to firms in crisis and their illegal nature.

For example, considering only the metal fabrication and machine construction industries, Gindin identified some 21 major advances by the state amounting to rs. 8.8 million in the years 1873–78, a period of financial crisis. During the decade of the 1880s, when the great manufacturing boom began, he identified an additional 12 major advances totaling rs. 19 million. Altogether, during the period from 1873 to 1892, Gindin cited some 48 major, illegal state loans to metal and machine manufacturing firms amounting to more than rs. 40 million (Gindin, 1960: 205). Were these interventions entirely arbitrary and thus open to crass favoritism and even corruption? Perhaps. Given that Kafengauz identified some 1,414 firms in this branch of industry with an annual output, by value, ranging from rs. 167 million (1887) to rs. 234 million (1892), the 48 rescues that actually occurred, and even the rs. 40 million that were advanced, seem likely to have been responses to special – possibly privileged – cases (Kafengauz, 1994: Table 8, 418). What seems clear is that there was no firm State Bank or Ministry of Finances policy, broadly agreed and scrupulously followed; on the contrary, the formal policy was that the practice was illegal.

Turning now to a consideration of the State Bank as a banker's bank, it is critical to note that, before the early twentieth century, the Gosbank was not only the lender of last resort to troubled commercial banks, it was also their competitor, stepping, as we have seen, into crisis situations that, in other circumstances (or in other countries) would have been addressed either by private banks or by a market that would have forced bankruptcy on firms in crisis. After the adoption of the gold standard in 1897 and the State Bank's assumption of the role of bank of issue, this situation began to change; Gosbank gradually became more recognizable as a banker's bank. Nevertheless, after emphasizing the size of the State Bank's liabilities to firms and individuals following the turn of the century, the author of one of the best studies of Russian finance policy could write that, "the Gosbank was certainly not just a bankers' bank during the period of inconvertible paper currency and after 1897 it became one only very gradually and incompletely."[6]

In addition to its roles as a lender of last resort (in which it aided commercial banks) and as a direct participant in commercial and capital markets (in which it competed with commercial banks), the State Bank was also a large purchaser of discount paper (i.e. it acted as a rediscounter) from commercial banks right up to the end of the Old Regime. In this respect the State Bank was a major source of liquidity for commercial banks. Among other advantages, this made the maintenance of commercial banks' obligatory reserves less onerous.

Commercial banks

In the next tier were the commercial banks, many of which were organized as limited liability corporations and registered as such with the state on what Owen describes as a "concessionary" basis (Owen, 1991b). This characteristic, which required specific state confirmation for the creation of each corporation and calls attention to the state's intrusive and paternalistic values, perhaps had more to do with the Russian bureaucracy's reluctance to allow the founding of corporations than it did with banking. This is a point of great importance to Owen. But the reader should note that the practice seems to have been common both in Europe and the United States during much of the nineteenth century. Finally, one might also include investment, or trading, houses in this group. However, while they were important sources of investment capital to some firms (especially in Moscow) these organizations did not conform to banking regulations and the Ministry of Finances did not consider them to be banks.[7]

During the entire early industrialization period, the numbers and fortunes of commercial banks rose and fell in tandem with the vigor of the economy. This fact alone emphasizes the irregular and somewhat unpredictable nature of the State Bank's backing of commercial banks. At the turn of the century the most important of these firms had their headquarters in St Petersburg (thirteen in all) with eight more in Moscow operating under somewhat different conditions; several of these maintained branches in other parts of the country. There were, in addition, some 30 commercial banks located in other cities throughout the Russian Empire by 1914 but these provincial banks were much smaller, on average, than those in the two capitals. (See Table 9.4, below.)

Gindin thought that state roles vis-à-vis commercial banks were divided into three main periods before the introduction of the gold standard. During the first of these (1860s) the state stimulated the growth of banks; during the second, it struggled to save only certain banks in the wake of the major crisis of 1873.[8] The result of this action was that the number of commercial banks declined from 42 in 1873 to 35 in 1884 (Gindin, 1960: 391). During the third period (1880s and 1890s), state policy settled into a system of management and oversight that restricted the formation of new banks and that effectively encouraged existing banks to take greater risks by investing in corporate shares and bonds, for example. Between 1878 and 1894 the State Bank's credits to commercial banks averaged rs. 35 million annually. In order to put these numbers into perspective it is useful to realize that, between 1880 and 1893, the number of commercial banks was reduced to 33 in Russia. Their total capitalization averaged a little more than rs. 122 million and their total deposits were approximately rs. 246 million.[9] Advances from Gosbank, in other words, constituted a substantial proportion of the worth of the commercial banks and compared very favorably with the backing offered to the metalworking industry during roughly the same period. Gindin, an Old Bolshevik with some of the instincts of a classical economist, thought that if the banks had been left to sink or swim without state support after the 1873 crisis, the entire system would have been stronger. This was his interpretation of the experience of banking in Germany following the same economic crisis of 1873 (Gindin, 1960: 392).

As Tables 9.1a and 9.1b indicate, commercial banks' role in the deposit and loan systems, while large, was not of a scale in the national economy that we might expect to find in more industrialized societies. In 1900 all of these institutions together accounted for about a quarter of deposits into the entire system and only about 12 percent of the loans. Tables 9.1a and 9.1b show that commercial banks' roles as repositories for deposits and as sources of capital were increasing – both absolutely and even by comparison with mortgage banks and the State Bank. Between 1900 and 1913, their deposits increased by more than four-fold and their loans increased more than three-fold. Similarly their ranking in the system rose – from a little more than 25 percent of deposits in 1900 to nearly 40 percent in 1913 and from 12 percent of loans to more than 20 percent in 1913. This shift was apparently achieved at the expense of most other types of institution; municipal banks, mortgage institutions and all small credit organizations suffered by comparison during the 1908–14 boom era. Even the State Bank, while its loans portfolio increased somewhat, experienced a relative decline in deposits.

Mortgage banks

On the next tier were the mortgage institutions, including two large, state-sponsored bodies – the Nobles Land Bank and the Peasants Land Bank. These organizations dominated certain banking roles, largely owing to the gross structure of the national economy whose income continued to depend heavily on land use. The state land banks depended for capitalization not upon depositors but principally upon the state, and the rules that governed their lending operations explicitly mixed social and economic policies (meant to support the social *status quo*) with economic tactics that were rooted in the market value of land. Thus, for example, both banks attempted to value mortgaged land at market prices but they were also constrained by rules that specified *who* could buy land and to whom it could be sold, a practice thought by some to have distorted the market.

In addition to the two large state-sponsored lenders, there was a small number of private mortgage (*ipotechnyi kreditnyi*) banks organized to make loans to holders of real estate. These included a few commercially organized and incorporated mortgage institutions (about ten in the early twentieth century); most of these bodies catered to the landed gentry and larger landholders throughout the empire and, perhaps, offered the opportunity to buyers and sellers of circumventing the rules that governed sales mortgaged by the big state institutions. While most of this business focused on rural property, a few firms served the needs of the growing population of private urban real property owners. These organizations were not numerous, but they grew rapidly in the twentieth century. One could also include among these firms that made loans secured by real urban property a few municipal communal banks (Anfimov and Korelin (eds), 1995: 164).

Small credit and deposit organizations: savings in Russia during early industrialization

The fourth tier of bank-like operations was occupied by so-called "small credit" organizations. There were thousands of these and the dynamics of the market and the state's intrusions into it seemed to have changed their structure and operation during the early twentieth century.

As Table 9.1b shows, the largest share of savings deposits was accounted for by the State Savings *Kassy* whose hundreds of teller windows led directly back to the State Bank, while a truly leonine share of domestic loans was accounted for by the state mortgage banks in this still largely agricultural economy.

Mutual credit, small loan-savings, and so-called petty credit associations grew very rapidly in the twentieth century, although, by comparison with commercial banks, they accounted for a relatively small proportion of banking business. For example, in 1900 there were some 117 mutual credit societies scattered mainly across European Russia. By 1914 there were nearly ten times as many (1,108). To some extent this shift was owing to a change in state policy in 1910. In response to criticism of the use that was being made of deposits in State Savings *Kassy*, new legislation mandated that rs. 20 million from state savings should be invested annually in small credit and loan-savings organizations (Miller, 1967: 91). As we shall see, *kassy* roles in banking varied, not only over time, but from one economic region to another.

Municipal banks began to be established following legislation introduced on behalf of towns and cities in the Russian Empire in 1870. They generally served the economic development needs of commercial enterprises in rapidly growing provincial towns and cities during industrialization. In 1900 there were 241 of these organizations with deposits of rs. 39 million; by 1914 their number had increased to 319 with deposits of rs. 46.2 million.

While savings deposited in small institutions accounted for only about one third of total deposits, they represented – with taxes, tariffs and foreign funds – one of the most important sources of investable capital. It is worthwhile, then, to look briefly at the distribution of these institutions across the western portions of the Empire. Following A.P. Korelin, we can divide them into three main types: cooperative credit and loan-savings associations, peasant small savings and loan communal associations, and land association (*zemstvo*) savings banks (Korelin, 1988: 91). Table 9.2 summarizes the relative financial importance of the different types of small credit institutions at the beginning of the second decade of the twentieth century. In the light of concern over the degree of continuing penetration of the state into the national economy after 1905, it is worth emphasizing that both the Loan–Savings Partnerships (*Ssudo-sberegatel'nyie Tovarichestva*) and the State Savings *Kassy* (*Gosudarstvennye Sberegatel'nye Kassy*) were chartered, financed and staffed by the state. Moreover, while the "Loan–Savings Partnerships" were cooperatives, or collectives, of investors and borrowers that would normally choose to focus their attention on local needs, the State Savings *Kassy* were straightforwardly organized as savings windows through which the savings of hundreds of thousands passed directly to St Petersburg.[10] These grew astronomically at the turn of the century to more than 8,000 by 1914. They were distributed in provinces throughout the Empire (and they survived, by the way, throughout the entire Soviet era). In the early twentieth century the *kassy* alone accounted for about 70 percent of all savings in savings accounts in the Russian Empire. Even after the policy change of 1910, noted above, this money was overwhelmingly invested in state long-term debt, railway loans and mortgages (Miller, 1967:

Table 9.2 Deposits in small savings, municipal and mutual banks in Russia, 1909–10.

Type of institution	Deposits: 1909–10 in roubles	Proportion of small institutions total
Zemstvo Kassy	9,878,339	0.5%
Peasant loan-savings partnerships	163,071,877	8.4%
Peasant societies for small credit	34,231,036	1.8%
Municipal banks	102,653,115	5.2%
Mutual credit associations	245,491,200	12.6%
State savings Kassy	1,390,260,281	71.5%
Total	**1,945,885,848**	**100.0%**

Source: Russia, *Ezhegodnik Ministerstva Finansov, 1911*, 388–93. Includes St Petersburg, Moscow, all provinces of European Russia and Poland but excludes Caucasus and Transcaucasus and Finland.

Appendix, Table K: 154). Rapid growth of the state-owned *kassy* must have been owing, in part, to favorable yield and hazard differentials combined with rising money incomes during industrialization. The law enhanced the competitiveness of these organizations by exempting savers from some capital gains taxes and registration fees. The state guaranteed deposits and the offices of these organizations were much more numerous and conveniently located than even those of mutual credit or city banks (Miller, 1967: 88–93, 153–6).

As Table 9.2 shows, the total in small institution savings accounts reached rs. 1.4 billion in 1909–10, or some 54 percent of Gregory's estimate of net investment.[11] To say whether Russian savings, early in the twentieth century, were "normal" for an economy at that stage of development is obviously difficult. If one combines savings deposits in all organizations with commercial bank deposits (rs. 1.7 billion) and divides by Gregory's figure for net investment in 1910 of rs. 2.6 billion, one finds that savings and commercial bank deposits amounted to about 1.4 times net investment (Gregory, 1982: Table A.2, 146–7). This figure is very high by comparison with other estimates for levels of savings in early industrialization.[12] Savings alone – that is, deposits in small institutions and loan-savings associations – in 1910 or 1911 were a bit more than 70 percent of net investment. Using rs. 1.9 billion as an estimate for savings, moreover, one finds that, in combination with commercial bank balances, the total equaled about 20 percent of net national product (NNP).[13] Savings alone, however, amounted to about 11 percent of NNP in Russia in 1910. In France, the same figure would have been about 18 percent of NNP, while in Germany it was much more, about 37 percent of NNP.[14]

Whether or not Russia may have been comparable to other early industrializers in terms of the propensity to save, we should emphasize the fact that the difference between the total of savings and net investment first of all shows that indigenous savers, small savers, and provincial savers played a significant role in economic investment in Russia during early industrialization. In the light of these observations one can more easily see where foreign investment capital, discussed below, went.

Table 9.3 Savings per capita in Zemstvo, non-Zemstvo and Polish provinces, Russia, 1909–10.

Regional group	Total of savings (1,000 of rs.)	Total of population (1,000s)	Savings per capita
Zemstvo (n=34)	1,373,794	85,458	16
Non-zemstvo (n=16)	454,450	35,130	16
Poland (n=10)	117,250	12,467	8

Source: see Table 9.2

It made up the difference between the comparatively meager resources of domestic savings and the needs of capital-hungry industry. But one can also see that, in terms of national or per capita income, there was significant domestic saving in Russia and that capital was available for investment independent of the money that foreigners were willing to risk.

We finally note, from Table 9.3, variation in savings input that appears to have been rooted in some set of regional differences in the Empire. Savings rates per capita during the last industrial spurt before World War I were the same (at 16 roubles, on average, per person per province) for the 34 ethnically Russian *zemstvo*, or self-governing, provinces and the 16 relatively non-Russian provinces without *zemstvo* administrations. The big difference was between these provinces and the 10 provinces of the former Grand Duchy of Warsaw where savings rates were half the per capita level of those elsewhere. This is unexpected since it can be shown that savings levels, across the whole of the western Empire, depended directly upon the size of urban population in a given province and factory output by value.[15] From the economic and demographic data, that is, one would have predicted that the relatively urban industrial provinces of central Poland would have had higher rates of savings than the non-*zemstvo* provinces and even many of the *zemstvo* provinces in European Russia proper. The fact that this was not the case underscores the need to penetrate beneath the surface of the national data and to take account of regional variation. In the following paragraphs we will see a much more striking example of the importance of regional variation when we focus on the difference in forms of finance for commercial and manufacturing enterprises.

Segmentation of the Russian banking market

From Tables 9.1a and 9.1b one can see that the Russian banking market was segmented, or compartmentalized, in the early twentieth century. Commercial banks wrote few mortgages; mortgage banks accepted no deposits. Moreover, if we consider real estate loans, for instance, we see a further illustration of segmentation; commercial banks could make advances with real estate as collateral but they tended to do so in limited quantities and for very limited purposes.[16] This huge market was left instead to the two government-sponsored (and subsidized) land banks and a few smaller private organizations that, probably owing to competition from the state banks which focused on rural property, were more successful in towns than in the country.

Small credit associations, the most ubiquitous form of bank-like organization, catered to the needs of small savers and short-term, retail borrowers. In addition, as we have just seen, there is some evidence that savings markets, at least, were segmented geographically or, perhaps, even culturally. Small savers in Russia (as opposed to, say, Poland) tended to take advantage of the security, convenience and higher rates of State Savings *Kassy*.

But this may have been changing. In 1900, 35 percent of all national savings were from small savers in the state savings *kassy* and only 26 percent were held by commercial banks. By 1913, the situation was basically reversed; 24 percent were in *kassy* and nearly 40 percent in the commercial banks. Of course, these latter were not likely to have been from small savers. Nevertheless, the change, discussed below, that saw commercial banks taking investment banking away from the State Bank was significant, finding additional resonance in the generally increasing role of commercial banks as repositories of savings, and giving these institutions greater flexibility as lenders.

At the end of the recession and political upheaval after the turn of the century, the big commercial bank companies operationally subdivided into two distinct categories (Gindin, 1948: 179). In a manner similar to previous recovery cycles, a small group of St Petersburg commercial banks became, during the twentieth century, what we might (by a stretch) today call "universal" banks, providing clearing house services, demand deposits and other commercial credits together with long-term resources to finance the fixed capital expenditures of large manufacturing and commercial enterprises, especially corporations. These last, since they increasingly involved accepting equities and bonds of debtor firms as collateral, involved the banks in underwriting corporate equities in a way that went beyond helping them to float share and bond offerings in the first place. The other commercial banks, including one large institution in St Petersburg (Volga-Kama) and most of those in Moscow, made relatively modest large-scale, long-term commitments of capital and securities-based investments – especially to corporations.

This division of interests is explained in the histories of Russian banking in several ways. First, note that the division described here argues that, while the state was the dominant player in these investment roles before the turn of the century, this function devolved into the hands of the commercial banks gradually after the turn of the century and, after the Revolution of 1905, rapidly into the hands of the nine St Petersburg banks. As Gindin shows, for example, the share of all commercial banks in the "main assets and liabilities" of the commercial credit system rose by 75 percent between 1893 and 1900 but that of the State Bank increased by 89 percent. Then, during the recession and civil strife of 1900–08, commercial banks' share rose by 45 percent while that of the State Bank actually declined by 20 percent. Finally, between 1908 and 1914, commercial banks' share rose by 176 percent while that of the State Bank increased by only 84 percent.[17]

The period 1905–08 was a moment of great vulnerability for the imperial state. The war with Japan was being lost; the gold standard was threatened; the state budget was under increasing pressure with no respite in sight, given the ongoing destruction of military equipment and economic infrastructure; riots and mutinies were common and, not surprisingly, foreign investors were leaving in droves.

Some historical narratives and memoirists of the day suggest that the strategies chosen by the Ministry of Finance to resolve the looming financial crisis played a role in the emergence of the nine universal banks in St Petersburg (Kokovtsov, 1935: 187–92; Crisp, 1976b; Crisp, 1976a: 141–7, Table 5.16). These banks had played a limited role as providers of long-term credit before 1908, but it is from that year forward that they became major forces in this market.

Still, the comparatively small interest of Moscow commercial banks in this form of investment requires explanation to which we shall now devote attention. Apart from the largest manufacturing corporations, enterprises in Moscow tended to be more closely held than those in St Petersburg. Family ownership, often through what we may call limited partnerships (*tovarichestva*), was prominent and conservative management was legendary (Ruckman, 1984: 48–108; Rieber, 1982: 133–218).

Questions that have to do with the formation of corporations in Russia turn out to be central to an understanding of the rise of universal banking. Owen says that each spurt of corporate formation in Russia was precipitated by a fall in rates and that savers, looking for better returns on their savings, chose corporate securities rather than savings accounts; this improved equities market, in turn, stimulated the formation of corporations (Owen, 1991b). The spurt of corporation and industrial growth of 1908–14 may not bear this perspective out.

First, Owen notwithstanding, savings increased substantially during this period that also witnessed corporate growth. It is true, however, that savings tended to move out away from state *kassy* and into commercial banks and mutual credit societies (see Table 9.1a). Second, this period actually coincided with renewed government efforts to attract foreign investors with high rates, as we shall see below. I am suggesting that it may be misleading to pin variation in corporation formation on interest rate policies in the twentieth century. Here we explore the possibility that the spurt in incorporation of firms from 1908 forward may have had more to do with the underlying conditions in which capital was available and with regional variations in the market.

We advance the hypothesis that, in St Petersburg, there existed a synergy of relation between corporate entrepreneurs and commercial bankers that interactively supported both the rapid rise of corporations and the rapid increase in long-term bank loans.[18] In Moscow, we suggest, alternative forms of commercial and manufacturing enterprise structure made such a synergy impossible – a circumstance that segmented the capital market and defended the self-interest of family-based commercial and manufacturing organizations. Slow corporation growth in Russia outside of St Petersburg and the national economic network dominated by Petersburg firms, we argue, may have had more to do with the self-interest of existing manufacturing firms (especially with the influential and powerful family firms in Moscow) than with the state's suspicion of new enterprise or variation in rates.[19]

In 1900, 17 percent of all factory labor in Russia was employed in Moscow Province and 16 percent of factory output by value originated there – far more than anywhere else in the Russian Empire (Vronkova *et al.*, 1992: 55–65, Table 30). Second place, in the same year, was occupied by St Petersburg where 8 percent of factory workers and 10 percent of output by value originated. By 1908 the ratios, but not the standings, had changed. Moscow still occupied first place. There were 1,295 manufacturing enterprises, with 314,476 workers (15 percent of the total) and 13 percent of output by value – nearly 600 million roubles. With 824 enterprises, 166,908 workers, and about rs. 450 million in output, St Petersburg retained its second place standing. Yet, in the 1906–13 period, almost twice as many corporations (473) were founded in St Petersburg as in Moscow (254).[20] Moreover, the corporations founded in St Petersburg were more than five times more heavily capitalized than were those founded in Moscow. Of course, some of this variation was reflected in the figures just presented; with only two thirds as many firms and a little over half as many workers, St Petersburg's output stood, nevertheless, at 75 percent of Moscow's, implying higher productivity both per firm and per worker.

But this finding still leaves us with a conundrum. If, as we have seen, Moscow was relegated to such inferior status with respect to commercial bank lending and numbers of corporations, how do we account for its leading position in the industrial activities of the national economy?

More common and more important than corporations in the Moscow region were manufacturing and commercial enterprises that were either privately held (*torgovye doma*) or organized as partnerships (*tovarichestva na vere*, or limited partnerships; and *polnye tovarichestva*, or full partnerships). A reading of the work of historians of entrepreneurship in Moscow suggests that there were several reasons for this.[21] First, keep in mind that entrepreneurial activity in Moscow long antedated that in St Petersburg, a city which was only founded by Peter I in the early eighteenth century. Second, recall that manufacturing and the sale of manufactured wares such as cotton, wool, silk and other consumer goods was well established in Moscow before the industrialization spurt of the 1880s. In much of the historical literature this fact is offered as an explanation for the backwardness of Muscovite entrepreneurial ways – the survival of guilds, the clannishness of merchant families, and the opaqueness of their business practices. The formation of corporations and massive investment in capital goods industries – especially railways – are broadly perceived as manifestations of Russia's belated industrial revolution, a view that is, today, associated with Gerschenkron. And, the reader is reminded, it was his measurement of the output of these new heavy industries that formed the foundation of Gerschenkron's conclusion that Russia's industrialization spurt began in 1885. Tenacious commitment to previously established commercial and manufacturing strategies is perceived as retrograde, a point of view that is not unique to twentieth-century historians of this era but that was also common in Russia throughout the nineteenth century and beyond the turn of the twentieth (Ruckman, 1984: 66–72).

Of course, one cannot quarrel with these perspectives when certain broad questions of industrial development are at issue. Large-scale, massively financed heavy manufacturing would seem to be indispensable to the economic development of a country such as Russia was in 1900. Given the degree to which the underlying technology of such activities depended upon foreign sources, the corporation – even the "concessionary" corporation of the nineteenth century – may well have been the ideal type of commercial structure. This does not mean, however, that no alternative approaches to industrial development and survival could be tolerated, any more than it means that alternative structures were necessarily so inefficient that they could not survive productively (Herrigel, 1996).

It seems to me that it is just as valid to read the story of Muscovite commerce and manufacturing as one of determined survival and successful adaptation to the political and cultural policies of the state and the marketplace. One of the foundation stones of the long-term, successful survival of Moscow commercial families, I suggest, was their ability to take advantage of legislation designed to monitor and control commerce and the reluctance of the state to allow the easy formation of corporations. A second foundation stone, it seems to me, was their consistent ability to take advantage of existing, traditional forms of social organization – Old Belief religious communities, and tenacious extended family ties, for example – that could be exploited into successful commercial activity.

The contrast between the St Petersburg and Moscow approaches to development was sharply underscored by differences in commercial banking activity. Table 9.4 shows that in 1913 more than 70 percent of all commercial bank assets were held by St Petersburg banks, 16 percent were held by Moscow banks and only a little over 12 percent by all other banks in the country.

In many ways the structure of commercial banking in Moscow during the nineteenth century was the mirror image of what, thinking of the German example cited by some writers, or following Gerschenkron's generalizations, one would expect in the most industrialized region of the country. Rather than a system in which universal banks partly covered the risk inherent in long-term exposure to manufacturers by direct participation on corporate boards, Moscow merchants and manufacturers tended to create their own "house banks" and it was the commercial and manufacturing business élite who sat on the boards of these banks. According to at least one writer, moreover, the work of financiers was not something which the business élite held in esteem (Ruckman, 1984).

The commercial banks created by the Moscow business élites during the nineteenth century tended not to be investment banks, but were focused instead upon short-term commercial operations such as discounting. This circumstance was of course linked to the way in which Moscow merchants raised investment capital. Their tendency was to do this out of revenues rather than out of share sales or from bonds. This did mean that investment and development were sometimes constricted; but it guaranteed an independence – both from the state and from foreigners – that seems to have been of the highest importance to Moscow merchants. Coupled with the strategy of self-finance was the tendency of the Moscow partnerships (the *tovarichestva*) to be very closely held, to trade only among investors who were known to one another, and to sell for exceptionally

Table 9.4 Assets of Russian commercial banks, 1907 and 1913 (millions of rs.).

	Net assets, 1913 (millions of roubles)	% Total commercial bank assets, 1913	Net assets, 1907 (millions of roubles)	% Total commercial banks assets, 1907
St. Petersburg				
Azov-Don Bank	487.1	8.8%		
Volga-Kama Bank	403.3	7.3%		
Foreign Trade Bank	598.6	10.8%		
Industrial-Commercial Bank	434.3	7.8%		
Asiatic Bank	705.5	12.7%		
Anglo-Russian Bank	16.2	0.3%		
Franco-Russian Bank	19.1	0.3%		
International Commercial Bank	622.3	11.2%		
Commercial Bank	47.8	0.9%		
Discount & Loan Bank	182.6	3.3%		
Private Commercial	137.1	2.5%		
Siberian Trade Bank	255.5	4.6%		
Credit Lyonnaise	73.0	1.3%		
Total	**3,982.6**	**71.7%**	**1,214.7**	**64.5%**
Moscow				
Moscow Bank	62.6	1.1%		
Merchant Bank	243.0	4.4%		
Popular Bank	2.4	0.04%		
Trade Bank	51.5	0.9%		
Discount Bank	64.0	1.2%		
Private Bank	36.3	0.7%		
Union Bank	294.2	5.3%		
Junker & Co.	124.3	2.2%		
Total	**878.2**	**15.8%**	**314.9**	**16.7%**
All others (28 banks)	691.0	12.5%	354.0	18.8%
Grand total	**5,551.8**		**1,883.6**	

Source: Russia, Ministry of Finances, *Ezhegodnik Ministerstva Fianansov. Vypusk 1913 g.*, 192–203.

high prices. Reflecting this difference, the Moscow stock exchange tended to trade commodities, not shares. So, Moscow banking – although there was undoubtedly some investment banking – was mainly commercial.

Moscow deposit banks, by contrast, seem to have operated in the same way as deposit banks elsewhere in Russia and they were apparently influenced by similar factors such as competition from state *kassy* and, occasionally, from commercial banks. According to Gindin's data, the assets of the Moscow mutual credit societies between 1875 and 1893 rose and fell roughly in an inverse relation to the large joint-stock banks and they never attained as much as 20 percent of the total of bank assets in the city (Gindin, 1997: 272).

In Moscow, as elsewhere, mutual credit societies recovered somewhat in the period just before World War I and this recovery seems to have been at the expense of both state *kassy* and municipals. In any case, according to Ministry of Finances data for 1909–10, funds on deposit in all of these institutions in Moscow Province – i.e. deposits in all small credit and savings organizations and excluding those in commercial banks and the Moscow branch of the State Bank – amounted to rs. 190 million. Of this sum three quarters (74.6 percent) was in the passbook accounts of the *kassy* and just under one quarter (24.47 percent) was on deposit in societies of mutual credit.[22] All other organizations, that is, accounted for less than 1 percent of deposits.

An additional contrast between Moscow and St Petersburg banking is found in evidence that individuals who controlled the St Petersburg commercial banks were often tied to government agencies such as the Ministry of Finances and the Ministry of Trade and Industry. Prominent names here included A.I. Vyshnegradskii (son of the former Minister of Finances and himself a former official), A.I. Putilov (son of the founder of the Putilev Works, a major government contractor, protégé of S. Iu Witte, and a world-class industrialist in his own right), and industrialist M.M. Fedorov to mention but three (Rieber, 1982: 364–71). Owen, Rieber and, once again, the indispensable Gindin, discuss the politics of these appointments at length and argue that these individuals were successful in large measure precisely owing to their close connections with former colleagues in state administration (Rieber, 1982: 364–71). Right up to the revolutionary year 1917, moreover, the State Bank and the Treasury competed with commercial banks for influence and control in industrial and commercial syndicates and large firms, not only using appointments in their management as posts for retired bureaucrats but even countenancing the illegal appointment of bureaucrats to positions in firms while they continued to hold official positions (Miller, 1967: 87; Owen, 1991a: 98–111).

If one looks at the record of bank deposits and loans together with evidence of what one might call the "finance culture", therefore, it seems that there were at least two distinct environments for big commercial banks during early Russian industrialization: one in St Petersburg and one in Moscow. As St Petersburg banks expanded into long-term corporate finance in the second decade of the twentieth century, they seem to have exploited the connection between the corporate form of organization and investment banking. As one grew, so did the other. In order to see this, note that Moscow commercial banks' assets rose, during the recovery of 1908–14, by about 2.8 times; St Petersburg banks' assets in the same period grew by 3.3 times on a much larger 1907 base. There were far fewer new corporations in Moscow (in spite of the higher concentration of manufacturing resources) and both new companies as well as existing ones found other sources than the commercial banks for their credit: mutual credit societies, private bank trading-house partnerships, self-financing and some level of participation of non-Moscow banks.[23]

First, consider mutual credit societies. In 1913 there were 28 of these in St Petersburg with net assets of rs. 150 million and 10 in Moscow with assets of rs.

92.5 million. Nevertheless, the total outstanding loans (of all durations, both secured and unsecured) of the Moscow societies were more than double those of the St Petersburg group: rs. 2.4 million compared with rs. 0.9 million.[24] Similarly, the trading-house partnerships were much more aggressively engaged in lending in Moscow than in St Petersburg. In a report published in 1910 the Ministry of Finances summarized the activities of bank trading-houses.[25] The report indicated that Moscow firms, while somewhat more solvent that those in St Petersburg, were also considerably more intensely engaged in securities investments (rs. 50 million compared with rs. 21 million in St Petersburg). One firm alone, Riabush-inskii Brothers, aggressively dominated the Moscow market by accounting for 60 percent of securities purchases (Anan'ich, 1996: 19). We have no hard data on the amounts of self-financing that were available to Moscow manufacturers. Estimates of their family fortunes, however, suggest a deep capacity for investment in new enterprise (Ruckman, 1984: 49–72).

We thus argue that segmentation of the *demand side* of the market for investment capital contributed to the concentration of universal banking in St Petersburg. If Moscow-style enterprise had dominated St Petersburg (as it perhaps did across the Central Industrial Region), or if St Petersburg-style corporate enterprise had dominated in Moscow, this market would likely have been fundamentally altered. As matters stood, the interlocking interests of corporate and ministerial management together with the comparatively great accessibility of publicly traded securities in St Petersburg appear to have made the extension of commercial banking into investment banking more attractive. At the same time, however, we have also seen that state roles on the *supply side* – such as backing from Gosbank and direct participation by former and even active state officials – contributed substantially to the development of universalism in St Petersburg. As we see in the following section, moreover, there is a further aspect of the state's role that shaped the structure of Russian banking before 1914.

Macro-strategies and the consequences of state roles

What were the implications of development policies, that now seem to have been engineered in, and for, St Petersburg, for the broad growth of the Russian economy during Russia's industrialization spurt? Some scholars have asserted that the accumulation of a large national debt or the transition to the international gold standard were impediments, on balance, to the growth of national income.[26] In particular, it is argued, this translated into more slowly rising standards of living than would otherwise have been experienced. This is thought to have been a consequence of restrictions on the growth of the money supply; a result of tariffs designed to constrain the purchase of foreign goods and to enhance the ingress of foreign capital; land and excise taxes that were meant to force the export of Russian agricultural products; and of programs aimed at stimulating domestic savings – especially through the state *kassy* – allowing the state to borrow huge sums from individuals who might otherwise have invested in local enterprise or simply increased consumption.

Partly, these critiques have arisen owing to the facts that this is an exceptionally complex issue and that reliable data necessary to resolve it are not easy to obtain. In part, however, the energy captured in these sometimes heated controversies is owing to the asserted connection between broadly experienced social emmiseration during Russian industrialization (if this actually occurred) and the revolutionary conflagrations of 1905 and 1917.

We have no space here to evaluate either the relevant data or the scholarship that has already addressed this issue. In any case, this has been done before.[27] We can only note that two of the best students of this question have cast doubt that, even among peasants, whose population was exploding, standards of living were in broad decline.[28] They have argued, moreover, that, while state roles were consistently central to the development of some Russian manufacturing and the creation of the necessary underlying capital markets, it is difficult to imagine an alternative policy that could simultaneously have produced an equally rapid record of development and a more equitable distribution of income in the given circumstances.[29] Gregory's assessment, however, is the more cautious:

> ... resource allocation in tsarist Russia already at the beginning of the industrialization era exhibited "Asian" features in terms of relatively high domestic investment and domestic savings rates, high government spending shares, and low personal consumption shares for a low income society. In this regard, Russia resembles Japan. The puzzle is the mechanism by which Russia achieved its "Asian" distribution, for in Japan almost one-half of capital formation was from public investment, whereas in Russia public investment (except in railroad construction) played a relatively minor role.
>
> (Gregory, 1982: 174–5)

Drummond goes so far as to suggest that, in the recovery following the 1900–08 recession, the Russian economy was so porous vis-à-vis markets and lenders in the rest of Europe that

> ... we should expect that Russia's own domestic monetary and credit conditions would be of little relevance to the cost and availability of credit within her borders ... The London discount market handled immense volumes of Russian trade bills. Russian commercial banks borrowed in London, Paris and elsewhere. Russian cities and companies came directly to the new-issue markets of the more industrialized powers. And so, of course, did the Russian state itself. Indeed, by borrowing abroad and piling up a large and growing balance with the Gosbank, the state provided a major channel by which foreign capital funds were transferred into Russia for relending to the Gosbank's thousands of private customers.
>
> (Drummond, 1976: 688)

In this assessment, Drummond, I think, solved Gregory's "puzzle": in addition to acting as both a direct investor and an indirect investor through Gosbank, the state built and maintained superlatively the avenues through which foreign capital penetrated the economy – more effectively, indeed, than Drummond seems to recognize.

For example, Crisp summarized the yield at issue for Russian and several other categories of bonds on the French market. She found that Russian bonds, by some margin, offered higher yields throughout the industrialization era than those of other foreign governments, French railways, the city of Paris, and even the French imperial colonies and protectorates.[30] Moreover, as Finances Minister Kokovtsov indicated in his memoirs, the situation did not ease for Russia later during the recovery in spite of the fact that, as a proportion of national income, state debt declined significantly from 32 percent of the budget in 1885 to 11 percent in 1913 (Gregory, 1982: Tables F1, 252; G1–G3, 261–3). Russian bonds continued to be floated at exceptionally high yields and, as Crisp shows, discounts to par that were accorded to the underwriting French banks made their sale abroad unusually profitable for the underwriters (Crisp, 1976c, Table 8.13). Throughout nearly the entire period of the industrialization spurt, the proportion of debt owed to foreigners exceeded that owed to Russians, and public and private access to foreign capital was both large and open as Drummond argues.[31]

According to the authors of the best study of international influence on the Russian banking system, moreover, in the last years before World War I state strategies to strengthen commercial banks involved foreign banks and capital intimately. The economic recovery after 1907, they conclude, "was characterized by a greater participation of foreign capital in Russian banks coupled with attempts of foreign banking groups to establish control over the premier Russian banks." The big St Petersburg banks, however, responded with enough vigor to maintain independence and to produce "still closer connections and collaboration of national and foreign capital."[32]

Conclusion

The industrialization spurt after 1885 clearly stimulated demand for long-term investment. In the case of Russia, however, this linkage requires careful qualification. Both the state and foreign investors played a large role in shaping both the long and short ends of the supply-side. The state, through Gosbank and directly, floated loans and guarantees of loans. As such, it was the indispensable source of investment, both direct and indirect, even as commercial banks' market share rose and became more universal. As a development strategy, moreover, this system was rooted in the peculiar structures and culture of the St Petersburg official and financial communities.

Nevertheless, one can argue that the most industrialized province of all – Moscow, with its textile mills and other consumer goods manufacturers – was but little affected by these strategies. This is seen by some as retrograde, constrictive, low-equilibrium "old capitalism," a capitalism that prevented large-scale mobilization of capital associated with "modern" economies. The fact remains, however, that industrialization as measured by numbers of factories and workers was more advanced in Moscow than anywhere else in the Empire.

180 *Don K. Rowney*

I am inclined to conclude that Moscow entrepreneurs must have been doing something right and that, whatever the costs of their not participating in the investment banking boom of 1908–14, they survived as a strong regional economy in comparatively autonomous form. Certainly, by these standards the demand side of the investment market was significantly compartmentalized in Russia and this seems to have held out the promise of alternative tracks to industrialization in the long run ... if there had been a long run.

Notes

1 For an excellent, short, authoritative summary see Gregory, 1994: 16–34.
2 Basic work on this subject has been done by Crisp, 1976a; Gindin, 1948; Bovykin, 1984; Shepelev, 1973.
3 As the range of materials cited in this study indicates, the literature on this subject is extensive, of surprisingly long duration, and – owing to long-term fundamental differences in economic perspective of Marxist and Western scholars – often difficult to interpret.
4 See Russia, Ministry of Finances, *Ezhegodnik Ministerstva Finansov* 1901, 1902, 1906, 1914.
5 Russia, *Polnoe Sobranie Zakonov*, II, 35, #35847.
6 Drummond, 1976: 666; see also Miller, 1967.
7 The organizations are referred to by Anan'ich as "banking houses". See Anan'ich, 1996.
8 See Gindin's table, "Kreditovanie gosudarstvennym bankom kommercheskikh bankov," Gindin, 1960: 367.
9 Bovykin and Anan'ich, 1991: Table 6.4, 142; also see Gindin, 1948: Tables 1–7, 66–72.
10 For foundation legislation, see Russia, *Polnoe sobranie zakonov*, III, 15, #11755.
11 See Gregory, 1982: Table 3.2, 58–9 where rs. 2.6 billion is the figure given for net investment in 1910.
12 See, for example, Kuznets, 1966: Table 5.5; but note that Kuznets uses "net savings," the meaning of which is not clear by comparison with the sum of commercial and individual savings deposits which we are using.
13 1.9 + 1.7 divided by rs. 17.2. This figure for savings is higher than the "savings deposit" figures of Khromov, 1950 and those given by Mitchell, 1975, who uses Khromov. Khromov's data are based, evidently, only upon the total deposits in savings *kassy*, leaving out deposits in all other savings institutions.
14 See Mitchell, 1975: 681–96, and Lévy-Leboyer and Bourguignon, 1985.
15 See savings data distributed across all of European Russia for 1905 and 1910 in Russia. Russia, Ministry of Internal Affairs, 1906: 444–7 and idem., 1911: 29–32.
16 Russia, Ministry of Finances, *Ezhegodnik. Vypusk 1906*. "Komercheskie banky", 1906, 216–23.
17 Gindin, 1948, Statistical Appendix, 406–53; also, see ibid. Table 26, p. 259.
18 Note Shepelev's reference to "industries of the October type" (a tag that was earlier used by Lenin) meaning firms that benefited, following the Revolution of 1905, from the continuation and, he suggests, intensification of policies that favored industry at the expense of workers, peasants and consumers. Shepelev, 1987: 8–117, 254–65. Partially reprinted as Shepelev, 1995.
19 For an illustration of the St Petersburg connections, see Rieber, 1982: 364–71, Figure 6.1. Also, see Gindin, 1960.
20 Owen, 1991b; for comprehensive listing of foreign and domestic corporations by industry type see, Anfimov and Korelin (eds), 1995: 185–6.
21 For discussion of the differences under Russian law, see Owen, 1991a.
22 Russia, Ministry of Finances, *Ezhegodnik*, 1911.
23 Ruckman, 1984: 49–72 and passim. As Deeg notes, the phenomenon of self-finance need not be limited to small, family concerns. He shows that it is increasingly common among contemporary large German manufacturing firms (Deeg, 1999: 86). Certainly there is a lot of evidence

that Russian closely-Sheld firms knew how to marshal cash for investment – see discussions in Rieber, 1982 and Crisp, 1976c of the connections between Moscow family firms and Moscow merchant banks.

24 Russia, Ministry of Finances, *Ezhegodnik*, 1913: 204–99.
25 Summarized in Anan'ich, 1996: 18–19.
26 For a summary of contemporaries' arguments, see Miller, 1967: 110–14. For a discussion of the broad negative impact of state macro-economic policies after 1861, see Volin, 1970, and Gerschenkron, 1965. For more recent critiques, see Barkai, 1973 and Kahan, 1989: 91–107.
27 An extended, well-documented discussion of the debate and data is in Gregory, 1982: 123–79.
28 Gregory, 1974; Gregory, 1982, chapter 7; also see Drummond, 1976.
29 In addition to works by Drummond and Gregory, see McKay, 1970.
30 Crisp, 1976b. See also Anfimov and Korelin (eds), 1995: 176–83, Tables 1, 1.1, 2.
31 On the ratio of foreign to domestic debt, see Gregory, 1982: Table M.2, 318–22.
32 Bovykin and Anan'ich, 1991: 158, see also ibid. 148–56 and 253–75.

10 Bank structures, Gerschenkron and Portugal (pre-1914)

Jaime Reis

I

European nineteenth-century financial history has tended to suffer from three shortcomings. Despite the early seminal works of Cameron, Goldsmith and Gerschenkron, until recently it has concentrated mostly on the study of sections of national financial systems, mainly commercial banks, rather than on these systems as a totality, thus leaving out the interaction between their constituent parts and giving less attention to other institutions such as non-profit banking or equity markets.[1] In the second place, notwithstanding a considerable amount of work cast in a comparative perspective, this approach has been less thorough and consistent than might be desired, largely because it has lacked the sound statistical underpinning needed for it and which has yet to be constructed. A good deal of quantification of financial activity at the national and local level is currently available but its international comparability has not been the object of enough research effort and therefore solid, statistically motivated conclusions are hard to draw.[2] Lastly, financial history on the whole has treated lightly the role of the legal and institutional framework in determining the shape, size and evolution of financial systems.[3] In virtually every study of this kind, one can find references to legislation and other forms of state regulation of financial activity, much of it focused on national reactions to crises, but this approach seldom occupies the center of the stage and rarely, if ever, goes into sufficient detail. Given the special importance of regulatory conditions for an economic sector such as this one and the exceptional weight, in this context, of the state as an economic agent, an incomplete picture is the inevitable result. This chapter seeks to contribute to all three of these aspects, taking Portugal during the second half of the nineteenth century as the object of study.

During this period all Western economies experienced the emergence of modern financial systems. Although these exhibited similar characteristics, the latter combined in such varied ways that throughout Europe structural divergence in this respect became pronounced. The classical dichotomy here was between the Continental and the Anglo-Saxon models as regards the prevalence of large specialized banks and equity markets. There were other important differences, however, such as size and importance of central banks, the relative weight of the non-profit sector and the diffusion of branch banking. Why so much variance should have arisen and then been maintained is an important but as yet not fully resolved issue for contemporary financial history.

In several recent papers, Daniel Verdier (1998, 2001, and in this volume) has grappled with this problem by proposing a revision of the paradigm that Alexander Gerschenkron advanced in the early 1950s. His suggestion is that the answer is best found in the comparative analysis of the state in its twin roles as major financial actor and as regulator of financial activity in general, as well as in the relationship between these two realities. The configuration of each system, in the mainstream view, arose as the optimal response to the difficulty in matching the demand for loanable funds with their availability through the traditional channels that is common in developing economies. Instead, according to Verdier (1999), the origins of the problem lie in political history, the critical variable being the degree of state centralization present in each country. This was in turn the result of the different paths in the process of state formation during the nineteenth century, or even before, which were significantly marked by the struggle between a core, which strove for control, and peripheries, which sought after ever-increasing autonomy or even secession. Not surprisingly, financial resources were an important dimension of this contest. Where the core was able to assert itself, political centralization opened the way for financial concentration, which was characterized by bank specialization, vigorous branch banking, strong equity markets and weak local financial institutions. In the cases where the core failed to achieve this predominance, unit banking and universal banks tended to prevail, financial decentralization was pronounced and markets for corporate equity were relatively weak. The key factor behind these differences was always the application of state power (or the incapacity to do so) in order to gain control over the savings of the community as these became transformed into financial instruments – deposits in particular – in accordance with laws and regulations that emanated from central or local authorities.

Daniel Verdier has underlined in his work that state centralization was not the only factor shaping banking structures and that several individual cases – the Netherlands, Spain, Norway and Denmark – deviate somewhat from the general lines of his model (Verdier, this volume). Portugal, which has not been a part of his sample, is another instance that fits poorly and may therefore be an interesting subject for in-depth study. During the nineteenth century, it was clearly a highly centralized state and, when modern financial institutions came into being on a significant scale, after the 1850s, the resultant system evolved into a concentrated one. Yet, contrary to what one would expect on the strength of the Verdier analysis, neither specialized commercial banking, nor a strong equity market manifested themselves, while branch banking was little more than minimal. Rather, universal banks dominated the scene and the stock market was rachitic. On the other hand, in two other respects, it conformed to expectations. A strong state bank was set up to gather savings in order to sustain public finance, and provincial banking was underdeveloped.

The argument of this chapter is that political factors may be generally important in explaining the shape that financial structures in Europe took over the course of the late 1800s. In this case however they are only partially helpful in accounting for the goodness of fit of this specific situation vis-à-vis the model under discussion. Other variables seem to have been of greater moment and this can be seen in the details of the Portuguese experience. First the chapter describes the main traits of Portugal's economy and society during the period and discusses the extent of political centralization. This shows Portugal as one of the most highly ranked from this point of view. This is followed by a section portraying the components of its financial system in terms of institutions, markets and instruments. In the next section there is a discussion of each of the aspects of this system and whether they deviate from or conform to the Verdier model. An explanation of this is advanced using factors other than political ones. By having recourse to the degree of economic development, income per capita, cultural characteristics and the nature of the country's public finance problem we seek to broaden the initial, mainly "political" terms of the analysis which was our starting point. A final section draws a conclusion.

II

Between 1850 and 1914 Portugal displayed four features that are important from the point of view of the problem that is being discussed here. In terms of the Western European standards of the time, it was one of the poorest countries, with an economic performance that was one of the least dynamic and revealed clear marks of structural underdevelopment. According to the latest real GDP per capita estimation by Prados (2000), in 1860 only Finland and Greece were worse off, with the Portuguese level at about 60 percent of the British one.[4] By 1913, this state of affairs had not improved. Rather, it had deteriorated relative to the more advanced countries, as well as to several other peripheral economies such as Denmark and Norway, owing to Portugal having had one of the slowest growth rates on the Continent in the course of these decades (O'Rourke and Williamson, 1999). This is hardly surprising when we consider that the economy's predominant sector, agriculture, was characterized by extremely low levels of productivity, while industry, which was mainly of the light variety, performed sluggishly by international standards and without the spurts that were common in the more dynamic economies of the time (Lains, 1995).

Naturally, in term of urbanization, around 1900, Portugal had fallen quite a lot behind the European norm of 36 percent of the population living in localities of more than 5,000 inhabitants. Its rate was a mere 17 percent instead. But its population was more than just profoundly rural. It also lived under conditions of considerable isolation from the forces of social and economic modernization. Although a small country, internal transport and communication were both difficult and costly. Roads and railways were thinly spread over the territory – about one third of the average European density – and only a fraction of agricultural production was marketed. Written communication with others, whether at home or abroad, was relatively infrequent. In 1900, 13.4 items per capita were mailed in Portugal, whereas the figure was 36.0 for Denmark, 20.8 for Italy, 26.0 for Norway and

19.4 for Spain (Mitchell, 1992). Among other reasons, this was the result of the abysmal state of ignorance in which most of the Portuguese population lived. Comparatively few of its children attended primary schools – in 1880, they were 476 per 10,000 of population compared with Spain, where the figure was double and France, where it was three times this. Low literacy rates were the inevitable outcome of this. Portugal's rate, persistently around 20 percent throughout these years, was one of the lowest in Europe and 10 to 20 percentage points lower than that of similarly less-developed societies of the time like Spain, Italy or Greece (Reis, 1993).

The broad lines of Portugal's political and institutional development are hardly exceptional in terms of European nineteenth century history. After a period of turbulence, between 1820 and 1850, which included a bitter civil war (1829–33), the country settled down peacefully to a parliamentary monarchical regime of a then fairly common stamp, with a strong executive role for the monarch, a two-chamber legislature and a small electorate qualified essentially by property. The degree of political centralism that emerged in the course of this process was quite pronounced. Notwithstanding an alleged and highly controversial claim of a strong municipalist tradition in previous centuries, this period does not seem to have witnessed a significant assertion of localism in politics. Whether in the countryside or at the provincial level, the trend appears to have been in the opposite direction.

The data available for replicating Verdier's (this volume) proposed index of political centralization indicate that Portugal possessed this characteristic to a considerable extent. At least during the 1850s and 1860s, the ratio of municipal fiscal revenues to those of the central state was around 10 percent, which would make it the most centralized country in the sample that Verdier has considered (Nogueira, 1856; Figueiredo, 1873). Thereafter, direct evidence for this is lacking but impressionistic evidence suggests that the situation did not change appreciably in the decades up to World War I. On the one hand, excepting Lisbon and Oporto, local government, which consisted of municipalities and parishes, generally had notoriously exiguous budgets and few administrative attributions that involved substantial spending. In contrast, central government revenues were large, covered a very wide scope of functions and represented a considerable proportion of GDP – in 1880, something of the order of 6 percent (Mata, 1993).

An equally helpful index for this would be one that reflected the capacity of central governments to mobilize, not revenue, as the above index does, but loanable funds through the utilization of public debt instruments. After all, the struggle between central and local government, as argued by Verdier, was not so much over income flows but over capital markets and savings, with the focus on central Treasuries' efforts to widen the circulation of state debt (Verdier, this volume). Table 10.1 constitutes an attempt to rank countries in the sample in accordance with this observation by showing the weight of the service of the Public Debt in total central government expenditure. It is not a perfect proxy for comparing the importance of the government's consumption of domestic savings in different countries given that the rates of interest and amortization differed over time and space (Homer and Sylla, 1996). But it does give us an idea of how significant this

Table 10.1 Debt service as a percentage of central
government expenditure in 12 European countries,
1880–1900.

	1880	1900
Belgium	36.4	37.5
Britain	31.5	16.1
Denmark	20.1	12.0
Finland	12.2	7.7
France	34.2	28.4
Germany	25.3	19.5
Italy	35.5	33.3
Netherlands	24.7	22.6
Norway	14.5	13.6
Spain	30.0	34.0
Sweden	12.4	9.5
Portugal	51.0	46.0

Source: Flora *et al.* (eds), 1983–87.

question was to central governments and to what extent they needed to get involved
in financial markets in order to solve budgetary difficulties. Moreover, it allows us
to gauge by how much the center of the political system was actually able to use
its power in order to muster non-fiscal resources to its ends.

Table 10.1 largely confirms previous findings on this issue. Portugal emerges
once again as the most centralized country, in the same class as Belgium, France,
Italy and Britain, while the remaining rankings tally reasonably well with those of
Verdier. The question this raises is whether the Portuguese financial system was at
all like those of the countries that were constituted politically in a similar fashion.
For this we must now turn to an examination of how this system was structured.

III

The Portuguese financial system was not out of keeping with the socio-economic
tableau we have just presented. It was small, developed only comparatively late
and, apart from an initial spurt of growth, expanded rather slowly over the years
1850–1913. On the other hand, if the analytic point of departure is a political/
institutional one, its main characteristics are hardly the predicted ones. In one
respect only – that of being heavily concentrated – did it fit with the predicted
centralized nature of the polity. Otherwise, it was based typically on unit banking,
when it was branching that should have prevailed; and most of its banking was of
the universal kind, when its vocation should really have been commercial.
Moreover, the evident weakness of its provincial institutions was certainly not
due to the centralizing pressures of the political authorities but rather to certain
social and economic features of the Portuguese periphery, as we shall see.

Some of this can best be grasped by comparing it with the situation in Denmark,
another small, essentially agricultural and peripheric economy, but, in contrast,

one with a considerably higher income per capita and a greater degree of social development. At mid-century, not untypically, the Portuguese system consisted of a fairly large, privileged national bank of issue in Lisbon and one small joint-stock bank in the country's second financial center, Oporto, where a third was added to the list in 1856. It was not until the mid-1860s that this situation changed with the creation of eight new banks, but by this stage Denmark already had sixteen commercial banks, a contrast which was still present in 1913, after several cyclical ups and downs. By this time Portugal had 27 such institutions to Denmark's 139. More important still was the volume of resources per head that each system was able to mobilize. Table 10.2 provides the relevant figures for various dates, converted to the same currency (sterling) at the going exchange rate. It takes into account not only commercial banks (including the respective national banks) but also non-profit savings and mutual credit banks, state savings banks and institutions dealing in mortgage credit. It shows that from the outset the difference not only was large but, by the turn of the century, had increased to a staggering per capita differential of 11:1, as a result of very contrasting growth experiences in all of these sub-sectors.

Table 10.3 takes this comparison one step further by factoring in additionally the financial resources gathered by the equity and bond markets and thus includes both the instruments issued by non-financial corporations and those pertaining to the Public Debt. The latter's price, in the Portuguese case, was prone to considerable fluctuation and they have consequently been valued at their current trading price rather than at their historical price of issue.[5] These data show Portugal still far behind Denmark but much less so than it would have been without the non-bank sector – the 1913 overall financial liability ratio between the two countries is still considerable but now of the order of 3.5:1. The reason is mainly that Denmark had a relatively small public debt whereas Portugal's was enormous and indeed

Table 10.2 Per capita liabilities of financial institutions: Portugal and Denmark, 1850–1910 (£ sterling).

	1850	1860	1870	1880	1890	1900	1910
Denmark	2.3	5.1	9.1	16.6	32.7	44.0	77.5
Portugal	n.a	1.4	2.9	5.0	5.7	6.8	6.9

Source: Reis, 1999a.

Table 10.3 Per capita liabilities of financial systems: Portugal and Denmark, 1850–1910 (£ sterling).

	1850	1860	1870	1880	1890	1900	1910
Denmark	n.a	n.a	18.6	28.4	n.a	59.4	95.7
Portugal	n.a	6.2	9.3	18.2	n.a	17.5	27.7

Source: Reis, 1999a.

overshadowed all non-state formal finance. In 1880, it represented one half of all financial liabilities whilst in Denmark this proportion was only 20 percent, a striking instance of the crowding-out effect the Public Debt can have on financial systems. Denmark, it is true, had an absolute superiority in non-financial corporate shares and bonds, which in per capita terms grew five-fold during the period 1870–1913. This did not have a major impact overall, however, because these instruments constituted roughly only 12 percent of this country's total liabilities.

External financial sources helped comparatively little the development of this system and this contrasts also with the Danish case, which was strongly favored by foreign investors from the late nineteenth century. Over the period, only a couple of foreign banks had a mildly significant presence – a London-based one and a branch of the Crédit Lyonnais – but their impact overall was weak. Foreign portfolio investment was small relative to population and to what it was in other countries, as might be expected given that growth prospects and financial policies were hardly attractive.[6] Too little is known about the sources of and the channels for the financing of foreign trade beyond the fact that domestic banks were involved in discounting these bills to some extent. It is likely that some of this should have also come from the country's trading partners, Britain in the first place, but it must be remembered that Portugal was not an open economy at this time and had one of the lowest ratios of exports to GDP in Europe. In the aggregate, this contribution was therefore probably not large.

The weak development of the stock market in Portugal was only one of the features of the general lack of progress of the financial structures there. Another one was the relative absence of a formal functional specialization in the banking sector and the consequent prevalence of general purpose banks. In the early twentieth century, local savings banks were few and far between – in 1913, there were only 11 and they were all minuscule, with the exception of the Montepio Geral, in Lisbon, which was unusually large in its class (Nunes *et al.*, 1994) – the same being true for institutions specializing in credit to small businesses, farmers, artisans and building. The Caixa Geral de Depósitos, which belonged to the state, was also quite large but had yet to develop a significant capacity to attract the savings of the popular classes, notwithstanding the state guarantee for its deposits. Its voluntary deposits in 1900 totaled only 5,000 contos, a mere 3 percent of the liabilities of all financial institutions. As a result of a legal monopoly enacted in 1864, there was only one mortgage bank – the Companhia do Crédito Predial Português – in the entire country, headquartered in Lisbon and with a share capital equal to only 1/40 of total bank subscribed capital. It dealt only in urban real estate and latifundiary landholdings in the south. Likewise, banks that were created specifically to provide long-term finance were a rarity. One only – the Sociedade Geral Agrícola e Financeira – emerged during the entire period and then it lasted for no more than 20 years, its activities ranging over a wide spectrum, which covered mining, agriculture and industry. Specifically agricultural banks, to help farmers with medium- and short-term credit to improve methods, seeds and equipment, were to have been created in provincial towns under a special law of 1867 but only three got off the ground. Their impact was minimal.

The financial fragmentation of this system offers some surprises, if we take into consideration the high degree of political centralization in Portugal and the concentration of modern economic functions in the country's two main commercial centers. We should expect center profit banking (in Verdier's terminology) to be anything but modest, to the detriment of provincial profit banks and the savings sector, but at first sight institutional statistics do not support this expectation. During the great surge of commercial bank creation of the 1860s and 1870s, 28 new establishments were set up in Lisbon and Oporto but 24 also came into existence in lesser towns. If we add to this number the handful of savings banks that were created in the meantime, the situation becomes one of virtual parity.

Table 10.4, which refers only to 1890, presents this distribution in terms of the respective shares of deposits and of total liabilities for each of these categories, and reveals rather different conclusions. First, if we consider deposits only, Portugal does not come out as having a highly concentrated system but one that is only moderately so. With 49.7 percent for its total fragmentation index (Verdier's terminology), it trails all the centralized states of Europe in the sample by at least 10 percentage points. Second, its level of state banking is modest by comparison with this group, except for Britain, whereas non-profit private banks are far stronger than those of Belgium, France or Britain. Within the profit-banking segment, however, the sign is of a high degree of financial concentration at the center. Lisbon and Oporto banks dominated by a ratio of more than 4:1 and the country bank sector obviously consisted of mostly small units with an apparently low capacity to attract deposits. On the other hand, if we switch to total liabilities as our gauge, financial concentration becomes more pronounced, given the importance of share capital in the overall picture of resource mobilization in Portugal. In this case, the non-commercial sector has only a 14 percent share of the total and the state savings bank's role is dwarfed even more, to 6 percent. Meanwhile, center profit banks' share of all financial institutions rises to two thirds and, if we put them together with the country banks, the figure becomes a crushing 85.9 percent.

In the sense that really matters, i.e. liabilities, the Portuguese corporate financial system was thus largely dominated by the commercial banks.[7] In contrast, at the turn of the century, the Danish commercial sector accounted for a mere 30 percent

Table 10.4 Deposits and total liabilities: shares of the four banking sectors, Portugal, 1890 (percent).

	Center profit banks	Country profit banks	State savings banks	Non-profit private banks
Deposits only	49.7	11.8	16.9	21.6
Aggregate liabilities	63.4	22.5	6.0	8.1

Note:
Non-profit private banks were mostly provincial. They were dominated however by the Monte Pio Geral which was Lisbon based.

Source: Portugal, *Annaes de Estatística*, 1894.

of the total liabilities of financial institutions, including the 7 percent corresponding to the National Bank, while the remaining 70 percent belonged to the strongly developed non-profit, non-state sector. Portuguese commercial banks varied a great deal in terms of size, age and location but displayed a surprising homogeneity as regards two characteristics that are particularly relevant to our analysis and to which we now turn. These concern their attitude towards branch banking and the essentially mixed nature of their operations.

The norm in Portugal prior to the 1950s, the period when branch banking began at last to experience a process of vigorous growth, was always very much the unit bank (Sérgio, n.d.). Consistent data are difficult to gather for earlier periods but we know that in 1920, 25 banks (not including the Bank of Portugal) had a mere 13 outlets other than their head office, and in 1939 the figure had crept up to 30 for a total of 21 such firms. During the time span we are considering, a similar quantification is impossible but the scattered evidence available suggests a like picture. Outside the towns and cities in which they were headquartered, commercial joint-stock banks never had more than one or two fully-fledged branches – often, the smaller, provincial ones had none at all – and if they were center banks, typically these branches would be located in the other major city and perhaps also one of the second-rank industrial towns such as Setúbal, Covilhã or Guimarães. Whatever business there was in the provinces was carried out through correspondents, usually local merchants of some standing who might represent several banks at the same time and whose functions were merely to make and receive payments on behalf of their principals. They never gathered deposits or undertook credit operations of any type. Only two financial institutions departed from this pattern and could therefore claim a national status. The Bank of Portugal and the Caixa Geral de Depósitos, which played significant official roles, opened branches for this reason alone in all 18 district capitals of the Continent from the late nineteenth century. The Bank of Portugal did so too on the islands of Azores and Madeira, while the Caixa had a total of twelve branches additionally in towns in the hinterlands of Oporto and Lisbon. The national coverage this implied was of the order of 0.1 branches per 10,000 inhabitants, at a time when in Britain it was 1.83 and in France at least 0.5.

As mentioned above, during this stage of its history, the Portuguese financial system reveals a low degree of functional specialization. The correlate of this, given that it was called upon to satisfy the needs of an already reasonably complex economy and that the equity market was underdeveloped, was universal banking and this was indeed the predominant form of profit banking during the second half of the nineteenth century. To financial historians this is a familiar category, which relates to all the many institutions in Europe at this time that "provided a complete range of commercial and investment banking services" and whose "industrial (*de facto* long term) credit and investment were financed by short-term resources" (Ziegler, 1998: 22–3).[8] It is not always easy, however, to establish the extent of its presence in a given situation and in the case in point we shall have recourse to four criteria for this.

The first is of a simple regulatory nature. After 1867, joint-stock limited liability banks were not only allowed to be constituted with a minimum of bureaucratic fuss but were free to engage in any business they wished. The law on joint-stock companies (including banks) of that year made no particular stipulations either about the aims of these institutions or about the manner in which they should conduct their business as long as they ensured full publicity for their acts. This meant that no barrier existed for banks as to how much long- or short-term lending they made, or as to the nature of its recipients[9]. An examination of the specific statutes of a number of these institutions shows that their founders had very much in mind the possibility of mixed banking as a long-term strategy. For example, the largest banks in Oporto – those that were created in the early 1860s – had as their general goal "to promote and help the country's trade and various industries".[10] In practice, they proposed to engage in virtually everything: the discount of all types of bills, the acquisition of Public Debt bonds, making advances on the security of a wide variety of assets, including mining concessions, corporate shares and bonds and even pending harvests, providing loans guaranteed by factories or their production, as well as mortgage loans backed by rural or urban property, allowing credits on current account and loans to other banks or joint-stock companies on the basis of reputation and, finally, issuing life insurance policies. In addition, they could buy and sell the shares of other companies, national or foreign, subscribe to them in new issues, and themselves promote bonds and shares on behalf of third parties.

Despite this impressive list of activities, it must be admitted that a large gap may have existed between intention and practice. A second way of establishing how much mixed banking there was in fact is by looking at the balance sheets of commercial banks for quantifiable signs of long-term lending that, in good banking theory, one would not have expected if they had been truly commercial institutions. The obscurity and lack of objectivity of bank balance sheets in nineteenth-century Europe has been stressed by many authors and Portugal is no exception to this rule.[11] We have tried nevertheless to make sense of them in this context by constructing two variables. One consists of rubrics which allegedly were short term, such as bills, current credit accounts and advances on security. The other includes those that were designated straightforwardly as "long-term loans" but also all those accounts which were vaguely described as "general debtors and creditors". According to Lumbralles (1926: 227), a contemporary expert on banking, these were "a sort of hold-all for all of those accounts that one does not really want to publish and which sometimes are of such a nature that they are called the 'dirty linen basket'". Our assumption is that they would mostly concern long-term applications of funds, at times possibly even of dubious liquidity. After 1894, new legal requirements forced banks to discriminate between holdings of Public Debt and corporate shares and bonds. For this later period it becomes possible to incorporate the second of these accounts into our long-term variable too. This is of interest on the grounds that it not only represents banks' direct involvement in railways, industry and mining but also one that could hardly be short term given that this type of paper was difficult to transact and had to be kept over long periods.

A comparison of the two variables for a sample of 13 banks of all types – center, provincial, large and small – points towards a generally strong "mixed" vocation in their operations. As can be seen from Table 10.5, the overwhelming majority in this group and also the largest part in terms of share of total assets were institutions where the long-term variable was at least half of the short-term one and, in six of them, it was equal to it or larger. Moreover, it is likely that this is an underestimate since many supposedly short-term operations covered up long-term ones and consisted of "rolled-over" bills and advances whose maturity date could be systematically extended over quite long periods. It is interesting to note that the only deviants from this universal pattern were two medium-sized provincial banks, one of which – the Banco da Covilhã – operated in a strongly industrial region.

A third way of analyzing this question takes us deeper but is inevitably patchy in its coverage. It consists of examining certain better-documented instances of bank–industry relationships using either the balance sheets of manufacturing joint-stock concerns, or the detailed data on the financing by banks of firms which for some reason – often a bankruptcy – were subject to particular scrutiny. This enables us to establish, at least for these firms, how dependent they were on external finance and often what form this took. Generally speaking, under-capitalization seems to have been a recurring problem, thus confirming the general opinion of industrialists noted in the 1865 and 1881 industrial enquiries to the effect that in many sectors

Table 10.5 Ratio of long-term to short-term credit of commercial banks, Portugal, 1865–1915 (averages for the period considered).

Banks	Ratio long/short credit
1865–1915	
Nacional Ultramarino	2.88
Vila Real	1.08
Comercial do Porto	2.41
Minho	0.99
Lisboa e Açores	1.45
Chaves	0.75
Douro	0.50
Comercial de Lisboa	0.46
Covilhã	0.09
Eborense	0.08
1865–1890	
Portuguez*	1.68
Lusitano*	1.42
União*	1.46

Note:
* indicates these banks failed in the wake of the 1891 crisis.

Source: Balance sheets of the respective banks.

companies were having to raise additional loans in the market up to 100 percent of the value of their share capital. Such cases also lend support to the widespread impression that large firms always managed to get credit from banks, though often at a high price, while the small ones, without reputation or collateral, struggled and ended up having to go to the usurer.

Share capital was the principal source of industrial finance in the case of joint-stock companies and, while some of it found its way into the portfolios of banks, the latter's position in this respect rarely seems to have been a strong one. The exception we are aware of was the Prado paper works, with 24 percent of its shares held by different financial institutions. This could be complemented by several other sources. One consisted of bond issues, infrequently promoted by banks or bankers, and not traded to any great extent on the stock exchange, but in some cases hardly insignificant in magnitude. In the early twentieth century, in the cotton industry, on aggregate they were equal to one quarter of the share capital (Oliveira, 1904). In addition, frequently informal loans were made to the company by some of its major shareholders. Besides this, a large part of the liabilities of these firms was in bills discounted by banks and concerned genuine commercial operations but one can only guess at how much of this in reality was concealed "roll-over" credit, having to do with fixed capital formation. Finally, we know of several instances where banks made large advances for periods of several years on the guarantee of bills drawn on the directors of the company, bonds, mortgages or simply personal surety. The Aliança Fabril, of Lisbon, owed the Banco Lusitano an enormous 280 contos (1 conto = £222) as part of a prolonged and intimate relationship that ended in bankruptcy for both of them in the early 1890s. The Nacional de Estamparia, also of Lisbon, borrowed an unknown amount from the Banco Lisboa e Açores in 1897 which was only paid back in 1904. The Salgueiros textile factory, in Oporto, took 40 contos from the Nova Utilidade bank in 1879 for four years, while the Nacional de Lanifícios, in Portalegre, had 177 contos of outstanding debits to six different banks for practically a decade when it went under in the 1880s. The Bank of Portugal, which is quite well documented in this respect, is an interesting example because, being a bank of issue, it should have been especially cautious with long-term industrial credit. And yet, among others, the Transtagana mining concern owed it 80 contos in 1883 from a debt contracted in 1878, the Huelva mining company owed it a substantial amount between 1887 and 1891, and the Tomar cotton spinning enterprise had a debit in 1873 of over 80 contos of bills that had been "rolled-over" for several years. A revealing register of loans guaranteed by securities compiled in 1903, which on statutory grounds were supposed to last for only three months, shows that about 60 percent were kept on for much longer periods of time, some for as long as ten years.

A close, supportive and sustained relationship between financial institutions and industrial firms that borrowed from them has traditionally been considered a further hallmark of universal banking. To test for this in the Portuguese case, information on directorships and membership of supervisory boards in both types of enterprise was examined. The result for 1883 is given in Table 10.6. It shows that altogether 184 of such places in the most significant non-financial joint-stock companies

Table 10.6 Supervisory and management board places occupied by bankers: Lisbon, 1883.

Banks	No. places	No. companies
1	35	21
2	20	16
3	18	13
4	22	17
5	12	10
6	30	20
7	9	9
8	8	7
9	5	4
10	3	3
11	4	4
12	10	9
13	8	8
Total	**184**	

Note:
The data are for the number of members of bank management or supervisory boards that also sat on management or supervisory boards of non-financial joint stock companies.

List of banks: 1-Lusitano; 2-Portugal; 3-Sociedade Geral; 4-Nacional Insulano; 5-Lisboa e Açores; 6-Lisbonense; 7-Nacional Ultramarino; 8-Comercial de Lisboa; 9-Crédito Predial; 10-Crédito; 11-Povo; 12-Caixa de Crédito Industrial; 13-Caixa de Empréstimos Lisbonense.

Source: Reis, n.d.

registered in Lisbon were held by persons who simultaneously occupied positions at board or supervisory board level in one or more of 13 principal Lisbon banks. Five of the latter accounted for 70 percent of the total. This strongly suggests a relationship that one could hardly describe as "arms-length", but it is not evident that it implies a close control by the financial side of the manufacturing partners in it, at least in the marked fashion that has been claimed for the German and Italian examples. It should be noted, in fact, that Portuguese bank directors did not take up these places so much as a consequence of the shareholdings of their banks but rather as a result of their personal shareholding. Moreover, there is as yet no proof – perhaps not surprisingly as Portuguese business history is still in its infancy – that banks with stakes in joint-stock companies tried to use their power to co-ordinate the latter's activities or to try and promote their technological progress, marketing or product development. On the other hand, their presence on company boards was not unrelated to the problem of information asymmetry which is such an important part of understanding the need for universal banking (Collins, 1998). This much at least is suggested by the scattered but not infrequent remarks in company annual reports to the effect that having bankers on their managing or supervisory boards was welcome for the reason that it enabled the bank to know their business well and to judge more easily whether to provide financial assistance and by how much.

Altogether, Portugal's commercial banks emerge unmistakably as having a universal vocation but in a version that was somewhat rudimentary by international standards. They mixed short- and long-term credits, often as services to the same firm, but only employed instruments such as shares and bonds to represent long-term credits occasionally, unsystematically and to a limited extent. As far as we can tell, they interfered relatively little in the running of these companies and did not nurse them through from foundation to maturity, unloading their shares and bonds on the market as they went along, though this conclusion could be reversed by future research. They managed to lessen the informational asymmetry quite effectively by their boardroom presence but were often caught nevertheless holding credits which had been unwisely granted or used and which took a long time to liquidate. In sum, they clearly combined the roles of commercial and investment bank.

IV

In what follows we try to establish how much of the configuration of Portugal's financial system was the result of politics and the role of the central state, and to what extent it was shaped instead by economic, social and cultural factors. The first of these hypotheses points towards a Verdier type of answer to this question. The second would lend support to a more Gerschenkronian vision of the problem. As suggested earlier, some aspects of Portugal's late nineteenth-century financial system conform to the Verdier model, others do not. One dimension that would appear to be in the first category is the coincidence of a highly centralized polity with a low degree of financial fragmentation (see Tables 10.1 and 10.4). But a closer look at the situation renders it less certain that a significant causal connection may have existed between these two aspects.

Conceivably, there were several ways in which the Portuguese state could have encouraged this financial concentration. The development of peripheral financial institutions could have been inhibited by means of regulatory devices aimed at impeding their access to the pool of available savings. The latter would thus be driven either into the state's coffers, or into deposits at institutions that the state controlled in some way. But there is little evidence that the state attempted such a strategy or that the underdevelopment of provincial banks was caused in these ways. The 1867 joint-stock company law was extremely permissive regarding commercial banks and merely stipulated (article 2) that corporations of any kind were to be established by "simply the will of the associates, without any dependence on a prior administrative approval of their statutes".[12] Other than the obligations regarding the transferability, ownership and voting rights of shares, the disclosure of internal information and the basic organization of the enterprise, it prescribed very little, particularly that was specific to banking. Above all, it made no distinction whatever between institutions operating in the center and in the periphery and consequently could not serve as an instrument of discrimination among them in the matter of the accumulation of deposits.

When it comes to savings banks, whose consistent absence from the Portuguese financial scene is so striking, it must be noted that during the entire period under consideration there was no specific legislation that covered their activity. *Caixas económicas*, as they were known, could therefore only come into existence with the approval of the central government, a cumbersome and deterrent process that required the petitioners to demonstrate that all the necessary guarantees for their depositors and members were given (Portugal, *Anuário Estatístico de Portugal*, 1875 and 1903). Since little is known about their history, in particular about how many sought authorization and were rejected, it must be admitted that this could have been used as an obstacle to their development. There are reasons, however, for not attributing much importance to this hypothesis. The first is the striking fact that those that did exist never grew much, the exception being the Monte Pio Geral, which was situated in Lisbon and whose assets increased by a factor of more than a hundred during 1860–1914 (Nunes *et al.*, 1994). This hints at the determining factor of success being social and economic, rather than regulatory, and connected to urban/rural differences in per capita income and saving habits. In the second place, even if there had been an anti-private savings bank inclination at the political center, there were legal ways of circumventing it. The 1867 law governing the creation of provincial agricultural and industrial credit banks – not to be confused with the joint-stock companies act of the same year already alluded to – not only conceded these institutions a tax-free status for all their operations, but also gave them the power to open *caixas económicas* in their territory and pay a competitive rate of interest for deposits (3.65 percent).[13] Had there been a local impulse to start up this form of savings institution in the countryside, this vehicle could have been more widely used than the mere three banks that were actually founded and then languished.[14] A further viable alternative to escape from central restraint would have been to foster local channels for savings in the context of mutual help associations. By the turn of the century, a large number of these existed – 162 in all, mainly in Lisbon and Oporto but also in smaller towns – and an unknown number managed to operate *caixas económicas* notwithstanding the fact that they were subject to central government regulation. Even so there is no evidence that they mobilized any significant amount of savings.[15]

If regulation did not matter, the state still had other ways of stunting the expansion of provincial financial institutions. Thus, arguably there was no need to asphyxiate them with the law because market mechanisms could be just as effective. Savings from the periphery could be drained directly by means of placing Public Debt bonds there under very competitive conditions, a hypothesis that gains plausibility when one considers the very heavy weight of the Public Debt in Portuguese finance. But the geographic distribution of the public's holdings of these bonds does not substantiate this view at all. The Junta do Crédito Público's (Public Debt Office) annual reports provide a detailed breakdown by districts and municipalities of the sums paid to bond bearers as interest on the internal debt. These payments (and the corresponding holdings of bonds) were heavily concentrated in the cities of Lisbon and Oporto, which together accounted for some 85 percent or more of the disbursement. In 1900, for example, this meant that the provincial population which was 85 percent of the country's total held only 15 percent of the Public Debt, while in the two main financial centers the same figures were respectively 15 and 85 percent. Under the circumstances, it is hard to believe that provincial deposits of whatever kind could have been crowded out by the Public Debt, when the dwellers of the two principal cities in Portugal held proportionately so much more in state bonds – 30 times more in fact – and still had a per capita level of deposits that was three or four times higher than provincial ones.

If crowding out was not the cause of the weak development of country deposit banking, then perhaps the state savings bank had some responsibility in the matter. After all, it had a fairly extensive network of offices in the provinces and its liabilities enjoyed the reassuring guarantee of the state. Had its volume of deposits been large, the Caixa Geral de Depósitos would certainly have been drawing away some resources from the provincial banks, commercial or otherwise. But the truth is that up to the first years of the twentieth century the total value of savings deposits at this institution was small. In 1890 it was in the region of 2,000 contos, a year in which total deposits in all types of banks came to about 40,000 contos, and it had reached only 8,000 contos by 1910.[16] About half of its deposits originated in Lisbon and Oporto, which means that in per capita terms it was diverting a minuscule 0.0001 contos per inhabitant from the commercial country sector. This would not account for the failure of provincial financial institutions to gather a significant volume of deposits.

The difficulties encountered by provincial institutions in raising funds locally were basically the same as those that prevented center banks from developing their business nationally, thereby forcing them to concentrate it instead at the central level. Considering what has been said about the country's social and economic characteristics, the explanation is fairly predictable. Low levels of income in the provinces coupled with a strong cultural resistance at all levels of society conspired to oppose the transformation of savings into the abundance of deposits that would render branches attractive to center banks. Lack of promising investment opportunities, both in terms of price and safety, complemented this, a reflection of the backwardness of agriculture, which was the dominant activity. Branching was also deterred by the high cost of information and the difficulty in monitoring asset performance in inaccessible places and in a highly segmented economy.

The well-documented experience of the Bank of Portugal is revealing of all these aspects.[17] It opened its 18 branches during the 1890s, very much against its will and as a result of a governmental imposition. The board's view was always that branches would not be profitable and would needlessly divert management effort from more lucrative tasks, and this is what happened. The situation gradually improved up to 1914 but profitability remained low for several reasons. On the demand side, business opportunities were considered unattractive because of the commercial backwardness of the interior, its low level of commercialization and of trading links with the outside, leading to a lack of good paper. Finding good and reliable clients proved difficult and an intolerably high number of more or less fraudulent practices had to be combated. Behind this lay a circumstance to which allusion has been made before: the lack of human capital in the country and in the periphery in particular. Filling both managerial and clerical posts turned out to be one of the chief problems of branch management and frequently had to be done from headquarters because suitable personnel could not be found locally. Moreover, problems emerged also with respect to standards of honesty, forcing the Bank repeatedly to dismiss and even pursue judicially some of its branch managers for gross fraud and embezzlement. Under these conditions, it comes as no surprise that frequently the board, in Lisbon, could not find out the debit position of its provincial clients and ended up extending credits well in excess of what it considered appropriate.

All in all, it is hard to pin on any centralizing urges of the state the responsibility for one of the salient characteristics of the Portuguese financial system, that is, its high concentration and the correlated weakness of its peripheral institutions. Rather it would appear that provincial savings were simply not there to be captured by any kind of institution, be it private or official, profit or non-profit. This conclusion is further reinforced by the contrast between the weakness of peripheral banking and the relative success of the Lisbon based Monte Pio Geral in mobilizing deposits from among an urban and better-off population. Can a similar reasoning be used for the second of these characteristics, namely the fact that commercial banking in Portugal evinced a strongly universal nature?

According to the Verdier model, universal banking would not have been anomalous in a situation where political arrangements could be characterized as semi-centralized. Commercial banks, in this case, would have had to face the competition of fairly developed profit and non-profit provincial banks both for deposits and for credits to certain sections of the economy. They would have been compelled to rely to a considerable extent on their own resources and to do business mainly with large clients, who would want long- as well as short-term credit. At the same time, their liability structure would have required high earnings, in order to satisfy shareholders, and this would have rendered necessary a greater share of long-term, riskier operations. But this is not how the Portuguese case can be described. Firstly, as we have seen, politically the situation was clearly centralized, not semi-centralized. In the second place, in terms of financial structures the periphery was very weak and could not be blamed for any barriers to business encountered by the center commercial banks. Once again, a closer look at the facts brings out the importance of social and economic factors in explaining this evolution, although this time the role of the state is not absent from the picture either.

On one thing there is undoubtedly agreement. The liability structure of these institutions, with its heavy dependence on low volatility resources (share capital and reserves), was strongly favorable to a credit policy that was weighted in favor of long-term operations. The banks in our sample could risk a high level of illiquidity and still not have to maintain large cash reserves because deposits did not represent a strong liquidity threat. This is borne out by the fact that it was the three of them with the largest proportion of deposits to total liabilities – Comercial de Lisboa, Viseense and Barcelos – that were the least "mixed" in our sample. Indeed, for the entire group that we have been able to study, the correlation between their shares of short-term credits in total assets and their shares of capital in total liabilities is an eloquent –0.78.

Interesting though this finding may be, it does not take us very far unless we are able to account for their liability structure itself, and here we have to resort to social and economic circumstances as well as to the state's role, though not in a regulatory mode. The crux of the matter lies once more not in any contest between center and periphery, or state versus profit sectors, for control of the country's deposits, but in a pronounced scarcity of deposits in general. As a result, even though the center banks obtained the lion's share of these funds, they were still left to finance most of their operations through own capital.

Three reasons can be invoked to explain this scarcity. A low income per capita by European standards is the first since it obviously determined both the savings propensity and the absolute value of per capita savings. While there is abundant evidence on the country's poverty, data on saving habits are not available. It is worth noting however that by 1950, when little structural change had occurred since the early twentieth century, at 7 percent, this propensity was still low – it was to rise rapidly thereafter, in a context of intense economic growth, to reach 20 percent and more. A possible indirect measure of the country's savings effort can be estimated by comparing the stock of all financial assets held by local residents (i.e. excluding foreign investments) with the Prados (2000) GDP per capita figures for circa 1900. If we attribute to Denmark a value in this exercise of 100, Portugal comes out of it at one half this level, a clear sign of a far poorer savings environment (Reis, 1999a).

Higher personal savings would have been only a necessary condition for a larger volume of deposits, however not a sufficient one. There was also a need to raise what might be termed the degree of financial sophistication of the population, which derived in turn from prevailing cultural and literacy levels, as well as from the amount of its experience in dealing with modern financial instruments. This relationship has been noted by several authors (Sandberg, 1978; Bordo and Jonung, 1987) and, in the Portuguese case, can be clearly perceived in the lukewarm reception accorded by the population even to basic financial instruments of everyday use. One aspect of this is its reluctant acceptance of bank notes. Between 1854 and 1891, when the gold standard was in force, though convertible without difficulty, notes were not a welcome medium of exchange. The Bank of Portugal did its best to push them into circulation but their share of the money stock (M0) never exceeded the 11 percent mark. When inconvertibility was ushered in, in 1891, and notes largely replaced gold and silver, obviously this had to change but illiteracy did not make matters easy. A foreign observer commented that "people of all classes even those who are incapable of reading a word or a number, made an effort to distinguish the different notes by their colors and only a few cases are known of illiterates having accepted the wrong one" (quoted in Reis, 1991). The use of checks, which was legal, was likewise restricted to a very small number. Their annual circulation in the early 1900s was of the order of 0.09 items per inhabitant, a plausible figure since only those who had bank accounts and who could read and write easily would normally have employed them (Reis, 1991).[18]

Finally, winning over economic agents to the habit of depositing their savings would have been feasible only in the presence of credit institutions that were more embedded socially than the predominant commercial banks which in reality catered to a small and socially superior stratum of society.[19] For the vast majority of the population and, in particular, its rural component, the path would have been considerably smoothed by a network of credit co-operatives and popular banks designed to overcome barriers and attenuate suspicions, as happened contemporaneously in many corners of Europe, where these flourished. It is worth remembering that in Denmark, at this time, local savings and mortgage banks were responsible for 70 percent of all financial liabilities. In Portugal, repeated efforts were made in this direction, with and without direct state support, but the result was no more than a handful of anemic rural credit institutions and the three agricultural and industrial credit banks that we have alluded to before (Castro, 1900). It appears likely however that rural Portugal lacked the social conditions that, in more developed areas of Europe, would foster co-ordination mechanisms between participants, which were widely trusted and accepted by them, and that would enable an efficient process of screening, monitoring and enforcement of credit contracts. A shortage of local human capital for running these operations and a lack of interest on the part of the local élite has also been recognized in other contexts as a powerful obstacle (Guinnane, 1994), and seem to have been present in this case too. In this respect, it is interesting that even the provincial wealthy in Portugal had a low preference for bank deposits. Helder Fonseca has shown that in late nineteenth-century Alentejo, landlords and big farmers kept only 19 percent of their financial assets in this form, while in Figueira da Foz, a second-rank port town, the proportion was even tinier (Fonseca, 1996; Cascão, 1989). The result was that informal capital markets thrived and there may even have been a growing propensity to hoard surpluses rather than to recycle them in the form of deposits through the formal financial system (Reis, 2000).

The state was important to the development of the country's corporate financial institutions, not as regulator of financial markets but rather as participant in them, as issuer of Portugal's Public Debt. With a value for this debt in 1910 that was nearly three times that of aggregate bank deposits, this emerges as a classic case of crowding out of banks and other financial actors. Informed public opinion never tired in fact of denouncing this situation, focusing in particular on the nefarious effect this had on direct credit to agriculture and industry, but it is obvious that all sectors of the economy suffered. The problem was that state bonds were safe, they gave a return of 5–6 percent, in contrast to the 2–3 percent earned by deposits, and they came in large denominations that targeted the well-to-do, who were essentially also the clientele of commercial banks. Surprisingly, this effect must have also hurt and delayed the development of the state's own savings bank, whose clients had a similar profile and included only a minority of workers and low-grade employees.[20] At the same time, it is important to stress that had there been a lesser absorption of savings by the Public Debt, this would probably not have entailed a stronger development of the periphery's financial sector. As noted earlier, an overwhelming share of these bonds was held by residents of Lisbon and Oporto and in this event they would have gravitated to alternatives such as center banks deposits or corporate stocks.

It is a matter for speculation whether a lesser pressure of the Public Debt on national resources would have changed the universal nature of the center commercial banks. At first sight, one might expect that if banks found themselves with a more volatile composition of their liabilities, i.e. a greater proportion of deposits, this would have driven them towards a more specialized and more commercial vocation, as should indeed happen in centralized states. But again, this is at best only a necessary condition. As was pointed out by two contemporary experts – Lumbralles (1926) and Cabreira (1915) – the resilience of mixed banking was determined not only by supply side conditions. There was also a demand side to the story. For both these authors, its principal cause lay in the exiguous dimension of the home market, which left little room for banks to specialize and forced them instead to engage in a wide variety of operations, hence their universality. On the basis of a reading of the archival material of the Bank of Portugal, one could add that pure commercial banking was hard to carry out properly owing to the general dearth of good quality short-term bills. In the provinces, in particular, commercial practice was still so backward that genuine trade bills, with good names and backed by real transactions, were hard to find, and the alternative was either to acquire other types of earning assets or do no business at all. This was a problem in the financial centers also, although to a lesser degree, and the conclusion that emerges is that even had resources been released from the stifling embrace of the Public Debt, banking might well still have remained essentially mixed.

Returning now to Verdier's model, the main lesson to be drawn from all of the above is that, as regards the prevalence of universalism, what matters is not simply the degree of centralization of the polity. The latter could have an impact on the shape of the financial system but this would depend on whether public finances were normally balanced or not. In Portugal, where there was a persistent deficit and a pyramiding of Public Debt, corporate financial activity of every kind was bound to be crowded out. Whatever happened in the periphery of the country, mixed banking was certain to arise as the dominant form of banking, particularly if the Public Debt outweighed the national saving capacity. Instead of center profit banks being out-competed by peripheral institutions, the picture here is one of their being driven away from the national savings pool by the state. The latter, however, did this not by using its regulatory clout but rather by employing its market power. In a centralized state financial concentration and bank specialization should only be expected to come together in the cases where a sound fiscal policy was also practiced.

Lack of space precludes an extensive treatment of two further points concerning the rise of a strong mixed banking sector in Portugal. One is whether the existence of a central liquidity guarantor, to ensure the liquidity of the components of the financial system as well as the latter's equilibrium as a whole, was a positive factor, if not in fact a necessity. The other is whether mixed banks only arose because the owners of shares in them, who provided most of their funding, required substantial dividends and this obliged center banks to deal prevalently in long-term, high-return and therefore riskier assets than if they had been commercial. As regards the first, the Bank of Portugal, though a competitor, certainly acted simultaneously as a fairly consistent lender of last resort. It often sustained individual banks in trouble and, during the two major banking crises of 1876 and 1891, it acted in a systematic way to bring back stability (Reis, 1999b). Why did it accept to play this game? In the first place, being by far the largest bank it had a vested interest in ensuring a stable financial system since any crisis of confidence was bound to affect it too. In the second place, as a privileged bank it came to be gradually regarded by the authorities and the public as having some public responsibilities. These were not laid down formally but were consensual and certainly included the Bank's duty to keep the monetary system convertible and to prevent any collapse of the financial system.

It is not evident, however, that universal banking emerged because bankers realized that this protection was available to them and felt therefore encouraged to participate in riskier types of banking. More likely it was the other way round. As the financial system grew and evolved, the Bank of Portugal found itself having to intervene every so often, as banks fell into difficulties that were caused, at least in part, by the riskier and less liquid mix of assets that they handled. And this led on to situations of moral hazard that could not but persist and grow, given that the Bank had no formal supervisory powers over the sector. The fact that Portuguese banking for profit suffered from quite a high mortality between 1860 and 1914 – of the 71 banks created only 23 still survived on the eve of the World War I – points in this direction. On the other hand, it does not necessarily mean that the liquidity guarantor performed inadequately, or that the risks taken by a great many banks were excessive. One reason is that the lender of last resort, understandably, tended to assist the larger financial corporations – those that were "too big to fail" – and let many small ones fall by the wayside. Except for the crisis of 1891, none of the big banks helped by the Bank of Portugal was ever allowed to fail, and therefore the system was essentially well looked after. The second reason is that if banks plunged recklessly into highly risky investments, characteristically they were not highly lucrative ones too. The record on dividends distributed by Portuguese banks from 1860 to 1892 reveals a sector where returns varied a lot over time and from bank to bank but overall were not impressive (Portugal, *Annaes de Estatística*, 1894). Modal values were only 5 to 6 percent a year, i.e. very similar to the return on Public Debt bonds, and for individual institutions they could vary over a range from 2–11 percent. Provincial banks paid a bit less, i.e. 3–4 percent, probably reflecting the poorer business opportunities in their territories.

Conclusion

Although it is tempting to end with a summary statement of the sort "neither Verdier nor Gerschenkron", it will be obvious to any reader how much both paradigms have helped to shape this account. Verdier's work has provided the incentive to focus on the role played by politics and the state in shaping financial systems. Gerschenkron's writings have stimulated this debate for decades and have provided us with stimulating reflections on the links between social and economic backwardness and the manner in which financial institutions arise and evolve. Grand models, however, when applied to concrete cases, are rarely immune to flaws and, in this particular instance, limitations have come to light suggesting that the original formulations of the problem at hand may have failed to take all aspects into consideration.

As a result, the Portuguese financial system, as depicted, ends up here displaying a rather poor fit relative to either of these interpretations. In terms of the Verdier model, its peculiarity lies in its domination by universal banks, its lack of branch banking and the weakness of its equity market. A centralized polity such as this one should have given rise to the opposite features. In this case however social, economic and cultural factors overshadowed the influence of the state's role in this matter and fostered an environment that was not encouraging either to commercial banks, to branch banking or to a strong stock exchange. All the same, the state did contribute to this outcome too, by managing to capture a large part of the already scarce financial resources of the community that, if otherwise employed, might have sustained the development of a very different situation. To do so, it did not need to use its regulatory capacity in order to block financial competitors. Instead, it was able to resort to its superior market power by issuing a crushing Public Debt that enabled it to make ends meet whilst running a permanently unbalanced budget. Probably, only a strongly centralized state could have done this but the argument here is that this was not enough. Only if it had followed such an unhealthy financial policy would it have needed to do so and this was not only characteristic of the situation in Portugal. In other countries of southern Europe, where public finances were similarly problematic, shades of this account are to be found as well, suggesting that Portugal was by no means an anomaly and that this approach to the study of its financial system may have some general validity.

The case described in this chapter also evokes interesting parallels with some of Gerschenkron's ideas on backwardness. As Sylla and Toniolo (1991a: 6) have pointed out, they included variables like "savings ratios, literacy, some technology related indicators (e.g. patents), per capita social overhead capital and even less measurable ones such as ideology". Gerschenkron was not interested, however, in all instances of backwardness but only in a particular kind, that of economies where a strong tension existed between obstacles to industrial development and the "great promise inherent in such a development" (Gerschenkron, 1962: 8). He was not concerned with countries that displayed a low potential for growth, i.e. where the "tension" would be weak, and therefore the southern European economies fell outside his scope. The key issue as regards Portugal is that universal banking arose not because growth-induced demand for finance was so strong that it was hard to meet by other means, but because it was so weak and compelled banks to diversify the nature of their assets. Moreover, on the supply side of banking, while he would have recognized the problem induced by the lack of savings, he was not concerned with the effect of an over-sized public debt that sterilized financial resources and blocked the development of commercial banking.

The final question that this chapter poses is whether the Portuguese case is singular or forms part of a coherent category that somehow has been missed by the two beacons that we have been following. The brief references made in the preceding pages to other countries in similar circumstances are a hint that the second hypothesis might be reasonable. Other polities faced difficult financial histories and their central authorities drained savings via the emission of a huge public debt. Domestic savings were scarce, economic agents were wary of the organized financial world and their economies languished at the bottom of the league tables for European economic growth. An answer to this here would require far more time and space than are available but might prove rewarding in the context of a comparative understanding of financial systems.

Notes

1   For examples of a departure from this state of affairs, see Levine, 1997 and some of the papers in Cottrell and Reis, 1998.
2   A symptom of this difficulty is the continued use of Goldsmith's work from the 1960s in spite of the progress there has been over the last three decades in historical statistics.
3   For a recent effort in this direction, see Sylla, Tilly and Tortella, 1999.
4   A more pessimistic view (Maddison, 1995) puts Portugal behind even Finland and Greece and attributes it a GDP per capita equal to 27 percent of the British one.
5   We have included both the internal and the external debts, the latter issued in London mainly and in gold, on the grounds that most of it was in fact held by Portuguese investors and was widely traded on the domestic stock market. For the sake of comparability, we have done the same for Denmark (Platt, 1980).
6   According to Flandreau, 1998 Portugal had one of the worst credit ratings attributed by the research department of the Crédit Lyonnais, along with Serbia, Argentina, Greece and Brazil.
7   Whether before or after 1891, when the Bank of Portugal became the country's sole note issuer, the state's banker and cashier, and a major creditor to the Treasury, its commercial activity was always pre-eminent and is included in this category. The same applies to the Danish National Bank.
8   See also Fohlin, 1998; and Tilly, 1995.
9   This considerable freedom suffered restrictions after legislation in 1894-96.
10   These statutes are transcribed in Ferreira, 1970.
11   See for instance Goodhart, 1986: chapter 2.
12   For the text of this law, see Portugal, *Diário do Governo*, 7 May 1867.
13   For the text of the law, see Portugal, *Diário do Governo*, 17 January 1867.
14   They were created in Viseu, Viana do Castelo and Faro. The last two failed during the 1890s.
15   See Portugal, *Anuário Estatístico de Portugal*, 1875 and 1903. They were governed by laws passed in 1891 and 1896 that placed them under the supervision of the local civil governor (Portuguese equivalent of the French *préfet*).
16   The Caixa Geral de Depósitos was founded in 1876 but started taking individual deposits only in the 1880s.
17   The following is drawn from archival sources and will be published as part of the second volume of the history of this institution.
18   The absence of a Chamber of Compensation for checks may have been an additional deterrent to their use but its introduction in 1926 did not seriously alter the situation.
19   One sign of this was the existence of minima for paying in or paying out of deposit accounts, which were entirely out of the reach of workers and even the lower strata of the middle class.
20   The annual accounts of the Caixa Geral de Depósitos provide details on the socio-professional background of depositors. Their deposits were typically of substantial amounts.

Works cited

Ahlström, G. (1989), "Riksgäldskontoret och Sveriges statsskuld före 1850-talet", in E. Dahmén (ed.), *Upplåning och utveckling. Riksgäldskontoret 1789–1989*, Stockholm: Allmänna Förlaget, 95–112.

Albrecht, C. (1990), "The decision to establish savings banks in Bohemia, 1825–1870", in J. Komlos (ed.), *Economic Development in the Habsburg Monarchy and the Successor States*, New York: East European Monographs, 75–87.

Albrecht, C. (1989), "Nationalism and municipal savings banks in Bohemia before 1914", *Slovene Studies*, 11(1–2): 57–64.

Aleotti, A. (1990), *Borsa e industria 1861–1989. Cento anni di rapporti difficili*, Milan: Edizione di Comunità.

Alieri, S., and E. Cerrito (1996), "Elementi per una settorizzazione dei bilanci delle aziende di credito", in F. Cotula, T. Raganelli, V. Sannucci, S. Alieri, and E. Cerrito (eds), *I bilanci delle aziende di credito, 1890–1936*, Collana storica della Banca d'Italia, Serie statistiche storiche, vol. 3, Bari and Rome: Laterza, 301–339.

Anan'ich, B.V. (1996), "Banking firms in the Russian Empire, 1860–1914: Topics in the history of private enterprise", *Russian Studies in History: A Journal of Translations*, Summer: 6–88.

Anderson, B.L., and P.L. Cottrell (1974), *Money and Banking in England: The Development of the Banking System, 1694–1914*, Newton Abbot: David & Charles.

Anfimov, A.M., and A.P. Korelin (eds) (1995), *Rossiia 1913 g.: Statistiko-dokumental'nyi spravochnik*, St. Petersburg: BLITS.

Aoki, M., B. Gustafsson, and O.E. Williamson (eds) (1990), *The Firm as a Nexus of Treaties*, London: Sage.

Arrighetti, A., and G. Seravalli (eds) (1999), *Istituzioni intermedie e sviluppo locale*, Rome: Donzelli.

Asajima, S. (1990), "Characteristics of the Japanese financial system during the inter-war period", in P.L. Cottrell, A. Teichova, and T. Yuzawa (eds), *Finance in the Age of the Corporate Economy: The Third Anglo-Japanese Business History Conference*, Aldershot: Ashgate, 1997, 79–93.

Aschauer, G. *et al.* (eds) (1984), *Standortbestimmung: Entwicklungslinien der deutschen Kreditwirtschaft*, Stuttgart: Deutscher Sparkassenverlag.

Ashton, T.S. (1945), "The Bill of Exchange and private banks in Lancashire, 1790–1830", *Economic History Review*, 15(1): 25–35.

Australia, Commonwealth Bureau of Census and Statistics (1908), *Official Year Book of the Commonwealth of Australia 1901–1907*, Melbourne: McCarron, Bird & Co.

Baker, M., and M. Collins (1999), "English industrial distress before 1914 and the response of the banks", *European Review of Economic History*, 3(1): 1–24.

Balogh, T. (1947), *Studies in Financial Organization*, London: Cambridge University Press.

Banking Almanac, The (1913), London: R. Groombridge and Sons.

Barclay's Capital (2000), *Equity-Gilt Study 2000*, London: Barclay's Bank.

Barendregt, J. (1999), "Towards national status, 1870–1914", in J. de Vries, W. Vroom, T. de Graaf (eds), *World Wide Banking, ABN AMRO Bank 1824–1999*, Amsterdam: ABN AMRO Bank, 127–184.

Barkai, H. (1973), "The macro-economics of Tsarist Russia in the industrialization era: Monetary developments, the balance of payments and the Gold Standard", *Journal of Economic History*, 33: 339–371.

Berend, I.T., and G. Ránki (1982), *The European Periphery and Industrialization, 1780– 1914*, New York: Cambridge University Press.

Bergh, T. (1975), *Fra Fædrelandssag til Storbank. Norges Postsparebank 1950–1975*, Oslo: Styret i Norges postsparebank.

Berghuis, W.H. (1967), *Ontstaan en ontwikkeling van de Nederlandse beleggingsfondsen tot 1914*, Assen: Van Gorcum.

Bernis, Francisco (1919), *La Hacienda Española*, Barcelona: Editorial Minerva.

Betänkande angående Sveriges ekonomiska och finansiella utveckling under åren 1834– 1860 (9 February 1863), Stockholm.

Bizet de Frayne, L.C. (1818), *Précis des divers manières de spéculer sur les fonds publics en usage à la Bourse de Paris*, 3rd edn, Paris: Delaunay.

Black, C.E. (ed.) (1960), *The Transformation of Russian Society: Aspects of Social Change since 1861*, Cambridge, MA: Harvard University Press.

Bloomfield, G.T. (1984), *New Zealand: A Handbook of Historical Statistics*, Boston, MA: Hall & Co.

Boksjö, A., and M. Lönnborg-Andersson (1994), "Svenska finanskriser: orsaker, förlopp, åtgärder och konsekvenser", *Uppsala Papers in Financial History*, no. 2, Uppsala University.

Bonin, H. (1993), "Frankreich", in H. Pohl (ed.), *Europäische Bankengeschichte*, Frankfurt a. M.: Institut für Bankhistorische Forschung, 250–262.

Borchardt, K. (1971), "Realkredit- und Pfandbriefmarkt im Wandel von 100 Jahren", in *100 Jahre Rheinische Hypothekenbank*, Frankfurt a. M.: Knapp, 105–196.

Bordo, M.D., and L. Jonung (1987), *The Long-Run Behaviour of the Velocity of Circulation*, New York: Cambridge University Press.

Bordo, M.D., and R. Sylla (eds) (1995), *Anglo-American Financial Systems: Institutions and Markets in the Twentieth Century*, Burr Ridge, IL: Irwin.

Born, K.E. (1983a), *International Banking in the 19th and 20th Centuries*, Leamington Spa: Berg.

Born, K.E. (1983b), "Vom Beginn des Ersten Weltkrieges bis zum Ende der Weimar Republik (1914–1933)", in Hans Pohl (ed.) *Deutsche Bankengeschichte*, vol. 3, Frankfurt: Knapp.

Born, K.E. (1977), *Geld und Banken im 19. und 20. Jahrhundert*, Stuttgart: Kröner.

Born, K.E. (1967), *Die deutsche Bankenkrise 1931*, Munich: R. Piper & Co.

Bouvier, J. (1988), "The Banque de France and the State from 1850 to the present day", in Gianni Toniolo (ed.), *Central Banks' Independence in Historical Perspective*, Berlin: Walter de Gruyter, 72–104.

Bouvier, J. (1973), *Un siècle de banques françaises*, Paris: Hachette.

Bouvier, J. (1968), *Naissance d'une banque: Le Crédit Lyonnais*, Paris: Flammarion.

Bouvier, J., and J.C. Perrot (eds) (1985), *Etats, Fiscalités, Economies*, Paris: Publications de la Sorbonne.

Bovykin, V.I. (1984), *Formirovanie finansovogo kapitala v Rossii*, Moscow: Sciences.

Bovykin, V.I., and B. Anan'ich (1991), "The role of international factors in the formation of the banking system in Russia", in R. Cameron and V.I. Bovykin (eds), *International Banking, 1870–1914*, New York: Oxford University Press, 130–158.

Boyce, G. (1992), "64thers, syndicates, and stock promotions: Information flows and fund raising techniques of British shipowners before 1914", *Journal of Economic History*, 52(1): 181–205.

Braudel, F., and E. Labrousse (eds) (1976), *Histoire économique et sociale de la France* III/1, Paris: Presses Universitaires de France.

Brewer, J. (1989), *The Sinews of Power: War, Money and the English State, 1688–1783*, New York: Knopf.

Brizi, R., and S. Petricola (1994), "Le stanze di compensazione dalle origini agli anni cinquanta", in S. Baia Curioni *et al.*, *Ricerche per la storia della Banca d'Italia*, Collana storia della Banca d'Italia, Serie contribuiti, vol 5, Rome and Bari: Laterza, 209–306.

Broz, J.L. (1998), "The origins of central banking: Solutions to the free-rider problem", *International Organization*, 52(2): 231–268.

Broz, J.L. (1997), *International Origins of the Federal Reserve System*, Ithaca: Cornell University Press.

Brück, C. *et al.* (1995), *Les caisses d'épargne en Europe*, Tome 1, *Les douze pays de l'Union européenne*, Paris: Les Éditions de l'Épargne.

Buist, M.G. (1974), *At spes non fracta: Hope & Co. 1770–1815: Merchant Bankers and Diplomats at Work*, Amsterdam: Nijhoff.

Burt, R. (1998), "Segmented capital markets and patterns of investment in late Victorian Britain: Evidence from the non-ferrous mining industry", *Economic History Review*, 51(4): 709–733.

Burt, R. (1997), "British investment in the American mining frontier", *Business and Economic History*, 26(2): 515–525.

Bussière, E. (1997), "Banks, economic development and capitalism in France", in A. Teichova, G. Kurgan-van Hentenryk, and D. Ziegler (eds), *Banking, Trade and Industry: Europe, America and Asia from the Thirteenth to the Twentieth Century*, Cambridge: Cambridge University Press, 113–130.

Butlin, S.J., A.R. Hall, and R.C. White (1971), *Australian Banking and Monetary Statistics 1817–1945*, Sydney: Reserve Bank of Australia, Occasional Paper, no. 4A.

Cabreira, T. (1915), *O Problema Bancário Português*, Lisbon: Imprensa de Libânio da Silva.

Cafagna, L. (1989), *Dualismo e sviluppo nella storia d'Italia*, Venice: Marsilio.

Calomiris, C.W. (1995), "The costs of rejecting universal banking: American finance in the German mirror, 1870–1914", in N.R. Lamoreaux and D.M.G. Raff (eds), *Coordination and Information: Historical Perspectives on the Organization of Enterprise*, Chicago: University of Chicago Press, 257–315.

Cameron, R.E. (1967), "England, 1750–1844", in Cameron *et al.* (eds), *Banking in the Early Stages of Industrialization: A Study in Comparative Economic History*, New York: Oxford University Press, 15–59.

Cameron, R.E. (1961), *France and the Economic Development of Europe, 1800–1914*, Princeton: Princeton University Press.

Cameron, R.E. (ed.) (1972), *Banking and Economic Development: Some Lessons of History*, New York: Oxford University Press.

Cameron, R.E., and V.I. Bovykin (eds) (1991), *International Banking, 1870–1914*, New York: Oxford University Press.

Cameron, R.E., with the collaboration of O. Crisp, H.T. Patrick, and R. Tilly (eds) (1967), *Banking in the Early Stages of Industrialization: A Study in Comparative Economic History*, New York: Oxford University Press.

Canada, Department of Agriculture (1890), *The Statistical Year-Book of Canada for 1889*, Ottawa: Brown Chamberlin.

Canada, Dominion Bureau of Statistics, Department of Trade and Commerce (various years), *The Canada Yearbook*, Ottawa.

Capie, F. (1995), "Prudent and stable (but inefficient?): Commercial banks in Britain, 1890–1940", in M.D. Bordo and R. Sylla (eds), *Anglo-American Financial Systems: Institutions and Markets in the Twentieth Century*, Burr Ridge, IL: Irwin, 41–65.

Capie, F., and M. Collins (1997), "Deficient suppliers? Commercial banks in the United Kingdom, 1870–1980", in P.L. Cottrell, A. Teichova, and T. Yuzawa (eds), *Finance in the Age of the Corporate Economy: The Third Anglo-Japanese Business History Conference*, Aldershot: Ashgate, 1997, 164–183.

Capie, F., and M. Collins (1996), "Industrial lending by English commercial banks, 1860s–1914", *Business History*, 38(1): 26–44.

Capie, F., and A. Webber (1985), *A Monetary History of the United Kingdom, 1870–1982*, London: Allen & Unwin.

Caprio, Jr., G., and D. Vittas (eds) (1997), *Reforming Financial Systems: Historical Implications for Policy*, Cambridge: Cambridge University Press.

Cascão, R. (1989), "Permanência e Mudança em Duas Comunidades do Litoral: Figueira da Foz e Buarcos entre 1861 e 1910", Ph.D. dissertation, University of Coimbra.

Cassis, Y. (ed.) (1992), *Finance and Financiers in Europe: 19th-20th Centuries*, Cambridge: Cambridge University Press.

Cassis, Y., G.D. Feldman, and U. Olson (eds) (1995), *The Evolution of Financial Institutions and Markets in Twentieth Century Europe*, Aldershot: Scolar Press.

Castro, A. de (1971), *A Revolução Industrial em Portugal no Século XIX*, Lisbon: Dom Quixote.

Castro, D.L. de (1900), "Le Crédit Agricole et le Mouvement Associatif Rural", in B.C. Cincinato da Costa and D.L. de Castro (eds), *Le Portugal au Point de Vue Agricole*, Lisbon: Imprensa Nacional.

Chaudhuri, K.N. (1978), *The Trading World of Asia and the English East India Company 1660–1760*, New York: Cambridge University Press.

Checkland, O. *et al.* (1994), *Pacific Banking, 1858–1959: East Meets West*, New York: St. Martin's.

Chlepner, B.S. (1943), *Belgian Banking and Banking Theory*, Washington DC: The Brookings Institution.

Chlepner, B.S. (1930), *Le marché financier belge depuis cent ans*, Brussels: Librairie Falk Fils.

Chlepner, B.S. (1926), *La banque en Belgique. Etude historique et économique*, Brussels: Lamertin.

Cincinato da Costa, B.C., and D.L. de Castro (eds) (1900), *Le Portugal au Point de Vue Agricole*, Lisbon: Imprensa Nacional.

Cleveland, H. van B., and Huertas, T.F. (1985), *Citibank 1812–1970*, Cambridge, MA: Harvard University Press.

Coleman, W.D., and H.J. Jacek (eds) (1989), *Regionalism, Business Interests and Public Policy*, London: Sage.

Collins, M. (1998), "English bank development within a European context, 1870–1939", *Economic History Review*, 51(1): 1–24.

Collins, M. (1991), *Banks and Industrial Finance in Britain, 1800–1939*, London: Macmillan.

Conant, C.A. (1927), *A History of Modern Banks of Issue*, 6th edn, New York: Putnam's Sons.

Confalonieri, A. (1982), *Banca e industria in Italia della crisi del 1907 all'agosto 1914*, 2 vols, Milan: Banca Commerciale Italiana.

Confalonieri, A. (1977–80), *Banca e industria in Italia (1894–1906)*, 3 vols, Milan: Banca Commerciale Italiana.

Conti, G., and G. Ferri (1997), "Banche locali e sviluppo economico decentrato", in F. Barca (ed.), *Storia del capitalismo italiano dal dopoguerra ad oggi*, Rome: Donzelli, 429–465.

Conti, G., and S. La Francesca (eds) (2000), *Banche e reti di banche nell'Italia postunitaria*, 2 vols, Bologna: Il Mulino.

Conze, W. (1973), "Möglichkeiten und Grenzen der liberalen Arbeiterbewegung in Deutschland: Das Beispiel Schulze-Delitzsch", in H.J. Varain (ed.), *Interessenverbände in Deutschland*, Cologne: Kiepenheuer & Witsch.

Cottrell, P.L., G. Feldman, and J. Reis, (eds) (forthcoming), *Finance and the Making of Modern Capitalism*, Aldershot: Ashgate.

Cottrell, P.L., and J. Reis (1998), *Finance and the Making of the Modern Capitalist World, 1750–1931*, Madrid: Fundación Fomento de la Historia Económica.

Cottrell, P.L. *et al.* (1997), *Finance in the Age of the Corporate Economy: The Third Anglo-Japanese Business History Conference*, Aldershot: Ashgate.

Cotula, F., and T. Raganelli (1996), "*Introduzione*", in F. Cotula, T. Raganelli, V. Sannucci, S. Alieri, and E. Cerrito (1996) (eds), *I bilanci delle aziende di credito, 1890–1936*, Collana storica della Banca d'Italia, Serie statistiche storiche, vol. 3, Bari and Rome: Laterza, 3–56.

Cotula, F., T. Raganelli, V. Sannucci, S. Alieri, and E. Cerrito (1996) (eds), *I bilanci delle aziende di credito, 1890–1936*, Collana storica della Banca d'Italia, Serie statistiche storiche, vol. 3, Bari and Rome: Laterza.

Crane, D.B. *et al.* (1995), *The Global Financial System: A Functional Perspective*, Boston: Harvard Business School Press.

Crisp, O. (1976a), "Banking in the Industrialization of Tsarist Russia, 1860–1914", in O. Crisp (ed.), *Studies in the Russian Economy before 1914*, London: Macmillan, 111–158.

Crisp, O. (1976b), "Russia's public debt and the French market, 1889–1914: A statistical assessment", in O. Crisp (ed.), *Studies in the Russian Economy before 1914*, London: Macmillan.

Crisp, O. (1976c), *Studies in the Russian Economy before 1914*, London: Macmillan.

Dash, M. (1999), *Tulipomania: The Story of the World's Most Coveted Flower and the Extraordinary Passions it Aroused*, New York: Crown.

De Cecco, M. (1974), *Money and Empire*, Oxford: Basil Blackwell.

Deeg, R. (1999), *Finance Capitalism Unveiled: Banks and the German Political Economy*, Ann Arbor: University of Michigan Press.

Dehing, P.W.N.M., and M. 't Hart (1997), "Linking the fortunes: Currency and banking 1550–1880", in M. 't Hart, J.P.B. Jonker, and J.L. van Zanden (eds), *A Financial History of the Netherlands*, New York: Cambridge University Press, 37–63.

De Mattia, R. (ed.) (1990), *Storia delle operazioni degli istituti di emissione italiani dal 1845 al 1936 attraverso i dati dei loro bilanci*, 3 vols, Rome: Banca d'Italia.

Denmark, Statistiske Undersøgelser (1969), *Kreditmarkedsstatistik*, no. 24, Copenhagen: Danmarks Statistik.

de Slechte, C.H. (1982), *Een noodlottig jaar voor veel zotte en wijze', de Rotterdamse windhandel van 1720*, The Hague: Nijhoff.

Deutsche Bundesbank (1976), *Deutsches Geld- und Bankwesen in Zahlen, 1876–1975*, Frankfurt am Main: Fritz Knapp.

de Vries, J., W. Vroom, and T. de Graaf (eds) (1999), *World Wide Banking: ABN AMRO Bank 1824–1999*, Amsterdam: ABN AMRO Bank.

Dickson, P.G.M. (1967), *The Financial Revolution in England: A Study in the Development of Public Credit 1688–1756*, New York: St. Martin's.

Dieckmann, J. (1981), *Der Einfluss der deutschen Sparkassen auf die staatliche Wirtschaftspolitik in der historischen Entwicklung*, Frankfurt: Rita K. Fischer.

Diederiks, H., and D. Reeder (eds) (1996), *Cities of Finance*, Amsterdam: North-Holland.

Dimsdale, N., and M. Prevezer, (eds) (1994), *Capital Markets and Corporate Governance*, Oxford: Oxford University Press.

Di Quirico, R. (1999), "The initial phases of Italian banks' expansion abroad, 1900–31", *Financial History Review*, 6(1): 7–24.

Dow, J., and G. Gorton (1997), "Stock Market efficiency and economic efficiency: Is there a connection?", *Journal of Finance* 52: 1087–1129.

Drummond, I. (1976), "The Russian gold standard, 1897–1914", *Journal of Economic History*, 36: 663–688.

Ecklund, G.J., and S. Knutsen (2000), *Vern mot kriser?: norsk finanstilsyn gjennom 100 år*, Bergen: Fagbokforl.

Edwards, J., and K. Fischer (1994), *Banks, Finance and Investment in Germany*, New York: Cambridge University Press.

Edwards, J., and S. Ogilvie (1996), "Universal banks and German industrialization: A reappraisal", *Economic History Review* 49(3): 427–446.

Egge, A. (1983), "Transformation of bank structures in the industrial period: The case of Norway 1830–1914", *Journal of European Economic History*, 2: 271–294.

Eigner, P. (1994), "Interlocking directorships between commercial banks and industry in interwar Vienna", in A. Teichova, T. Gourvish, and A. Pogány (eds), *Universal Banking in the Twentieth Century: Finance, Industry and State in North and Central Europe*, Aldershot: E. Elgar, 260–294.

Eisfeld, C. (1916), *Das niederländische Bankwesen*, The Hague: Martinus Nijhoff.

Eistert, E. (1970), *Die Beeinflussung des Wirtschaftswachstums in Deutschland von 1883 bis 1913 durch das Bankensystem*, Berlin: Duncker & Humblot.

Elias, J.E. (1963) [1903–05], *De vroedschap van Amsterdam 1578–1795*, Amsterdam: Israel.

Fase, M.G., G.D. Feldman, and M. Pohl (eds) (1995), *How to Write the History of a Bank*, Aldershot: Scolar.

Faust, H. (1977), *Geschichte der Genossenschaftsbewegung*, Frankfurt: Fritz Knapp.

Federico, G., and G. Toniolo (1991), "Italy", in R. Sylla and G. Toniolo (eds), *Patterns of European Industrialization*, New York: Routledge.

Feinstein, C. (ed.) (1995), *Banking, Currency, and Finance in Europe between the Wars*, New York: Oxford University Press.

Feldenkirchen, W. (1991), "Banking and economic growth: Banks and industry in Germany in the nineteenth century and their changing relationship to industry", in W.R. Lee (ed.), *German Industry and German Industrialization*, New York: Routledge.

Feldenkirchen, W. (1982), *Die Eisen- und Stahlindustrie des Ruhrgebiets, 1879–1914: Wachstum, Finanzierung und Struktur ihre Grossunternehmen*, Wiesbaden: F. Steiner.

Feldenkirchen, W. (1979), "Banken und Stahlindustrie im Ruhrgebiet. Zur Entwicklung ihrer Beziehungen 1873–1914", *Bankhistorisches Archiv*, 2: 27–52.

Feldman, G.D. (1991), "Banks and the problem of capital shortage in Germany, 1918–1923", H. James, H. Lindgren, and A. Teichova (eds), *The Role of Banks in the Interwar Economy*, New York: Cambridge University Press, 49–79.

Ferreira, A.C. (1970), "A Banca Portuense 1850–75", Licenciate thesis, Oporto University.

Figueiredo, A. de (1873), *Le Portugal – Considérations sur l'État de l'Administration des Finances, de l'Industrie et du Commerce de ce Royaume et de ses Colonies*, Lisbon: Lallemant Frères.

Financial Times, The, (1888–), London: MacRae, Curtice & Co.

Flandreau, M. (1998), "*Caveat Emptor*: Coping with sovereign risk without the multilaterals", Discussion Paper No. 2004, London: Center for Economic Policy Research.

Flora, P. *et al.* (eds) (1983–87), *State, Economy and Society in Western Europe, 1815–1975: A Data Handbook*, Frankfurt am Main: Campus.

Fohlin, C.M. (2000), "Economic, political, and legal factors in financial system development: International patterns in historical perspective", *Social Science Working Paper 1089*, Pasadena: Division of the Humanities & Social Science, California Institute of Technology.

Fohlin, C.M. (1998), "Capital mobilization and utilization in latecomer economies: Germany and Italy compared", *European Review of Economic History*, 3: 139–174.

Fohlin, C.M. (1997a), "Universal banking networks in pre-war Germany: New evidence from company financial data", *Research in Economics*, 51: 201–225.

Fohlin, C.M. (1997b), "Bank securities holdings and industrial finance before World War I: Britain and Germany compared", *Social Science Working Paper 1007*, Pasadena: Division of the Humanities and Social Science, California Institute of Technology.

Fohlin, C.M. (1997c), "Bank securities holdings and industrial finance before World War 1: Britain and Germany compared", *Business and Economic History*, 26(2): 463–475.

Fonseca, H. (1996), *O Alentejo no Século XIX. Economia e Atitudes Económicas*, Lisbon: Imprensa Nacional-Casa da Moeda.

Forstmann, W. (1996), "Frankfurt am Main, a city of finance: Banking systems in Frankfurt in the 18th and 19th centuries", in H. Diederiks and D. Reeder (eds), *Cities of Finance*, Amsterdam: North-Holland, 181–188.

Forsyth, D.J. (1993), *The Crisis of Liberal Italy: Monetary and Financial Policy, 1914–1922*, New York: Cambridge University Press.

Forsyth, D.J. (1991), "The rise and fall of German-inspired mixed banking in Italy, 1884–1936", in H. James, H. Lindgren, and A. Teichova (eds), *The Role of Banks in the Interwar Economy*, New York: Cambridge University Press, 179–205.

Fratianni, M., and F. Spinelli (1996), *A Monetary History of Italy*, New York: Cambridge University Press.

Fridenson, P., and A. Straus (eds) (1987), *Le capitalisme français 19e-20e siècle*, Paris: Fayard.

Fritschy, J.M.F., and R. Liesker (1996), "Overheidsfinanciën, kapitaalmarkt en 'institutionele context', in Holland en Overijssel tijdens en na de Spaanse Successie-oorlog", in C.A. Davids, W. Fritschy, and L.A. van der Valk (eds), *Kapitaal, ondernemerschap en beleid, studies over economie en politiek in Nederland, Europa en Azië, afscheidsbundel voor prof.dr. P.W. Klein*, Amsterdam: NEHA, 165–196.

Fritschy, J.M.F., and R. van der Voort (1997), "From fragmentation to unification: Public finance, 1700–1914", in M. 't Hart, J.P.B. Jonker, and J.L. van Zanden (eds), *A Financial History of the Netherlands*, New York: Cambridge University Press, 64–93.

Fritz, S. (1987), *Affärsbankernas aktieförvärvsrätt under 1900-talets första decennier*, Stockholm: Almqvist & Wiksell International.

Gall, L., G.D. Feldman, H. James, C.-L. Holtfrerich, and H.E. Büschgen (1995), *The Deutsche Bank, 1870–1995*, London: Weidenfeld & Nicolson.

Gebhard, H. (1928), *Die Berliner Börse von den Anfängen bis zum Jahre 1896*, Berlin: R.L. Prager.

Gehr, M. (1959), "Das Verhältnis zwischen Banken und Industrie in Deutschland seit der Mitte des 19. Jahrhunderts bis zur Bankenkrise 1931", Ph.D. dissertation, University of Tübingen.

Gerschenkron, A. (1965), "Agrarian policies and industrialization, Russia 1861–1917", in H.J. Habakkuk and M. Postan (eds), *The Cambridge Economic History of Europe*, vol. 6, *The Industrial Revolutions and After: Incomes, Population and Technological Change* (part two), Cambridge: Cambridge University Press, 706–800.

Gerschenkron A. (1962), *Economic Backwardness in Historical Perspective: A Book of Essays*, Cambridge, MA: Harvard University Press.

Gerschenkron, A. (1960), "Problems and patterns of Russian economic development", in C.E. Black (ed.), *The Transformation of Russian Society: Aspects of Social Change since 1861*, Cambridge, MA: Harvard University Press, 42–72.

Gerschenkron, A. (1947), "The rate of industrial growth in Russia since 1885", *Journal of Economic History*, Supplement, 7: 144–174.

Gindin, I.F. (1997), *Banki i ekonomicheskaia politika v Rossii (XIX-nachalo XX v.). Ocherki istorii i tipologii Russkikh bankov*, Moscow: Sciences.

Gindin, I.F. (1980), "Antikrizisnoe finansirovanie predpriiatii tiazheloi promyshlennosti (konets XIX-nachalo XX v)", *Istoricheskie zapiski Akademii Nauk SSSR*, 105: 105–149.

Gindin, I.F. (1960), *Gosudarstvennyi bank i ekonomicheskaia politika tsarskogo pravitel'stva, 1861–1892 gody*, Mosow: Gosfinizdat.

Gindin, I.F. (1948), *Russkie komercheskye banky. Iz istorii finansovogo kapitala v Rossii*, Moscow: Gosfinizdat

Goldsmith, R.W. (1985), *Comparative National Balance Sheets: A Study of Twenty Countries, 1688–1978*, Chicago: University of Chicago Press.

Goldsmith, R.W. (1969), *Financial Structure and Development*, New Haven: Yale University Press.

Gömmel, R. (1992), "Entstehung und Entwicklung der Effektenbörsen im 19. Jahrhundert bis 1914", in H. Pohl (ed.), *Deutsche Börsengeschichte*, Frankfurt am Main: Knapp, 135–210.

Gonjo, Y. (2000), "La Banque de France et la déconcentration du crédit (1880–1920)", communication au colloque du Bicentenaire de la Banque de France, Paris, unpublished.

Gontard, M. (2000), *La Bourse de Paris (1800–1830)*, Aix-en-Provence: Edisud.

Goodhart, C.A.E. (1988), *The Evolution of Central Banks*, Cambridge, MA: MIT Press.

Goodhart, C.A.E. (1986), *The Business of Banking 1891–1914*, Aldershot: Gower.

Gorton, G., and G. Pennacchi (1990), "Financial intermediaries and liquidity creation", in *Journal of Finance*, 45: 49–71.

Great Britain, Committee on Finance and Industry (1931), *Report of the Committee on Finance and Industry*, London: H.M. Stationery Office.

Gregory, P.R. (1994), *Before Command: An Economic History of Russia from Emancipation to the First Five Year Plan*, Princeton: Princeton University Press.

Gregory, P.R. (1982), *Russian National Income, 1885–1913*, Cambridge: Cambridge University Press.

Gregory, P.R. (1974), "Some empirical comments on the theory of relative backwardness: The Russian case", *Economic Development and Cultural Change*, 22: 654–665.

Groeneveld, F.P. (1940), *De economische crisis van het jaar 1720*, Groningen: P. Noordhoff.

Gueslin, A. (1992), "Banks and State in France from the 1880s to the 1930s: The impossible advance of the banks", in Y. Cassis (ed.), *Finance and Financiers in European History, 1880–1960*, New York: Cambridge University Press, 63–92.

Guex, S. (1993), *La politique monétaire et financière de la Confédération suisse, 1900–1920*, Lausanne: Payot.

Guinnane, T.W. (1997), "Regional organizations in the German cooperative banking system in the late 19th century", *Research in Economics*, 51: 251–274.

Guinnane, T.W. (1994), "A failed institutional transplant: Raiffeisen's credit cooperatives in Ireland, 1894–1914", *Explorations in Economic History*, 31: 38–61.

Habakkuk, H.J., and M. Postan (eds) (1965), *The Cambridge Economic History of Europe*, vol. 6, *The Industrial Revolutions and After: Incomes, Population and Technological Change* (part two), Cambridge: Cambridge University Press.

Hájek, J. (1994), "Origins of the banking system in interwar Czechoslovakia", in A. Teichova, T. Gourvish, and A. Pogány (eds), *Universal Banking in the Twentieth Century: Finance, Industry and State in North and Central Europe*, Aldershot: E. Elgar, 22–31.

Hansen, P.H. (1994), "Production versus currency: The Danish Central Bank in the 1920s", in A. Teichova, T. Gourvish, and A. Pogány (eds), *Universal Banking in Twentieth Century Europe: Finance, Industry and State in North and Central Europe*, Aldershot: E. Elgar, 59–76.

Hansen, P.H. (1991), "From growth to crisis: The Danish banking system from 1850 until the interwar years", *Scandinavian Economic History Review*, 39: 20–40.

Hansen, S.A. (1982), "The transformation of bank structures in the industrial period: The case of Denmark", *Journal of European Economic History*, 3: 575–603.

Hardach, G. (1984), "Banking and industry in Germany in the interwar period 1919–1939", *Journal of European Economic History*, Supplement: *Banks and Industry in the Interwar Period*, 203–234.

't Hart, M., (1993), *The Making of a Bourgeois State: War, Politics, and Finance during the Dutch Revolt*, Manchester: Manchester University Press.

't Hart, M., J.P.B. Jonker, and J.L. van Zanden (eds) (1997), *A Financial History of the Netherlands*, New York: Cambridge University Press.

Hashimoto, J. (1990), "Japanese industrial enterprises and the financial market between the two World Wars", in P.L. Cottrell, A. Teichova, and T. Yuzawa (eds), *Finance in the Age of the Corporate Economy: The Third Anglo-Japanese Business History Conference*, Aldershot: Ashgate, 1997, 94–117.

Henning, F.W. (ed.) (1980), *Entwicklung und Aufgaben von Versicherungen und Banken in der Industrialisierung*, Berlin: Duncker und Humblot.

Henze, W. (1972), *Grundriss für die Sparkassenarbeit: Grundzüge der Geschichte des Sparkassenwesens*, Stuttgart: Deutscher Sparkassenverlag.

Herrigel, G.B. (1996), *Industrial Constructions: The Sources of German Industrial Power*, New York: Cambridge University Press.

Hertner, P. (1984), *Il capitale tedesco in Italia dall'unità alla prima guerra mondiale*, Bologna: Il Mulino.

Hertzberg, E., and N. Rygg (1907), *Den norske Creditbank 1857–1907*, Christiania: W.C. Fabritius & Sonner.

Hicks, J. (1969), *A Theory of Economic History*, London: Oxford University Press.

Hicks, J. (1965), *Capital and Growth*, London: Oxford University Press.

Hildebrand, K.G. (1992), *Swedish Iron in the 17th and 18th Centuries. Export Industry before the Industrialization*, Jernkontorets Bergshistoriska Skriftserie 29, Stockholm: Jernkontoret.

Hiler, D. (1993), "De la Caisse d'épargne à la banque universelle: l'exemple de la caisse d'épargne de Genève", in Y. Cassis and J. Tanner (eds), *Banques et crédit en Suisse (1850–1930)*, Zurich: Chronos, 185–198.

Hilferding, Rudolf (1981) [1910], *Finance Capital: A Study of the Latest Phase of Capitalist Development*, Boston: Routledge & Kegan Paul.

Hoffman, P.T., and K. Norberg (1994a), "Conclusion", in P.T. Hoffman and K. Norberg (eds), *Fiscal Crises, Liberty, and Representative Government, 1450–1789*, Stanford: Stanford University Press, 299–312.

Hoffman, P.T., and K. Norberg (eds) (1994b), *Fiscal Crises, Liberty, and Representative Government, 1450–1789*, Stanford: Stanford University Press.

Holtfrerich, C.-L., J. Reis and G. Toniolo (eds) (1999), *The Emergence of Modern Central Banking from 1918 to the Present*, Aldershot: Ashgate.

Homer, S., and R. Sylla (1996), *A History of Interest Rates*, 3rd rev. edn, New Brunswick: Rutgers University Press.

Horne, H.O. (1947), *A History of Savings Banks*, Oxford: Oxford University Press.

Hovland, E., and H.W. Nordvik (1997), "Det industrielle gjennombrudd i Norge 1840–1914 med samtidens og ettertidens øyne", in B. Basberg, H.W. Nordvik, and G. Stang (eds), *I det lange løp. Essays i økonomisk historie tilegnet Fritz Hodne*, Bergen: Fagbokforlaget.

Imset Matre, H. (1992), *Norske kredittinstitusjoner 1850–1990. En statistisk oversikt, 1914*, Rapport no. 10, The Norwegian Research Council for Applied Social Science.

Ingham, G. (1984), *Capitalism Divided? The City and Industry in British Social Development*, Basingstoke: Macmillan.

Israel, J.I. (1990a), "Een merkwaardig literair werk en de Amsterdamse effectenmarkt in 1688: Joseph Penso de la Vega's '*Confusion de confusiones*'," *De zeventiende eeuw*, 6: 159–161.

Israel, J.I. (1990b), "The Amsterdam stock exchange and the English revolution of 1688", *Tijdschrift voor geschiedenis*, 103: 412–440.

Jacklin, C.J. (1987), "Demand deposits, trading restrictions, and risk sharing", in E.D. Prescott and N. Wallace (eds), *Contractual Arrangements for Intertemporal Trade*, Minneapolis: University of Minnesota Press, 26–47.

Jacquemard, P. (1911), *Les banques lorraines*, Paris: A. Rousseau.

James, H., H. Lindgren and A. Teichova (eds) (1991), *The Role of Banks in the Interwar Economy*, New York: Cambridge University Press.

James, J.A. (1978), *Money and Capital Markets in Postbellum America*, Princeton, NJ: Princeton University Press.

Jeidels, O. (1905), "Das Verhältnis der deutschen Grossbanken zur Industrie mit besonderer Berücksichtigung der Eisenindustrie", *Staats- und sozialwissenschaftliche Forschung*, 24(2): 1–271.

Johansen, H.C. (1985), *Dansk historisk statistik 1814–1980*, Copenhagen: Gyldendal.

Jones, C. (1997), "Institutional forms of British foreign direct investment in South America", *Business History*, 39(2): 21–41.

Jones, G. (1993), *British Multinational Banking 1830–1990*, Oxford: Clarendon Press.

Jones, S. (1994), "Origins growth and concentration of bank capital in South Africa, 1860–92", *Business History*, 36(3): 62–80.

Jonker, J.P.B. (1999), "The cradle of modern banking: Finance in the Netherlands between the Napoleonic era and the first commercial banks, 1813–1870", in J. de Vries, W. Vroom, and T. de Graaf, (eds), *World Wide Banking: ABN AMRO Bank 1824–1999*, Amsterdam: ABN AMRO Bank, 49–94.

Jonker, J.P.B. (1997), "The alternative road to modernity: Banking and currency, 1814–1914", in M. 't Hart, J.P.B. Jonker, and J.L. van Zanden (eds), *A Financial History of the Netherlands*, New York: Cambridge University Press, 94–123.

Jonker, J.P.B. (1996), *Merchants, Bankers, Middlemen: The Amsterdam Money Market during the First Half of the 19th Century*, Amsterdam: NEHA.

Jonker, J.P.B. (1995), "Spoilt for choice? Statistical speculations on banking concentration and the structure of the Dutch money market, 1900–1940", in Y. Cassis, G.D. Feldman, and U. Olsson (eds), *The Evolution of Financial Institutions and Markets in Twentieth-Century Europe*, Aldershot: Scolar Press, 187–208.

Jonker, J.P.B. (1991), "Sinecures or sinews of power? Interlocking directorships and bank–industry relations in the Netherlands, 1910–1940", *Economic and Social History in the Netherlands*, 3: 119–132.

Jonker, J.P.B., and K. Sluyterman (2000), *At Home on the World Markets: Dutch Trading Houses from the 16th Century to the Present*, The Hague: Sdu Uitgevers.

Kafengauz, L.B. (1994), *Evoliutsiia promyshlennogo proizvodstva Rossii (posledniaia tret' XIX v. –30e gody XX v.)*, Moscow: RAN.

Kahan, A. (1989), *Russian Economic History: The Nineteenth Century*, R. Weiss (ed.), Chicago: University of Chicago Press.

Kauch, P. (1950), *The National Bank of Belgium 1850–1918*, Brussels: Société Belge d'Imprimerie Sobeli.

Kennedy, W.P. (1987), *Industrial Structure, Capital Markets and the Origins of British Economic Decline*, New York: Cambridge University Press.

Khromov, P.A. (1950), *Ekonomicheskoe razvitie Rossii, XIX-XX vv*, Moscow: Gospolitizdat.

Kindleberger, C.P. (1984), *A Financial History of Western Europe*, London: Allen & Unwin.

Kindleberger, C.P. (1978), "The formation of financial centers", in C.P. Kindleberger (ed.), *Economic Response: Comparative Studies in Trade, Finance, and Growth*, Cambridge, MA: Harvard University Press, 66–134.

Kindleberger, C.P. (ed.) (1978), *Economic Response: Comparative Studies in Trade, Finance, and Growth*, Cambridge, MA: Harvard University Press.

Klüpfel, W. (1984), "Entwicklungslinien im Sparkassenrecht", in G. Aschauer *et al.* (eds), *Standortbestimmung: Entwicklungslinien der deutschen Kreditwirtschaft*, Stuttgart: Deutscher Sparkassenverlag.

Kluthe, K. (1985), *Genossenschaften und Staat in Deutschland*, Berlin: Duncker und Humblot.

Knutsen, S. (1992), "Banker og næringslivskunder under ekspansjonsfaser 1890–1913", in S. Knutsen, E. Lange, and H.W. Nordvik, *Bankstruktur og kundeforhold i langtidsperspektiv*, The Norwegian Research Council for Applied Social Science, Report no. 31/1992.

Knutsen, S. (1991), "From expansion to panic and crash: The Norwegian banking system and its customers 1913–1924", *Scandinavian Economic History Review*, 39(3): 41–71.

Knutsen, S. (1990), "Bank, Samfunn og Økonomisk Vekst ", in S. Knutsen and H. Nordvik, *Bankenes rolle i norsk industriell utvikling 1850–1914,* Rapport no. 10, The Norwegian Research Council for Applied Social Science.

Knutsen, S., E. Lange, and H.W. Nordvik (1992), *Bankstruktur og kundeforhold i langtidsperspektiv,* The Norwegian Research Council for Applied Social Science.

Knutsen, S., and H.W. Nordvik (1990), *Bankenes rolle i norsk industriell utvikling 1850– 1914,* Rapport no. 10, The Norwegian Research Council for Applied Social Science.

Kocka, J. (1981), "Grossunternehmen und der Aufstieg des Managerkapitalismus im späten 19. und frühen 20. Jahrhundert: Deutschland im internationalen Vergleich", *Historische Zeitschrift,* 232: 39–60.

Kocka, J. (1978), "Entrepreneurs and managers in German industrialization", in *The Cambridge Economic History of Europe,* vol. 7, Peter Mathias and M.M. Postan (eds), *The Industrial Economies: Capital, Labor, and Enterprise,* part 1, *Britain, France, Germany and Scandinavia,* New York: Cambridge University Press, 492–589.

Kokovtsov, V.N. (1935), *Out of My Past: Memoirs of Count Kokovtsov,* Stanford: Stanford University Press.

Korelin, A.P. (1988), *Sel'skokhoziaistvennyi kredit v Rossii v kontse XIX-nachaleXX v,* Moscow: Nauka.

Kuznets, S. (1966), *Modern Economic Growth: Rate, Structure, and Spread,* New Haven: Yale University Press.

Kymmel, J. (1996), *Geschiedenis van de algemene banken in Nederland, 1860–1914,* vol. 2, Amsterdam: NIBE.

Lains, P. (1995), *A Economia Portuguesa no Século XIX: Crescimento Económico e Comércio Externo, 1851–1913,* Lisbon: Impresa Nacional–Casa da Moeda.

Lamoreaux, N.R. (1994), *Insider Lending: Banks, Personal Connections, and Economic Development in Industrial New England, 1784–1912,* New York: Cambridge University Press.

Lamoreaux, N.R., and D.M.G. Raff (eds) (1995), *Coordination and Information: Historical Perspectives on the Organization of Enterprise,* Chicago: University of Chicago Press.

Larsson, M., and H. Lindgren (1992), "The political economy of banking: Retail banking and corporate finance in Sweden, 1850–1939", in Y. Cassis (ed.), *Finance and Financiers in Europe: 19th-20th Centuries,* Cambridge: Cambridge University Press.

Laufenberger, H. (1940), *Enquête sur les changements de structure du crédit et de la banque, 1914–1938. Les banques françaises,* Paris: Sirey.

Lazonick, W.R., and M. O'Sullivan (1997), "Finance and industrial development: Evolution to market control", Part II: "Japan and Germany", *Financial History Review,* 4(2): 117–134.

League of Nations, Economic Intelligence Service (1931), *Memorandum on Commercial Banks, 1913–1929,* Geneva: League of Nations.

Lee, W.R. (ed.) (1991), *German Industry and German Industrialization,* New York: Routledge.

Lehmann, P.J. (1997), *Histoire de la Bourse de Paris,* Paris: Presses Universitaires de France.

Lescure, M. (2000), "La formation des systèmes de crédit en Europe et le rôle des banques d'émission, 1850–1914", Communication au colloque du Bicentenaire de la Banque de France, Paris, unpublished.

Lescure, M. (1995a), "Banking in France in the inter-war period", in C. Feinstein (ed.), *Banking, Currency and Finance in Europe Between the Wars,* Oxford: Clarendon Press, 314–336.

Lescure, M. (1995b), "Banks and small enterprises in France", in Y. Cassis, G.D. Feldman, and U. Olsson (eds), *The Evolution of Financial Institutions and Markets in Twentieth Century Europe*, Aldershot: Scolar Press.

Lescure, M. (1992), "Les banques et le financement des PME en France pendant les années 1920", *Entreprises et Histoire*, 2.

Lescure, M. (1985), "Banques régionales et croissance économique en France au XIXe siècle: l'example de la Société Marseillaise de Crédit", in *Banque et investissements en Méditerranée à l'époque contemporaine, Actes du colloque de Marseille des 4–5 février 1982*, Marseille: Chambre de Commerce et de l'Industrie de Marseille–Provence.

Lescure, M., and A. Plessis (eds) (1999), *Banques locales et banques régionales en France au XIXe siècle*, Paris: A. Michel.

Levine, R. (1997), "Financial development and economic growth: Views and agenda", *Journal of Economic Literature*, 35: 688–726.

Levine, R., and S. Zervos (1998), "Stock markets, banks, and economic growth", *American Economic Review*, 88: 537–558.

Lévy-Leboyer, M. (1976a), "L'apprentissage du marché", in F. Braudel and E. Labrousse (eds), *Histoire économique et sociale de la France*, vol. 3/1, Paris: Presses Universitaires de France 391–430.

Lévy-Leboyer, M. (1976b), "L'évolution insitutionelle", in F. Braudel and E. Labrousse (eds), *Histoire économique et sociale de la France* III/1, Paris: Presses Universitaires de France, 347–390.

Lévy-Leboyer, M. (1976c), "La spécialisation des établissements bancaires", in F. Braudel and E. Labrousse (eds), *Histoire économique et sociale de la France* III/1, Paris: Presses Universitaires de France, 431–471.

Lévy-Leboyer, M., and F. Bourguignon (1985), *L'économie Française au XIXe siécle. Analyse macro-économique*, Paris: Economica.

Lévy-Leboyer, M., and M. Lescure (1991), "France", in R. Sylla and G. Toniolo (eds), *Patterns of European Industrialization: The Nineteenth Century*, London: Routledge.

Lilja, K. (2000), "Utav omsorg och eftertanke. En undersökning av Falu stads sparbanks sparare 1830–1914", Licentiate dissertation, Uppsala University.

Lindgren, H. (1999), "Preindustrial financial markets: Estimates based on microdata", Paper given at the Institutet för Ekonomisk Historisk Forskning seminar, Stockholm School of Economics.

Lindgren, H. (1991), "Swedish historical research on banking during the 1980s: Tradition and renewal", *Scandinavian Economic History Review*, 39(3): 5–19.

Lindgren, H. (1990a), "Affärsbankerna – näringslivets herrar eller tjänare?", *Pecvnia. Skrifter i mynt- och penninghistoriska ämnen utgivna av Kungl. Myntkabinettet*, vol. 1, Stockholm: Kungl. Myntkabinettet.

Lindgren, H. (1990b), "Long-term contracts in financial markets: Bank–industry connections in Sweden, illustrated by the operations of Stockholms Enskilda Bank, 1900–70", in M. Aoki, B. Gustafsson, and O.E. Williamson (eds) (1990), *The Firm as a Nexus of Treaties*, London: Sage, 266–270.

Löb, E. (1896), "Kursfeststellung und Maklerwesen an der Berliner Effektenbörse", in *Jahrbücher für Nationalökonomie und Statistik*, 3(11): 237–273.

Lucas, R.E. (1988), "On the mechanisms of economic development", *Journal of Monetary Economics*, 22(1): 3–42.

Lumbralles, J.P. da Costa Leite (1926), *Organização Bancária Portuguesa*, Coimbra: Livraria França Amado.

Lundstrom, R. (1994), "Continuity and change in Swedish banking", in A. Teichova, T. Gourvish, and A. Pogány (eds), *Universal Banking in the Twentieth Century: Finance, Industry and State in North and Central Europe*, Aldershot: E. Elgar, 3–11.

McKay, J. (1970), *Pioneers for Profit: Foreign Entrepreneurship and Russian Industrialization*, Chicago: University of Chicago Press.

Maddison, A. (1995), *Monitoring the World Economy 1820–1990*, Paris: OECD.

Maddison, A. (1991), *Dynamic Forces in Capitalist Development: A Long-Run Comparative View*, Oxford: Oxford University Press.

Magnusson, L. (1988), *Den bråkiga kulturen. Förläggare och smideshantverkare i Eskilstuna 1800–1850*, Stockholm: Författarförlaget.

Marichal, C. (1997), "Nation building and the origins of banking in Latin America, 1850–1930", in A. Teichova, G. Kurgan-van Hentenryk, and D. Ziegler (eds), *Banking, Trade and Industry: Europe, America and Asia from the 13th to the 20th Century*, New York: Cambridge University Press, 339–358.

Marmefelt, T. (1998), *Bank–Industry Networks and Economic Evolution*, Aldershot: Ashgate.

Martín-Aceña, P. (1995), "Spanish banking in the inter-war period", in C. Feinstein (ed.), *Banking, Currency, and Finance in Europe between the Wars*, New York: Oxford University Press, 502–527.

Martín-Aceña, P., and J. Reis (eds) (2000), *Monetary Standards in the Periphery: Paper, Silver and Gold, 1854–1933*, Basingstoke: Macmillan.

Mata, E. (1993), *As Finanças Públicas Portuguesas da Regeneração à Primeira Guerra Mundial*, Lisbon: Banco de Portugal.

Mayer, C. (1994), "Stock markets, financial institutions, and corporate performance", in N. Dimsdale and M. Prevezer, (eds), *Capital Markets and Corporate Governance*, Oxford: Oxford University Press.

Meier, J.C. (1992), *Die Entstehung des Börsengesetzes vom 22. Juni 1896*, St. Katharinen: Scripta Mercaturae.

Merrett, D.T. (1997), "Capital markets and capital formation in Australia, 1890–1945", *Australian Economic History Review*, 37(3): 181–201.

Merrett, D.T. (1995), "Global reach by Australian banks: Correspondent banking networks, 1830–1960", *Business History*, 37(3): 70–88.

Merton, R.C., and Z. Bodie (1995), "A conceptual framework for analyzing the financial environment", in D.B. Crane *et al.*, *The Global Financial System: A Functional Perspective*, Boston: Harvard Business School Press, 3–31.

Michel, B. (1976), *Banques et banquiers en Autriche au début du 20e siècle*, Paris: Presses de la Fondation Nationale des Sciences Politiques.

Michie, R.C. (forthcoming, a), "One world or many worlds: Markets, banks and information flows in the nineteenth and twentieth centuries", in T. de Graaf (ed.), *European Banking Overseas in the 19th and 20th Centuries*, Amsterdam.

Michie, R.C. (forthcoming, b), "Stock exchanges and economic growth, 1830–1931", in P. Cottrell, G. Feldman, and J. Reis (eds), *Finance and the Making of Modern Capitalism*, Aldershot: Ashgate.

Michie, R.C. (2000), "The early UK equity market", in Barclay's Capital, *Equity-Gilt Study 2000*, London: Barclay's Bank, 9–17.

Michie, R.C. (1999), *The London Stock Exchange: A History*, New York: Oxford University Press.

Michie, R.C. (1998a), "The invisible stabilizer, asset arbitrage and the international monetary system since 1700", *Financial History Review*, 15(1): 5–26.

Michie, R.C. (1998b), "Anglo-American financial systems, 1800–1939", in P.L. Cottrell and J. Reis (eds), *Finance and the Making of the Modern Capitalist World, 1750–1931*, Madrid: Fundación Fomento de la Historia Económica.

Michie, R.C. (1994), "Introduction", in R.C. Michie (ed.), *Financial and Commercial Services*, Oxford: Oxford University Press.

Michie, R.C. (1992a), *The City of London: Continuity and Change 1850–1990*, Basingstoke: Macmillan.

Michie, R.C. (1992b), "The development of the stock market", in P. Newman, M. Milgate, and J. Eatwell (eds), *The New Palgrave Dictionary of Money and Finance*, vol. 1, London: Macmillan, 662–668.

Michie, R.C. (1988a), "The Canadian securities market, 1850–1914", *Business History Review*, 62(1): 171–179.

Michie, R.C. (1988b), "Different in name only? The London Stock Exchange and foreign Bourses c. 1850–1914", *Business History*, 30(1): 46–68.

Michie, R.C. (1987), *The London and New York Stock Exchanges, 1850–1914*, London: Allen & Unwin.

Miller, M. (1967), *The Economic Development of Russia 1905–1914*, New York: Kelley Reprints.

Mitchell, B.R. (1998), *International Historical Statistics*, 4th edn, New York: Stockton Press.

Mitchell, B.R. (1992), *International Historical Statistics: Europe, 1750–1988*, 3rd edn, New York: Stockton Press.

Mitchell, B.R. (1983), *International Historical Statistics: The Americas and Australasia*, Detroit: Gale Research Company.

Mitchell, B.R. (1975), *European Historical Statistics*, New York: Columbia University Press.

Moss, M. (1997), "L'exemple du Royaume-Uni (1810–1914)", in B. Vogler (ed.), *L'histoire des Caisses d'épargne européennes*, vol. 3, *Conjoncture et crises 1850–1914*, Paris: Editions de l'épargne, 133–146.

Mura, J. (1987a), *Entwicklungslinien der deutschen Sparkassengeschichte*, Stuttgart: Deutscher Sparkassenverlag.

Mura, J. (1987b), "Krisen und Kontinuität der Sparkassen (1908 bis 1931)", in J. Mura (ed.), *Die Entwicklung der Sparkassen zu Universalkreditinstituten*, Stuttgart: Deutscher Sparkassenverlag.

Mura, J. (ed.) (1987c), *Die Entwicklung der Sparkassen zu Universalkreditinstituten*, Stuttgart: Deutscher Sparkassenverlag.

Myers, M.G. (1936), *Paris as a Financial Center*, London: P.S. King.

Natmeßnig, C. (1994), "The establishment of the Anglo-Czechoslovak bank: Conflicting interests", in A. Teichova, T. Gourvish, and A. Pogány (eds), *Universal Banking in the Twentieth Century: Finance, Industry and State in North and Central Europe*, Aldershot: E. Elgar, 96–115.

Neal, L. (1994), "The finance of business during the Industrial Revolution", in R.F. Floud and D. McCloskey (eds), *The Economic History of Britain Since 1700*, 2nd edn, vol.1, *1700–1860*, New York: Cambridge University Press, 151–181.

Neal, L. (1990), "The Dutch and English East India Companies compared: Evidence from the stock and foreign exchange markets", in J.D. Tracy (ed.), *The Rise of Merchant Empires: Long-Distance Trade in the Early Modern World, 1350–1750*, New York: Cambridge University Press, 195–223.

Nederlandsche Bank (1987), *Financiële instellingen in Nederland 1900–1985: balansreeksen en naamlijst van handelsbanken,* DNB Statistische Cahiers, no. 2, Amsterdam: De Nederlandsche Bank, NV.

Neuberger, H., and H.H. Stokes (1974), "German banks and German growth, 1883–1913: An empirical view", *Journal of Economic History* 35(3): 710–730.

Newman, P., M. Milgate, and J. Eatwell (eds) (1992), *The New Palgrave Dictionary of Money and Finance,* 3 vols, London: Macmillan.

Newton, L. (1996), "Regional bank–industry relations during the mid-nineteenth century: Links between bankers and manufacturing in Sheffield, 1850–1885", *Business History,* 38(3): 64–83.

Nilsson, G.B. (1988), "Kreditens jättekraft. Svenskt bankväsende i brytningstid och genombrottstid vid 1800-talets mitt", *Uppsala Papers in Economic History, Research Report no. 18,* Uppsala: Department of Economic History, Uppsala University.

Nilsson, G.B. (1981), *Banker i brytningstid. A.O. Wallenberg i svensk bankpolitik 1850–1856,* Stockholm: Institutet för Ekonomisk Historisk Forskning.

Nishimura, S. (1995), "The French provincial banks, the Banque de France and bill finance, 1890–1913", *Economic History Review,* 48(3): 536–554.

Nogueira, J.F.H. (1856), *O Município no Século XIX,* Lisbon: Typ. Do Progresso.

Nordvik, H.W. (1993), "The banking system, industrialization and economic growth in Norway, 1850–1914", *Scandinavian Economic History Review,* 41, no. 1: 51–72.

Nordvik, H.W. (1990), "Industrialization and economic growth in Norway, 1850–1914: The role of the banking sector", in S. Knutsen and H.W. Nordvik, *Bankenes rolle i norsk industriell utvikling 1850–1914,* Rapport no. 10, The Norwegian Research Council for Applied Social Science.

Nordvik, H., G. Nerheim, and T. Brandal (1989), *Penger spart-penger tjent. Sparebanker og økonomisk utvikling på Sør-Vestlandet 1839–1989,* Stavanger: SR-Bank.

North, D.C. (1990), *Institutions, Institutional Change and Economic Performance,* New York: Cambridge University Press.

North, D.C., and B.R. Weingast (1989), "Constitutions and commitment: The evolution of institutions governing public choice in seventeenth-century England", *Journal of Economic History,* 49(4), 803–832.

Norway, Central Bureau of Statistics (1949), *Statistical Survey 1948,* Oslo.

Norway, Central Bureau of Statistics (1915), *Private banks 1912 and 1913,* Kristiania.

Norway, Norge Statistisk Centralbyra (1975), *Historisk Statistisk: 1968,* microfilm edn, Cambridge: Chadwyck-Headley.

Nötel, R. (1984), "Money, banking and industry in interwar Austria and Hungary", *Journal of European Economic Review,* 13(12): 137–202.

Nunes, A.B., C. Bastien, and N. Valério (1994), *Caixa Económica Montepio Geral. 150 Anos de História 1844–1994,* Lisbon: Montepio Geral.

Nygren I. (1989), "När lång upplåning blev korta krediter 1840–1905", in E. Dahmén (ed.), *Upplåning och utveckling. Riksgäldskontoret 1789–1989,* Stockholm: Allmänna Förlaget, 190–210.

Nygren, I. (1985), *Från Stockholms Banco till Citibank. Svensk kreditmarknad under 325 år.,* Stockholm: Liber Förlag.

Nygren, I. (1983), "Transformation of bank structures in the industrial period. The case of Sweden 1820–1913", *Journal of European Economic History,* 12(1), 29–68.

Nygren, I. (1967), *Svensk sparbanksutlåning 1820–1913: En analys av de större sparbankernas kreditgivning,* Meddelanden från ekonomisk-historiska institutionen vid Göteborgs universitet, 9, Göteborg.

Oliveira, L.F. d' (1904), *Indústria Algodoeira, 1887–1903*, Oporto: Typ. Empresa Guedes.

Olsson, U. (1997), *At the Center of Development: Skandinaviska Enskilda Banken and its Predecessors 1856–1996*, Stockholm: Skandinaviska Enskilda Banken.

O'Rourke, K., and J.G. Williamson (1999), *Globalization and History: The Evolution of a Nineteenth-century Atlantic Economy*, Cambridge, MA: Harvard University Press.

Owen, T.C. (1991a), *The Corporation under Russian law, 1800–1917: A Study in Tsarist Economic Policy*, New York: Cambridge University Press.

Owen, T.C. (1991b), "The population ecology of corporations in the Russian Empire, 1700–1914", *Slavic Review*, 50: 807–826.

Pantaleoni, M. (1998) [1895], *La caduta della Società Generale di Credito Mobiliare Italiano*, Turin: UTET.

Passion, L. (1991), "La Caisse d'épargne de Paris: 1818–1848", in B. Vogler (ed.), *L'histoire des Caisses d'épargne européennes*, vol. 1, *Les origines des Caisses d'épargne 1815–1848*, Paris: Les Éditions de l'Épargne, 89–109.

Paulet, E. (1999), *The Role of Banks in Monitoring Firms: The Case of the Crédit Mobilier*, London: Routledge.

Pecorari, P. (ed.) (1995), *Finanza e debito pubblico in Italia tra '800 e '900*, Venice: Istituto veneto di scienze lettere ed arti.

Penso de la Vega, J. (1957) [1688], *Confusión de confusiones*, selected and translated by Hermann Kellenbenz, Boston: Baker Library, Harvard Graduate School of Business Administration.

Petersson, T. (2001), *Framväxten av ett lokalt banksystem. Oppunda sparbank, Södermanlands enskilda bank och stationssamhället Katrineholm 1850–1916*, Uppsala Studies in Economic History 56, Uppsala: Acta Universitatis Upsaliensis.

Petersson, T. (1999), "Kreditmarknad i omvandling. En studie i sparbanksverksamhet på lokal nivå: Oppunda härads sparbank och stationssamhället Katrineholm 1881–1916", Licentiate dissertation, Uppsala University.

Petersson, T. (1998), "Utlåningen i de svenska sparbankerna 1820–1900", *Uppsala Papers in Financial History*, no. 6, Uppsala: Department of Economic History, Uppsala University.

Petzina, D. (ed.) (1990), *Zur Geschichte der Unternehmensfinanzierung*, Berlin: Duncker & Humblot.

Phimister, I. (2000), "Corners and company-mongering: Nigerian tin and the City of London, 1909–12", *Journal of Imperial and Commonwealth History*, 28(2): 23–41.

Platt, D.C.M. (1980), "British portfolio investment overseas before 1870: Some doubts", *Economic History Review*, 33: 1–16.

Plessis, A. (1996), "Le développement des activités financières à Paris au xixe siècle", in H. Diederiks, and D. Reeder (eds), *Cities of Finance*, Amsterdam: North-Holland, 167–180.

Plessis, A. (1987), "Le 'retard français': la faute à la banque? Banques locales, succursales de la Banque de France et financement de l'économie sous le second empire", in P. Fridenson and A. Straus (eds), *Le capitalisme français 19e-20e siècle*, Paris: Fayard.

Plessis, A. (1985a), *La politique de la Banque de France de 1851 à 1870*, Geneva: Droz.

Plessis, A. (1985b), "Les concours de la Banque de France à l'économie (1842–1914)", in J. Bouvier and J.C. Perrot (eds), *Etats, Fiscalités, Economies*, Paris: Publications de la Sorbonne, 169–180.

Pogány, A., "The industrial clientele of the Hungarian General Credit Bank, 1920–26", in A. Teichova, T. Gourvish, and A. Pogány (eds), *Universal Banking in the Twentieth Century: Finance, Industry and State in North and Central Europe*, Aldershot: E. Elgar, 215–228.

Pohl, H. (1983), "Die mittelständische Wirtschaft und ihre Finanzierungsprobleme bis zum Weltkrieg", *Die Sparkasse*, 100(8): 301–305.

Pohl, H. (1982a), "Das deutsche Bankwesen (1806–1848)", in Pohl, H. (ed.), *Deutsche Bankengeschichte*, vol. 2, Frankfurt am Main: Fritz Knapp.

Pohl, H. (ed.) (1982b), *Deutsche Bankengeschichte*, 3 vols, Frankfurt am Main: Fritz Knapp.

Pohl, M. (1986), *Entstehung und Entwicklung des Universalbankensystems*, Frankfurt am Main: Fritz Knapp.

Pohl, M. (1976), *Einführung in die deutsche Bankengeschichte*, Frankfurt am Main: Fritz Knapp.

Polsi, A. (2001), "L'articolazione del sistema bancario italiano fra scelte di mercato e intervento delle autorità monetarie (1900–1936)", in G. Conti and S. La Francesca (eds), *Banche e reti di banche nell'Italia postunitaria*, vol. 1, Bologna: Il Mulino, 217–262.

Polsi, A. (1997), *Il mercato del credito a Piacenza. Storia della Banca Popolare piacentina (1867–1932)*, Piacenza: Banca di Piacenza.

Polsi, A. (1995), "Sportelli bancari e sistema creditizio in età giolittiana", *Storia e problemi contemporanei*, 16: 47–65.

Polsi, A. (1993), *Alle origini del capitalismo italiano. Stato banche e banchieri dopo l'unità*, Turin: Einaudi.

Portugal, *Annaes de Estatística. Volume I. Serie 1 – Finanças. No. 1–Estatística Bancária (1858 a 1892)* (1894), Lisbon: Imprensa Nacional.

Portugal, *Anuário Estatístico de Portugal* (1875 and 1903), Lisbon: Imprensa Nacional.

Portugal, *Diário do Governo* (various dates).

Prados de la Escosura, L. (2000), "International comparisons of real product, 1820–1990: An alternative data set", *Explorations in Economic History*, 37: 1–41.

Reis, J. (2000), "The Gold Standard in Portugal, 1854–91", in P. Martín-Aceña and J. Reis (eds), *Monetary Standards in the Periphery. Paper, Silver and Gold, 1854–1933*, Basingstoke: Macmillan.

Reis, J. (1999a), "Was there a Mediterranean financial system in the 19th century? A comparison with Scandinavia", unpublished paper.

Reis, J. (1999b), "The Bank of Portugal's first century: From 1846 to the Second World War", in C.–L. Holtfrerich, J. Reis, and G. Toniolo (eds), *The Emergence of Modern Central Banking from 1918 to the Present*, Aldershot: Ashgate, 144–160.

Reis, J. (1993), *O Atraso Económico Português em Perspectiva Histórica: Estudos sobre a Economia Portuguesa na Segunda Metade do Século XIX, 1850–1930*, Lisbon: Imprensa Nacional–Casa da Moeda.

Reis, J. (1991), *A Evolução da Oferta Monetária Portuguesa 1854–1912*, Lisbon: Banco de Portugal.

Reis, Jaime (n.d.), "Os Bancos Portugueses, 1850–1913", *Conferência de História de Empresas 1991. Anais*, Rio de Janeiro: Universidade Federal.

Rieber, A.J. (1982), *Merchants and Entrepreneurs in Imperial Russia*, Chapel Hill, NC: University of North Carolina Press.

Riesser, J. (1911), *The Great German Banks and Their Concentration, in Connection with the Economic Development of Germany*, Washington DC: Government Printing Office.

Riesser, J. (1910), *Die deutsche Grossbanken und ihre Konzentration in Zusammenhang mit der Entwickung des Gesamtwirtschaft in Deutschland*, 3rd rev. and enl. edn, Jena: G. Fischer.

Riley, J.C. (1980), *International Government Finance and the Amsterdam Capital Market 1740–1815*, New York: Cambridge University Press.

Robinson, J. (1952a), "The generalization of the general theory", in idem., *The Rate of Interest and Other Essays*, London: Macmillan.

Robinson, J. (1952b), *The Rate of Interest and Other Essays*, London: Macmillan.

Rokkan, S., and D.W. Urwin (1983), *Economy, Territory, Identity: Politics of West European Peripheries*, London: Sage.

Rousseau, P.L., and P. Wachtel (1998), "Financial intermediation and economic performance: Historical evidence from five industrialized countries", *Journal of Money, Credit and Banking*, 30(4): 657–678.

Ruckman, J.A. (1984), *The Moscow Business Elite*, DeKalb: Northern Illinois University Press.

Rudolph, R.L. (1976), *Banking and Industrialization in Austria-Hungary: The Role of Banks in the Industrialization of the Czech Crownlands, 1873–1914*, New York: Cambridge University Press.

Russia (1881–1913), *Polnoe sobranie zakonov Rossiiskoi Imperii*, 3rd collection, St. Petersburg: Gos. Tip.

Russia (1825–1881), *Polnoe sobranie zakonov Rossiiskoi Imperii*, 2nd collection, St. Petersburg: State Publishers.

Russia, Ministry of Finances (1901–1914), *Ezhegodnik Ministerstva Finansov*, St. Petersburg.

Russia, Ministry of Internal Affairs (1911), *Ezhegodnik Rossii na 1910*, St. Petersburg.

Russia, Ministry of Internal Affairs (1906), *Ezhegodnik Rossii na 1905*, St. Petersburg.

Rybczynski, T.M. (1997), "A new look at the evolution of the financial system", in J. Revell (ed.), *The Recent Evolution of Financial Systems*, Basingstoke: Macmillan, 3–15.

Sandberg, L. (1978), "Banking and economic growth in Sweden before World War I", *Journal of Economic History*, 38: 650–680.

Saunders, A., and I. Walter (eds) (1996), *Universal Banking: Financial System Design Reconsidered*, Chicago: Irwin.

Sayers, R.S. (1976), *The Bank of England 1891–1944*, 3 vols, Cambridge: Cambridge University Press.

Schäfer, K.C. (1993), *Deutsche Portfolioinvestitionen im Ausland 1870–1914. Banken, Kapitalmärkte und Wertpapierhandel im Zeitalter des Imperialismus*, Münster: Lit.

Schmitz, C. (1997), "The nature and dimensions of Scottish foreign investment, 1860–1914", *Business History*, 39(2): 42–68.

Schön, L. (1989), "Kapitalimport, kreditmarknad och industrialisering 1850–1910", in E. Dahmén (ed.), *Upplåning och utveckling. Riksgäldskontoret 1789–1989*, Stockholm: Allmänna Förlaget, 227–246.

Schulz, W. (1994), *Das deutsche Börsengesetz: Die Entstehungsgeschichte und wirtschaftlichen Auswirkungen des Börsengesetzes von 1896*, Frankfurt am Main and New York: P. Lang.

Schumpeter, J. (1911), *The Theory of Economic Development*, Cambridge, MA: Harvard University Press.

Sérgio, A. (n.d.), *O Sistema Bancário e a Expansão da Economia Portuguesa (1947–1959)*, Lisbon: Banco de Portugal.

Shepelev, L.E. (1995), "Business organizations in the Russian Empire, 1906–14", *Russian Studies in History*, 34: 40–87.

224 *Works cited*

Shepelev, L.E. (1987), *Tsarizm i burzhuaziia v 1904–1914 gg. Problemy torgovo-promyshlennoi politiki*, Leningrad: Sciences.

Shepelev, L.E. (1973), *Aksionernye kompanii v Rossii*, Leningrad: Sciences.

Sheppard, D.K. (1971), *The Growth and Role of UK Financial Institutions 1880–1962*, London: Methuen.

Siepmann, Jürgen Dietrich (1968), *Die Standortfrage bei Kreditinstituten*, Berlin: Duncker und Humblot.

Sieveking, H. (1934), "Die Hamburger Bank", in J.G. van Dillen (ed.), *History of the Principal Public Banks*, The Hague: M. Nijhoff, 125–160.

Sjögren, H. (1997), "Financial reconstructions and industrial reorganizations in different financial systems – a comparative study of British and Swedish institutions during the interwar period", *Business History*, 39(4): 84–106.

Sjölander, A. (2000), "Att reglera eller inte reglera – en undersökning av sparbanksfrågan i riksdagen 1882–1939", Uppsala Papers in Financial History, Report no. 13, Uppsala: Uppsala University.

Skånland, H. (1967), *The Norwegian Credit Market Since 1900*, Oslo: Central Bureau of Statistics.

Smith, A. (1976) [1776], *The Wealth of Nations*, Chicago: Chicago University Press.

Smith, M.F.J. (1919), *Tijdaffaires in effecten aan de Amsterdamsche beurs*, The Hague: Nijhoff.

Sneller, Z.W. (1934), "Boedelinventarissen van Twentsche entrepreneursgeslachten uit het laatst der 18e eeuw", in *Bijdragen en mededelingen van het Historisch Genootschap*, 55: 33–118.

Söderlund, E. (1964), *Skandinaviska Banken i det svenska bankväsendets historia 1864–1914*, Stockholm: Almquist & Wiksell.

Sommarin, E. (1942), *Svenskt sparbanksväsen 1834–1892*, Lund: Ohlssons boktryckeri.

Steinherr, A. (1996), "Performance of universal banks: Historical review and appraisal", in A. Saunders and I. Walter (eds), *Universal Banking: Financial System Design Reconsidered*, Chicago: Irwin, 2–30.

Štiblar, F. (1994), "Universal banking in the Slovene Region, 1900–1945", in A. Teichova, T. Gourvish, and A. Pogány (eds), *Universal Banking in the Twentieth Century: Finance, Industry and State in North and Central Europe*, Aldershot: E. Elgar, 44–58.

Stonehill, A. (1965), *Foreign Ownership in Norwegian Enterprises*, Oslo: Central Bureau of Statistics.

Story, J., and I. Walter (1997), *The Political Economy of Financial Integration in Europe: The Battle of the Systems*, Cambridge, MA: MIT Press.

Streeck, W. (1989), "The territorial organization of interests and the logic of associative actions: The case of *Handwerk* organization in West Germany", in W.D. Coleman and H.J. Jacek (eds), *Regionalism, Business Interests and Public Policy*, London: Sage, 59–94.

Streeck, W., and K. Yamamura (eds) (2001), *The Origins of Nonliberal Capitalism: Germany and Japan*, Ithaca: Cornell University Press.

Stünkel, F.D. (1938), *Die Arbeitsteilung der Banken in Norwegen*, Würzburg-Aumühle: Konrad Triltsch.

Sweden, Sverige Statistika Centralbyran (1914), *Statistisk Arsbok för Sverige*, Stockholm.

Switzerland, Département Fédéral de l'Economie Publique (1927), *La Suisse économique et sociale*, Zurich: Benziger.

Sylla, R. (1996), "Notes on universal banking in history", in A. Saunders and I. Walter (eds), *Universal Banking: Financial System Design Reconsidered*, Chicago: Irwin, 118–121.

Sylla, R., R. Tilly, and G. Tortella (eds) (1999), *The State, the Financial System and Economic Modernization*, Cambridge: Cambridge University Press.

Sylla, R., and G. Toniolo (1991a), *"Introduction"*, in idem, *Patterns of European Industrialization: The Nineteeth Century*, London: Routledge, 1–28.

Sylla, R., and G. Toniolo (eds) (1991b), *Patterns of European Industrialization: The Nineteeth Century*, London: Routledge.

Szász, Z. (1994), "Banking and nationality in Hungary, 1867–1914", in A. Teichova, T. Gourvish, and A. Pogány (eds), *Universal Banking in the Twentieth Century: Finance, Industry and State in North and Central Europe*, Aldershot: E. Elgar, 32–43.

Taylor, G.V. (1962), "The Paris Bourse on the eve of the revolution, 1781–1789", *American Historical Review*, 67: 951–977.

Teichova, A. (1997), "Banking and industry in Central Europe, 19th to 20th century", in A. Teichova, G. Kurgan-van Hentenryk, and D. Ziegler (eds), *Banking, Trade and Industry: Europe, America and Asia from the Thirteenth to the Twentieth Century*, Cambridge: Cambridge University Press, 214–228.

Teichova, A., T. Gourvish, and A. Pogány (eds) (1994), *Universal Banking in the Twentieth Century: Finance, Industry and State in North and Central Europe*, Aldershot: E. Elgar.

Teichova, A., G. Kurgan-van Hentenryk, and D. Ziegler (eds) (1997), *Banking, Trade and Industry: Europe, America and Asia from the Thirteenth to the Twentieth Century*, Cambridge: Cambridge University Press.

Thomes, P. (1995), "German savings banks as instruments of regional development up to the Second World War", in Y. Cassis, G.D. Feldman, and U. Olson (eds), *The Evolution of Financial Institutions and Markets in Twentieth-Century Europe*, Aldershot: Scolar Press, 143–162.

Tilly, C. (1990), *Coercion, Capital, and European States AD 900–1900*, Oxford: Blackwell.

Tilly, R.H. (1999), "Public policy, capital markets and the supply of industrial finance in nineteenth-century Germany", in R. Sylla, R.H. Tilly, and G. Tortella (eds), *The State, the Financial System, and Economic Modernization*, New York: Cambridge University Press, 134–157.

Tilly, R.H. (1998), "Universal banking in historical perspective", *Journal of Institutional and Theoretical Economics*, 154: 7–38.

Tilly, R.H. (1995), "How to write the history of a bank – Belgium, Holland, Germany, Luxemburg, Switzerland", in M.G. Fase, G.D. Feldman, and M. Pohl (eds), *How to Write the History of a Bank*, Aldershot: Scolar Press, 68–85.

Tilly, R.H. (1986), "German banking, 1850–1914: Development assistance for the strong", *Journal of Economic History*, 15(1): 113–152.

Tilly, R.H. (1980a), "Die politische Ökonomie der Finanzpolitik und die Industrialisierung Preussens, 1815–1866", in idem, *Kapital, Staat und sozialer Protest in der deutschen Industrialisierung*, Göttingen: Vandenhoeck und Ruprecht, 55–64.

Tilly, R.H. (1980b), "Banken und Industrialisierung in Deutschland: Quantifizierungsversuche", in F.W. Henning (ed.), *Entwicklung und Aufgaben von Versicherungen und Banken in der Industrialisierung*, Berlin: Duncker und Humblot.

Tilly, R.H. (1980c), *Kapital, Staat und sozialer Protest in der deutschen Industrialisierung*, Göttingen: Vandenhoeck und Ruprecht.

Tilly, R.H. (1967), "Germany, 1815–1870", in R.E. Cameron (ed.), *Banking in the Early Stages of Industrialization: A Study in Comparative Economic History*, New York: Oxford University Press, 151–182.

Tilly, R.H. (1966), *Financial Institutions and Industrialization in the Rhineland*, Madison: University of Wisconsin Press.

Tobin, J. (1984), "On the efficiency of the financial system", *Lloyds Bank Review*, 153: 1–15.

Tortella, G. (1999), "The role of banks and government in Spanish economic development, 1850–1935", in R. Sylla, R. Tilly, and G. Tortella (eds), *The State, the Financial System, and Economic Modernization*, New York: Cambridge University Press, 158–181.

Tortella, G. (1974), *La Banca Española en la Restauración*, vol. 2, *Datos para una Historia Económica*, Madrid: Servicio de Estudios del Banco de España.

Tracy, J.D. (1985), *A Financial Revolution in the Habsburg Netherlands: Renten and Renteniers in the County of Holland, 1515–1565*, Berkeley: University of California Press.

Tracy, J.D. (ed.) (1990), *The Rise of Merchant Empires: Long-Distance Trade in the Early Modern World, 1350–1750*, New York: Cambridge University Press.

Trende, A. (1957), *Geschichte der deutschen Sparkassen*, Stuttgart: Deutscher Sparkassenverlag.

Tullio, G., and J. Wolters, (1996), "Was London the conductor of the international orchestra or just the triangle player? An empirical analysis of asymmetries in interest rate behavior during the classical gold standard 1876–1913", *Scottish Journal of Political Economy*, 43(4): 419–443.

Ullmann, H.P. (1986), *Staatsschulden und Reformpolitik. Die Entstehung moderner öffentlicher Schulden in Bayern und Baden 1780–1820*, Göttingen: Vandenhoeck & Ruprecht.

United States, Department of Commerce (1976), *Historical Statistics of the United States: Colonial Times to 1970*, Washington DC: Government Printing Office.

United States, Federal Reserve, Board of Governors (1942), *Banking and Monetary Statistics*, Washington DC.

United States, National Monetary Commission (1911), *German Bank Inquiry of 1908–9*, Stenographic Reports, Proceedings of the Entire Commission on Point VI of the Question Sheet, vol. 2, Washington DC: Government Printing Office.

Urquhart, M.C., and K.A.H. Buckley (eds) (1965), *Historical Statistics of Canada*, Cambridge: Cambridge University Press.

van der Wee, H. (1982), "La politique d'investissement de la Société Générale de Belgique, 1822–1913", *Histoire, Economie et Société*, 1(4): 603–619.

van Dillen, J.G. (1930), "Isaac le Maire en de handel in actiën der Oost-Indische Compagnie", *Economischhistorisch jaarboek* 16: 1–165.

van Dillen J.G., (ed.) (1934), *History of the Principal Public Banks*, The Hague: M. Nijhoff.

van Gor, L., and J. Koelewijn (1995), "Le système bancaire néerlandais. Etude rétrospective", in Ministère de l'Economie, des Finances et du Plan, Comité pour l'Histoire Economique et Financière de la France (ed.), *Les banques en Europe de l'Ouest de 1920 à nos jours. Colloque tenu à Bercy les 7 et 8 octobre 1993*, Paris: Impremerie nationale, 153–175.

Vanthemsche, G. (1991), "State, banks, and industry in Belgium and the Netherlands, 1919–1939", in H. James, H. Lindgren, and A. Teichova (eds), *The Role of Banks in the Interwar Economy*, New York: Cambridge University Press, 104–121.

van Zanden, J.L. (1997), "Old rules, new conditions, 1914–1940", in M. 't Hart, J. Jonker, and J.L. van Zanden (eds), *A Financial History of the Netherlands*, New York: Cambridge University Press, 124–151.

Varain, H.J. (ed.) (1973), *Interessenverbände in Deutschland*, Cologne: Kiepenheuer & Witsch.

Vasta, M., and Baccini, A. (1997), "Banks and industry in Italy, 1911–36: New evidence using the interlocking directorates technique", *Financial History Review*, 4(2): 139–159.

Verdier, D. (2002a), *Moving Money: Banking and Finance in the Industrialized World*, New York: Cambridge University Press.

Verdier, D. (2002b), *How and why financial systems differ: A survey of the literature*, European University Institute Working Papers, SPS No. 2002/2.Verdier, D. (2000), "The rise and fall of state banking in OECD countries", *Comparative Political Studies*, 33(3): 283–318.

Verdier, D. (2001), "Financial capital mobility and the origins of stock markets", *International Organization*, 55(12): 327–56.

Verdier, D. (1998), "Domestic responses to capital market internationalization under the Gold Standard 1870–1914", *International Organization*, 52(1): 1–28.

Verdier, D. (1997), "The political origins of banking structures", *The Policy History Newsletter*, Bowling Green State University, Dept. of History, 2(3).

Verdier D. (1996), "Gerschenkron on his head: Banking structures in 19th-century Europe, North America, and Australasia*", EUI Working Papers*, no. 96/3.

Verdonk, D.D. (1994), "The Wiener Bank-Verein and its customers in the 1920s and 1930s", in A. Teichova, T. Gourvish, and A. Pogány (eds), *Universal Banking in the Twentieth Century: Finance, Industry and State in North and Central Europe*, Aldershot: E. Elgar, 194–207.

Vidal, E. (1910), *The History and Methods of the Paris Bourse*, Washington: Government Printing Office.

Vitols, S. (2001), "The origins of bank-based and market-based financial systems: Germany, Japan, and the United States", in W. Streeck and K. Yamamura (eds), *The Origins of Nonliberal Capitalism: Germany and Japan*, Ithaca: Cornell University Press, 171–199.

Vitols, S. (1995), "German banks and the modernization of the small firm sector: Long-term finance in comparative perspective", *Wissenschaftszentrum, Berlin, Discussion Paper*, FS, 1: 95–309.

Vittas, D. (1997), "Thrift deposit institutions in Europe and the United States", in G. Caprio, Jr. and D. Vittas (eds), *Reforming Financial Systems: Historical Implications for Policy*, Cambridge: Cambridge University Press, 141–179.

Vogler, B. (1991), "Les caisses d'épargne en Alsace de 1831 à 1870", *Bankhistorisches Archiv*, 17: 82–98.

Vogler, B. (ed.) (1997), *L'histoire des Caisses d'épargne européennes*, vol. 3, *Conjoncture et crises 1850–1914*, Paris: Editions de l'Épargne.

Vogler, B. (ed.) (1991), *L'histoire des Caisses d'épargne européennes*, vol. 1, *Les origines des Caisses d'épargne 1815–1848*, Paris: Éditions de l'Épargne.

Volin, L. (1970), *A Century of Russian Agriculture*, Cambridge, MA: Harvard University Press.

Vronkova, S.V. *et al.* (1992), *Promyshlennost' Rossii na rubezhe XIX–XX vv. Metody izucheniia territorial'nogo razmeshcheniia i protsessov kontsentratsii promyshlennosti*, Moscow: ROU.

Weber, A. (1902), *Depositenbanken und Spekulationsbanken. Ein Vergleich deutschen und englischen Bankwesens*, Munich and Leipzig: Duncker und Humblot.

Weinberger, B. (1984), "Die Bedeutung der Sparkassen für die Entwicklung des kommunalen Raumes", in Günter Aschauer (ed.), *Standortbestimmung: Entwicklungslinien der deutschen Kreditwirtschaft*, Stuttgart: Deutscher Sparkassenverlag.

Weir, D.R. (1989), "Tontines, public finance, and revolution in France and England, 1688–1789", *Journal of Economic History*, 49: 95–124.

Wellhöner, V. (1989), *Großbanken und Großindustrie im Kaiserreich*, Göttingen: Vandenhoeck & Ruprecht.

Whale, P.B. (1968) [1930], *Joint-Stock Banking in Germany: A Study of the German Credit Banks before and after the War*, New York: A.M. Kelley.

White, E.N. (1999), "Making the French pay: The costs and consequences of the Napoleonic reparations", *NBER Working Paper 7438*, Cambridge, MA: National Bureau of Economic Research.

White, E.N. (1995), "The French Revolution and the politics of government finance, 1770–1815", *Journal of Economic History*, 55: 227–255.

Wixforth, H. (1995), *Banken und Schwerindustrie in der Weimar Republik*, Cologne: Boehlau.

Wixforth, H. (1988), "The relations between the banks and the Westphalian heavy industry, 1918–1932: Three case studies", *Uppsala Papers in Economic History*, Working Paper no. 4, *Report from the Vienna Banking-Industry Symposium*, Uppsala: Department of Economic History, Uppsala University.

Wixforth, H., and D. Ziegler (1995), "Bankenmacht: Universal banking and German industry in historical perspective", in Y. Cassis, G.D. Feldman, and U. Olsson (eds), *The Evolution of Financial Institutions and Market in Twentieth-Century Europe*, Aldershot: Scolar.

Wysocki, G. (1983), *Untersuchungen zur Wirtschafts- und Sozialgeschichte der Sparkassen im 19. Jahrhundert*, Stuttgart: Deutscher Sparkassenverlag.

Wysocki, J. (1997), "Croissance et conjoncture (1850–1914)", in B. Vogler (ed.), *L'histoire des Caisses d'épargne européennes*, vol. 3, *Conjoncture et crises 1850–1914*, Paris: Editions de l'épargne, 17–28.

Wysocki, J. (1987), "Die bankmässige Entwicklung der Sparkassen (1908–1931)", in J. Mura (ed.), *Die Entwicklung der Sparkassen zu Universalkreditinstituten*, Stuttgart: Deutscher Sparkassenverlag.

Wysocki, J. (1985), "Der öffentliche Auftrag der Sparkassen im Zeitalter der Industrialisierung", in J. Mura (ed.), *Der öffentliche Auftrag der Sparkassen in der historischen Entwicklung*, Stuttgart: Deutscher Sparkassenverlag.

Yudanov, A. (1997), "The role of banks in establishing a community of firms in Russia", in A. Teichova, G. Kurgan-van Hentenryk, and D. Ziegler (eds), *Banking, Trade and Industry: Europe, America and Asia from the 13th to the 20th Century*, New York: Cambridge University Press, 277–294.

Zamagni, V. (1995), "Alcune riflessioni sul finanziamento dell'industria in età giolittiana", in P. Pecorari (ed.), *Finanza e debito pubblico in Italia tra '800 e '900*, Venice: Istituto veneto di scienze lettere ed arti, 137–152.

Ziegler, D. (1998), "Universal banking in Continental Europe, 1830–1938", in P.L. Cottrell and J. Reis, *Finance and the Making of the Modern Capitalist World, 1750–1931*, Madrid: Fundación Fomento de la Historia Económica.

Ziegler, D. (1997), "The influence of banking on the rise and expansion of industrial capitalism in Germany", in A. Teichova, G. Kurgan-Van Hentenryk, and D. Ziegler (eds), *Banking, Trade and Industry: Europe, America and Asia from the Thirteenth to the Twentieth Century*, New York: Cambridge University Press, 131–156.

Ziegler, D. (1990a), *Central Bank, Peripheral Industry: The Bank of England in the Provinces 1826–1913*, London: Leicester University Publishers.

Ziegler, D. (1990b), "The origins of the 'Macmillan gap': comparing Britain and Germany in the early twentieth century", in P.L. Cottrell, A. Teichova, and T. Yuzawa (eds), *Finance in the Age of the Corporate Economy: The Third Anglo-Japanese Business History Conference*, Aldershot: Ashgate, 1997, 184–208.

Zimmerman, R. (1987), *Volksbank oder Aktienbank? Parlamentsdebatten, Referendum und zunehmende Verbandsmacht beim Streit um die Nationalbankgründung 1891–1905*, Zurich: Chronos.

Zysman, J. (1983), *Governments, Markets, and Growth: Financial Systems and the Politics of Industrial Change*, Ithaca: Cornell University Press

Index

agricultural interests 3, 12, 109, 117, 128,
   133, 142, 188
Ahlström, G. 128
Albrecht, C. 24, 41
Aleoti, A. 112
Alieri, S. and Cerrito, E. 111
American system 47
Anan'ich, B.V. 181
Anderson, B.L. and Cottrell, P.L. 46
Anfimov, A.M. and Korelin, A.P. 167, 180
Arrighetti, A. and Seravalli, G. 110
Asajima, S. 63
Ashton, T.S. 42

Baker, M. and Collins, M. 55
Balogh, T. 56, 58
Bank of England 9, 11, 42n, 46, 47, 71,
   72, 74
Bank of Portugal 190, 193, 197, 200
banks, assets/demand-side factors 3–4, 9,
   18, 19, 117, 143; and availability of
   funds 53–6; center/periphery
   relationship 72–3, 77, 92, 117, 189,
   190, 195–8, 201; competition with
   securities market 50, 56; crises in 59;
   cross-national variations 23, 72–4;
   development of 44–5, 62–3; direct state
   intervention 17; environmental
   incentives/constraints 8; functionality/
   stability of 13; and government
   regulation/structure of national deposit
   markets 2; historical period 7;
   importance/role of 43–4; and industrial
   investment 111–12; and
   industrialization/economic growth
   156–60; influence of 89–90; and
   information asymmetry 121–2; lack of
   trust in 18; legal barriers to security
   holdings 138–40; liabilities/supply-side

factors 4–5, 117, 143; liquidity
   problems 26–7, 80; loans by 19, 60;
   networks 89; patterns of 65; political
   centralization of 17; and problem of
   over-lending 61; and provision of loans
   to brokers 58–9; regulation/supervision
   of 153–4; relationship with industry
   191–5; relationship with securities
   market 60, 62; second revolution in 79;
   segmentation of 2–3, 13, 118–22,
   170–7; spread of 50–1; state-centered/
   market-centered choices 5–6, 9;
   strategic decision-making 3–6, 8; three-
   sector system 92–101
Banque de France 13–14, 75, 77, 122,
   124–5
banques de dépôt 13, 14
banques d'affaires 13, 79
Barendregt, J. 70
Barkai, H. 181
Berend, I.T. and Ránki, G. 157
Bergh, T. 155
Berghuis, W.H. 85
Berlin Banks 87–8, 89, 93, 99–100, 101,
   104n
Bizet de Frayne, L.C. 76
Boksjö, A. and Lönnborg-Andersson, M.
   138
Bonin, H. 77, 79, 86
Borchardt, K. 86
Bordo, M.D. and Jonung, L. 199
Born, K.E. 56, 63, 88, 100, 103
Bouvier, J. 27, 42, 119, 123
Bovykin, V.I. 180; and Anan'ich, B. 22,
   180, 181
Boyce, G. 62, 63
branch networks 65, 119, 120, 121;
   development of 131, 132; Portuguese
   190–5, 197–8; rise of 25–7, 124;